# Steal Me Blind!

The Complete Guide to
Shoplifting & Retail Theft
...and how to stop it
*without getting sued*

R.W. Helena

BlueLight
📖
**Charleston**

> A $1,000 reward will be paid for information leading to the conviction of any individual, group, company or corporation violating or infringing upon this work and applicable copyright laws.

# Steal Me Blind!
## The Complete Guide to Shoplifting & Retail Theft
## ...and how to stop it without getting sued

Library of Congress Catalog Card Number 96-95433
Registered in accordance with Title 17, United States Code
Copyright © 1995-2000
by Richard Winston Helena. All rights reserved.

Revised 1996, 1997, 1998, 1999, 2000
Sixth BlueLight Printing

Previously: Steal Me Blind!
The Complete Guide to Shoplifting
and how to stop it without getting sued.

Printed in the United States of America.

International Standard Book Numbers
ISBN 0-9654637-2-9  Soft Cover Text

Except for brief quotations or passages for review purposes, no part of this book may be reproduced or stored in any form, including electronically, without written consent of the author.
For information write:
BlueLight Publishing, Box 39205, Northbridge Station, Charleston, SC, 29407
or e-mail to bluepub@internetx.net

Quantity discounts are available.

This book reflects actual experience. It is designed primarily to aid retail management & loss prevention and members of the law enforcement community. Since laws vary and are constantly revised, it is neither expected nor recommended that information in this book be considered legal advice. In every case, applicable laws and ordinances should be researched, then methods adapted to conform.
Whether engaged in retail operations, farming, or medicine, the degree of success depends in large part upon circumstances and upon the personalities, histories, and skills of those involved. Variables affect results. This book contains information that may not be suitable for use by every reader in every situation. Judgment and caution *must* be exercised. The publisher, seller, and author disclaim any liability, loss or risk incurred as a direct or indirect consequence of any application. If expert assistance is required, the services of a competent professional should be sought.

*Steal Me Blind!*
*The Complete Guide to Shoplifting & Retail Theft*

**Dedication**  This book is dedicated to Winston because it has to be. It was his inspirational faith and sacrifice that got us around the corner. I suppose it's possible that someone, somewhere, has a better son; but probably not.

**Acknowledgments**  If you like this book, I'll take full credit. If you don't like it, well...one way or another and whether they meant to or not, all these people helped. So blame them.

- Chris Hodgdon of Winthrop University, SC (computer consultant),
- Noah J.R. Moore, Mall Security Director, founder & Director of the Greater Charleston Loss Prevention Task Force,
- Ken 'Kenny Stealth' Dean, Private Detective & Surveillance Expert (Chas., SC),
- Detectives Keith 'Slim' Wiggins & Jose Diaz, Gwinnett County PD, (GA),
- Sgt. David Fair, CPD (SC) Vice President of the SC Fraternal Order of Police,
- Sgt. Kevin Hux & Sgt. Alfonso Scott, NCPD (SC), Corporal Tommy Smith, CPD (SC) & Officer Harwood Beebe CPD (SC),
- Loss Prevention Officers Steve Smith (also, SCSTP), Brad Norvell (SCDPPP), Pete Wright, Lynda Austin, Annette Allen-Lindayen, and Ken Horne,
- Chief Detective James Josey, Evidence expert & Director of Admin. Services, MPD (GA),
- Bob Moorefield, Alpha Academy of Dog Training, Atlanta, GA. (P.O.S.T. Certified Police K-9 Instructor; obedience training & consultant; founder of GA's Police Dog Assoc.),
- Mrs. Dorothy Hardie, Ret. Secretary to Chief of Police, MPD (GA),
- Juanita 'Nita' Birmingham, investigative reporter & adventurer,
- Herby Black, Rusty Wagner, Chief Osborne, Capt. Wolfe, Robert Goocher, Larry Milner, Bill Farris, Eddie Harris, Curtis Moore, Sgt. Kendricks, Randy Hartzell, & the other boys in the band; plus, of course, 'Sister,' and 'Favors' (MPD, GA),
- Jerry Whidby, Special Agent, Georgia Bureau of Investigation,
- Nancy Atkinson, Esq. & Phil Carr, Esq. (GA), Harry Belk, Esq. & Jon Mercereau, Esq. (SC),
- Doug Thompson, Former Director, GA Law Enforcement Training Center,
- Isaiah Daise, Artist & Entrepreneur (SC),
- Lillie Manning, Certified SC Number Cruncher (When asked, 'What does 1.0 mean?' She responds, 'What do you want it to mean?')
- Lowell Corbin and Kyle Ripley, Innovative shrinkage-aware managers & superb back-up,
- Col. 'Fat Jack' Martin (Ret.), Golden Gloves boxer, professor and philosopher,
- William 'The Sandman' Thrasher,
- Luchenbach II (Luke), MPD,
- my Mother, who always had a home fire burning,
- and Carmel Hallex & Alex's Restaurant for hundreds of gallons of wee-hour coffee.

Also, I want to thank the several E.R. staffs who sewed me back together.

## ABOUT THE AUTHOR
by
William R. Thrasher

---

Graduating from The Citadel in Charleston, SC, the author of Steal Me Blind!© entered the retail industry with the F.W.Woolworth Company. Almost immediately he came face to face with shoplifting, and years later Rich Helena is not that same person.

He received training in basics such as merchandising and advertising, but his interest was drawn to the security aspects of retail. Manuals he read from corporate sources were filled with carefully phrased what-to-do's and what-not-to-do's; impossible to successfully apply in practice. Always pursuing practical solutions, Rich eventually drew the attention of a local police recruiter.

I was the recruiter, and I sensed Rich was happiest when apprehending shoplifters, and that he could make the transition to a Georgia city cop. So I talked him into taking a new job with a built-in pay cut. Six months later Rich graduated first in his class, the only officer from our 190-year-old city ever to be the police academy's Honor Graduate.

While he did little to endear himself to those administrators who felt a police officer's job was writing traffic tickets, he did much to make our city's thieves lose a lot of sleep. He quickly developed a reputation for resourcefulness and excelled almost immediately in a field that normally requires substantial start-up time. Within four years, he had worked in conjunction with a dozen other Georgia and federal agencies, had participated in over 200 drug arrests, and had been wounded several times in the process.

(During one fracas, he misplaced an ear. Found later by another officer it was reattached--for the most part--at a Macon (Ga.) trauma center. While that particular arrest technique will never be included in any manual as the "right" way to do things, the perpetrator *was* locked in Rich's squad car when back-up units arrived; *the job got done.* When asked in court to describe his ears before the incident, Rich--now called "One-Ear" by some--said that when he entered the house he had "a matching pair.")

Rich was the City's first-ever canine handler, and with three colleagues (Bob Moorefield and Terry Cook from Atlanta and Jerry Whidby from Putnam County) formed the Georgia Police Dog Association. Tirelessly, Rich worked to design and implement a number of unique and very effective detection and interdiction programs aimed at the burgeoning drug traffic in our city, and he was appointed the sole department representative to the Atlanta Law Enforcement Exposition.

He prosecuted a thousand cases in Georgia courts, was described by the media as one of two unquestionably honest police officers in the city, was twice elected vice-president of the Fraternal Order of Police, and, during my tenure as his supervisor, was the only officer from our city to be awarded a Senate Commendation (for meritorious service to the State). On the side, he raised cows on his mini-ranch.

Moving to Charleston, SC, he began investigating federal disability claims. Over half of his cases involved individuals with varying degrees of mental disorders and anti-social conduct, and he prepared thousands of cases, often reviewed by administrative law judges.

In 1990, he turned his attention back to crime, became a state-certified private investigator, and fashioned counter-theft techniques. In 1992 those ideas were put to the ultimate test: in a 4-million dollar retail operation with security averaging one shoplifting stop a week, Rich averaged a stop every 2.9 *hours*.

With grand larceny and repeat-offender cases, his thieves all entered guilty pleas with no concessions from the company. To date, he has engaged 500-plus individuals, prosecuting cases with a perfect record. No gnashing of teeth or sleepless nights and, more importantly, *no lawsuits*. *And* all this was accomplished without a single claim of false arrest or a single complaint, questioning letter, or phone call from any attorney alleging any sort of improper conduct or procedures. Very clean; and I would have thought it impossible in this age of litigation.

With a unique blend of experience in retail sales, police work, psychology, and commercial loss prevention, Rich has produced a system of methods and techniques *that work*.

Without a doubt, Steal Me Blind!© is the most powerful and cost-effective weapon yet devised for combating the thieves *within* your gates. Not only does he clearly state what *needs* to be done, he describes in detail *how to do it*. If I was in retail or had anything to do with shoplifting and couldn't afford to buy this book...I damn well might *steal* it.

William R. "Bill" Thrasher

Bill Thrasher is a law enforcement veteran and rose through the ranks to become a Captain. He was the author's supervisor during much of his police career. Bill is an acknowledged expert in the fields of loss prevention and loss control and, based in Rome, Georgia, his operations extend throughout the continental US and counts many of the nation's largest insurance carriers and industrial/retail giants among his clients.

# CONTENTS

**ABOUT THE AUTHOR IV**
*(by William R. Thrasher)*

**TABLE OF CONTENTS VI**

**CHAPTER 1** Overview...1

| | | | |
|---|---|---|---|
| 1.01 | Why thieves steal 2 | 1.03 | Roots 4 |
| 1.02 | Why others *don't* steal 4 | 1.04 | Sun Tzu meets Jimmy Johnson 5 |

**CHAPTER 2** Thieves and Deceivers...7

| | | | |
|---|---|---|---|
| 2.01 | Who steals 8 | 2.06 | Employee theft 15 |
| 2.02 | Categories of thieves 8 | 2.07 | Cash shortages and tracking 17 |
| 2.03 | Professionals 9 | 2.08 | Venders and jobbers 18 |
| 2.04 | Amateur types 11 | 2.09 | With a little help from their friends 18 |
| 2.05 | Refunds and exchanges 13 | 2.10 | Employee Screening and training 20 |

**CHAPTER 3** State and Local Laws...23

3.01 Shoplifting laws in Concealment & Non-Concealment states 23
3.02 Refund laws 25
3.03 Inappropriate versus criminal 25

**CHAPTER 4** Policy versus Law...29

| | | | |
|---|---|---|---|
| 4.01 | Policy A 31 | 4.04 | The human factor 34 |
| 4.02 | Policy B 33 | 4.05 | Approach examples 35 |
| 4.03 | Policy-world 33 | | |

**CHAPTER 5** Liability (Lie-ability)...39

| | | | |
|---|---|---|---|
| 5.01 | Actions and alternatives 40 | 5.06 | Payment for stolen merchandise 49 |
| 5.02 | Victimhood 42 | 5.07 | Accomplices 49 |
| 5.03 | Games people play 45 | 5.08 | Questions of liability 50 |
| 5.04 | Minimizing risk 47 | 5.09 | Harassment and Honey Traps 51 |
| 5.05 | Insurance 49 | | |

**CHAPTER 6** The Mechanics of Theft...53

| | | | |
|---|---|---|---|
| 6.01 | Thieves' tools 53 | 6.04 | Profiles and red flags 65 |
| 6.02 | Tactics and devices 56 | 6.05 | Site hardening 67 |
| 6.03 | Intimidation 61 | | |

**CHAPTER 7** The Shoplifting Act...69

| | | | |
|---|---|---|---|
| 7.01 | Location 69 | 7.04 | Counter-surveillance 75 |
| 7.02 | Examples 71 | 7.05 | *Dee-fense* 76 |
| 7.03 | Shoplifting rituals 73 | 7.06 | Employee Sabotage 78 |

## CONTENTS (CONT.)

### CHAPTER 8  Surveillance...79

| | | | | |
|---|---|---|---|---|
| 8.01 | Technique 80 | | 8.07 | Cameras 90 |
| 8.02 | Watching and seeing 83 | | 8.08 | Projections from observation 90 |
| 8.03 | Physical descriptions 85 | | 8.09 | 2nd-hand information 91 |
| 8.04 | Security windows 86 | | 8.10 | When to let go 92 |
| 8.05 | Fire Lanes (Kill Zones) 88 | | 8.11 | Uniformed security 92 |
| 8.06 | Mirrors 89 | | | |

### CHAPTER 9  Beyond Prevention...95

| | | | | |
|---|---|---|---|---|
| 9.01 | Location of the stop 95 | | 9.06 | Offensive tactics 106 |
| 9.02 | The Third Option offense 97 | | 9.07 | Stops and detention 109 |
| 9.03 | Whoops! (Bad stops) 102 | | 9.08 | Weapons and accessories 110 |
| 9.04 | In-store codes 104 | | 9.09 | Gangs & Cliques 112 |
| 9.05 | Necessary roughness 104 | | | |

### CHAPTER 10  Reports and Processing...113

| | | | | |
|---|---|---|---|---|
| 10.01 | Searches 113 | | 10.06 | Friends and family 121 |
| 10.02 | Interrogations 114 | | 10.07 | Acknowledgment and release 121 |
| 10.03 | Obtaining Confessions 115 | | 10.08 | Records and report writing 122 |
| 10.04 | Special requests 119 | | 10.09 | Evidence 125 |
| 10.05 | Juveniles 120 | | | |

### CHAPTER 11  Prosecution, Police, and Court...127

11.01   When to prosecute, when not to  128
11.02   Court  131
11.03   Jury trials  138

## CHAPTER NOTES...141

## APPENDIX...149

| | | | |
|---|---|---|---|
| 1. Acknowledgment | 150 | 8. Shopper's Report | 165 |
| 2. Civil Release | 151 | 9. Refunds/Exchanges Report | 166 |
| 3. Criminal Trespass | 152 | 10. Wind in your Sales | 167 |
| 4. Stop Log | 153 | 11. Credit Card Fraud | 170 |
| 5. Incident Reports | 155 | 12. Floor-Walking | 172 |
|     Supplemental Report | 158 | 13. Covert Tape-Recording | 173 |
|     Witness Narrative | 159 | 14. LP Newsletters | 175 |
| 6. Loss Prevention Checks | 160 | 15. Internet & Other Sources | 177 |
| 7. Thieves' Manual | 161 | 16. Employee Orientation | 180 |

## GLOSSARY
## WORDS, TERMS & USAGE...189

## INDEX...207

# ILLEGITIMI NON CARBUNDUM.

(DON'T LET THE BASTARDS GRIND YOU DOWN.)

# Chapter 1: Overview

In South Carolina and Georgia, it's "Shoplifting." Elsewhere, it might be Theft by Taking or Petty Larceny. Everywhere, though, it's definitely out of control.

Shoplifting is the Number One growth field in the larceny industry, and the U.S. has more shoplifters than many entire countries have people. Our twenty million shoplifters equal the combined state populations of Alaska, Wyoming, Delaware, Hawaii, Idaho, Vermont, New Hampshire, North Dakota, Montana, Rhode Island, South Dakota, Maine, Georgia, South Carolina, *and* the District of Columbia.

Whether shoplifting, fraud, or employee theft, when sociologists and academicians examine "the multi-faceted problem" of why Johnny steals, they study "trends and root causes" and "address the needs of everyone concerned." This manual, on the other hand, is insensitive to thieves' personal problems and whining..

Despite vast resources, most Ivory Tower experts exhaust their expertise, homilies complete, before addressing shoplifting performed by thieves fewer than a million or so in number. They leave it to *us* to deal with all the individual Johnnies who, when taken together, steal us blind.

One sermon many experts never tire of preaching is that to decrease thievery we must create millions of new jobs. (As if you or I could personally handle that little chore on the way home after work: "Gee, Ward, you're late for supper. Was traffic bad?" "No, dear, I just got some gas and made a few million jobs. Sorry I didn't call.") That may be a valid theory, but a Wilson and Hernstein study indicates job scarcity is not the problem:

"During the 1960's, one neighborhood in San Francisco had the lowest income, the highest unemployment rate, the highest proportion of families with incomes under $4,000 a year, the least educational attainment, the highest tuberculosis rate, and the highest proportion of substandard housing. That neighborhood was called Chinatown. Yet in 1965 there were only five persons of Chinese ancestry committed to prison in the entire state of California."

U.S. unemployment was at record lows in the 90's, but shoplifting continued to rise.

Do shoplifters and others have to steal to survive? In Cambodia or Rwanda, maybe, but in the United States? No way. Here, dishonesty is a choice. Millions of Americans live in identical or worse circumstances than our shoplifters and other thieves, but struggle desperately and maintain an honest life; *not* one based on self-deception, illusion, and theft.

> Asked why he shoplifts, one young man--who, I believe, speaks for *many*--replied, *"Because I can."* Why hassle total strangers? *"I just told you, man. Because I can."*

After stealing designer clothes, jewelry, and hundred-dollar shoes, *our* thieves ride or drive to homes with telephones, televisions, and food in the 'fridge. It's rare to find a mother rustling baby-formula, but common to find one poaching earrings. They don't steal because they need to, they steal because they want to. One thief put it this way: "What's the point of being a thief if you have to live like normal people?" Feel sorry for them if you please, but don't forget there ain't but so much actual help to spread around.

The value of stolen items ranges from pennies to hundreds of dollars, but the total loss is staggering: perhaps fifty-billion dollars annually. (Can you even imagine fifty-thousand million?) If that figure seems high, the low-ball estimates range from ten billion annually to twenty-five million every day (plus at least another five million lost to dishonest employees, every day).[1] (See Chapter notes, Number 1, pg. 141)

If a pair of $5 earrings is stolen, what is the cost to the store in terms of "dollar-sales?" For an accurate answer, look to the profit margin. With a 4 percent "bottom line" (net profit), $4 represents the profit from $100 in sales, $2 represents $50 and so on (at a

25 to 1 ratio). If one shirt is stolen, twenty-five more must be sold just to stay even. If one $40-piece of merchandise is lost, that is the profit from one thousand-dollars of sales (the loss times twenty-five). And I've seen over $1,000 of merchandise walk out the door with a single shoplifter (a loss which represents all the profit from *$25,000* in sales).

The true extent of losses can't be known without a count or inventory, but to keep pace with a 4% net (which is about normal for retail; less for grocery), 25 sales are needed for every 1 item lost. Otherwise, you might have a year of sales without profit; a waste of investment, time, and effort called "feeding the monkey just to watch him crap."

Of course, the average thief doesn't steal just $1 per theft. Estimates place the average between $10 and $200, depending on such variables as the type of thief and store. In 1992 I arrested Kimberly P., 29 years old, with $8 of concealed merchandise. In 1994, in a different town, I busted her with $40-worth. Not recognizing me, she wailed and swore it was the first time she ever tried to steal. Were these her only two attempts at shoplifting in two years or just the only two times she was caught and prosecuted?

> **Who steals?** Margo Adams, tell-all female companion of baseball's Wade Boggs, with a $258 designer jacket from a California department store.   --*Time* magazine, 3 April 89

In 1989, Hurricane Hugo announced his imminent arrival off the Carolina coast with a gentle, harmless breeze--so it seemed to me--but eight hellish hours later, losses were in the billions. Many thieves, too, often appear pleasant to the untrained eye, but working largely undetected they slam American business like one Hugo after another.

For many years I didn't understand why people steal when they can afford to buy; why they feel no remorse, are seldom stopped, and are normally not noticed even by store security. To get a handle on these things, I interviewed hundreds of thieves and spoke with judges, lawyers, police, store security and detectives, retail managers, employees, and thieves' families. I studied security programs and videos; I experimented. Throughout all that, I suffered no shortage of enthusiastic volunteers: the procession of thieves is endless. Believe it or not, sometimes they even arrive by the *busload*.

> **Who steals?** Former Mayor of Cleveland and one of the nation's first black big-city mayors, Carl Stokes was involved in not one, but two shoplifting incidents. The first involved a $2.39 screwdriver, the second a 20-pound bag of dog food.
> --Time magazine, 19 June 1989
>
> (A couple of phone calls to Cleveland revealed that Mr. Stokes admitted taking the screwdriver. His dog food caper went to jury trial where he successfully pled absent-mindedness.)

## 1.01 Why Thieves Steal

Ordinarily, motives for shoplifting and other types of theft are addressed by non-profit sociologists and bottom-line politicians. Aside from distraught parents, they're about the only ones who have the time (or inclination) to worry about it.

But if we set those experts and parents aside--just for a moment, please--the rest of us might all agree that professional thieves are in it to make money, and most other thieves steal so they don't have to spend money. (At least that's what they *say*.) That sounds reasonable to most of us, but a few deep thinkers will never accept it: "Far too simplistic!" huff sociologists; "Too much Pavlov and not enough Freud," puff psychiatrists.

In the first place, they don't like input from pesky, "non-professional sources;" plus, they don't think that police and loss prevention know enough about psychology and the "unique" political-socioeconomics of deceivers to have a legitimate opinion anyway. Or we don't know as much as politicians like, oh...the Hero of Chappaquiddick, for example. They may be right, but the fact remains that a nod's as good as a wink to a blind horse.

> Employees of a large department store were left speechless by four "shoppers" in their 20's. Roaming from one display to another, making one mess after another, the quartet gaily sang a song to the tune of "We Are The World." The lyrics--as they sang them--went like this: "We are the world, we are the children.
> To make our world a better place
> we do our stealin'."
>
> These "customers," one after another (none of whom made a purchase, by the way), occasionally shouted, "We ain't stealin' nothin'!" The group then laughed riotously and swung into another chorus.

A Georgia police officer was asked why he shot a man six times. After thinking, he said, "Because I didn't have time to reload." When asked why he stole two shirts, a teenager replied that he "couldn't hide more." A girl who stole a $3 item said she wanted "lots," but didn't think she could get away with lots. That's why she stole just one.

Thieves subscribe to the **SWAT Principle**: Steal What's Available Today. They steal a pocketful because they can't get a sack full, a sack full because a crate full is too risky or impractical. If they don't steal all you have, it's not because they wouldn't.

A teenager told me that he and some chums, while skateboarding, once noticed a shirt displayed in a store window. One of the crew dipped inside and moments later reappeared wearing a new shirt over his own. "It was totally awesome." In 1955, Albert Cohen wrote, "...stealing is not just another way of getting something. In the delinquent subculture the stolen dollar has an odor of sanctity that does not attach to the dollar saved or the dollar earned." The problem wasn't resolved. Instead, it spread and mutated.

> Many shoplifters ask, "Are you going to call the police? Am I going to jail?"
> They seem shocked when I reply, "Of course you're going to jail. You stole something." When I ask what they expected, they say, "Not that."
> "What?" I say, "What did you expect?" So many times, they blurt, "I thought you'd let me go."
> Why on earth would they think that? [2] (See Chapter Notes, Number 2, pg. 141)

**A rose by any other name.** In college, I failed botany and zoology numerous times. Philosophy, I'm proud to say, was a brighter star in my academic constellation. There, somewhere between the Greek alphabet and rationalizations for cannibalism, lay a topic I *really* sank my teeth into: "**THE ARGUMENT OF THE BEARD**." The thesis, in essence, is how many individual hairs make a beard?

If we begin with a full beard and pluck hairs out one by one, an argument will eventually arise as to whether or not the beard is still a beard. At some point, the removal of a single hair from hundreds or thousands precipitates the argument. But where?

When I ask amateur shoplifters if they'd steal a $100 item, they usually answer "no." Why? "That's different." How about $90? On we go, until inevitably we learn that we don't know "exactly" what our personal dollar-limit might be, and never mind the legal limit is always *zero*.

Many people debate what really constitutes stealing and at what dollar-level theft should be punished. Parents say, "I don't want to see my son in trouble for such a small thing." Would they rather see him in trouble for a big thing? No...they're saying it's just shoplifting so let's not treat it like a crime.

Some parents actually say they don't feel their child stole "enough" to be prosecuted. When I ask them to define "enough" with standard units of measure--like miles or dollars-- we encounter the Argument of the Beard. (And that type always becomes angry.) "It's a little thing," they say. "I can't believe you're making a big deal out of it!" (Shame on me!)

To millions, shoplifting is not only no big deal, it's socially and morally acceptable; a non-criminal activity that magically breaks the curse of "wait until you can afford it." As one shoplifter explained on national television, "The key word is *shop*. It's not the same as stealing." In order to have, you can buy, trade, or shoplift. It's *all* OK. [3] (See Chapt. Notes, No. 3, pg. 141)

**The making of Frankenstien.** It's common for juveniles to enter adulthood possessing neither personal experience in responsible planning or decision-making nor even the habit of weighing consequences. ("Life skills," they're called.) Like doting parents, society conditions them to expect protection from even the most predictable and natural consequences of bad choices. So great is this expectation that they believe it's a "right."

Unfortunately, nature's law holds that good judgment comes from experience, and experience comes from bad judgment. That's nature's way: all bad decisions are pregnant with negative consequences. But like Dr. Frankenstien, we like to tinker with natural law.

Our creation--our monster--is millions of demanding, irresponsible "adult-children" who are high on sugar-plum "rights" with no inner core of personal responsibility. They make poor choices and when (inevitably) confronted with negative consequences, they become genuinely confused, even enraged. They cry foul: "It's not fair!" But what they actually mean is it doesn't *feel* good.

Our 24-, 34-, and 44 year-old adult-children frequently equate the assignment of personal responsibility with harassment. To them, any arrested thief is presumed a poor, sad victim. Assuming, of course, he was stealing from someone else.

Ayn Rand, in *Atlas Shrugged,* presented the concept of trading "Value for Value" as being an indispensable thread in our economic tapestry. That's not rocket science. In fact, it's common activity at every lunchroom table in schools world wide. Unfortunately, we've got tens of millions of thieves who prefer the concept of income redistribution by virtue of speed, deception, fear and force.

From mountains to valleys and sea to sea, the landscape is choked with kudzu masquerading as lilies. They get, but toil not; take, but pay not.

## 1.02 Why Others *Don't* Steal

In addition to interviewing thieves, I asked non-thieves "Why not steal?" Socially fashionless and shamefully unscientific to be sure, but...hey, so what?

While shoplifters conjured up rationalizations for theft that ranged from remarkably naive to incomprehensibly bizarre, paying-customers provided remarkably simple reasons not to steal. The most common reason had only two words: "Stealing's wrong." Not illegal, mind you, but wrong.

Who's teaching morals here? Why do some people have a clear idea of right and wrong while others are genuinely confused or even clueless? Ten year-old Ricky paid for his candy because "stealin's bad." How did he know that? "My mom and dad tell me."

I know, I know: that's not enough. In our society it's not enough that kids think stealing is wrong; they must think it wrong for the right reasons. Before we embrace moral values they must be "explored" and thoroughly examined from every conceivable angle. Until the exploration is complete and consensus reached, honesty can mean nothing.

Well, Captain, if *that's* the way you think, I will *personally* be the most enthusiastic hat-waver on the dock when you and your ship of exploring fools go sailing away.

## 1.03 Roots

Typically, many problems go unaddressed until there's a "fire in the hole." It's certainly necessary to put fires out, but is it your plan to allow problems to fester until they require emergency action? Do you find yourself putting out the same fires again and again? What root issues allow them to rekindle? In most companies, for every ten people whacking away at the branches of problems there might be one person digging at roots.

Is it better to catch every burglar or to eliminate burglary altogether? Effective programs aggressively identify and resolve root issues and, as a result, hundreds of "situations" are never handled...because they never arise.

How issues are resolved depends on such things as available time and resources and degrees of cooperation and resistance. (You can expect that any solution requiring any degree of personal inconvenience will be resisted.by someone.) Certain behaviors are essential to resolve any issue, and those essential behaviors are called "requirements."

## 1.04 Sun Tzu meets Jimmy Johnson

Many shoplifters and other retail thieves have hundreds of hands-on thefts behind them. Highly skilled in battle for cash and merchandise, they operate as though guided by principles of war developed by the ancient Chinese warlord Sun Tzu: use a variety of offensive and defensive tactics; use spies to learn the enemies' secrets; study their dispositions and exploit their weaknesses. Strike where they are not. Play to win.

Jimmy Johnson also plays to win. His college and professional football teams included players from fashionable suburbs as well as dirt-poor streets. But that's not uncommon. What *is* uncommon--and made Jimmy Johnson legendary--is that from the raw material of groups and individuals, he molded cohesive, disciplined *teams* that *won*.

**Teams & Groups.** On the food chain of endeavor, teams are at the top and feed on everything below. Groups, crowds, mobs, and individuals are all usually "below."

Teamwork is so powerful and the word "team" has become so symbolic in our culture that virtually every business has eliminated their management and sales staffs and replaced them with "management teams" and "sales teams." Predictably, most of that effort accomplishes very little because not every group can *be* a team, and simply calling a group "a team" does not make it one. Teams have certain essential characteristics.

Essential to the success of teams are open communications, commitment to shared goals and value systems, trust between individuals, self-discipline, adherence to standards, subordination of individual personalities to "the team," and team-oriented reward systems.

One of Johnson's fundamental success "secrets" with the Dallas Cowboys and Miami Dolphins was an uncompromising dedication to exceptional standards (requirements). That same "secret" was practiced twenty-five centuries earlier by the military genius Sun Tzu, also a coach of sorts, who went eighty seasons undefeated in a very tough conference. (The best edition of his book, I think, is *The Art of War* forwarded and edited by James Clavell.)

**Requirements.** By definition, requirements (standards) are not requests. When those words are used interchangeably or people don't know which is meant, the result is trouble. How to tell one from the other? Where "failure to comply" is not excused or ignored, but is consistently punished, a requirement exists. If failure to comply is ignored or *not* punished, then the "requirement" is, in fact, only a request or suggestion. (Maybe even *fantasy*, but whatever the label, it's foolish and silly to call it a requirement).

When a "requirement" is implemented, there is much more at risk than semantics. Whenever a requirement is violated and your reaction is to "back off," bad things happen. Those employees who followed your instructions usually include the better ones, the new ones, and the borderline. At the very least, they will suffer frustration, disillusionment, or confusion. They did as you instructed because they believed in you or your office. Then you made fools of them. If they harbor resentment, you are to blame.

Another result is that employees who did not do what you "required" (and some who did) will consider you a weak and stupid leader who doesn't know his own mind and who can be directly and successfully challenged on his own turf. That, naturally, ensures future challenges. Meanwhile, your worst and dishonest employees have an easier time swaying your "borderliners" and your best people become tolerant of dysfunction.

Every such battle that you lose--and they *are* battles lost--exacts an ever increasing toll in respect and credibility. Eventually, you lose the ability to successfully initiate any meaningful reform and may even put yourself in a precarious position--legally--to enforce *anything*. The first rule of rules, then, is "Rules are enforced." It follows that you must never make rules or initiate requirements that you will be unable or unwilling to enforce.

Consequences may change with time, but rules for victory do not. Players not meeting Jimmy Johnson's requirements had their names dropped. Those not meeting Sun Tzu's had their heads lopped. If something is a requirement, enforce it. Or modify it to something you *will* enforce. Otherwise, openly announce what everyone already knows: that it's only a request and does not carry the weight of policy. It might be painful to operate that way, but it's honest and essential to order, credibility, and victory.

**Breaking orbit.** A satellite requires more energy to break out of Earth's orbit--a thousand miles, more or less--than it needs to travel the next ten million miles through space. Changing existing patterns of behavior also requires the most effort at the front end. Without the resources and determination ("resolve") to break orbit, leaders often give up or become distracted before the new course is firmly set. There follows a costly and discouraging "back-slide," making future efforts much more difficult.

There is no "silver bullet" to eliminate theft, and every loss prevention (LP) person I know--myself included--struggle daily with many of the issues identified in this book. The ultimate goal, though, is not perfection. It is the step by step, issue by issue creation and day to day growth and maintenance of the most effective, secure, and profitable operation possible. No more can be asked and no more given.

As you read these pages, constantly ask yourself, "How does this apply to my own situation? How can I adapt this?" Take your time, but don't dawdle; the clock is ticking. If you have something of value, sooner or later thieves will come; and some will come again and again.

**Your Alternative.** Without planing, discipline, and resolve, retail operations risk slipping into a deep funk that I call "sleep-walking to inventory."

Eventually, employees get raises and promotions despite engaging in what *should* be intolerable behavior. Teams dissolve into groups with conflicting agendas, key players cannot agree on how to proceed, and long-range planning and goals become jokes.

Proactive work decreases as people simply react to whatever seems most pressing that particular day. Confused employees must guess at what to do, and often guess incorrectly. Hardly immune, loss prevention becomes ineffective and able to deal only with thieves who are even worse. (And no store is lucky enough to have only totally incompetent thieves.)

Then, the most amazing thing happens: even *that* cheery situation degenerates.

Fortunately, though, before things reach that point, anyone with even the slightest hold on reality has time to write a resume.

**"Wise men learn by others harms, fools by their own."**
                                                                                        -- B. Franklin

StealMeBlind

---

A Clarification to Placate a Friend:

It's been pointed out that here or there I seem to imply that some criminal defense attorneys view victims of crime as mere inconvenient bodies of evidence, perhaps as obstacles in the path to a winning (or profitable) season.

I truly regret any misunderstanding. In point of fact, I firmly believe that no one who knows as much as I know about defense attorneys could *possibly* have a higher opinion of them than I do. And in *my* opinion they're about as

# Chapter 2
# Thieves and Deceivers

Shoplifting is the doorway through which most career criminals pass *en route* to "serious" crime; things such as burglary and armed robbery. It's the common entry to the World of Crime, and the door is usually wide open and unattended.

Where they exist, commercial security officers, plain-clothes and uniformed, stand watch as clocks tick and salaries mount. Average hourly wage for a security guard: $9.00. By the year? $19,000 plus expenses. The number of thieves actually arrested by an average security guard during an average 8-hour watch? None.

> Most shoppers don't steal, but those who do demand judicious attention. One study found that of 20-million active shoplifters, nearly 60 percent admitted stealing at least once a month, and nearly 30 percent from once a week to once a day.

In 1989, seven million shoplifters were arrested. What number escaped? Few stores estimate they catch even ten percent, and most estimate fewer than one percent. Consider these internal memos of a national retailer that spends millions annually to counter shoplifters:

"Shoplifting continues to be our most serious external form of shrinkage. We must focus our attention on this serious problem daily. Through strong awareness and improved customer service, we have our best chance of controlling this evil profit-reducer. Everyone must...strengthen and fortify our shoplifting defenses."

A memo from a store (with a good LP staff) with a national chain: "We estimate that in 1993 some 4,000 shoplifters will come through (this store). We can expect to apprehend about 10 percent."

Whether theft in a particular store occurs once a month or dozens of times daily depends in part on the location, size and configuration of the store, the number of employees on the sales floor, the season, type of merchandise, class of clientele, and quality of security programs. Some factors are controllable, some are not. Among the controllable are three that ultimately determine whether you win or lose: (1) customer-service skills of store personnel, (2) their *perception* of the shoplifting, internal theft, and the overall loss control problem, and (3) their personal role, as *they* perceive it.

> Two women arrested for shoplifting were toting an 18-month-old child. They agree that, when stealing, a baby "is a bigger problem than employees." Amateur thieves consider routine "good customer service" to be an ineffective hindrance to stealing, and it doesn't bother professional thieves at all.
>
> "Good customer service" keeps today's under-12 crowd honest, but that's about it.

To deal successfully with today's shoplifters, "good customer service" must be replaced with excellent customer service; far more than just can-I-help-you and well-let-me-know-if-I-can. It requires multiple, indirect follow-up contacts and teamwork. In actual practice in the retail community, "good customer service" is usually self-service.

Once upon a time, a good school staff kept us from chewing gum in class and smoking cigarettes behind the gym. Today, an exceptional staff keeps kids from dealing dope in halls and shooting each other. Society evolves, and most retailers, like school administrators, are way outside the curve. In fact, the entire criminal justice system is reeling from tides of juveniles, many quite violent, now swelling the ranks of street gangs and other professional and semi-professional criminal operations. *Ah, mi vida loca.*

Drawn by the lure of easy money, juveniles "turn pro" as young as ten years of age, and adults employ them to an extent undreamed of only ten years ago. Why? Because kids don't do hard time. They can be caught with felony loads of stolen goods or drugs and never scratch their names on a cell wall. While many shoplifters are fairly young, at the opposite end of the scale some areas see a significant rise in shoplifting among the elderly, adults in their 60's and 70's. [4 (Chpt. Notes, pg.141)]

## 2.01 Who Steals?

By way of an answer, I'll list categories not yet personally encountered: no nuns or priests, retail managers, cadets from military schools or officers in the Armed Forces. No doctors or dentists. I <u>have</u> arrested shoplifters ranging from 8 to 82, blacks, whites, Hispanics, Orientals, Gypsies, an American Indian from an obscure Northwest tribe, and a tourist from Scotland and her little friend too. But despite the vast range of shoplifters, general characteristics do exist (with *lots* of exceptions).

- The lower the level of education, the more likely to shoplift.
- About 85 percent of shoplifters are under age 35.
- The lower the level of personal income, the more likely to shoplift.
- The lower an individual's class, the more likely to steal. [5 (Chpt.Notes, pg.141)]

"Shoplifter profiles" differ from store to store on the same city block, and profiles vary for different departments within a single store. To pick thieves from a crowd, profiles help. (Obviously, though, if all your customers are elderly, your shoplifters are going to be elderly, too. For profile purposes, age, then, is moot.)

## 2.02 Categories of Thieves

Anyone who has seen the movie classic *Oliver Twist* knows what thieves looked like back when robbers said quaint things like "stand and deliver." Times have changed. It's now extremely difficult to spot an Artful Dodger simply by the cut of his clothes or his grammar. But some things change very little, and at this point I should mention Gypsy crime groups. All gypsies are sometimes called the Rom or "Travelers," but are not the same as "Irish Travelers,' another non-conventional crime group. (Gotta watch them, too.)

Thousands of criminal Gypsies exist, often traveling the US by caravan. Superb at deception and distraction, the dishonest teach even the youngest to help steal. If they come, don't take your eyes off your jewelry, cash office, and safes for a second, even if they're locked. Also, beware Gypsies snatching cash from open tills or out of your hands. If they do, they palmed some (and will often *act* ignorant or mental). If 6 to 12 enter (often by 2's and 3's), call the police immediately and tell them you think you're about to be robbed.

Traditionally, female Gypsies do most of the hands-on retail stealing. Children act as distractions, and males plan, back up, drive, etc. The women's clothes are becoming more conventional, but they still often wear long skirts with "booster aprons" beneath. If you detain or arrest Gypsies, expect shenanigans and <u>do not</u> take your eyes off of them.

Besides criminal Gypsies (and several other non-conventional but organized criminal groups), there are four broad, if imprecise, categories of shoplifters: the Professional, the Recreational/Social, the Disturbed, and the Situational. But lines blur and categories mingle. Even after an arrest and investigation, it's often impossible to be sure what type you've got. Good thieves are good actors, and some are Hollywood quality. When a professional is caught, he might portray the bumbling amateur. When an amateur's caught, *he* pretends it's the first time he ever tried to steal. It's all a part of their game.

> The world of loss prevention is a cross between war and sports; an arena where Sun Tzu blends with Jimmy Johnson in daily battles for profit and survival.

## 2.03 Professionals

"Obviously, crime pays or there'd be no crime." --G. Gordon Liddy, 1986

Professionals are in it for money which represents their entire earned income or a significant percentage of it. (In this, shoplifters are like prostitutes. A few are "full-time," but most are "part-time;" semi-pro.) Some professionals travel extensively--Atlanta today, Charlotte tomorrow--but *all* towns are home to professionals and local shoplifting rings.

Some thieves get advance orders from their customers or from a "fence" who buys and sells stolen goods. He can be an individual or a store-front; waiting just outside the store, down the street, or many miles distant. A thief may service several fences and other buyers, all of whom may appear quite respectable. A bait-and-tackle shop, for example, may not be particular about how it acquires $500 worth of reels for only $100, and how many school kids happily buy $15-CD's for five bucks and $40 jeans for ten? (Also, many restaurants buy and sell stolen food.) Buying from a fence is like watching a low budget movie: if you want to enjoy it, don't ask questions. (Also, see Gangs & Cliques, page 112.)

The American Black Market flourishes. Everywhere, professionals and semi-pros provide the underground economy with quality merchandise at substantial savings. Hundred-dollar sweaters go for $25 and you can pick the color. Books, jewelry, cosmetics, toys, VCR's, antiques...just name it, and take 25-80 percent off Suggested Retail. Many consumers don't care. Others, even if suspicious, still shop the lowest price. It's supply and demand, "the politics of contraband." And honest merchants pay at both ends; their merchandise is stolen, then sold to their own customers by thieves.

Some people sell their blood every couple of weeks to get some extra cash. Others occasionally buy stolen items from their local thief, then return the item to the store to "earn" the difference between what they paid and what the store will refund. (These people say that since *they* didn't steal it, it's OK. And besides, the store already lost it.)

> Michelle typifies retail thieves. Since moving from her parents' home into her own apartment, she shoplifts once or twice a week "to save money." She's done it "about fifty times," and has eight friends who've done it "hundreds" of times. Did she worry about employees? "It never even crossed my mind." Why not? "Nobody ever gets caught." (Coming as it did from someone in handcuffs, I thought that was a little ironic.)

Two Hours and $700.00    Two girls (thirteen and fourteen) "handled" by an adult aunt hit six stores before taking a break at a fast food restaurant. They had no way of knowing, but three loss prevention (LP) officers from two stores were on their case. (And the girls paid no attention to a woman who followed them in for some tea.)

An hour earlier while "shopping" in one of the stores, the girls had asked a clerk hold their bags behind a checkout. The clerk took the bags and then called Loss Prevention. Suspicious, the LP manager decided to personally protect the girls' property and move the bags to a safer place. While doing so, the clumsy man tripped and spilled the contents all over the floor. (Purely accidental, of course, but my, oh, my, what do have we here?)

The girls "hit" a couple of stores with high-tech security, but got nailed "the old-fashioned way." When arrested, they had five large sacks of stolen merchandise. Each girl wore stolen clothes and each carried a stolen purse crammed with loot. Also recovered was a tool used to remove security devices.

As it goes, the girls weren't even taken to the police station, but were released into their aunt's custody within an hour of being "arrested." If it goes to trial, it could easily be a year or more before it happens. (Where will the witnesses be in a year?)

Professionals, regardless of age, often work alone, but usually work in twos or threes. This does not mean they enter the store together, nor does it mean they're the same sex, race, age, or even dressed alike. (Amateurs commonly work singly or in pairs, usually entering the store together.) Pros frequently use false names and false ID (or none). They might use birth-dates and social security numbers they know are "clean," like those of an honest niece or cousin. Some arrange in advance to "make bond" in case they're arrested.

Some "case" a place (look it over), leave, then return, snatch and go. Others "pay off" (bribe) employees with a flat fee ($20 to turn your back); some bribe by the piece ($x per item), or pay a percentage of the "take" or "score." Some pay employees with drugs.

The 1990's witnessed the rise of a brutal phenomenon called "carjacking," a no-nonsense variation of Grand Theft, Auto. Some professional shoplifters, overshadowed by their more media-grabbing cousins in the automobile industry, likewise have a more up-front style of doing business: three or more thieves descend like locusts and in a flurry of activity move, handle, drop, and pile merchandise. Or they just snatch it and go: any number of bags and pockets, and six to twelve hands, each with more moves than a Rolex. No clerk can monitor the activity, and the looting thieves know it. (They may even hit your stockroom or office. If discovered, he'll say he was looking for a restroom.)

If any serious attempt is made to oversee the chaos, the group often employs intimidation by cussing, getting loud, threatening, etc. They know that you know they are thieves, but what you think is irrelevant. They care only about what you do, and they leave only after getting what they want, or if it becomes clear they will not get it.

The words "time to go" mean employees are too bothersome or the desired items have been successfully concealed. (Once you get what you want, it's time to go.) If someone arrives on scene who appears willing to go toe-to-toe or who (God forbid!) just tells them to get out, it's definitely time to go. It's *de rigueur*--considered the "proper" thing--to posture and cuss on the way out, especially if an attempt to steal was thwarted.

Many conventional professional teams operate with Swiss precision. Members of the group (even children) distract employees while others select merchandise; or some bag while others help conceal that. Still others may be look-outs ("help look") or distractions ("tricksters"), help with doors, block pursuit, or have a car(s) waiting. One may enter and browse, gathering items for a "bagger" who arrives later, sometimes hours, sometimes minutes. (A good bagger, with bag, baby buggy, or whatever tool it is, might enter, get the loot, and be gone in under two minutes. 120-seconds doesn't give you much reaction time.)

How do shoplifters become so efficient? By practice and rehearsal, study, trial and error. Professional thieves, regardless of age, take their techniques as seriously as you take cash control. It's their livelihood. I've seen and heard shoplifters practicing with new thieves and teaching them the ropes. [6 (See Chapter Notes)] (Also, see Appendix 7.)

## *"Most of what I own, I got from stealing."*

For years, Alethia has been a professional shoplifter and flimflam artist who occasionally takes conventional short-term jobs here and there. At one time, she worked in South Carolina as a store security guard, and when asked if she stole from that store, she burst out laughing. "Of course!" Several times we drank coffee far into the night while she shared stories and answered questions.

"You watch a store for two days before you steal. You look at the employees, what you want, where things are, and how they do things. You look for cameras and security and stuff. You go in when they're busy, always when they're busy, not when they're standing around talking to each other. You send a clerk on a goose chase if you have to, and you get what you want.

Only after "learning the employees" (who is dangerous, who doesn't care, etc.) does she feel confident stealing frequently from any particular store. She works alone because she doesn't trust the quality of other thieves' work. ("I don't want to go to jail for someone else's stupidity.")

To Alethia, employees are either stupid or dangerous, and she believes most are stupid. She shoplifts "when the stupid (slack, incompetent) ones are there," and she uses several different methods to target inexperienced cashiers for cash-withdrawals. Common to all of her tactics for short-changing are, (1) Request change or exchange denominations of bills, and (2) "Distract 'em...keep 'em distracted. Talk to 'em. It's a mind-game."

She has personally stolen "hundreds of times" and claims to have made $1,500 on her "best day." Based on friends' and personal experiences, she estimates the "average" shoplifter is caught only one time for every hundred times he steals and gets away.

Whether they have a shopping-list or not, come alone or in a group, are looking for "the sort of things" that make their customers happy or just out stealing for themselves, if you give professionals half a chance, they'll do you like the James Gang did banks.

## 2.04 Amateur types

"It ain't no sin if you crack a few laws now and then, just so long as you don't break any." --Mae West

**A. Recreational and Social Shoplifters** These thieves sometimes steal just for fun or the thrill (the "rush") of doing something dangerous; bungee-jumping for a prize. It may be a response to peer-pressure, to "fit in" or to "prove themselves." Many amateurs truly believe that "everybody does it, nobody's hurt, and nobody ever gets caught."

If a speed limit's 65, won't you drive 70 or 75, if you're in a hurry? Probably. But the limit is still 65, *not* "65-plus-a-little-more-if-you're-in-a-hurry." So why not do 90? Is it OK to break the law a little but not a lot? Or is it OK to break the law as much as you figure you can get away with? I asked a teenage shoplifter, "As long as you were out stealing, why didn't you try to steal a pin-ball machine from the arcade?" His response: "That'd be stupid." Then came the kicker: "It's too big. I'd never get away with it."

He wouldn't try 90 in a 65 zone, but he'll sure do 70. Most recreational and social shoplifters believe a little larceny is OK the same way a little speeding is OK; that no one will miss the little bit they steal. "Yeah, sure it's illegal, but it's not the sort of thing that'll bother my conscience. I mean, it's not like something serious."

To millions, it's a "victimless" crime. The theft is from a store, which is a "what" rather than a "who;" from a building, a pile of cinder blocks. And who ever heard of victimizing a cinder block? As for employees, "They get paid whether I steal or not."

Once someone decides to be a shoplifter, the moral hurdle is overcome and stealing becomes just another way of "getting." They *do* continue to entertain reasons for not stealing, but those reasons have nothing to do with morality. Reasons not to steal include mechanical problems such as too little time, too small a bag, etc. "Getting caught" is a minor concern. "Just don't be real stupid," one says, and the chance of getting caught is "less than getting hit by a car" (presumably while crossing a street).

**B. The Disturbed** This distressing group needs some serious counseling. To a dangerous degree and for a variety of reasons, their perception of reality is sadly distorted. Nevertheless, most should be prosecuted.

In 1992 I arrested a man in his mid-20's for stealing watches. Initially, all went well, but suddenly, he lashed out with a foot, kicking me and causing considerable pain. When I demanded an explanation, he responded by snarling, "You kidnapped my family!"

I told him I didn't recall doing that, but if he'd tell me a little more about it, maybe it'd come back to me. The floodgate opened: "You Caucasian (expletive) kidnapped my ancestors 400 years ago! I got a *right* to take from you!"

A ten-year-old with a stolen football stuffed in his overalls was *very* belligerent. Crying real tears, he repeatedly screamed, "I hate cops!" It was too odd. I called his mother and the police, and then dug deeper. Much deeper.

Two days before that, he was caught stealing candy from a drug store, but was released after being lectured. He hadn't told them, but he *wanted* to be arrested. My young desperado was from a broken home and in the legal custody of his mother. The father wanted custody, and many painful battles were fought. Weary, the father persuaded the boy to get into trouble in hopes the law would send him to live with Dad.

Failing at the drug store, the persistent youngster escalated. If I, too, had simply put him out, what mischief would he have tried next? (Notice the word "mischief." He's no thief.) With the help of a good police officer and conscientious social worker, this particular story had a happy ending. The next time I saw my new friend--a couple of months later--he was creeping into my security office, grinning ear to ear. No question: extra time and effort with little humans makes life better all around.

"Roses are red, violets are blue. I'm schizophrenic, and I am, too." Compelling "voices" might convince schizophrenics to steal, and drunks apparently think they're invisible when stealing. Another type of disturbed individual, but rare, is the kleptomaniac ("the guy who helps himself because he can't help himself"). A stolen item represents some unrelated object or experience, a "symbol" which may provide sexual gratification. (Obsessive-compulsive disorders--very common--probably account for more mental-health-related shoplifting than kleptomania. "Addiction" to shoplifting is another problem.)

Most kleptomaniacs are female, about 20 to 40. This condition is *so* rare, though, that if a person claims to be one that pretty much means she isn't. The only one I've caught who was adamant about being a klepto couldn't produce a note from her doctor. (It's incidental, of course, but she also claimed to be a nurse when she isn't stealing socks.)

Other disturbed people feel they have a "duty" to steal from Big Business or from "the oppressors of the people," and God only knows what evil thing you do with your ill-gotten profits. In their minds even the "mom and pop" corner grocery could be an integral part of some evil conspiracy that will be thwarted, apparently, if enough people steal beef jerky and Ding Dongs.

Some people who may or may not belong in the "Disturbed" category are generic juveniles from about 12 to 14 years old. Ordinary kids steal an incredible assortment of things for any number of juvenile reasons. They even steal things they don't *want*. [7] ("Alas! Regardless of their doom, the little victims play." --T. Gray)

> Most shoplifters are amateur and situational. This means no ingenious plan, no tricky coats or booster boxes. They come in and just stuff things into pockets, pants or bags. They are less professional than you are, so the advantage is yours.

### C. The Situational Shoplifter

This type shoplifter--often labeled "Impulsive"--can be a real curiosity. He's the $40,000-executive stealing a $2 pen; the average guy who could easily pay, but steals anyway. Impulsiveness does seem common in their thefts, and they say things like, "I just don't know what came over me."

Sometimes it's, "I've been under a lot of stress lately," or "The check-out line was too long," or "Right then it just seemed OK." Like other thieves, the Number One Reason they give for stealing is "I don't know." And that's pure lie; they *do* know why they did it. (Incidentally, the check-out line reason is common. When lines are short and moving, some thefts are deterred.)

Situational temptation gets the best of these folks and sympathy might come easy, especially since they seem so sincere when they say it's their "first time." Unfortunately, the claims of these twice-wed virgins don't sit well with mathematics. The chance of being caught during a first and only attempt at shoplifting is *so* small as to make it statistically insignificant. In truth, temptation gets the best of them more often than they care to remember.

### 14 Shoplifting Tips From a Professional Thief

1. It's always best to have a store employee help you.
2. Concentrate on "stupid" employees: they're slow and don't pay attention. Go in when they're working.
3. If you need to, make up something for a clerk to do. Send him on a "goose chase."
4. Go in when there are more customers than employees. (Note: Some pros hit when a store is opening or closing, when employees are preoccupied with registers and other first or last minute chores; or during lunch hours, when stores are short-handed.)
5. Before you steal from a new place, check it out for a couple of days. (Find cameras, mirrors, dressing rooms. Notice how they do things. Learn who works there. If they have plain-clothes security, see when they work.)
6. Before you go in to steal, know where the items are that you want. Know exactly where you'll steal them and exactly how you're going to do it.
7. A really large pocketbook (purse) is best for stealing, coats are equally good. Bags attract attention.
8. Figure out who's around and wait till you see them distracted. If they don't get distracted, distract them yourself. Then steal.
9. For flimflams and short-change switches, use a cashier you know is new or stupid. (Talk a lot; ask questions; keep him from focusing on the money and what's happening. Do the same when you slide things past a cashier, so he won't notice he hasn't rung them up. Keep him from looking at what's happening.)
10. Unless employees are stupid, never go in when it's really slow. They might look at you and think about you. (**Note:** Others like a slow store where employees get occupied with "work" and pay no attention to "customers.")
11. Stay away from places with cameras and security people who dress like customers. (Get other people to steal from these places for you. *You* go to safer places.)
12. If there's more than one of you, know exactly what everybody's supposed to do.
13. It's a mind game. Don't let them organize their thoughts.
14. Before you go in to steal, know how you're going to leave.

   \* As mentioned, Alethia is a professional shoplifter operating mostly in New York City, the State of New Jersey, the Richmond, Va. area, and Charleston, SC.

## 2.05 Refunds and Exchanges

A thief might make a purchase *and* steal. The purchase provides a store bag for future stealing and might confuse anyone who was watching. "Well, I thought her purse was smaller when she came in, but she's buying something so maybe she's honest," or "Maybe what she's buying is what I thought she stuck in her purse." Also, thieves try to demonstrate "honesty" so they'll be trusted (and ignored) in the future. And what's the harm? They can just bring the purchase back for a refund.

Thieves take every advantage of refund and exchange policies and, unfortunately, these are areas where honest shoppers routinely have their feelings hurt. (Even when employees suspect an item was stolen, they must be diplomatic.)

Some thieves steal what's handy (easy), and return it later for something they *really* want, like cash. Or they have it returned by an accomplice, addict, unsuspecting relative, or a go-fer for hire. To prevent a plague of stolen merchandise returned for cash, the best policy is just don't do it without a sales receipt. (Yeah, *right*.) But whether cash or straight exchange, to deter and slow thieves down you must require *real* identification and get as much info as possible. (But always: no receipt and no ID means no refund or credit.)

Determine a reasonable rate (one a week, one a month, one a quarter...) for refunds without receipts and, if a customer reaches that limit, politely advise him that there will be *no* future refunds without a receipt. Advise him also, that because of his history (volume) of returns, even future *exchanges* will be "very difficult." If he returns for an exchange, give a different size or color only; not a different item. After that, no receipt, no nothing.

Don't expect a thief and the "returner" to be the same person. Nonetheless, *do* get good physical descriptions (height, weight, etc.) and *lots* of information (driver's license number, address, DOB, etc.). On all refunds, get a signature on a receipt for the money, and *personally* check the ID. See if the signature on the refund receipt matches the signature on the ID. Always compare signatures on charge cards, checks, and paper media, and *always* compare ID pictures and information to the customer who presents it.

Again, an employee must personally record the info off the ID. *Do not* let customers do that. They lie. Also, don't ask if the address or phone number in your records is "still correct." Get the info then compare and verify it later. If employees get refunds, track their information in the same manner. Always keep employees' personal information current and check it against refunds from customers to see if any frequent refunders share an employee's name, address, telephone, or credit card numbers. (See Refund Laws, pg. 24.)

> Giving cash refunds without receipts *invites* thieves. By returning merchandise to the the store, they get full retail rather than a discounted street price. (Much more profitable.)

An invaluable tool for refund tracking, minimizing bad checks, and exposing fraud is a city cross-reference directory with telephone numbers to match street addresses, and addresses to match phone numbers. (One source: City Publishing Co., Independence, KA, 316-331-2650) Look for refunds to different names, but with matching addresses or phone numbers: you might find many people living together who constantly "lose" receipts *and* seem to have lots of parties where presents need returning. That is a den of thieves.

Whenever possible, check phone numbers and other information before you give anyone a significant amount of cash. Does the person answering the phone deny knowing the person returning the merchandise? Is the phone disconnected? If so, no refund.

If a customer becomes testy while you verify information, you might point out that "everything's getting complicated." Play it light, (usually). I explained to one irate man that "the store is set up to have merchandise go one way and money the other. Things get complicated when they go against the flow. We try to get it right the first time so there won't be a problem later. You want to just forget about it?" It was his third questionable return in one week, so he could take it or leave it. I was cutting him off anyway.

Most customers happily cooperate if things aren't terribly complicated or time consuming. Some, however, honestly don't seem to grasp a store's need for information. With these, try, "When our auditors come, they need to spot-check refunds and exchanges." Also, it may help to say that keeping records helps with customer service, and sometimes random mailings are sent out. "Since customer satisfaction is so very important to our company, these forms are necessary, thank you."

Refunds and exchanges are for purchases, not stolen items. Letters should be sent to specific individuals, anyone receiving a refund from a suspicious employee, all names from a particular day (perhaps Monday, then two weeks later all names from Tuesday, etc.), refunders without receipts, and/or refunds over x-number of dollars. An important function is address-verification. Think hard about future no-receipt refunds or exchanges for people whose mail is returned as undeliverable, not known, no such street number, etc.

If a thief works with a dishonest employee, sales receipts are easy to get, and thieves often have a string of returners-for hire. That makes effective refund tracking *much* more difficult. Mailings help identify these employees. For refunds *with* receipts, does the receipt indicate the item was purchased by cash, check or bank card? Does any employee have a much higher than average number of refunds with cash or credit card receipts? Also, check the *dollar amount* of refunds. Does anyone have a much higher than average dollar figure?

A computer is best, but no-receipt refund logs can be three-ring binders with homemade forms (Appendix 9). Keep forms in alphabetical order. When you cut a person's refund privilege, note that on the refund form as "apology," and the employee who advised the customer signs and dates it. Also, keep a tally of the quantity of refunds each employee gives (plus $-value and noting with or without receipt). Does anyone stand out?

Yours is not the only store that your thieves visit. Identify other stores carrying identical or similar merchandise and go introduce yourself. Make friends. Ask them to call if they think someone's out stealing or passing bad checks. Get names, ID numbers and descriptions of thieves and suspects. Look at pictures. (Note: Be careful with name and information sharing. Be aware that you might have no idea how discreetly the other party handles it. Even if you can legally share, have the ground rules laid out up front.)

## 2.06 Employee Theft

Two hundred years ago, Benjamin Franklin wrote, "The open foe may prove a curse, but a pretended friend is worse." Theft by employees is not normally "shoplifting" per se (though it may qualify as such in some circumstances). It's usually considered another type of larceny such as 'breach of trust.' Though this manual deals primarily with non-employee theft, employees can play a significant role in losses. In a worst-case, an employee--even a school kid--can hit a store for a thousand dollars of merchandise a day.

Some people simply will not work where they cannot steal. A rule of thumb for personnel: 10% of employees will not steal from you come hell or high water. They just won't. Another 10% steal regardless of generous wages, a splendid personal financial situation, and apparent sterling personal integrity. They just do. [8] (See Chapter Notes, pg. 142)

Some dishonest employees help others steal. One popular method is the "under-ring" (also called "sliding"). Friends, family, and other dishonest employees take merchandise to registers where dishonest cashiers ring only a fraction of the ticket price or don't ring some items at all. (Every item should be rung in turn, one thing at a time. Watch for merchandise being bagged or slid across the counter en masse or too fast, *especially* before the register sings. And watch for personal visitors at cash registers; don't tolerate that.)

Professional dishonest employees sometimes freelance their way from store to store. Connie is an excellent example. Her job application shows she worked three years with a small retail store that closed, followed by a year-long gap in employment that she explains as being pregnant and time with her baby. Before retail, she was a part-time college student. Her personal references speak highly of her, she seems sincere, is punctual, dresses well, and is eager to work.

She works several days and all goes well. Saturday, she leaves in a rush because her child is sick. By coincidence, the register comes up short. Could cash-pulls dropped at the bank be over? The manager can't know for sure until Monday. She calls in Sunday to say her husband doesn't want her working, so she won't be back. What really happened?

She lined up two cashier jobs the same week and worked about 20 hours at each. The stores had about $400 in cash shorts and only The Shadow knows how much sliding and under-rings were done, credit card numbers stolen, hot checks taken, or stolen credit cards used. (She was all smiles collecting paychecks, and skipped town a short time later.)

A shocking cash shortage always grabs attention, but small cash overages--$1.35, 81¢ and the like--can signal a worse problem. Dishonest cashiers sometimes make false voids in the amount of a previous sale. The size of voids depends on the cashier's greed and fear, but they normally steal even-dollar amounts. So...if the fraudulent void is $11.35, they pocket a ten-dollar bill or two five's, leaving the register $1.35 *over*. If you look only for shorts, this can go on for a very long time indeed.

It's been said that the devil's greatest trick was convincing the world that he doesn't exist. Likewise, the MO of some thieves and 'till tappers' includes creating the illusion that nothing was stolen. One way thieves do this is by removing a few bills from the middle of wrapped stacks (bundles), without breaking the wrapper (or seal). They leave loose bills in place, untouched. At a glance, nothing's amiss.

A day (or week or month) later when that particular wrap is broken and each bill is counted, the "shortage" is discovered. But was it theft or a bank error? When did it even happen? How many people had access to it and since when...for how long?

> Shoplifters create a "nothing stolen" illusion by exchanging merchandise before attempting a refund. If they might not get cash for an easily stolen item, they first exchange it for something *very* difficult to steal; perhaps from a locked case. Later, someone returns that item for cash. Since it "couldn't" have been stolen, the cash refund is approved. (If a thief's not stealing right now, he's engaged in a bigger scam.)

(A national chain provides the following advisory.)

## Most Common Methods of Theft from Cash Registers

- **Under-ringing** (not ringing all items at correct price), but collecting correct amount of money from customer. Often, a notebook or piece of paper is used to calculate the correct total amount of the sale. In most cases the money is placed in the register and removed later.
- **"No-Sale" ring** and/or working with an open cash drawer. This would apply to under-ringing. It is the most common method of a solo thief.
- **Cash theft.** Salesperson removes money from the register and conceals it.
- **Holding register receipts** used later to prepare "phony" void/over-ring or used for a **fraudulent refund.**
- **The most costly method** of theft at the register occurs when a sales-person fails to ring up merchandise being purchased by an accomplice (friend, relative, or other employee). Items taken to the register are rung at a greatly reduced price, and some not rung at all. (Often called "sliding.")

**How to catch a cashier skimming.** This method eliminates the need for lengthy surveillance. Get someone trustworthy, *whose face is totally unknown to the clerk*, to make what is called an "exact-change purchase." Decide in advance what item the "shopper" will purchase, and he should know exactly where it is located. It should be a "low-profile" item that no one would miss, *not* something noticeable or unique. It should not require more than about $20. More might be considered "entrapment." (Not good.)

Have his watch synchronized with the register's internal clock. He waits outside and out of sight with his beeper. When no customers or employees are present at the cash area other than the suspected clerk, the manager *pages* the shopper. He enters in a rush, quickly gets his item and hurries to the register. (There must be no witnesses nearby that could worry the cashier.) It doesn't matter if the clerk is behind the register or not; he gets her attention, shows the price sticker, puts the cash in her hand or on the counter, and *leaves*.

He should leave a bit extra, but not more than about a dollar too much. If the purchase comes to $4.65 (tax included), he can drop a $5-bill and quietly tell her, "Here. I'm in a *big* hurry. Keep the change. Thanks a lot." He leaves quickly, before she reacts. He notes the time, and *never looks back*. Later, check the register tape to see if the transaction is recorded. (Recording the serial number on the bill[s] beforehand is helpful in some cases.) In addition, a second person could watch the operation from hiding and see what happens; or you could have the whole thing (video) recorded. However you do it, remember this: if the cashier catches on or is badly spooked, you'll get no decent second chance.

## 2.07 Cash Shortages and Tracking

Cash shortages are maddening. They can be caused by dishonest cashiers or bookkeepers, errors making change, voids, or refunds, botched bank deposits, lost checks, dishonest people taking change to registers, dishonest managers, short-change artists, or thieves who get their hands in a register or grab cash from the office.

Most cash discrepancies work themselves out, but always act quickly. Check inside the register and under the drawer; around and under the register; check change bags, trash, the floor, inside the safe, and everywhere money is counted. Is a bank deposit over? If still missing, it might show up--somehow--the following day. If not, *maybe* it was stolen.

"Maybe," because I once saw an honest cashier give $60 too much change. She was handed $20 for an $8 purchase and gave $72 back. Why? Well, why does anybody do a dumb thing? Before you blame register operators for shortages though, the first step, *always*, is to make sure the office people are competent and honest. Can they steal or make errors that throw you off by making registers or tills appear short?

Some people track shortages as small as $5, others track only $20 or more. It's your decision. If you track only shortages above $10 or $20, cashiers hitting you for lunch money (and even more) slip through the net. *But,* if you do much volume, registers are bound to be a little off one way or another. Whatever the limit, use a log for each register.

Whether it seems theft or error, track who handled cash, made change, and ran the register, and who else did and did not work that day. It may become necessary to stagger schedules if two or more strong suspects work the same hours or days. (Tip: Compare hire-dates against $-shorts.) In the example below, five cashiers run the same register.

On Saturday the 16th, four cashiers work and it's $29 short. Is it lost, stolen, or paper error? Log it. Wednesday, you're $31 short. You log it and wonder about Lee and Aynsley. Before things get any worse, make sure no one is making honest mistakes with procedures [such as voids] that make registers appear cash-short.

When you see the shortage on Friday, you think Lee has to go, but be patient. Even if it's costly, you need a longer (better) track record.

Saturday the 23rd creates a dilemma. You thought Lee was your thief, so what happened? Be patient and maybe stagger schedules. In a couple of weeks you see that the 20th was probably some sort of error. Whatever's going on, William *is* your man.

Analyze shortages and overages, and study his voids, no-sales, refunds, and any bad checks he took from customers. After *all* your homework is done, set up the arrest or termination. For a non-controversial exit, find a legal reason (pretext) to replace him or lay him off without bringing up the "stealing" issue.

| Register Number #2 | Location: Back check out | | | | | | | | |
|---|---|---|---|---|---|---|---|---|---|
| Day | Sat | Wed | Fri | Sat | Mon | Wed | Tues | Thur | Sun |
| Date | 3/16 | 3/20 | 3/22 | 3/23 | 3/25 | 3/27 | 4/2 | 4/4 | 4/7 |
| Amount | $29 | 31 | 21 | 24 | 23 | 31 | 25 | 27 | 22 |
| Cashier: | | | | | | | | | |
| Leslie | x | | | x | x | x | | | x |
| Aynsley | x | x | | x | | | | x | |
| Lee | x | x | x | | | | x | x | |
| William | x | | x | x | x | x | x | x | x |
| Drayton | | | x | | x | x | | | x |

**Defense against the short-change artist.** Never allow the amount tendered to change in the middle of a transaction. That is _the_ rule. The "change due" shown on the register is exactly what the customer gets. Nothing else. If the drawer opens and $3.60 is owed to the customer--especially for a small purchase--he gets $3.60 and that's it. Close the drawer. If he says, "Oh, let me give you...." don't do it! Give him $3.60 and _close the drawer_.

Elements of short change theft include being friendly (relax the cashier and create trust), and chatting (mentally distract the cashier). Typically, the thief makes a simple, modest purchase and then acts confused; or starts to walk away while the cashier still owes him money. He'll say he thought he gave the her a different denomination or _meant_ to give another. (The short-change game has begun.) Or he might drop money on the floor or pocket some; or ask the cashier to exchange denominations of bills. Don't even listen to the stories, just give the amount due and _close the drawer_. Keep the transaction simple.

Then if you must break a bill for change or whatever, do it as a new transaction, but _never_ alter the amount tendered, the "change due," or the denominations being handled. Never, _ever_ let it become a three or four-step process. With short change artists, the simplicity of the original purchase or initial request is the set-up. (Till tappers: Some snatch bills from the drawer, babble or act crazy, palm some, then give the rest back, pretending the whole thing was a stupid mistake. Some just grab the money and run.)

## 2.08 Venders and Jobbers

**Vendor theft** is a close kin of employee theft and can be worse than professional shoplifters. They trick employees into signing for full deliveries when only a fraction is delivered. They stock merchandise and remove it from the store unsupervised. "Jobbers," cleaners, and repair men are problems too. Do they have access to stockrooms and sales areas? Will they readily agree to arbitrary checks of coats and baggage? Are they bonded? Ask the honcho, "Are you putting temporary help in here or full-time people?" (You should assume that anyone with out-of-state ID is a new-hire or temp.)

Basic to a defense against all thieves are locked doors. All office, freight, stock and storage doors should close and lock automatically. (But that's pretty pointless if the door takes Visa. (Opens by sliding in a credit card or driver's license.) Check all door locks.

Whether vender, jobber, or employee, "a problem with your back door" affects profit far out of proportion to the number of thieves involved. Lowell Corbin of the Woolworth Company, one of that company's best shrinkage-aware managers, was the first I heard say, "Shoplifters steal your profits, but an employee will steal your business."

**Is throwing out trash a management function?** Yes. Some dishonest employees conceal merchandise in store trash, throw it in the dumpster and come back for it later. Others steal while removing trash from the store. Inspecting trash and supervising its removal, plus frequent, surprise inspections ("walk-throughs") of trash collection areas, closets, and stockrooms are imperative. A retail chain distributed this bulletin:

"Reports are continuously received from managers on individuals who were caught attempting to steal merchandise concealed in the store trash. If your store's trash is put in an outside container (not compactor), you are extremely vulnerable to this method of internal theft." The following suggestions were made:

- All cartons and boxes should be broken down.
- Clear (transparent) trash bags should be used.
- Stockroom trash-holding area should be separate from merchandise storage area.
- Trash holding-area should be rigorously spot-checked for merchandise.
- Trash removal from store should always be closely monitored by a supervisor.
- Do not remove trash during evening business hours.

## 2.09 With a little help from their friends

One professional shoplifter says she nearly always uses store clerks for "back-up." Given a time-frame the clerk may not know who is coming, only that someone will. The clerk is paid to collect items in prearranged locations, supply bags, or have merchandise bagged and waiting. If something goes wrong, the employee isn't easily connected with the thief. ("I didn't see him.") It's sometimes part of a dishonest employee's "job" to ensure nothing goes wrong. (You must notice and question merchandise out of place on the floor, at cash registers, and in stockrooms, and bags laying around, disappearing employees, etc.)

**Thieves get a wealth of information from dishonest employees**: Internal policies, up-to-the-minute warnings, descriptions of security personnel, work and break schedules, and information about cameras and other security tools. They "drop a dime" when security or management is off the sales floor. (Some thieves use codes and coordinate with personal pagers and cellular phones. Do not allow these things on the salesfloor.)

In countless ways, dishonest employees help their friends steal: with fraud refunds, approving fraud refunds, entering false ID info, removing security tags, and distracting honest employees at the right times. ("Come help me with this," or "Cover this area for me while I run to the restroom.") To keep friends from getting caught, they shout at security or slow them down with conversation, false "hot tips," or questions. Obviously, the more employees you have "looking out for friends" the more difficult it is to identify and catch thieves. And these employees make hideous witnesses. The situation is desperate if LP must hide from employees while trying to catch shoplifters and other thieves.

**Management's Dilemma.** Most businesses operate with a "zone defense" with each employee assigned to a specific task or area. As in sports, this works <u>only</u> if every player stays in his zone and pays attention. It's not optional. Do you want a right fielder who thinks, "Gee. That batter doesn't look like he'll hit a ball. I think I'll go shoot the breeze with the first baseman?"

It's axiomatic that employees on the sales floor are the first and most important line of defense to protect profits. Unfortunately, many employees are--as psychiatrists say-- passive-aggressive. Their intentional *in*action allows problems to bloom. They may not *personally* steal, but they let it happen. (Maybe "it serves you right.")

How do you distinguish dishonest employees from honest ones who have no mental security mode? Or an honest one who is truly afraid of thieves or might do better with additional training? Why is it <u>really</u> that Herman never sees anything suspicious or seems bothered if security checks his area? What are his true intentions? Whose side is he on?

No matter what the New York experts say, deciphering human intentions is still a freaking black art. You may as well toss chicken bones. Besides, it's irrelevant which side an employee *says* he's on. What matters is which side he behaves like he's on. That's #1. You cannot reach your goals and potential (<u>win</u>) with people on your team whose loyalties and dependability vacillate from play to play.

So do not "split hairs" arguing "intent." If--for whatever reasons--an employee does what thieves like, that employee should be corrected, retrained or both. If he doesn't, can't, or won't come around, find a legal way to ditch him (and quick). You'll occasionally toss an honest one who just can't do the job, but helping thieves is intolerable.

If an employee's true goal is to help thieves, expect him to leave areas unattended and distract other employees; to *not* call management or LP about odd people and activity, and to side-step refund, exchange, check-acceptance policies and other LP directions. Is that a "good employee?" No. (And even if his "sales" are good, he'll cause a long-term disaster.)

"But just because he does wrong things for us and right things for thieves, that doesn't prove he's dishonest or bad." Maybe, but if you're under a bridge and you hear what sounds like horses galloping above you, it probably is horses. Sure, it might be giraffes, but if it was important, how would you bet? Are shrinkage and profit important?

Internal thieves, sorry employees, and those making excuses for poor performance are like card cheats: they pull issues from up their sleeves. If a register is short and you investigate, they say the "real issue" is you don't like them personally; or it's policies or attitudes to blame. Those might be problems, too, but the real issue is still missing money.

> When a trained employee--however "good" a worker--frequently acts as though he is on a thief's payroll, maybe he is! And if he's "honest," how many thousands of dollars in stolen merchandise and lost sales will his bad habits cost you? Find someone better.

Ordinarily, someone must do something to commit a crime, but sometimes a crime is committed because someone does not do something. Ergo, two basic categories of crime: crimes of commission (doing something) and crimes of omission (not doing something).

Most employees who help thieves do it unintentionally. But so what? While on the clock employees are paid to make your goals their goals. If they can't do that or just don't or won't do it, then they are bad. It's really that simple. And when you fail to insist that they do what you say, you encourage everyone to take advantage of you, undermine your own training and goals, and you allow theft to bloom.

The three basic types of crime are crimes against people (murder, etc.), against property (stealing, etc.), and crimes of personal disorganization (drugs, gambling, etc.). Just as many criminals reveal their nature through crimes of "personal disorganization," many dishonest employees reveal themselves by late arrivals (or not at all), cutting corners with policies, leaving early, personal visitors, etc. Few plan to stay with you for long, so they're often disinterested in promotions or long-term benefits. (Some thieves make themselves "small;" so low-profile and well-behaved that people pay them little attention.)

Don't confine yourself to catching thieves in the actual act of stealing. Police seldom catch a (drug) dealer in the actual act of dealing; much easier to get him for disorderly conduct or a motor vehicle violation. Then he's ID'd and searched. Enforcing all policies complicates thieves' work and stiffens slack employees who--even if honest--create problems every day by wasting payroll, wasting LP and management time, and putting extra work on dedicated crew members. And that's not to mention their effect on morale.

## 2.10 Employee Screening and Training

**Drug Testing.** "We provide a drug-free work environment. The applicant agrees to participate in pre-employment drug screening. If hired, the applicant agrees to additional testing at random, without cause, and without notice while employed. The applicant understands that a failure to appear or the detection of restricted drugs may be grounds for termination, and the applicant agrees to hold the Company harmless."

Every business should include a similar note on applications. One of the best employment screening tools is a pre-hire drug test, and some companies require random tests. If you hire someone with a nose-problem (cocaine), they'll steal for sure, and create other problems as well. Ask local hospitals or clinics for information about testing.

**Criminal Records Checks.** If an applicant will be in position to steal anything or will do any driving for your company--even to the post office--check his records.

For a small fee, applicants can go to a police station or sheriff's office and receive a copy of their own criminal and driving records. Then give it to you. (But did they alter it?) Another way is to have a "release" on your application stating that the applicant authorizes you to check his record. (The date and his signature must be there.) Then for a small fee, the local police will usually provide a copy of the record directly to you.

Problem: Some checks provide only *local* criminal records, not records of upstate larceny convictions or anything at all in a neighboring state. But the deeper you check, the more it costs. (Most police detectives or chiefs can tell you how to dig deeper.)

If you obtain criminal and driving records through a private detective or security agency, what are you paying for? Local, state, or nation-wide? Felonies, misdemeanors, or both? Convictions and arrests? If there's a conviction, was the original charge reduced?

It's usually easy to get information from applicants and new-hires, so while at that stage, get it. If they will be engaged in credit sales, get their major credit card numbers to safeguard yourself against 'charge-credit' fraud. Also, get the names, addresses, and phone numbers for three non-family, non-employer "personal references." These are normally trusted friends which, for criminals, are often trusted accomplices. (Watch for them to show up on refunds and other transactions.)

Check on all applicants, or be selective. If selective, establish criteria such as those with time between jobs, employment that can't be verified, "job hopping," or applications for high-risk positions (stock, customer service, fine jewelry, electronics, cash handling, etc.). Personally, I favor checking everybody. (Also, see Prevention: Hiring, page 112.)

Criminal, credit, and driving records and drug tests might seem expensive, but checking fifty is cheap if it saves hiring even one thief or addict. If you can't afford these things, at least have applicants sign authorizations. Just thinking you check will deter some of the minions from across the River Styx. Whether you do criminal checks or not, you *must* verify past experience and investigate gaps in work histories. Hire right, then train right. If things cannot be verified, don't hire! (An excellent cost-effective program for basic background screening is CLEO from USATRACER. See page 197.)

**Training.** Few employees understand proper LP operations or the LP mentality, neither do they (or many managers) have a clue as to what constitutes security or what it takes to maintain it. Therefore, they must be treated like puppies: show them the ball *before* you throw it. Explain basics; that just as they work for personal profit, the store, too, "works" for profit and no business is profitable without discipline, good people, customers, and loss control. (See Employee Training, Appendix 16.)

Tell them that employees are shepherds and merchandise is sheep and it's essential (if they want to keep their job) that they keep little lambs from wandering off. Explain that you don't expect them to fight wolves or thieves, but if one is around, shepherds are expected to notice <u>and</u> call for help <u>before</u> sheep disappear. If they whine, "But I get busy." Remind them that if a school teacher has twenty students, she can't totally ignore nineteen just because she's busy with one; even a bad one.

→ **Explain** that LP is *supposed* to "look for trouble." It's their job to examine every type thing and be suspicious *before* there's anything concrete to be suspicious about. Any fool knows you've been robbed after ten-thousand dollars of locked-down merchandise or cash disappears, but LP--if allowed to do its job--can often spot the opportunity to avert trouble *before* it reaches the point where things go missing.

→ **Explain** that everything is checked not just for theft, but for consistency, training opportunities, and to catch and correct honest mistakes. And explain that when LP examines a register tape, it may be to check a transaction that occurred ten minutes or two hours ago and have nothing to do with the cashier *or* the current or last customer.

→ **Explain** that employees don't know every shopper's individual history in the store, who each shopper associates with, if a shopper arrived in a car with paper tags now waiting in a fire lane with the motor running, or if a shopper matches a police or other BOLO. Or if you or someone else just happened to see the customer do something odd.

→ **Explain** that some things are checked just to "touch base" or to eliminate possibilities related to other matters, and that LP checks many things that don't even occur to non-LP employees (just like clothing, cosmetics, jewelry, and electronics experts routinely deal with issues that LP personnel don't even know exist).

**"Just looking around."** Internal checks and investigations serve *three* functions. First, problems and opportunities for hiring, training, and improving procedures are identified. Second, thieves and slothful employees are identified. (Both cause loss of merchandise, time, and money.) The third function is that LP helps identify dependable, trustworthy employees suitable for raises, promotions and increased responsibility.

LP professionals don't "assume" anyone is honest or dishonest, competent or incompetent, consciences or not. An LP rule of thumb, therefore, is before you trust them you *prove* them trustworthy. Everyone begins in the "don't know, yet" category.

Tell employees, also, that LP investigates actual crime, and if they provide specific reasons for what they're doing, a mere suspicion or routine investigation might become public knowledge and suggest dishonesty where none might actually exist. That causes *beaucoup* troubles. In sum, even asking LP what they're looking for is asking too much.

If employees "second-guess," circumvent, or interfere with LP, it inevitably helps thieves. If an employee does so, take a minute (when it's convenient) and explain what specific behavior is a problem. Then explain how it *needs* to be done or how to avoid it. Make it clear that you *expect* mistakes and that everyone has both strong and weak areas; that "making a mistake" does not make him a "bad person." But bad habits must change.

It's sometimes helpful to stand with an employee, point to someone and ask, "If he wanted to steal, how could you help him?" Then help the employee verbalize different ways he could help a thief steal. (Not greet him, ignore him...) This is training and retraining. If they say, "Oh, you're on that again," say, "Not again. We're STILL on it."

Complying with policies and fully cooperating with internal investigations aren't just "nice things to do." They're essential. Therefore, if repeated conversations are necessary with non-compliant individuals, put notes in personnel files. Train, correct and re-train, but once they demonstrate they can't, won't or just don't comply, move 'em or fire 'em.

**"Feelings."** Dishonest, immature, and poor-quality employees ordinarily view LP the same way that thieves do. If LP even looks in their direction, they're being "bothered" or "harassed." They claim that "all security does is try to catch employees."

Some honestly think (more likely, <u>feel</u>) they are violated by LP "sneaking around," and some forget that it's impossible for LP--or anyone else--to be liked by everyone. People differ. But there are other, **sinister** reasons for wanting LP to stay away. Some employees say, "It hurts my feelings to be treated like a thief," or they truly believe "checking on my work means you think I'm stealing." If they even say that, they're too intellectually immature or too paranoid to be on a payroll. Or they *are* a thief.

Think. If a cop sees a dead body on a porch, he might knock on the door and say, "I'm sorry to bother you, but do you know anything about the dead guy out here?" Then he checks with neighbors. That is NOT the same as treating people like criminals or accusing them of murder. Questions and interviews are necessary. Crime flourishes where police don't get cooperation, and it's the same in stores with LP. If employees are permitted to intimidate or persuade LP into ignoring violations or curious situations, they can then make mistakes, intentionally screw up the works, or steal. Allowing one to do it empowers others. You must not let it take root. (See "Employee Sabotage," page 78.)

Stress heavily that employees must not take business matters personally or react to business matters unprofessionally. It is very, *very* important to get that point across. Finally, make it clear that intentional challenges to LP are neither tolerated nor forgiven.

From then on, anyone hindering investigations, or harassing or interfering with LP or LP goals should be viewed as dangerous. Even if they're not thieves, they will ignore theft, sow confusion, hate, and discontent, <u>and</u> they will be hostile witnesses to anything that happens. Put up with that, and defecation will eventually contact the rotary oscillator.

**"He who wants his garden tidy, doesn't reserve a plot for weeds."** --Dag Hammarskjold

## *"Thou shalt not steal."*
## --God

# Chapter 3
# STATE and LOCAL LAWS

Warning: Until an individual can demonstrate to a very knowledgeable person that he has a proper understanding of the concepts and laws in this chapter, it is advised that he have nothing whatsoever to do with any type of "security stop" or confrontation. (It's *that* important. Any court can provide names of prosecutors and police.)

## 3.01 Concealment & Non-Concealment States

In addition to specific shoplifting and refund laws, most states have merchant-friendly "concealment laws." These laws may be called nothing in particular, *or* they may go by one of several names including "willful concealment." Concealment law may be a separate clause *or* may be incorporated into shoplifting law (as in SC and GA).

**It is of the utmost importance that you know if your state has a concealment clause or law.** If it does, as SC and GA do (and those laws are found on the next page), it means that merchants, employees, and loss prevention (LP) in those states can approach and arrest a thief inside their stores <u>as soon as the thief conceals store merchandise</u> (in a purse, coat, bag, pocket, or whatever). Most states are "concealment states."

**Understand this: if your state has a concealment law, there is no legal requirement to wait to make an arrest until after a thief exits the store.** SC and GA laws are excellent examples of typical laws in concealment states. Other concealment states include Washington, Iowa, Virginia, Michigan, Tennessee, and Florida.

Sadly, there are states without concealment laws. Among these "non-concealment states" are Nevada and Texas. (Retailers and LP there should lobby their State-houses.)

Whatever state you're in, though, you play by company and state-house rules. If your state has no concealment law (e.g. Nevada or Texas) the thief--I'm told--must pass at least the last possible point of purchase (cash register, service desk, etc.) and be on his way out the door--or actually outside the store--before a legal arrest can be made. The Las Vegas PD advised me that it's actually outside the store, so maybe that's right.

**Wherever you are, check with local police, a municipal judge, and a local solicitor.** There are many reasons to check with all three. Learn what is legal and what is illegal, what you must tolerate, at what point you can legally react and/or escalate, in what circumstances police will make arrests (and for what), and in what circumstances and for what offenses you are legally empowered to use physical force. [9 (Page 142)]

**A common, misconception in concealment states such as SC and GA is that a thief must leave the store before he can be legally detained and charged with shoplifting.** That is simply not true. If he intentionally conceals an item without consent or having paid for it, that is **prima facie evidence** that his intent was theft. He has committed a shoplifting act, right then and without leaving the store. (Much more on this later.)

**Regardless of the state law, many large companies prefer that a thief leave the store before being arrested.** I've heard that some loss prevention officers legally get around that. If a thief conceals an item, they "crowd him" or "burn him out" by saying something like, "Hey! Are you going to buy something or <u>leave</u>?" If he produces the item, they might put him on criminal trespass notice or just order him out. If he leaves with the item concealed, they bust him when he hits the door. (Maybe it's just rumors.)

## Code of Laws of South Carolina

**16-13-110. Shoplifting.**

(A) A person is guilty of shoplifting if he:

(1) takes possession of, carries away, transfers from one person to another or from one area of a store or other retail mercantile establishment to another area, or causes to be carried away or transferred any merchandise displayed, held, stored or offered for sale by any store or retail mercantile establishment with the intention of depriving the merchant of the possession, use or benefit of such merchandise without paying the full retail value; or

(2) alters, transfers or removes any label, price tag marking, indicia of value or any other markings which aid in determining value affixed to any merchandise displayed, held, stored, or offered for sale in a store or other retail mercantile establishment and attempts to purchase such merchandise personally or in consort with another at less than the full retail value with the intention of depriving the merchant of the full retail value of such merchandise; or

(3) Transfers any merchandise displayed, held, stored or offered for sale by any store or other retail mercantile establishment from the container in which it is displayed to any other container with the intent to deprive the merchant of the full retail value.

**16-13-120.** Presumption from concealment of unpurchased goods.

**It is permissible to infer that any person willfully concealing unpurchased goods** or merchandise of any store or other mercantile establishment either on the premises or outside the premises of the store **has concealed the article** with the intention of converting it to his own use without paying the purchase price thereof **within the meaning of 16-13-110.** It is also permissible to infer that the finding of the unpurchased goods or merchandise concealed upon the person or among the belongings of the person is evidence of willful concealment. If the person conceals or causes to be concealed the unpurchased goods or merchandise upon the person or among the belongings of another, it is also permissible to infer that the person so concealing such goods willfully concealed them with the intention of converting them to his own use without paying the purchase price thereof within the meaning of Section 16-13-110.

## Georgia Code

**16-8-14. Theft by Shoplifting.**

**(a)** A person commits the offense of theft by shoplifting when he alone or in concert with another person, **with the intent** of appropriating merchandise to his own use without paying for the same or to deprive owner of possession thereof or of the value thereof, in whole or in part, does any of the following:

**(1) Conceals or takes possession** of the goods or merchandise of any store or retail establishment; **(2) Alters the price tag** or other price marking on goods or merchandise of any store or retail establishment; **(3) Transfers the goods or merchandise of any store or retail establishment from one container to another; (4) Interchanges the label or price tag from one item of merchandise with a label or price tag for another item** of merchandise; or **(5)** Wrongfully **causes the amount paid to be less than the merchant's stated price** for the merchandise.

---

In GA and SC (concealment states), the finding of a concealed item is considered prima facie evidence of willful concealment *and* intent to deprive the store of the item.

## 3.02 Refund Laws

Few law enforcement officers or judges are familiar with refund laws. In the South Carolina Criminal Law Handbook, it's in Crimes and Offenses, Section 16-13-440. In my Georgia Handbook, it's Section 16-9-56 and essentially the same as the SC code. *But please*, don't take my word for it. Look it up! Refund laws vary from state to state, and states with (or without) concealment laws may or may not have a refund law. Then too, laws are changed, evolve over time, and are affected by "case law," those seemingly daily court decisions and interpretations from the Supreme Court, other Federal courts, State courts, etc. (A source for state code books: Gould Publications, FL, phone 407-695-9500.)

After you read it, go to a local judge (or magistrate for your location) and the local prosecuting attorney (both!). Ask how this refund law would play in their court. (They probably never even read it, much less tried one.)

Ask what evidence your local judge and solicitor would require to support the charge. If a defendant claims you misunderstood what he said and wrote the wrong thing, or she gave a maiden name, or she returned it for a friend, and it was her name, what then? Ask them to imagine problems and describe their idea of an "air-tight" case (or at least one that's excellent). The SC code:

**16-13-440. Use of false or fictitious name or address to obtain refund.**

(A) It is unlawful for any person to give a false or fictitious name or address, or to give the name or address of any other person without that person's approval, for the purpose of obtaining or attempting to obtain a refund from a business establishment for merchandise.

(B) Any person who violates the provisions of subsection (A) of this section is guilty of a misdemeanor and, upon conviction, shall be punished by a fine of not to exceed two hundred dollars or by imprisonment for a term not to exceed thirty days.

There it is. Notice there is no stated requirement that the merchandise being returned for refund is stolen, can be proved stolen, might be stolen, or is even thought to be stolen.

> **Warning:** Refund law is a loaded gun. Study up and do the leg work before using it. Even if you don't prosecute, it can be an excellent **pretext** for other action.

This manual applies in its entirety to concealment states such as South Carolina. *However*, most information applies to non-concealment states as well. Readers operating in non-concealment states must make those adjustments necessary to apply certain of our methods to their unique situation.

**Again...readers in concealment states (SC, Georgia, Washington, Michigan, Iowa, etc.) may read on and freely apply whatever they choose.**

## 3.03 Inappropriate Versus Criminal

- **Situation:** A woman picks up a scarf, takes it to a secluded place, unzips her purse and puts it in.
  **Situation:** A man strips a ball-point pen from its package and clips it beside his own in his shirt pocket. He discards the package on the counter and walks away.
  **Assessment:** In concealment states, both of these individuals have probably done enough to be convicted in court, and both would probably say the same thing: "I was going to pay for it." Judges frequently hear this tired lie because thieves often say it in even the most flagrant cases. (What else can they say?)
- **Situation:** A three-year-old child picks up an item and drops it in the mother's shopping bag without her knowledge. They leave the store.

**Assessment:** Neither the child (because of age) nor the mother (aware of no wrong-doing) is guilty of anything in any state. The mother did not intentionally remove merchandise from the store. You must view "intent" and the totality of the circumstances!

> **Who steals?** Born in Dublin, Ireland, singer Sinead O'Conner was packed off to reform school after getting busted for shoplifting. --*Time*, 16 April 1990

- **Situation:** A female takes earrings from a display and walks around the store. While doing so, she takes them off the card and puts them on her ears. She "palms" the card in her hand so it can't be seen. She wanders past a trash can and without pausing drops the earring card (with the price tag attached) into the can.
  **Assessment:** For now, she's guilty only of poor judgment. It's possible she may yet pay, but the smart money is on thievery afoot. If arrested at this point, she would need to convince the judge or jury that discarding the card in the trash was absent-minded and highly regrettable, but that she did intend to pay.
- **Situation:** This same woman walks past the check-out toward the exit. She walks out the door and makes no effort to retrieve the card from the trash or to pay.
  **Assessment:** At this point, she has no significant chance in any honest court.
- **Situation:** A man picks up a pair of sunglasses, walks around, peels off the price tag and drops it on the floor. He keeps walking, glasses in hand.
  **Assessment:** Same as the earrings: be patient and watch. (Get the price tag.) Sure, he's going to steal them, but you need to let the case develop. (If you spook him, he might leave considerably faster than he came in. Be ready.)
- **Situation:** A woman in an antique store selects a sterling silver flask, circa 1900. She discreetly puts it down her pants, covering the bulge with her sweater.
  **Assessment:** If she pleads "not guilty" in court, she'll have no real chance. If, however, she has a coat draped over her arm and holds the flask so that the coat conceals it, it is definitely wait-and-see. (Go to her and suggest you keep the flask or coat at the checkout so she'll be less burdened while browsing. Tell her it's no trouble at all, and with both hands free to shop she might spend more money, *ha-ha-ha*. (Sound cheerful.)

If a person intentionally conceals merchandise and it's not an iffy situation, the concealment is prima facie evidence of shoplifting. Life is simple when thieves put merchandise into purse, pocket or pants. Of course, you have to know it, and, most importantly, it must *be there* when you go to retrieve it.

> **AN IMPORTANT CONCEPTUAL POINT:** "Should be" is one thing, and "is" is quite another. Most civil suits arise from someone equating "should be" with "is."

In most situations, a person is legally detained precisely because the *item is* concealed. They must not be detained if it merely "seemed as though" something was concealed; not because it "felt like," and not because there "should be."

Doing is one thing, "appearing to do" is quite another. Most illegal things can "appear" to be done with impunity. If concealment is a legal element of a case or crime, the person must actually conceal something. If he merely appears to conceal it, he's guilty of nothing and if you stop him you might wake up on the wrong side of the badge.

"Appearing" to conceal merchandise creates confusion. For example: a woman at a cosmetic counter needs lipstick that *must* match her own. She drops things in and pulls things out of a bottomless purse. She may be stealing, but may not be, and there's really not much an employee or security person could say or do that won't reek, "I think you're trying to steal." Sometimes, your best reaction is Rolaids and a change of scenery.

If it's just too much, a diplomatic (safe) course is for someone to stand very near, do busy-work, and "softly" monitor the activity. If anything's said, keep it light.

An aggressive response is to stand just 3 or 4 feet away, and keep glancing at her hands. Do that, and things progress rapidly. She pretends to ignore you (but acts more responsibly), or she says something like, "Do you think I'm stealing?" Answer that question or don't, but be careful, and *never say yes*. What people *mean* is often very different from what they say. Before answering, grasp what is really being said.

**A.** Did she not realize that she was acting suspiciously? Is she apologetic? If she appears to genuinely regret it, be friendly. She'll appreciate your levity, probably make a purchase, and return another day. If she *might* notice "follow-up," forget it; let it go. Do *not* make her "feel like a criminal;" make her feel trusted. You want her to come back.

*Or* **B**, did she mean, "I can act as I please, and there's nothing you can do about it. If you even look my way again I'll make a major scene." Whether she was stealing or not, she's trouble. Employees have every right to investigate suspicious behavior within the store, and the "right" is often incorporated in state law under what is sometimes called *"a merchant's privilege."* [10 (Page 142)] (Mostly, though, it's called common sense.)

When thieves are interrupted, they often try verbal intimidation because--why else?-- it's effective. The most common line is, "Do you think I'm stealing?" If I think so--and have a peephole handy--I act timid and get to it. Usually, though, I go in-their-face overt.

Some suspects get a "shopping shadow" as long as they stay (which isn't normally long once I crash the party). They may say, "Go somewhere else," but anyone telling me where I can or can't stand *will* get my undivided attention, and I say so. Remember, shoplifters and jerks leave *only* after they get what they want...or it's clear they won't.

Some say, "I'm not telling you where to stand, just don't hang around looking at me." Same as above. If you tell me what I must or must not look at, you better have a badge or majority stock certificate in your back pocket. When someone says that, one option you have is to say nothing and continue to look. Your silence will probably irritate them. (They know they can leave if they don't like it, so there's no need to remind them.)

A second option is somewhat provocative (but I like it and use it a lot): "You're in public. If you don't want anybody looking at you, all I can say is stay home, lock the door, and pull the curtains real tight." In effect: If you want to dance, we'll dance.

> *The law*: Employees may not be threatened, harassed, intimidated, cussed out, or otherwise prevented from freely and peacefully engaging in their legal business.

Employees can freely conduct business within legal guidelines, and for society to maintain order we must all peacefully submit to certain norms, laws, and policies even if it doesn't "feel" good. Laws vary from city to city, but there are certain constants, and included in these are **"Disorderly Conduct"** ordinances covering such things as unruly and inappropriate behavior such as interfering with others engaged in lawful activities.

It's essential that you learn the germane statutes and ordinances in your area. Be better versed than the average citizen, because shoplifters commonly violate ordinances, especially "Disorderly Conduct." Then, they're too absent-minded to consider *your* legal options. If someone is "disorderly," you are within your rights to ask and then *demand* that they leave. (Yes, your store is a "public place," but it's private property, nonetheless.)

Encounters result in lessons taught and lessons learned. You want trouble-makers to learn four things: (1) your store does not cater to thieves and ne'er-do-wells, (2) trying to steal or damage merchandise in your store is not pleasurable, (3) trying it in your store is dangerous, and (4) they don't make the rules in your store. Damaging or throwing merchandise, horseplay, insulting behavior or language, threats...one way or another, all these can be "Disorderly Conduct." (Also, see Intimidation, page 61.)

A young man rips open two packages of underwear and tosses the contents and torn bags down on the counter. He's joined by another man, and after a couple of minutes I'm *convinced* they're thieves. I don't want them ripping packages, stealing or coming back later. My inclination is to wait and arrest them, but my dance card's full so I just want them gone *quickly*. Also, I want them to learn a lesson. I approach, pick up the damaged bags and say, "This is quite a mess. Are you going to buy these?"

"No," says the one who ripped them. "I'm just looking for my size."

"No, you're not," I say, matter-of-factly. "Looking is one thing, ripping things apart is something else."

"Hey,(expletives aplenty)," says his intellectual friend.

Bingo! "In the State of (which ever) and the City of (whatever), it's against the law to go in a store, rip things up, and cuss at people. You need to shop somewhere else." If one dawdles, I keep the ball bouncing: "You're wasting your time. You can shop or break the law, but not both. It's time to go."

Create an "effect." Bluff. If they don't head for the door, I might pick up a phone and "pretend" to call the police (and I *will* call if they escalate). What would I tell the police? What's the legal problem? "These guys are damaging our merchandise and when I asked them to stop, they cussed me out. I asked them to leave and they won't go." Simple as that. If thieves ask me who I called, I tell them all the same thing: "My Mama."

Do not allow thieves to draw you into their weird conversations, and do not try to argue with their slogans.[11] Just settle into a few "standard lines," then stick with 'em. I respond to most things by pulling from my Book of Common Response. (Example: "This is not a debate, discussion or negotiation. It's time for you to go.")

Many trouble makers are *already* in trouble with the law or have a history of petty disorderly conducts or other such things. If there's no profit in staying or they're worried that the cop they irritated yesterday might show up today, they'll leave. If they're irritated, that's fine. You want "persona non grata" to leave...and not want to come back.

By nature, people seek pleasure, avoid pain, and follow the path of least resistance. Consider burglars: While a police officer, I worked countless burglaries, but only one where a dog had been indoors. Burglars can just burgle, *or* they can burgle *and* mess with a dog. Since *not* messing with a dog is easier, thieves look for houses without dogs.

Dog 'em. If trouble-makers do any cussing, that's a pretext to be their shadow; maybe even evict them. If they say you're picking on them personally, a good response is, "No I'm not. I'm talking to you because you're the kind of person who uses filthy language around old ladies (or little children...). (See "Single Issue Offense," pg. 63.)

Again, the goal is not to "stop them from stealing;" you can't really do that. What you *can* do is motivate them to inflict themselves on someone else. Make their visit distasteful. Frustrating. Prevent them from stealing *this* time and maybe find some legitimate reason to kick them out. Or, perhaps, catch them stealing and arrest them.

Thieves and other trouble-makers often know their own rights--God knows they've heard 'em enough--but these people seldom know the full extent of *your* rights. Therefore, you can surprise 'em and astonish 'em with things they never even thought of. But while you're out there surprising and astonishing, remember these two things: 1. The Prime Directive is 'Don't get sued,' and 2. If you can't ride him, don't saddle him.

**"When you dance with the law, let it lead."**

# Chapter 4
# POLICY versus LAW

I observed a young man steal a tape from a mall music store and discard the package (which I retrieved). I took it back to the store and told the manager, but "company policy" was to do nothing unless he personally saw the theft. Happily though, the thief entered *my* store about five minutes later; now with a chum. Obligingly, he quickly grabbed something and stuffed it in his pocket.

I stopped him and (of course) he denied taking anything. I handcuffed him anyway while his friend loudly (of course) protested his pal being harassed "for no reason whatsoever." I recovered my item and while patting him down felt the tape in a pocket. A spontaneous confession was unlikely, but I had nothing to lose by trying. "What about the tape?" Predictably, he replied, "What tape?" I announced the title and artist, and my thief's babbling friend immediately turned silent.

I pulled the tape from the thief's pocket and, playing the crowd, handed it to a witness, asking her to read the label. *Suspense*. Then everyone seemed delighted when she read it. Well, almost everyone. My thief's speechless friend just backed away; fearful, perhaps, of my x-ray vision.

My stunned thief was arrested, handcuffed, embarrassed and afraid, and **RICH'S AMAZING MIRACLE OF THE TAPE** was simply more than he could bear. Eyeballing him, I said, "Gee. How'd I know?"

"I got it from the tape store before I came in here."

"Got it?" I asked. My syrupy tone made my implication clear.

"You're right, I stole it. Who *are* you?" T.K.O. (No great piece of work, by the way. Any decent street cop or loss prevention officer could do it in his sleep.)

He repeatedly confessed to both thefts, not only to us and the police, but also to his family who arrived a little later. Back to the music store, I told the clerk that we had witnesses, tape, thief, and multiple confessions, all bolstered by my own iron-clad case. "*Now* do you want to prosecute?"

I thought he'd be happy, but he was obviously troubled. "No. I don't think I'm supposed to. We might get sued."

---

As a "safety measure," a new (*new*) police chief ordered officers not to exceed 65 mph *no matter what*. Some of these cops could bootleg at 50 on a two-lane black-top while smoking and talking on the radio, all without spilling coffee, but no matter: 65 became the police ceiling while anyone else in the Western Hemisphere could do 70.

As frustrated officers in cars that could nearly out-run the Word of God obediently broke felony chases at 66 mph, it became apparent the novel measure was flawed.

In this same vein, shoplifting policies should be "safe," but not counter-productive. Shoplifting policies that are "too-safe" create problems and encourage theft.

---

Every state has laws concerning speeding and shoplifting. Cities create their own laws--ordinances--which are valid so long as they do not violate State or Federal laws. Most ordinances concern misdemeanors, and actually duplicate state laws, so in most cities shoplifters are charged with violating a city ordinance rather than a state law. That has two significant results. The first is quick court dates, normally within a week. The second is that the city keeps the fine if defendants are found guilty. (Think about that.)

"Speeding" is a good example. A state conducts a study of a particular city street to determine the maximum speed for normal traffic. If the determination is 40 mph, anything *over* that would violate state law. The city, however, can legally post a limit under 40, so their traffic department, in conjunction with police and city council, might post 30. One reason for the lower limit could be a nearby playground, but regardless the reason, police can issue tickets to any driver doing over 30.

However, city policy may also dictate that no tickets are issued for speeding unless a violator is in excess of 10 mph over the posted limit. (Maybe they want to avoid a "speed trap" reputation.) The legal limit becomes 30, but drivers can usually do 40 without seeing a blue light in the rear-view. If you own a delivery business, what do you do?

One company tells drivers to do the limit, 30 mph. Others tell drivers to go as fast as they can, "but don't get a ticket"; they do 40. Another company, however, might want to be as safe as possible: its drivers stay 5 mph under any posted limit, thereby avoiding tickets, accidents, and any possibility of success in the pizza delivery business.

> **News Flash:** IBM and Blockbuster Entertainment announced a joint venture to develop a new way to deliver CD's. They will be recorded one by one on demand right at the store, eliminating the need for inventory and the possibility of shoplifting.
> 
> *Time* magazine, May 1993

**No Policy.** If problems arise from a shoplifting stop and you have no written policy, an allegation could be made that you do not even *try* to take minimal precautions to safeguard against unreasonable and illegal behavior by store personnel. With a policy in place and employees familiar with the parts germane to their particular job(s), you could demonstrate a reasonable, "good faith" effort to train your work force to protect the public while on your property and to comply with the law. (It might even help with shrinkage.)

> Fascinated, I watched a clerk price hundreds of little promotional items with 5/$1.00 stickers. While she did *her* work, two shoplifters were in the area doing *their* work (before I arrested them). The clerk noticed neither the thieves *nor* their arrest.
> 
> It took hours for her to price the little items, but it would have taken her only five *minutes* to discourage the thieves enough to go steal somewhere else. At the end of the day, 3,500 promo items would need to be sold to cover what the thieves tried to steal.
> 
> Had they *not* been caught, the store would have been financially better off to have simply thrown all the promo items out with the trash and been done with it. Then the clerk could have spent her shift straightening or providing proper customer service. She may even have tried a quaint tactic to increase sales called "Suggestive Selling."
> 
> As it was, she "did her job" while thieves did theirs; and even though the clerk "got lots of work done" the company nearly suffered a severe net dollar loss.

The Point-of-Purchase Advertising Institute suggests that if your business is one where customers come to browse and buy, you should consider your aisles to be your trenches. That's where the battles for dollars are and where the shoplifting war is won or lost. Complex policies allow blame for situations that go south to roll far down the hill. Deflecting "blame"--rather than preventing shoplifting--seems an unspoken goal of some policies, policy writers, and overseers. A better idea is to fix the problem, not the blame.

Some companies have strict policies while others have "guidelines." Either way, an effective shoplifting policy and loss prevention (LP) operation must maximize strengths while minimizing those of opponents, both internal and external.

Controversy still rages over the "Rules of Engagement" used by our troops during the war in Vietnam. Experts on both sides of the issue agree that horrendous damage resulted from lower echelons attempting to implement unrealistic policies dictated from high upon a distant mountain. Carrying that analogy further, we can draw significant parallels between shoplifters and guerrilla fighters. These parallels might explain why a Vietnam vet [Bill Thrasher] is among the nation's most successful loss-control specialists.

At any rate, the war against a largely invisible army of shoplifters, con-artists, and employee thieves will ultimately be won or lost in retail trenches by loss prevention personnel. These true capitalist foot-soldiers--God bless 'em--struggle daily against the odds with Rules of Engagement dictated from high above.

---

**17 Parallels Between Shoplifters and Guerrilla Insurgents**

1. They lack their enemy's financial resources.
2. They're usually outnumbered.
3. They rely on stealth.
4. They avoid set battles.
5. Their tactics are simple.
6. Their actions are offensive in nature.
7. Their enemy is technologically superior.
8. They travel lightly.
9. They're often feared by their enemy.
10. They're highly imaginative.
11. They're relentless.
12. They're highly motivated to succeed.
13. Their enemy is poorly motivated to resist.
14. They enlist younger recruits than their enemy.
15. They're patient.
16. Their enemy is poorly trained in counter-tactics.

The 17th Parallel: They steal as much as they can.

---

## 4.01 Shoplifting Policy A

Common among major national retailers, this six-step policy requires far more from employees than does *any* state law:

"Before a person can be detained or arrested for shoplifting, the following conditions will exist:

1. The Agent (employee) must see the subject approach the fixture or area of display from which the article is taken.
2. The Agent must see the selection of the article.
3. The Agent must see the article become secreted or concealed.
4. The Agent must then keep the subject under continual surveillance, without interruption, until the subject leaves the store.
5. The subject must have failed to pay for the article in question and must have left the physical confines of the store.
6. At the time of the stop the Agent must know exactly where the article is in the possession of the subject."

On paper, it's safe, tidy and reasonable (i.e., *efficient*), but shoplifters aren't model airplanes where instructions in one box work for all the other models too. With shoplifters, one size *never* fits all, and attempts to force all shoplifting situations into a common mold usually result in longer dockets in civil courts, chaos in the trenches, and, of course, increased shrinkage. Efficient policies aren't necessarily effective policies.

---

**Tip de jour:** Shoplifters are frequently nervous, and that nervousness often manifests itself in an inability to remain still. Be on the lookout for nervous feet.

**The following is the step by step stated logic behind Policy A.**

1. *(Approach)* To insure you see the selection. This prevents error if someone enters the store with his own property that could be confused with store merchandise. If he puts it in a bag, it won't be alarming.
2. *(Selection)* As above. Also, note that "second-hand information" should *seldom* be relied upon. The *same person* should see the selecting of the merchandise *and* the approach to the display.
3. *(Concealed)* If you can't see the article being concealed, then conceivably you can't see it being replaced on a counter, discarded or handed-off to a third person.
4. *(Continual Observation)* Insure the "customer" does not change his mind and discard the stolen item during a second or two of interrupted observation. Also, to insure the item is not "passed" to an accomplice or other third party.
5. *(Non-Payment)* You must know that the suspect did not pay for the item, and also that *no one else* did. For example: Subject X stuffs a pack of chewing gum into his pocket and tells his pal, Subject Y (in a check-out line), to pay for it. X leaves the store while Y pays for the gum along with his own purchase. What if Subject X is arrested outside?
6. *(Exact Location of the Item)* If you don't know exactly where the item is, then it might be anywhere; maybe inside on a counter.

**Problems with Policy A are covered here point by point (as outlined in 4.01):**

1. (*Approach*) You can't be *everywhere* and have your eyes fixed on *every* customer's hands while they move from area to area, display to display.
2. (*Selection*) As above. Per policy, it's not enough to see him walk empty-handed to a display case, open it, and walk away with a few cordless telephones with your price tags attached. You must actually see him remove the phones from the display. You let him go or violate policy.
3. (*Concealed*) Imagine the man (above) holding the dozen phones in one hand and a flat (empty) plastic bag in his other. He stands in front of you and turns his back to you for about five seconds. You hear the bag rustle.

    He turns again--now facing you--and the phones are gone. The bag is full, and there is no way he discarded the phones. By policy, you don't have a case because you didn't *see* the phones go in the bag. You didn't see it, so you must let the gentleman go about his business...or policy is violated. (Is this really what the policy-maker wants?)
4. (*Continual Observation*) Same as No. 1. Remember that per policy you must never lose sight of the (concealed) merchandise. Does never mean never? If so, you must turn every corner at exactly the same time, and maintain this strict surveillance for as long as the "customer" remains in the store. This may be five minutes or twenty-five.
5. (*Non-Payment*) Can you realistically query everyone who may have purchased the item(s) on someone else's behalf? Or who might be about to purchase it? Or others who might be about to enter a check-out line with the intention of eventually paying for it?
6. (*Exact Location of Item*) Again...is a small item like jewelry in the purse, the bag, or the coat? Which pocket? If you're not certain, policy requires you let 'em walk.

Policy A seems to touch every base and certainly looks good on the surface. But like blueberry packages in the grocery, it looks so good because all the pretty berries are on top. When Policy A is followed to the letter, arrests are few and lawsuits inevitable.

But Policy A is not the only show in town. There is also a very interesting program that I call 'Policy B.' Widely used throughout the US, it could have originated only in one of three places: (1) San Francisco, (2) Washington, DC, or (3) Woodstock.

## 4.02 Shoplifting Policy B

1. We prevent shoplifting with customer service.
2. Do not attempt to detain any customer whom you may suspect of shoplifting.
3. Do not attempt to detain anyone whom you may have seen conceal any item.
4. Do not attempt to detain anyone who is leaving or has left the store who was seen by anyone, including yourself, with merchandise which is thought to be stolen or concealed.
5. Avoid any such question as "Has that item been paid for?" (No matter how politely phrased, if a question could imply wrong-doing, avoid it.)

Personally, I find it hard to believe that anyone would operate with Policy B, but managers who do (use it) assure me in a matter-of-fact way that their losses (often hideous in volume) are covered with a high gross "and we never get sued." Maybe not by shoplifters, but what are the long-term effects of such generosity? What message is sent and what message heard? The following is attributed to former New York City police commissioner Raymond Kelly:

"There is an expectation of crime in our lives. We are in danger of becoming captive to that expectation, and to the new tolerance to criminal behavior, not only in regard to violent crime. A number of years ago there began to appear, in the windows of automobiles parked on the streets of American cities, signs which read: 'No radio.' Rather than express outrage, or even annoyance at the possibility of a car break-in, people tried to communicate with the potential thief in conciliatory terms. The translation of 'no radio' is: 'Please break into someone else's car, there's nothing in mine.' These 'no radio' signs are flags of urban surrender. They are hand-written capitulations. Instead of 'no radio,' we need new signs that say 'no surrender.'"

## 4.03 "PolicyWorld"

During the past 30 years or so, juries have awarded incredible dollar-damages for false arrest and the like. One result has been to make lawsuits a career of choice for some retail "customers."[12] Corporations generally respond with increasingly restrictive policies which hobble LP efforts and frequently reduce management to fear-driven or weak-kneed responses to shoplifting and internal theft. That in turn, *encourages* shoplifting and internal theft and results in "Catch 22" situations: for fear of being sued, companies allow thieves to set them adrift in a sea of red ink.

Like most policies, A and B probably reflect the writer's or companies' fears more than their desired goals because they seem totally reactionary procedures rather than serious, proactive attempts to effectively eradicate theft. If a shoplifting policy sets tougher standards than the applicable state law or city ordinance, a reasonable and perfectly legal case could *also* be a serious policy violation. That can put LP in an awkward position because virtually all shoplifting arrests violate the written letter of some step of Policy A.

Policy A is commonly used today; possibly more than any other in the US. It is so restrictive, though, that some managers who use it tell LP to "follow the policy, but use common sense." That means "follow the policy sometimes" which is a very dark alley indeed. If a boss says this but doesn't pass out flashlights (read: spell out what he means), it probably means he wants "numbers," but, when problems arise he'll blame others for "violating policy" or "not using common sense." He will sell his people down river.

More savvy managers who recognize inherent policy flaws tell LP to know the policy, understand it, and be guided by it. They see the obvious: if Policy A is strictly observed "with no deviation whatsoever," there can be *very* few arrests (if any) unless someone cheats. (And the temptation is strong.) If it's a "guideline," call it that.

A play on words? No. Even if no evidence was "planted," consider this: some defense attorneys do *not* attack the *legality* of an arrest, but focus instead on the fact that your actions, the stop, and the arrest were all in violation of your own policy.

Laws and policies are drafted and implemented by people. Enter Murphy. It's a rare law or policy, however well-written or well-intended, that covers every legal wound it's meant to bandage. But, 'Oh,' you say, 'how about Policy B, the one that says ignore it all?' Well, do you really believe those companies expect (or even *want*) employees to stand idle as thieves steal? One clerk discovered the answer isn't "no," it's "Hell, no!" [13]

Policy B is simple, the clerk followed it to the letter, and--quite predictably--thieves stole jewelry. She was unquestionably compliant and then unceremoniously fired. Why? "She should have used common sense." Maybe so, but do folks implementing such a policy imply even a casual interest in individual judgment? The policy alone makes me wonder, but they also made it clear when she was hired that violation of that policy would result in termination. So what's a girl to do?

Policy B, the "High Gross" policy comes highly recommended in some quarters and certainly eliminates--as well as any policy could--confusion and unpleasantness. But, of course, it has a fairly obnoxious, if not intolerable down side.

Policy A allows stopping and prosecuting, but parts of it are so restrictive as to frustrate even the most conscientious employee trying to "do it by the numbers." One excellent clerk misinterprets management's literal adherence as being a lack of concern. She says, "If the company really worried about shoplifting, they'd do something about it." She's not really wrong, but she *is* really discouraged.

---

I arrived at a store and became interested in a man strolling in the same manner as a security officer or floor supervisor. He had told an employee that he was "killing time waiting for someone," and the assistant manager told me that he'd been in and out "for hours." "Since he doesn't want any help, everybody's just leaving him alone."

Right. In the following fifteen minutes, I watched him steal two small items. "Just don't be too obvious," said one man I arrested. "They'll get busy with something."

---

## 4.04 The Human Factor in an Imperfect World

Some people love to say, "The law's the law" or "policy is policy." Ignored by that mind set, however, is the fact that we have a right--at times a duty--to take extraordinary measures in extraordinary situations. Sometimes, illegal things must be done for a higher good while legal things must not be done. **The Letter of the Law** rubbing against **The Spirit of the Law** sometimes generates enough friction to require a legal bucket brigade to handle the resulting conflagration.

You are in your car, stopped at a red light. You hear a horn blast and look up to see a tractor trailer doing about a hundred coming straight at you. If it's about to flatten your car, the only rational thing to do--state motor vehicle laws notwithstanding--is get your assembly out of the way. No "average prudent person" will fault you. In the real world, unpredictable circumstances arise, roads abruptly veer, and wheels guided by human hands just don't make the curve. Sometimes we break rules, adapt, improvise, or die.

The term "*the totality of the circumstances*" is found throughout this book. Effective policies are flexible and allow the freedom to react in a reasonable way to the variables of individual situations and to any unpredictable circumstances which may arise. As any case progresses, it must be constantly analyzed in context of the totality of the circumstances. Many excellent cases require frequent fine-tuning and adjusting from beginning to end. An inflexible, one-size-fits-all policy does not allow such freedom and in extreme cases will be about as helpful as straightening deck chairs on the Titanic.

> **Successful shoplifters *and* loss prevention personnel
> who are successful against internal and external thieves
> make maximum use of six "S" factors:**
>
> **Speed**
> **Secrecy**
> **Security**
> **Surprise**
> **Simplicity**
> **Surveillance**

## 4.05  Six Approach Examples

The following examples were selected to demonstrate variety. Ordinarily, the stop begins in a non-threatening, pleasant manner. You never want a thief to panic. Ordinarily, you want a thief to maintain his customer persona and cooperate until you control the evidence and the entire situation.

For maximum effectiveness (and to avoid preposterous outcomes), policies must allow LP and management to adjust to odd and surprising case developments. (Two highly unusual situations with surprising developments--and their outcomes--are described on pages 84, 85.) Note: 1-5 (below) are all "let 'em go" according to Policy A and Policy B. However, all <u>seven</u> perps were easily convicted. (Case 5 involved a professional thief.)

**Situation 1:**  From a peephole, I watch a female stuff cosmetics into her blouse after her friend looks around and says, "Go ahead." As they leave the department, it takes me only seconds to meet them, and it's certain they couldn't *possibly* have returned the merchandise to its proper display. I stop about two feet in front of them--facing them--so they have to pull up short to avoid a collision.

Me:  "Excuse me, ladies. I work for the store. We've misplaced some cosmetics."

They know what I'm talking about and I know they know, but it seldom hurts to be nice, cautious, and vague. It gives them a chance to deny knowledge of the items, and that ultimately bolsters my case. Also, I can easily back away from what I said (if I'm wrong).

Woman A:  "What cosmetics?"  She's the one I saw steal. Ignoring her question, I let them stew a few seconds as I look each in the eyes. They now know that I know more than they thought anyone knew, and they're wondering how much *more* I know. Was there a camera? They're scared and have no plan.

Woman A:  "You mean the ones I have?"  She accented the word "I" which is very interesting. Did the second woman steal, too? The talker obviously knows she's busted, but she's fishing for information. Why? I look at Woman B and hold her eyes a few seconds, then address A, their chief negotiator.

Me:  "I mean *all* the merchandise."  I switch from "cosmetics" to "merchandise" to follow her juicy lead; I don't have any idea what else they may have, but if I'm right, there's something, so I use a "shotgun" approach. They don't know what I know, or how little I know.

They say nothing. I've got Woman A with concealed merchandise and a pretty strong case that Woman B is a "bustable" accomplice. Plus, I feel that B has something concealed. I wait a couple of seconds and put a lot more force in my voice. Looking at Woman A, I cut to the chase.

Me:  "Don't jerk me around. I want *all* the merchandise, and I want it *now*."
Immediately, both reach in their blouses.

Me: "Stop!" (They freeze.) "Do both of you have ID in your purse?" (Both nod.)

"*Slowly,* give me your purses, and don't do anything else with your hands unless I tell you to." I don't want them to fill my hands with merchandise and then run, so I get purses first. If Woman B had run right then, I would have let her go because she was still too iffy for a chase. (She has something, but is it from this store or from another?)

I want them to think I know what I'm doing; that I have everything under control and no thinking is necessary on their part. They just need to follow my simple directions one step at a time. My voice is reassuring, quiet, and firm.

Some people who have ID lie and say they don't; but, if they say they do, it's ordinarily so. I get the purses and concealed merchandise from each, then we walk. Detainees *always* walk in front or beside you, never behind. If you are right-handed, it's usually best to keep them to your left. Watch them--especially their hands--*very* closely. If they walk too fast, say, "Slow down a bit;" too slowly, "Let's walk a little faster."

**Situation 2:** A woman looks around and stuffs three items into her purse. She hangs it from her shoulder and walks away. Five seconds later, about fifteen feet from the display, I'm in her face. I proceed quietly, but very forcefully.

"I work for the store. You're under arrest for shoplifting. Do you need to be handcuffed? Good. We're going to walk slowly to the manager's office, and I'm going to hold your sleeve just like this while we walk. We'll talk when we get there. Right now, stay <u>right</u> with me. Walk now."

Total silence from her. She was out of view for less than two seconds and could not *possibly* have ditched the merchandise. When asked about the handcuffs, she just shook her head "no." She knew by my approach and words that she was inescapably caught. She believed, and rightly so, that unquestioning compliance was her sole rational option. The danger here could be that she'd panic, or a friend might arrive and try to be a hero.

**Situation 3:** A man takes a pair of sunglasses from a display and browses over to a different area of the store. He rounds a counter, and, when he reappears, the sunglasses are gone. With-out checking his path, I go straight to him with a smile.

"Did you change your mind about the sunglasses?"

"Yeah, I changed my mind."

"How 'bout tell me where you left them so I can get 'em back where they belong?" Friendly voice and disarming demeanor, I don't want him overly worried--just yet--because I need his cooperation.

"Oh, I left them on the rack."

This, I know, is not true. He's now "very suspect" rather than "suspicious."

"Not those. I'm talking about the pair you had when you were over there. How 'bout show me where <u>that</u> pair is so I can get 'em back where they belong."

"I left 'em over there." (Pointing to the last corner he had rounded.)

His story has definitely changed. Anything could happen at any time. If he's runner or fighter, he could unwind any second. On the other hand, it's still *possible* he's an honest shopper, just confused--or stoned, maybe--and needing a minute to get himself on track. (I figure him for a thief.)

"How about <u>show</u> me where they are." Still nice, but force in my voice. He can see that I'm insisting.

"They're right over there... ."

We stroll in the direction he chooses, but can't seem to find the glasses. I stay close, not for a second letting him out of my sight or reach. I see his hands go from his sides to his front (out of my sight) and his elbows bend to 90-degrees. My bet is he's going into his pants for sunglasses. I literally jump ahead and just off to one side, facing him. Sure enough, one hand holds his waistband, the other is in his pants.

"Hold it! I want the sunglasses now!"

A thief hears, "The game's over." He thinks you know he's a thief and where the sunglasses are. He thinks the sluggish process is just "rules being followed." He doesn't know that I provide the rope, but he puts it around his neck. When the sunglasses are handed to me, I say, "Thank you."

"Can I just pay for them and leave?"

"Before you leave, you have to apologize to the manager for what you did." I want his cooperation, so I give him hope. "Oh, boy!," he thinks. "All I have to do is act sorry, BS some fool, and I'm outta here!" After he confesses he'll leave, true enough, but in the back seat of a squad car. (He should ask more precise questions is all *I* can say.)

**Situation 4:** A teenager--about 18--stuffs a baseball cap into the crotch of his pants and then grins at his chums. He looked left and right about a half dozen times and did all the right things, but he just didn't see sneaky me. Approaching him, my body language and tone of voice were too intense; two bad mistakes.

"I work here. Could you show me where you put the hat?"

Not a word. He instantly feinted to his left and broke right. I got a piece of his arm, but he twisted away, bolted, and half way across the parking lot, I gave up. Frustrated and empty-handed, I walked back to my office not knowing that Lady Luck had smiled.

A plain-clothes security officer from another store (who I dealt with from time to time) saw the chase and picked up where I left off. The thief must have been anchor-man for his high school track team, but young Matt chased him to a nearby highway where a North Charleston police officer happened to be working a fender-bender.

If the thief had known Officer Offenbacher like I do, he probably would have turned around right then and walked back to my store, beating himself in the head all the way for being stupid. But with Offenbacher in pursuit, he kept running.

Back in my office, I was still picking up pieces of the broomstick I'd beat my file cabinet with, when I was surprised by Ray's familiar voice at my door. "Hey, Rich. This guy look familiar?"

Certainly dirtier and nowhere near as cocky, but it was my thief. I had the hat, the thief, and--just twelve hours later--a conviction. There *is* justice in the world.

**Situations 5 & 6:** "Damn the Torpedoes! Full Speed Ahead!"
(Sometimes, you just attack.)

5. I noticed a man who matched a description of someone who had gotten away with a sack full of pants a few days before. I followed him to the men's department and saw him pull a 50-gallon plastic trash bag from his pocket. He filled it with dozens of shirts, threw it over his shoulder and sped toward the door.

As he rounded a corner, I grabbed him. Before he had a second to react, I told him he was under arrest, had him up against a wall, and the cuffs went on.

*Yes*, I had a few seconds lapse in surveillance. However, he had taken so many shirts that he had to be a professional and probably wouldn't cooperate in being arrested. There was no way bags were switched. Also, I didn't want him to have time to think, or time for an unseen accomplice to react.

6. A teenager entered a store, grabbed a can of Pringles and stuffed it in his pants. Thirty seconds later he was in handcuffs. Nothing to it.


**"The most exquisite folly is wisdom spun too fine."**
-- B. Franklin

**Pre-hire and Training Tip:** Incident reports and report writing skills are extremely important, and any type video (even a favorite movie) can be a useful tool in this regard. For pre-hire screening and in-store training, I use a particular training video of a shoplifting incident with two loss prevention officers making an arrest involving a brief scuffle. The video is in color and about three minutes in length.

Without telling them why they'll be watching, I show it to LP job applicants (and to employees who are already on-board). Afterwards, I give them fifteen minutes to write about what took place; a narrative with as much detail as possible in their descriptions of what happened, the people involved and everything that was said.

In reviewing that, I learn if they can organize and relate their thoughts and observations on paper in a literate, professional manner; if they can "zero in" on important facts and details. *And* I find out if they're color-blind. (A lot of people are.) Also, I check spelling and handwriting.

We are in the communication business, and rambling nonsense, poor spelling and illegible handwriting are confusing, misleading and highly distracting. Time spent translating and rewriting such things is totally wasted, and I just don't have time for it.

**Web-site Tips:** These sites are good for researching or browsing Federal, state and local laws, case-law, and opinions, with links to all sorts of retail, risk management, loss prevention, and law enforcement-related issues and subjects: aele.org (Americans for Effective Law Enforcement), and law.indiana.edu In addition to everything else, the Indiana site has links to all U.S. Circuit courts. Example: Fourth Circuit is law.emory.edu (Also, see Appendix 15, page 176-177.)

- A very nice web-site library is that of the International Association of Professional Security Consultants at iapsc.org. Topics include a fascinating <u>History of Private Security</u>, <u>The Acquisition, Care and Feeding Of Security Consultants</u>, <u>Body Language</u>, <u>Cargo Theft</u>, <u>Employee Theft</u>, and many, many others. Going into this site will probably make you late getting somewhere.

- For basic descriptions of some interesting street cons and scams, the congames.com site of Travis Dacolias is quite good. The fraud-watch.com site does very well with employee accident fraud. Finally, the National Consumers League's National Fraud Information Center site at fraud.org is a fine service with excellent information.

---

### Card-Carrying Crooks:
### This tough judge forces shoplifters to wear signs!

Sticky-fingered first offenders are given a choice between 60 days in jail or five hours marching back and forth in front of the store they ripped off wearing a sandwich board sign that reads: "I was caught shoplifting. This is part of my punishment."

Most choose the signs and are so embarrassed, they choose never to shoplift again, says Judge Edwin Keaton of Camden, Arkansas.

He says he adopted this policy ten years ago because fines didn't have the desired effect: "An efficient shoplifter may have taken $500 or more worth of goods before they got caught, so they just viewed it as a cost of doing business.

It wasn't a deterrent when they knew all that would happen when they got caught was they'd have to pay a fine. Back then, we had a lot of repeat offenders. Now we have very, very few repeat offenders."

*--Examiner,* 28 February 1995

# Chapter 5

# LIABILITY (or, Lie-ability)

Bungled situations can usually be smoothed over if you stay calm, think, and graciously accept a tongue-lashing. A really botched stop, though, can result in two types of problems: civil and criminal. The former costs money, perhaps lots, while the latter (criminal) might cost money *and* see you in jail. For either problem to haunt you, someone must first be "wronged." * As owner, manager, or LP, courts expect your actions to be reasonable and legal. You might stray a bit, but never with both feet out of bounds. If, for any reason, you accuse and arrest someone, you'd better be able to make a case.

Professional con artists and others *want* to be "wronged." "Slip and fall guys," for example, arrange an in-store accident with a fractured bone. Actually, it was a pre-existing injury (yes, even a freshly broken arm) and you might be the third or fourth business "responsible." They use different names, identifiers and social security numbers, cut off the cast as soon as they exit the ER, and move on to another store. Their accomplice is sometimes the "independent witness." **

Other con-men use the "bait and switch" or a "sting." They conceal merchandise, "dump" it or pass it off to an accomplice, then tempt and deceive you into mistakes. They wrong you to provoke an overreaction, a "greater wrong." Then they sue and settle.

Even if an action is legal, it can cause problems if it is not "reasonable." And vice versa. "Reasonable" is often defined as what an average prudent person would believe or do in similar circumstances, and "average prudent person" is *not* "average prudent LP" or "average prudent retail manager." Just because you personally think some little thing is reasonable does *not* mean the next person in line won't think it's absolutely outrageous.

A friend of mine once went positively bonkers because I *may* have eaten an egg. She shook me awake, showed me a gift box of candy, and asked what I ate for breakfast. I couldn't recall. She demanded that I concentrate: brek-fust, brek-fust...and I remembered, sort of. I remembered a color: breakfast was yellow; I ate yellow. Wrong answer.

In the hurricane that followed, "clogged arteries," and "dimwit boyfriends," flashed like lightning, but the rest of her storm just shook me like explosions of nearby thunder. Ordinarily, I would have recognized her tirade as being a demonstration of love and concern, but *ordinarily* I wasn't hospitalized in ICU and massively drugged.

Oddly though, her tirade helped me to focus--but on the chocolates, of all things--and I dreamily wondered why she wasn't opening the box. I probably asked, because that would explain why it hit my head...which caused me to panic, jerk the IV from my arm, tumble out of bed, careen into a bathroom, and sit against the door, totally disoriented. Some time later, a nurse coaxed me out, and by then my cheerful visitor had gone.

Egg-eating is legal in South Carolina, but, even so, is it reasonable? One juror sure doesn't think so, and *one* juror can ruin a case in court. Are chemicals (poisons) in the store's bathroom? That's legal, but is it reasonable to let a small child in unattended? It's probably *legal* to handcuff an 8 year-old, but is it reasonable? (Do it, and a lawyer will explain the finer points and a jury will define "unreasonable" in terms of dollars.) [14]

* Technically. Generally, however, people might sue not only for "wrongs," but for *perceived* wrongs, and whether they can realistically expect to win or not.
** Ask the "victim" <u>and</u> witnesses for their place of employment, phone number, address, and social security number. Also, try to get their city and state of birth, plus their *previous* place of employment and *previous* address. Follow them and get car tag numbers. This additional information often exposes con artists for what they really are.

## 5.01 Actions and Alternatives

Before someone is arrested for stealing an unconcealed item, he normally passes the "point of purchase" (Also called point of sale, POS, the check-out or even the door).

Situation: A teenage boy puts on one of your hats and hangs around the front of the store. He keeps glancing from the cashier to the door and is obviously nervous. If he walks to the door and opens it, would it be premature to grab him or arrest him?

What if you do, and he says, "I was just looking out the door to see if my Mom's here yet with some money. She said she'd be here ten minutes ago." And a few minutes later, mom arrives and says, "I left my son to pick out a hat. Why is he saying he's been arrested?" His parents would later say their boy was embarrassed and humiliated, has developed terrifying nightmares, and his school performance has crashed. Afterwards, a jury would say your assumption was unreasonable and your arrest was even worse.

If your goal is prevention, you should approach him, but don't mention "stealing" or "thief." Be diplomatic. Once he passes the checkout, stop him with a forceful "Excuse me." If he runs with the hat, you can arrest him. If he stands silently and watches what you do, be careful. (Always be careful.) Safe questions are, "Are you ready to pay for the hat?" and, "Have you already paid for the hat?" Perhaps the safest and easiest thing to do is go to him, look him in the eyes and say, "Nice hat." Then see what kind of kid he is.

**Five card draw.** It's a game of nerves, skill, and luck. If he says the hat is his (but you know it's yours), his lie indicates an intent to steal. Be ready for action. If his bluff fails, he might bolt. (To a thief, "bolt" follows "bluff" both alphabetically and in the natural order of the universe.)

After saying the hat is his, he may add, "You think I stole it?" In a poker game, he "saw your bet and raised." He may think *you* are bluffing, or he may hope there's enough doubt in your mind to make you "fold," leaving the "pot" (the hat) to him. Another possibility is he might think he can intimidate you into letting him have it. (After all, he doesn't know what, to you, is a hat's worth of trouble.) If he can't decide what to do, he might stall and hope that something will come along and help him. Regardless of what he thinks, if he says your hat belongs to him, you ordinarily have at least three options:

**Option 1.** "It's my hat. Are you going to pay for it or what?"

He'll buy it, discard it, hand it to you or run. You implied he could leave without paying, so even if he gets verbal, an actual arrest for shoplifting is pretty much out unless he tries to take the hat. If he gets ugly, take the hat and, if he doesn't leave quickly, call the police. If he's more or less polite, but doesn't want to buy it, take it and keep things quiet: "If you come in here again, the police might take you out."

**Option 2.** Get the hat and detain him. "Come on over here with me. We're going to talk about this hat."

Once off to the side, tell him quietly and briefly, "What you did was wrong. Do you want me to call your mother, or call the police?" He may whine, but don't let that dissuade you. If you let him go, there's often hell to pay after he goes home and lies to the family about how he was accused and manhandled when he didn't even touch a hat.

**Option 3.** Arrest him. "You're under arrest for shoplifting. Come now."

Be ready for him to come unglued. ("You're under arrest" are what some police call "The Magic Words." Strange things happen; transformations occur. If it looks like a fight is likely, get a squad car rolling before you even approach him.) Then take him where you detain people and do the paperwork.

**Get the Hat.** Even the simpler situations can be horribly mangled, but no matter what: if he doesn't buy the hat and you can prove it's yours…get it. If he runs, get it if possible. If he throws it and runs, get it first, then chase him (if you want to), but get the hat. If he throws it or drops it, it might get lost, replaced on a display, or stolen in the confusion. Get it. In court, "This is the hat" is infinitely better than, "There was a hat."

**To *prevent* the hat theft:** Provide excellent customer service as soon as he gets to the hat display (or begins "rubber-necking"). "What kind of hat are you looking for?" (Open-ended questions.) When he makes a choice or takes a hat away from the display, talk to him again: "That's an excellent choice." If your strategy is prevention, make customer service so thick you could pour it on a waffle.

If you want an arrest, think liability, what his lies will likely be, and how your case can be made stronger. Even if State law allows you to arrest someone who strips the price tag off a hat and then takes it for a walk, you can make the case much stronger (and maybe save a world of anxiety) by waiting for him to conceal it or carry it out the door.

Even then, could it be a "set up?" Did he buy the item elsewhere, then bring it in your store with the tag still on it for the purpose of confusing and provoking you? Was the item already purchased from you, or some sort of legitimate exchange? Does he have an explanation that can be verified? One that might be a problem later if you ignore it now?

When prevention is the goal, act quickly. Try, "Excuse me. Did the price tag come off?" If you're certain it's yours but he says it's his, his claim is a good demonstration of an intent to steal. If he says, "Oh, gee, I guess it did fall off," you have options: He can pay now ("Yeah, right. I watched it fall off. Let's get it paid for right now before anything else falls off."). Or you can be his shopping buddy and stick right with him; or you can take the item to a cashier; or you can say, "Here's the price tag. If you change your mind about buying it, how about bring it to me so I can fix the tag?" It all depends.

**Example:** You interrupt an obvious attempt at theft, but she hasn't done quite enough to be arrested. She's lucky. She dodged a bullet, but she's irritated because she can't steal what she wants. Naturally, she "gets in your face" and cusses like the proverbial sailor. Then, naturally, you want to slap her somewhere into next week.

However nice it might feel to slap her, don't *you* be the one to serve up dessert. If you hit her first, you'll need an attorney. She'll swear out warrants and sue. If she had friends present, they'll swear to God and the magistrate that your attack was *totally* unprovoked. Police will sympathize, but they may have to arrest you anyway.

Regardless how obscene her cussing gets, do not hit her. Instead, employ **"The Single Issue Offense,"** order her to leave, and/or call the police. Or take her picture. (More about pictures later.) Just don't let her provoke you into something stupid. [15 (Chapter Notes, pg. 143)]

**Example:** A nice woman in custody asks for coffee. Hey, why not?

Because she'll throw it in your face and break the hard cup on your gullible head. Or she'll spill it and "burn herself." Or pour it on the floor, then slip and fall and "twist her back." New issues might be created, so the rule is don't provide drinks, food, or anything that could be used for choking, throwing, sticking or hitting. Provide no tools for anything.

**Example:** Someone in custody asks for an aspirin.

Do not dispense any drug unless you use a stethoscope at your day job and everyone there calls you "doctor."

**Example:** A prisoner claims he needs water for the medicine in his pocket.

First, suggest waiting for police. If he says he needs it now, that implies you might cause a medical problem by withholding it. You are not a pharmacist, and we already know you're not a doctor. What you *are* is a non-expert facing a combination medical-legal decision with a patient who is a liar and thief. Do you see a potential for trouble?

If you let him take it, have a witness, provide plenty of water (you do *not* want him to choke), and prepare for a trick or seizure. Be ready to call 911. Document how much was consumed, when and why, and tell the police everything. (Do *not* let anyone ingest anything from a plastic baggie, *especially* powder or weird-shaped "little rocks.")

Think. If someone is arrested and dumb enough to possess contraband, *and* he knows the police are coming, he might (1) try for some privacy near a sink or commode, (2) "ditch" the item(s) or pass them to a friend, or (3) ingest them. But how are you to know?

Just be alert to what's happening and take reasonable action in any given situation. If someone shakes and falls to the floor, call EMS. If someone asks for a knife to clean their fingernails, say, *"Let's hold off on that a few minutes."* You make the arrest, and the thief sits still until police arrive; use common sense and try to keep it simple.

> Ultimately, how things are handled depends on the overall situation (the totality of the circumstances). There is no One Way. In addition to how your legal case is progressing, you must always consider how your opponent's case might play in court.

## 5.02 Victimhood and Mud-slinging

Mark Twain said that the main difference between dogs and people is if you pick up a starving dog and make him prosperous, he won't bite you. Main difference or not, no matter how nicely you treat some thieves or how appreciative they appear that you don't prosecute, their feelings were hurt. To them, that means their "rights" were violated.

They lie and tell half-truths to friends and family who then pressure the "victim" to sue. Will their witnesses lie? You bet. They might get a piece of the settlement. Besides, didn't you choose to "humiliate" their friend when you could have ignored it or handled it with more 'sensitivity?' Aren't you "big business messing with little people?"

In addition to lying and deceiving, some thieves actually develop "selective-memory." They truly convince themselves that they didn't put the item in their pocket at all, really, but were about to put it back on the shelf when they were set upon for no reason whatsoever by lying brutes passing as employees.

**Assertiveness Training Gone Mad** What will your insurance pay if you lose a hand or a leg? Twenty-grand? Fifty? It's reported that in 1976 a New York woman received a million dollars for being a "victim" of false arrest. A *million*?

The old Oklahoma Land Rush is positively dwarfed by today's Victim-Certification Rush, and the US is now teeming with 90's-style "victims." Millions of people now actually *want* to be victimized for the simple reason that being a victim can remove pressure to succeed or be productive. (Whereas if you're *not* a victim, you've got no *excuse*.) Most victims expect to be rewarded or have their lives financially underwritten, while many others feel that being a recognized victim is a sort of validation.

This trend is encouraged by our recently developed habit to use the word "victimized" in place of "offended," a word which is often more appropriate. The result of this new-speak? Yesterday's woman who was offended by Gomer Pyle's auto shop wall-calendar is today's "victim" of a sexist mechanic.[16] Americans are capitalists, and capitalists go after money. When "victim equals money," what's a good American to do? [17 (Chapter Notes, pg. 144)]

I suspect that most people who sue retail stores are not actually bad people, just people badly infected with America's victim-lawsuit virus.

> If it's true that "a hundred hoods with machine guns can't steal as much as one lawyer with a briefcase," it's more true that a hundred thieves with grocery bags can't steal as much as one shyster with a grief case.

**Acknowledgment and Release.** A detained thief should not leave the store with the impression he bullied or intimidated you into not prosecuting. Nor should he leave thinking that "failure to prosecute" is weakness and/or proof the stop was somehow illegal. Instead, he should believe that he's lucky, and you are either very generous or very naive.

That outcome may take some work. If, for example, he thinks he's not guilty because he didn't leave the store, explain *why* he is guilty, help him understand that a judge *will* convict him* and give him a criminal record ("the gift that keeps on giving").

An acknowledgment (Appendix 01) is a confession; the thief admits he did, in fact, shoplift by law. With a Release (Appendix 02), the thief promises that no legal action will result from the stop. Both Acknowledgment and Release are completed *and signed* before the non-prosecuted shoplifter leaves. It's that or jail, with few exceptions. (See pg. 121)

**Family Arriving for a Juvenile.** Ideally, you want a juvenile to confess to witnesses *before* his family arrives (a real priority!), and then confess to the family. When the family arrives, they *may* want facts, but they'll eventually reach one or two of Four Standard Conclusions: the child is the "bad-guy," you are the "bad guy," both, or neither. It's usually pretty obvious how they view things. If they think their kid is the bad-guy, there's no problem. If they reach the second or fourth (you or both), *watch out*.

If parents appear suddenly or unexpectedly, invite them outside the room to speak with you for a minute. Discuss the case briefly before they talk to the juvenile. If he initially denied having the item, tell them so. Never argue "intent" with parents. If they question it, just say, "The law is simple: when he put it in his bag, that very second, he broke the law. In this state, putting... it... in... the... bag...is against... the law."

And don't argue with a kid who's lying or call him a liar, especially in front of family. Be firm, but don't appear overbearing. It's not a debate or negotiation, so politely dictate and, if you choose, offer options. It's OK to get a handle on the family before deciding whether or not to prosecute, but make the phone call quickly if that's the way of it. [18]

> Once the decision is made to prosecute, you enter a legal adversarial relationship. A good rule is, don't discuss cases pending in court with a defendant, his family, or his friends except to get a confession or more ammunition for court. Give up nothing.

**The Bad and the Ugly.** If family members talk false arrest or try to "cross-examine you," or threaten you, call you a liar, or cuss you out, it means they consider you a bad guy. They might even be drunk or unruly; or refuse to sign the Acknowledgment or Release. Or they might demand a lawyer before they "commit" to anything. Don't argue. Remain polite. If they *don't* think you're the bad guy, those things usually mean they don't take you seriously or--more likely--they're probably too stupid to be reasoned with.

"Filters," too, cause illogical, cockeyed behavior. Our upbringing, education, personal experiences, and associations...our entire life experience affects our interpretation of everything we see and hear. These filters--mental maps--sometimes lead us astray.

An exception is an adult who is truly ignorant and, perhaps, illiterate. Be patient and try explaining things in elementary terms. Some people, particularly those with low or borderline IQ's, have trouble grasping concepts. They may honestly fear signing papers and be unable to understand legalities. If so, try to find someone to "translate." It might help to say, "Let's get a police officer to explain it and give you some advice."

You do not have to answer and normally you should <u>not</u> answer questions like, "Did you see him take it?" or "Did he leave the store?" You are obliged only to say he didn't pay for the item, you're prosecuting for shoplifting, and the police will answer their questions. (More about this later.) Even if they show a complete lack of manners, stay cool. It's obligatory to be civil to superiors, common courtesy to be civil to equals, and a quality individual is civil to strangers and the rest. Be professional, not emotional.

* If you *are* going to prosecute, the psychology is "no big deal." Don't educate him and, hopefully, he'll tell police and witnesses that he concealed it, but didn't leave the store. You don't want him so badly rattled that he clams up or thinks he needs a lawyer. You want Stupid to confess, pay the fine and forget it, or represent himself in court.

> A **"shrinkage box"** is useful when a thief or family member whines about the small dollar value of merchandise stolen as opposed to the "big deal" you're making of it. Keep a cardboard box at some convenient location. As merchandise is stolen and the empty packages are found, toss them in the box. Occasionally tally the value of the contents. Eventually, the accumulated packages and dollar total become a striking demonstration of how "little stuff" adds up.
>
> Another use for the box is to illustrate what is being stolen and when and where it's being done. This is valuable information for security purposes.

**Perception versus Reality.** Some thieves are prosecuted and others are not. If you don't do them all, you are engaged in "selective-prosecution" and (sooner or later) you may have to explain to someone why you prosecuted Billy for stealing the same amount of merchandise as Bobbie Sue whom you turned loose. "I felt sorry for Bobbie Sue" won't answer, particularly if the two were a team.

If both are the same race, many reasons might be fine: "I just prosecuted the one who actually bagged the merchandise," or "...the one who screamed and threatened us." If the suspects are different races, however, expect allegations of racism regardless the reasonableness of criteria used in prosecuting only one. (It's called "reality.") Racism is a frequent allegation, and there's unimaginable animosity just below many a peaceful surface.[19] Regardless of your race, you will be attacked. It's as inescapable as it is sad.

Personally, I think most people see what they look for, which is often just a reflection of their own bias. As it is, some whites and Asians believe that all blacks are "morally depraved" (bad people) and some blacks believe all whites and Asians are "inherently racist" (bad people). Some people believe that "fat people are lazy" (bad), or that people who eat an occasional New York Strip are "murderers" (bad to the bone). Living that way saves mental work, but real problems result from the blind faith these people have in a god that I call Ignorance. It's a deity that demands--and gets--frequent human sacrifice.

Accusations of racism, sexism and the like are too often justified, but, many times, the true intent is to intimidate or distract by turning shoplifting incidents into racial incidents, or policy violations into sexual encounters. Everyone present ordinarily knows that the person making the allegation has no idea what the other person's actual, life-long history or personal philosophy may be, and, curiously, it never seems to matter.

Next they will claim that whatever started the ruckus (stealing, trying to steal, breaking policies or whatever) is merely a secondary or inconsequential issue; at worst, a misunderstanding or irrelevant mistake. As a rule, don't bother trying to convince the Inquisition that you're not a racist, or an "oreo," a sexist, "banana," "apple," or whatever heresy you're accused of. In truth, they don't care. Besides, you'll only appear clumsy, and probably stick your foot in your mouth, too. Sure it's absurd, but like "Loose Willie" Shakespeare, these people are not the type who let facts get in the way of a good story.

What you *must* do is act in a professional manner. For starts, don't *do* sexist, racist and other idiot things. Beyond that, be cautious, take each case on its own merit, and do not play Tit-for-Tat. (It's proven by psychologists that people who play Tit-for-Tat long enough are sure losers.[20]) Like you, I didn't start all this; but, like me, you have to live with it. Until something breaks, all you can do is be straight-up and take hits anyway.

Even thinking about all that can be nerve-wracking. Since we don't control employee, customer or area demographics and can't special order certain kinds of thieves, we have to take what we get. It can be frustrating to have a lengthy run of only one particular type thief, but if all you get is juveniles, don't back off kids. Rather, simultaneously pay more attention to adults. (Never do I pass up a solid case.)

Another thing you *can* do is make a point of letting everyone--particularly potential critics--see that you go after people of all ages, races, etc. Put out in-store BOLOs on every type of suspect. One way or another, be involved and get everyone else routinely involved in such a way that they see and believe that you, personally and professionally, are concerned with only two categories of customers: honest and dishonest.

---

**"American college students disgrace their school and flabbergast Japan"**

**Who Steals?** For more than a week the story went unreported, and for the reputation of Texas Southern University in Houston that was good news. Then the Japanese media disclosed that on Dec. 7 (Pearl Harbor Day, of all days) members of the university's marching band, on a goodwill trip to Japan, turned their Tokyo tour into a shoplifting spree, making off with $22,000 in loot from stores.

When Japanese police told the Americans that the buses would not leave for the airport until the items were returned, more than 80 CD players, pocket recorders, miniature televisions, and electric razors suddenly--and anonymously--were handed over to the police. The incident has profoundly embarrassed the historically black university and given rise to concerns that the students' behavior will further tarnish the negative opinion of blacks already held by many Japanese.   --*Time* magazine, 28 Dec 1992

---

**Guidelines.** Selective prosecution can be legal or illegal. You *can*, for example, use *dollar value* as a criteria and prosecute anyone who steals more than x-amount of merchandise. If you prosecute by dollar-value, remember that "if a man will steal your eggs, he'll steal your chicken." Cases, personalities, and circumstances vary so much that dollar-value alone is a questionable (and occasionally stupid) determinant for prosecution.

If you choose, you can prosecute thieves who appear experienced or use actual shoplifting tools such as a booster-box; or thieves who create an ugly scene. Legally, you have great leeway, but whatever your criteria, *deal from the top of the deck*.

I suggest prosecuting anyone you physically hit or wrestle. Shoplifters, especially unruly ones, exaggerate any physical contact and vehemently deny that you had any reason to touch them. If they steal they lie, and exceptions are rare. Any physical contact opens the door to allegations of "assault" or "excessive force." The assertion may be ridiculous, but shoplifters tell outrageous lies to judges and their own families even when literally covered with indisputable evidence to the contrary. [21] (Chapter Notes, pg. 144)

You must have a reasonable, legal response to "Why did you prosecute Billy Joe, but not Bobbie Sue?" You're free, occasionally, to prosecute when you usually don't and be generous when usually tough, but a pattern (or even a single case) of demonstrable discrimination or malicious prosecution will justify a visit from an attorney from hell. Protect yourself with an in-depth defense: well chosen words, discreet conversation, correct actions, solid witnesses, quality reports, good records...and integrity.

## 5.03 Games People Play

To be safe, decide to watch overtly (openly) or covertly ("spying"). If you were covert and a suspect saw you twice, consider your cover blown--you're "burned." You might be burned if he saw you just once, but if twice, you're foolish to think he doesn't suspect you. (And while you're watching your suspect, is a friend of his watching you?)

Average customers pay little attention to who watches them shop, but thieves pay *lots* of attention. When you walk past a shoplifter, he often looks up as you approach *and* looks to see if you look back at him as you walk away. If he sees you looking back, he suspects that you suspect him. That can start Trouble (with a capital T) because some shoplifters play a game called "Who Screws Who?" This type thief *loves* trouble.

**Going After The Big One.** A shoplifter wants a shirt here or a C.D. there, but all the while he *prays* for the hit that delivers a *huge* piece of the pie. Pros and semi-pros dream about it. But to land "The Big One," he needs your help. He needs to be arrested when he's not holding stolen property. Then he can scream to the world and its juries, "Oh, God! I've been wronged!" For that to work for him, *you* must do something very wrong.

The problem begins if he knows you're watching, but you don't know that he knows. Then he conceals something in such a way you're sure to notice. You think he's stupid, but his plan is to ditch the item before he gets stopped. If you arrest him before he ditches it, he gambled and lost. For him, that's "one of them bummers."

If he was able to ditch it, though, he'll be happy if you stop him, but he won't appear so. He'll encourage you to escalate. He *wants* to be "humiliated and terrorized." He may let you search him or he may not. He might remain in the area "under guard" or he might walk away so someone will grab and "drag" him back. He wants witnesses, too.

Sure, you saw him conceal something, but he ditched it. Sure, he acted nervous and guilty--the better to reel you in, my dear. Sure, some merchandise ought to be there, but it's not. And sure, he's guilty; but you can't prove it. Sure, sure, sure, but "Who Screws Who?"

> "I was looking back to see if she was looking back to see if I was looking back to see if she was looking back at me."

If a thief discards merchandise or passes it to a cohort (either in the store or outside), you better know it happened. It's like a shell game, and the more time he has to shuffle the shells--huddle with other people, walk around counters and displays, up escalators and into bathrooms--the greater the chance you will lose.

After processing information missed by your conscious mind, your subconscious may sound an alarm. Once properly programmed, it won't forget to avoid lawsuits. If you "feel bad" about a stop, respect yourself. A hunch or bad feeling may not be logical, but it may be right anyway. Don't ignore it.

> Maintain and study your records. They should reflect legal guidelines.

If a suspect tries to snooker you into stopping him but you don't do it, he may come back and try again. And again, and again. Eventually, his antics may become complex and involve purchases, exchanges, refunds, etc. Finally, everyone watches him closely, monitoring everything he does every time he comes in. Suddenly, he switches gears and claims he's being harassed. This catches you totally off guard.

To avoid being blind-sided, document his activity very discreetly all along the way. He may use an accomplice, perhaps even an employee. Initially, that person's job is to complicate your job. Later, the accomplice listens for you to say something libelous, "I know that sucker's a thief. I know he's stealing, but I just can't catch him." He passes this tid-bit along to his friend, and now you might be looking at a civil suit. ("Oh, poor, innocent me! I've been spied upon, harassed and slandered!")

Your notes should demonstrate that his refund and exchange activity was more frequent than the norm; that he moved merchandise around and left it out of place, constantly came and went, etc. Document everything abnormal (i.e., different from the average shopper). While doing it, be careful of what you say and do around anyone. It's a small world, and who knows what person might play both sides against the middle. (Watch for anyone spying on you to document that his friend is actually "being watched" and "spied upon" while in the store.)

If anything comes of all this, you want to be able to demonstrate that his abnormal behavior warranted special attention: that it was reasonably considered suspicious.

That's Plan B. Plan A is tackle the situation as soon as red flags appear. "Hi, there. I've noticed you have a problem finding what you want. How can I help you?" Smother him with kindness and excellent customer service.

If there's a problem with merchandise, you need to know. If it's some sort of con, acting quickly and decisively keeps it from becoming a protracted cat-and-mouse game. The longer an unpleasant, abnormal situation drags on, the greater the chance it turns into real trouble. (And what is a potential problem? It's a potential problem if it *could* create trouble downstream. If it *does* create trouble downstream, it *is* a problem. Simple as that.)

**Penny Ante.** Three boys tried to "jack" some candy bars, but rather than arrest them, I interrupted and asked if they'd like some free candy for giving me a hand. I wrote up a list of sports cards and told the three if they'd run to a competitor, check his prices against ours and let me know what's up, I'd give them each a candy bar and a soda. Fifteen minutes later, my intelligence agents reported back and got their groceries. The next time they came in, my friends went to the candy and then to the checkout.

Young kids and teenagers sometimes pretend to conceal merchandise for the thrill of worrying adults. The best thrill comes if an adult get all excited and upset. Kids are unlikely to pursue a law suit, but they can sure ruin your day.

Unless you're dealing with real thieves or delinquents (or you want to make a statement for them to spread around), don't spend a lot of time with kids who are obviously playing. Try "I *really* want to help y'all find exactly what you want." (While talking, look at hands, bags, and anywhere else they were pretending to hide things, just in case.) Sound sarcastic or condescending. Treat them like three-year-olds, and they'll probably quit and leave or quit and buy something. If you're no fun, the game's no fun.

Sometimes you can play, too. After seeing a pair of teenagers steal packs of gum *and laugh,* I approached with a smile and told them they looked like real sports; and maybe there was a game all three of us could play..."like cops and robbers." Silence.

I asked one if he had a badge. He just stood there staring, and I got the same non-response from his partner. "OK," I said, "since I got a badge (which I pulled from my pocket), I'll be the cop. You guys can be the robbers. Are we havin' fun yet?" Talk about scared stiff, those two kids could have passed for mannequins.

How juveniles are treated depends, also, on whether or not they have parents in the store. I often begin encounters with kids by asking if they have a parent in the store. If so, "You need to stick with your mother." Pleasant.

If they consider it at all, most kids who create problems don't consider it serious. Don't *assume* juveniles are smart alecks, thieves, or thugs, but don't assume they're not. Most outgrow it; so, even if you give 'em marching orders, be pleasant. If you make friends, who knows? I've had kids I made friends with point out shoplifters to me.

> According to William Bennett in his fascinating book *"The Index of Leading Cultural Indicators,"* 99% of us are victims of theft at least once, and 87% have property stolen three times or more.

## 5.04 Minimizing Risk

Most important is personal safety; yours and that of innocent people. Risk of physical harm is not entirely avoidable, but it can be minimized. First, and very important, is this: seldom should you descend like some avenging angel, racking, stacking, and dragging people to the office. You don't have to.

Most shoplifters are surprisingly docile. Verbal, maybe, but not inclined to physically resist. And even if they do, ninety percent resist "by the numbers." Just as you use only enough force to detain them, they use only enough force to escape. (Civilized, ain't it?)

Second, keep stops quiet. It's *rarely* to your advantage for things to be loud. I sometimes ask a suspect to step aside with me so his friends can't hear what's being said. (Then they don't have to worry so much about being "cool.") Also, "insulting" a person without a witness is one thing--legally speaking--but the same words, more or less harmless in private, may be legally libelous or slanderous if overheard by a third party.

Third, it's seldom good for a stop to drag on and on. Long stops draw spectators, a pool of potentially hostile witnesses who might even physically interfere.

**Movement.** Can the situation be resolved without the suspect moving more than a few feet? That decreases allegations of, "He forced me to go with him." If you make an arrest, of course, you would take him to another location, and by force if necessary. Try to time stops so that the suspect is physically removed from bystanders (unless, of course, that would be advantageous to *you*.)

**The Set-Up.** Be tactful and control the conversation. Use a soft approach to entice the person to agree (admit) that he had the item in his possession and that he moved it from where it had been. A thief will usually admit those things if he thinks he'll walk away free.

The question, "Do you think I stole it?" is easily handled without a yes or no. Try, "Pardon me? I asked you where you *left* it, *not* where you have it. Would you mind telling me where you left it?" A more assertive way is, "I didn't ask you where you have it. I want you to tell/show me where you left it after you moved it."

I've responded to, "Do you think I stole it?" with, "No, but you should know where it is, which is why I'm asking you," and "No, but since you moved it from where it was, that makes you the logical person to ask where it is." Remember: a thief wants to maintain an "ordinary shopper persona" or put you on the defensive. If you act dumb and ask "innocent questions," thieves become confused. They wonder how a "real shopper" would answer. Faced with an unusual stressful dilemma, they must improvise. (And that is something they do poorly.) Take them outside their normal game plan.

"There's nothing wrong with moving things around as long as you put them back or say where you left them. You have no right to come in here and hide things or rearrange them any way you want." The words "wrong" and "right" give thieves anxiety attacks. This approach also makes an issue of common courtesy. "Having things where they belong" is not an unreasonable expectation in any state. 22 (Chapter Notes, pg. 144)

Evading questions is common for shoplifters. If he says, "I didn't hide anything," try "Well, I don't see it." If he says, "You haven't looked for it," try "I shouldn't have to look for it. What's the big deal? If you don't want it, just tell me where it is so I can put it back. Where'd you leave it?"

(Or), "I asked you where you left it. Do you think when I ask my son where he left the remote control for the TV that I think he stole it? He was the last one with it, so I ask him where it is. We just want our stuff where it belongs. Show me where you left it. Is it a secret?" (Pushy, for sure, but not lawsuit material.)

From time to time, you'll get nasty tongue-lashings. (No big deal. Back when they shaved my head every week I got cussed out 20 times before breakfast *every* day.) Don't take it personally. Just accept it in good humor (if possible) and remember that it beats a lawsuit. Some risk is unavoidable, but don't set yourself up by moving too fast, being overbearing, or losing your cool. The Prime Directive is, "Don't get sued."

**Teenagers.** The 12-16 crowd is approached like others: ask where they left it. If they stole it, no problem. If they discarded it somewhere out of place, talk to them about "putting things back where they belong." Tell them that shopping is one thing, but messing things up makes a lot of extra work for employees. "It's just common courtesy."

Maybe you're worried they might steal, but you don't have time to wait and watch. Don't say, "You have to leave because you're trying to steal." Instead, find something "reasonably unacceptable" about their behavior and make an issue of it.

"Making a mess" is one reason (a pretext) for telling them to find a different playground. If you think they're thieves, a single item set down anywhere other than exactly where they got it might constitute an intolerable mess. Your issue of choice (pretext) can be ripping open sealed packages, *any* profanity (verbal or printed on clothes), inappropriate comments, being too loud, spraying too much perfume...the list is endless. Whatever the issue, use it to "get in their face" and remain nearby, or encourage their exit.

Moving in close--for any reason--discourages thieves. They absolutely do not want that, and making an issue quickly of something like cussing will often obviate the need later to deal with a possible theft where your legal ground may be shaky. But whatever is happening and whatever else you're thinking, always think subterfuge. A couple of people acting up in one area may be cover for someone else stealing you blind in another.

> Surprisingly, most shoplifters cooperate fully if they are approached correctly.

## 5.05 Insurance

If you run a stop sign, are you "willfully" putting life at risk? Always remember that something you consider accidental could be perceived by others as pure negligence.

Are you liable for what a disgruntled employee does, or an officer of a private agency who is working under contract in your business? Does the security company have its own insurance? Can you be responsible for what a certified city police officer does? Can you be liable for the actions of a total stranger?

You catch a juvenile, talk to him, "give him a break" and let him leave. He runs happily off, but misses his ride home. He hitchhikes and gets hit by a car. Are you liable? Many questions need answering, and foremost is "Will your insurance cover you?" To assure you don't find yourself insurance-impaired, get your policy checked, cross-checked and double-checked by a qualified attorney and insurance agent.

## 5.06 Payment for Stolen Merchandise

A demand for money linked in any way with a real or implied threat is worrisome. *As a rule*, do not accept payment for recovered merchandise. Either prosecute them, or release them without accepting money. The reason for this involves the concept of "extortion."

If you say or imply that a payment of cash will result in your not prosecuting the case, your words could reasonably be construed (twisted) as being, "If you give me money, you can go; but if you don't, you'll have trouble." And if that is twisted, it might be made to sound like, "If you give me money, I'll leave you alone and you can go. But if you don't, I'll have to break your legs."

A judge can order "restitution" for goods damaged or lost, but only if you prosecute. Absorbing the cost of damaged merchandise is usually a drawback with a non-prosecuted case. Individual judges and jurisdictions differ considerably, but the rule of thumb is do not threaten to prosecute anyone for not giving up money even if he gets merchandise. Once an arrest is made for stealing, it's too late to buy or sell.

Be safe. Check with the local solicitor and make sure your lemonade stand can't be construed as being Big Al's protection franchise.

## 5.07 Accomplices

**"The hand of one is the hand of all,"** is legal theory which--generally--means that a thief's friend can be arrested *if* he assists the crime in a *truly significant* manner. More than just "looking around," there must be a strong demonstration of active participation. Simply because two people were together at a particular place is *not* proof--in and of itself--that both were involved.

Ideally, they enter together, go to the display together, and stand together when the item is concealed. *And* the accomplice is "active," which means he provides a bag, handles the merchandise, etc. If they split up, both can say they thought the other one paid.

What initially passes as a "good-enough" accomplice case can easily degenerate into a false-arrest nightmare. At trial, the thieves may know the primary thief (the one "most obviously guilty") has a hopeless case. If so, they might work together to have the lesser thief found "not guilty." (Not innocent, mind you, just not guilty, i.e., not enough evidence to convict.) Working with a sharp attorney, this lesser thief--poor soul--might later sue for false arrest. He was, after all, found not guilty, and that might sway ignorant jurors in a civil court. When two work together, you usually have to let one go.

A rule of thumb is if you're not arresting someone, you don't want him around. (And if there's not enough evidence to convict him, only a fool would arrest him.) If you allow a prisoner's friend or accomplice to walk with you and your thief to the office, they might later lie and twist the story by saying you forced the friend to come. Don't let third parties weasel their way into your case, *especially* an accomplice whose participation you let slide.

> Whenever a suspect protests or offers an explanation, listen to him. What he says must be examined in light of a courtroom defense. Consider the potential effect on a judge or jury of what he says. If he offers an explanation that can *reasonably* be investigated prior to formally charging him, by all means look into it.

## 5.08 Questions of Liability

False arrest, anguish, and the entire catalogue of wrongs suffered by "customers" all fly contrary to the Prime Directive: "Don't get sued." It's the J.O.B. to ensure encounters don't degenerate badly and Benjamin Franklin's sage advice will help: "Make haste slowly."

If you are mistaken (or probably mistaken) or for any reason want to end a stop, try to have the following questions answerable with a "No:"

Was the person--
...touched?
...accused of theft in so many words?
...accused of theft in the presence of others?
...ordered to "stop," "come here," or "go there?"
...approached by a uniformed guard?
...searched or told to empty pockets, purse, bag, etc.?
...forced to return to the store/business?
...(Was he) loud enough to attract attention, or spoken to too loudly?
...(Was he) confronted outside the store?
...confronted for more than a minute (i.e., 60 seconds)?
...confronted by more than a single employee whose presence was obvious?
...confronted by police or uniformed security along with plain-clothes employees?

Hopefully, the following questions can be answered "Yes:"

- Aside from theft, was there another, ostensible reason (pretext) to justify a stop?
- Could there have been?
- Can there be?
- Was there some (other) legal reason that he *should* have been stopped?
- Did he act in a manner that reasonable people would think suspicious?
- Was he provocative?
- If he opened his bag for inspection, did he do so without prodding, demand, or suggestion by an employee?
- Was the conversation heard by only the suspect and employees?

- Were employees the only witnesses to the conversation?
- To impartial witnesses, did the employee seem friendly and polite?
- To a casual observer, did the stop look like a casual conversation?
- Did the suspect seem to take it all in stride, exhibiting no anger, etc.?
- Did he admit to any inappropriate behavior?
- Did he verbalize an understanding of the employees' actions by saying (in effect), "I would have done the same as you."

If the first set of questions receive a "no," and the second set a "yes," it's very unlikely certified letters will arrive, *if* the truth is told.

After any worrisome or unusual situation and *any* time you're in the wrong (or not entirely right), get statements from witnesses to bolster your position. (This is "damage control.") Record what people say--friendly and otherwise--even if they say they saw nothing. (If they later testify for the defendant, you can assert that current testimony is inconsistent with statements at the time of the incident.)

"Leading-questions" can result in faulty answers. "Did you see a purse in her hand," is a leading-question. That can result in what labs call a "false positive" (which, I can't deny, can sometimes be a good thing). Instead, try "Did you see anything in her hands?"

In written statements, all relevant points are addressed, and it's perfectly acceptable to ask a witness to write about a certain point(s). If a witness alludes to a certain time, ascertain if he means exact or approximate. Also, it's especially important that witnesses perceive you as a nice person just doing his job. From the beginning and throughout, be as nice as possible (considering the totality of the circumstances).

**Note:** Also see "Whoops!" (Bad stops), pg 102.

## 5.09 Harassment and Honey Traps

Sexual harassment, personality disorders, and dirty tricks can strike anyone. Many promising police, management, and loss prevention careers have been--and will be--*trashed* because a legal line was crossed or was perceived to have been crossed. Some jerks or fools intentionally cross, some people are tricked or seduced into crossing ("honey traps"), some are naive and blindly stroll across, and some people just accidentally trip and fall across. If you cross the line, it probably won't matter why. LP exists to solve problems, not create them, so even if everyone else crosses a line, LP must not.

LP must inspire confidence and develop sources of information. To do so demands the reality and the perception of professionalism. Flirting, dating, "meeting," suggestive comments, and physical contact are all contrary to LP goals. LP and management must go out of their way to avoid even the appearance of "hitting" on employees and customers. If a person even *might* profit from a sexual harassment *allegation*, don't be in a room alone with them. Without a witness, don't even get on an elevator with them. Be *that* careful.

It doesn't really matter if employees hit on LP or LP hits on employees. If you don't act to stop it, you condone it. Condoning is a form of participation, so it would be fair to say that you're a part of the problem. Besides, do you think people hit on you just because you're that irresistible? No. Most are trying to sink a hook.

Some employees are actually afraid of authority (which is what LP represents and what management *is*). Employees like this will absorb a lot of abuse, and may even feel obligated to flirt. Taking advantage of these people is simply unconscionable.

Dishonest thieves want to play you, and some employees have minor (or major) personality disorders. An employee may want to "one-up" another, or be friendly to distract you. A disgruntled employee might try to set up a lawsuit or justify a resignation. Some have marriage problems (maybe a jealous and violent spouse), and others fish for information. Some want on your good side so you'll let minor (or major) infractions slide.

Even if flirting or touching, dating, etc., seems "harmless," the potential for personal, professional, or legal problems is inescapable. (But remember the Godfather: Keep your friends close and your enemies closer. It's a balancing act.)

Don't comment on a mini-skirt, need for a diet, or tell off-color jokes. Over time, you might develop friendships, but have them honest. Until you know the players *real* well, if an employee talks about their personal life, run away. Even a perception of harassment or "playing around" can compromise or decrease your effectiveness. One result--of many--is decreased respect, trust and confidence of honest employees.

Two basic rules: 1. Don't foul your own nest, and 2. If you want a pet, buy a dog. If you chat with young employees, chat with old ones, too. If you pat young ones on the back, pat old ones. If you chat only with "beautiful people" or "power people" you are slighting or insulting all the rest and there *will* be pay-back.

If you engage in sexual harassment, have a fling with an employee, or flirt and touch, you are a liability. You're incompetent, undisciplined, immature, unprofessional or all the above. Sooner or later you, and probably others too, will pay for your transgressions.

## *Golly, it's a small world!*

Serving "no-knock" search warrants on drug houses can be tricky. On one occasion, the dealers inside were alleged to be well-armed users, so our plan was to sneak into the house about four a.m. and take them in their sleep. Good plan, but our locksmith couldn't jimmy the locks. It was then decided that *someone* should try going through a second story window, make his way through the house, and open the door from the inside.

The climb and entry went well, but once inside I had to pass an open bedroom where a naked man was sleeping on his back, head propped up on a pillow, facing the doorway. On his night stand were bags and bags of green leafy stuff, and a pistol lay on the bed just inches from his left hand. With my service revolver in both hands and pointed at his face which was about ten feet away, I was silently passing his room en route to the front door of the house when his eyes suddenly popped opened and looked straight into mine.

Drugged and startled as he certainly was, he didn't panic and jump (thank God!) so even with a gallon of adrenaline coursing through me, I didn't start blasting away. Instead, he lay there totally motionless (except for his eyes, which kept flicking back and forth from my eyes to the yawning barrel of my .357 magnum). This was yet another scenario not specifically covered at the police academy.

Not knowing how many of his friends were home or what the "right" move was, I held a finger to my lips (motioning him to keep silent), whispered, "Rise and shine,--- ----," (expletive deleted) and then motioned him to come to me. A minute later he opened the tricky door and the troops poured in. While they "cleared" the house my guy sat on the cold, tile floor stark naked, hands cuffed behind him, and looking pretty glum, I thought.

Now to the "point:" It's been said that we all are just six people removed from anyone else in the country-- that we know someone who knows someone, etc.--and for that reason we can never guess who even a five-word, off-the-cuff conversation might be repeated to. It's a good idea, therefore, to always be as light and polite as time and situation allow.

Later the same day (as the drug raid), I learned that the highly-embarrassed dealer who, at the point of my gun was rousted out of bed with an obscenity and then handcuffed and parked naked on the floor, just happened to be the son of a very senior--and very unforgiving--law enforcement official.

**When a liar tells the truth, it's often some part of a bigger lie.**

StealMeBlind

# Chapter 6

# The Mechanics of Theft

32,000 variations and combinations of just three basic colors (red, blue and green) make possible the works of great masters and six-year-olds everywhere. Eight basic literary plots (e.g., "Lonely boy with cut finger meets passionate girl with Band-Aid") provide countless books and movies, and an alphabet with just 26 letters provides the U.S. Copyright Office with over half a *million* new manuscripts *every* year.

By themselves, chemical elements such as hydrogen, sulfur, and oxygen are pretty benign, but problems arise when some elements combine with certain others. ("Little Willie was a chemist. Little Willie is no more. What he thought was $H_2O$ was $H_2SO_4$.")

Crime occurs when three basic elements combine. These elements are means, desire, and opportunity. Eliminate any one of those and you prevent crime. It's really that simple. We can do little about a thief's *desire* to steal, because "lust" is, after all, a problem of Biblical proportion. Much can be done to eliminate opportunity, but more on that later. This section deals with means, the first of the three elements.

"Means" includes not only shoplifting tools, but also tactics which are the "how" of thievery. Several have been mentioned in previous chapters (including the "carjacking" variation). Tactics involve the actual use of tools and how shoplifters (and dishonest employees) work, both when alone and as members of a team. Basically, thieves have two types of tools: containers and body parts. Just two, but diversity, tactics, variations, and combinations provide an impressive and sometimes bewildering array of means.

## 6.01 Thieves' Tools

**1. Paper and Plastic Bags.** Very popular is the type with a pull-string top. Plastic bags and sacks are folded small and brought in by hand, pocket, or purse, or carried inside another bag, itself in plain view. Bags used for stealing are often nicked, worn, and/or quite rumpled. (Prior to bagging, a thief often "rolls" clothes around his forearm.)

A bag brought in openly might contain items already purchased (or stolen) or contain an empty box for concealing stolen merchandise. A bag that appears full might be filled with nothing but air or wadded up pieces of paper.

**2. Shopping Bags With Handles.** These rectangular bags--with string handles--have large cargo capacities and are custom-designed for "sliding" and "dropping." They free-stand on the floor while the thief slides merchandise off a counter with his hand or sleeve into the bag's gaping mouth. It takes only a second. But they're not without problems. Store personnel can easily look down into the bag and see the contents, and--thieves often forget--you can *hear* merchandise hit bottom.

Owning a bar is a common fantasy among police officers. Bill Thrasher and I were talking about that when I mentioned pool tables. He immediately said no. No pool tables. "You gotta be crazy to give a stick to a drunk." But stores give bags to thieves.

**3. Purses.** Full- and part-time professionals often use **"trash purses"** that contain no ID or anything of personal value so they can throw (it) down to divert pursuers. They commonly steal purses and fill them with merchandise stolen from the same store.

**4. Pants.** The most popular "containers" for small or easily folded items. Males *and* females stick merchandise down the front of pants about as often as they use pockets. (Front pockets are used much more than back pockets.)

Shirt-tails hanging out cover bulges made by items stuffed down the front of pants, and if the item protrudes above the waistband, the shirt covers that, too. CD's, socks, books, scarves, baseball caps, shirts, jewelry, cosmetics and a great deal more go inside pants. (A few weeks before this writing, I stopped a teenager with a can of Pringles chips in the crotch of his pants. His baggy clothes covered the bulge, but it was just a bad day to be a thief.)

Wearing two pairs of pants is popular. Holes are cut in the outer pants' pockets and items are placed through the outer pants into the pockets of the inner pants. If stopped, the thief happily turns pockets inside-out and protests his innocence. This ruse usually works because it's initially so unnerving.

Another reason thieves wear two pairs of pants is to confuse pursuers. The initial description of the thief is near useless if he strips off his outer pants. A man with black pants instantly becomes a man in red ones with a greater chance of escape.

**5. Skirts.** Female shoplifters wear strong "booster girdles" under skirts, and after stealing, they appear pregnant or overweight. (One woman drew stares from everyone she passed. Shameless observers pointed and laughed at this unfortunate but brave mother-to-be who appeared pregnant with a large, presumably mutant *square* baby about the size of a toaster oven.)

On a more typical occasion, a woman concealed a leather coat under her maternity blouse inside a hand-made girdle used exclusively for theft. (This is a Gypsy specialty.) If a skirt is a long, flowing one, even a camcorder will show only a small bulge.

**6. Jackets and Coats.** I've arrested *many* shoplifters by seeing a coat when everyone else wore only a shirt. *Notice this*! It's too flagrant and stupid to pass undetected.

Naturally, pockets (both inside and out) are used, but thieves might also cut the inside lining and fill it with loot. By using the lining, the thief can "prove his innocence" by opening the jacket front and pulling empty pockets inside-out.

With the pocket linings *and* inside linings of a large coat cut, a thief can lean over a display and appear to have his hands in his coat pockets. In reality, hidden hands snatch items off displays. Large or loose-fitting coats and jackets "hang," making visibility difficult from the sides. From behind him, of course, nothing at all can be observed. If he faces a display, standing closely, all his bases are covered.

Large items are held under arms inside coats or stuffed into sleeves. Jackets can be mostly unzipped, but secured at the waist, so items can be safely dropped in the jacket.

Some coats are custom-fitted with hooks inside to hold items or with **"deep pockets."** The manufacturer's pocket is cut and fitted with a bag-like device that allows for remarkable storage. If the coat is ankle-length, items even two or three feet in length can be concealed. Because **"deep-pocket coats"** often have merchandise hanging below hip-level, there may be no apparent bulge hinting at the theft of a rifle, curtain rods, or a tightly rolled Oriental rug. (Even bulkier items such as a camcorder won't show much of a bulge.)

**7. Garments.** Coats and other garments carried over the shoulder or over the arm provide an excellent place for concealment of items under or within the folds of the garment, or stuffed into the sleeves. Umbrellas are used for this purpose, too. Small items are just dropped down the open end. (You must pay attention! Concealing an item can take only a second or two.)

**8. Booster Boxes.** An empty box is gift-wrapped or disguised to *appear* sealed, but one of the six sides has a "door" rigged to open and shut. If it's professional-quality, the door has a mechanism (or spring) that causes it to close after something is inserted. With a slit on one side, this idea works for bags, also. Booster boxes *and* large purses are sometimes lined with aluminum foil. The purpose, of course, is to get past electronic sensors at doors.

**9. Booster Pants.** With strong elastic at the ankles, pants "catch" items dropped down the waist or through a hole in the pocket. Athletic pants are great for this. To be even safer, a thief may secure the ankles with rubber bands, tuck the ankles into socks, or wear the pants' leg up around his calf.

**10. Shirts.** Loose-fitting shirts (and sweaters) are tucked in at the waist, and inside the "floppiness" of the shirt--as it hangs over the belt--is a safe haven for small or "soft line" items such as socks and scarves.

**11. Booster Sleeves.** Booster sleeves are shirt or jacket sleeves with strong elastic or rubber bands at the wrist. Thieves slide merchandise up a sleeve like an uptown hustler slides cards, or they drop an item from inside the jacket at the armpit down into the sleeve. (You *must* watch hands.)

**12. Backpacks.** School backpacks and carry-alls are popular, especially with the younger set. (Watch for zipping, unzipping, putting on and taking off.)

**13. Baby Buggies.** The more deluxe the model, the more pouches and flaps. When a buggy canopy is closed--pulled back--a nice little kangaroo pouch is created. People also conceal merchandise under the child, if, in fact, there's even a child in the buggy. I've seen buggies with nothing but stolen merchandise under a baby blanket.

**14. Store Buggies.** Merchandise is concealed in a buggy, covered with a sale-paper (or something else that's handy) and a large, bulky item or, perhaps, bags or boxes from another store are then put on top. Few cashiers bother to check buggies closely, so the thief asks to use it to carry things to his car.

**15. The Book Club.** Newspapers, magazines and books are used to conceal merchandise slipped in their pages. If the thief has a stack of reading material, items are placed between magazines or books. A variation is the old-fashioned, if rarely used, **hollow book**: an ordinary book--usually quite thick--has the pages cut with a razor so that the book is actually a box.

**16. Fast Food Cups.** Cups with plastic lids are an unexpected hazard. I've encountered several thieves--all female teenagers--who use empty cups for small items like jewelry and cosmetics. (Not a bad idea, actually, and the girls played it up by sipping on the straw.)

**17. The "Customer Persona."** A shoplifter's second most important tool is the use of "illusion." He creates an illusion of normalcy. This is his "con," his "gimmick." To this end, he assumes a customer persona. He dresses, acts, and sounds like a normal shopper to convince you his illusion is reality.

**18. Confusion.** Combined with illusion, that's really about all it takes. Whether the game is shoplifting, cons, swindles or fraud. Whenever thieves deal with loss prevention, store personnel or even the police, one of their primary goals are illusion and confusion. These are true Gypsy specialties.

---

The "Number One Tool" used by thieves has yet to be discussed. It's reasonable to say that without it there can be *no* theft. Although most thieves use two, this obvious tool is virtually ignored by store personnel.

---

**19. The Number One Shoplifting Tool.** Male employees look at women's legs, derrieres, *everything,* it seems, but hands and what they hold. (Female employees do no better.) Ask an employee what that last man to pass them held in his hands, and almost always the answer is, "I don't know" or (much worse) "What man?" Thieves walk out with piles of clothes and even TV's because no one sees what they are holding.

*Hands!* Losses would be cut dramatically if employees were trained to look at customers' hands when they enter and exit a store or department; what customers hold as they turn away from displays, and what they hold as they stroll around. And *more* losses could be prevented if employees noticed what customers don't have in their hands.

> I observed a man, about 35, walk to a candy bar display and casually make a selection. He took it into a swarm of shoppers and tore the package off, discarding it on the floor. The "evidence" was immediately trampled by the crowd, and he began eating.
>
> I retrieved the package and caught up to him. Stepping in his path, I said, "You dropped this." (Just a simple statement of fact to see how he wanted to play.)
>
> Conjuring a "mean" look, he stepped closer and parried, "Did I?" (He wanted to see if I'd back down easily and let him steal or if I was willing to push it.)
>
> "Yes. You did." (Yes, I'll push it. Whether I'll go to war or not, he now *thinks* that I might. That's now reality *for him*, so he has to factor it into his thinking.)
>
> Plan A (steal and leave) and Plan B (bluffing and a "mean look") both failed, so he must think, fight, or run. He has the physical advantage, but much can go wrong and this is clearly not his lucky day. Is there an off-duty cop around? Am *I* an off duty cop? Who might recognize him? How might others react if he creates a problem?
>
> Concluding that a loud scene was too risky, he went with the "careless, honest shopper routine." Almost humbly, he said, "I wasn't paying attention." A lie. (His problem was fear: not of me, personally, but of all the unknowns; his response told me so.)
>
> "I was," I said. (Again, just matter of fact.) Wordlessly, he took the wrapper, then walked straight to a cashier and paid. Note: I could have let it go at any time.
>
> (He worked at a nearby store, and I had suspected him before. Now he knows that in *this* store he's no longer the Invisible Man, he is a *marked* man.)

Look at the obvious. If someone's at a shoe counter, look at their feet; at an earring display, look at their ears. Is it their own purse they're holding at a purse display? And *always* check people at umbrella displays when it's raining. Notice how people are dressed and what they hold when they approach a display (before they start playing with merchandise). Then scrutinize them when they walk away.

Many people (especially thieves) have much to lose if arrested for *anything*. They "talk the talk," but if they think that security or police are nearby, they won't "walk the walk." They understand that the law's arm is usually longer than a thief's legs, so play on their fear. Often it's enough to just pick up a phone, talk to the dial tone and look a suspicious person in the eyes while you do it. Whatever you do, do *something*.

Employees see activity that anyone should consider odd, but don't call management or security until it's too late. True story: "He was here for ten minutes. I asked him if he needed anything, and his eyes were real red. He must have been on drugs. Then he kept messing with his bag and every time I got close to him, he moved to a different place. When he left, I know his bag was a lot bigger than it was when he got here. You can still catch him. He just walked out the door a second ago." Sad, sad, sad.

> **Shoplifters depend on employees.**
> They depend on employees *not* to notice and *not* to go out of their way. They depend on employees *not* to consider the significance of what they or *not* to care. They depend on employees *not* to call for help soon enough. Or not to call at all.

## 6.02 Tactics and Devices

17-year-old Melanie says that "most all" of her friends shoplift and she's personally done it "hundreds of times." Small, exclusive shops are easiest, she says, and she prefers "expensive places." What about employees? "In small shops they don't have as many and you can always get what you want. They'll get busy or have to ring somebody up or answer the phone. They'll go away long enough."

How about larger stores? Are employees a problem? "No."

Are they at least inconvenient? "No. Employees are really all the same. I don't think they care. Everybody shoplifts and nobody ever gets caught. Nobody watches." (Ironically, she was wearing handcuffs throughout this conversation.)

**1. Price Switching.** Tags with lower prices replace correct tags. This is encouraged by inattention to detail and a cavalier attitude toward control and accountability of price guns, stickers, and labels. Price stickers (the Monarch type used in price guns) are put on some merchandise in such a way that thieves can obviously easily peel them off and attach them to something else. (That employee error is as common as it is stupid.)

Still, a thief's favorite price is "free." Some stores put large "paid" stickers on bulky items instead of bagging them. These stickers are often used to stick a receipt to a large box or piece of luggage. Are the stickers rationed out daily, or are they found laying around at unattended cash registers and other places? Are entire rolls free for the taking?

And what is the safest place in the store for changing prices and other mischief? Where are thieves guaranteed a few minutes of privacy?

**2. Dressing Rooms.** Three items in, one returned; six in, two returned, the rest worn by thieves under their own clothes, in purses, or in shopping bags. Customers in fitting rooms provide an excellent opportunity to increase sales through customer service, but instead, fitting rooms are often ignored and are havens for thieves.

> If what a customer takes into the dressing room is not actually seen and <u>handled</u> by an employee, it's <u>impossible</u> to know if all merchandise is returned.

Melanie loves dressing rooms: "It's just so easy! You just take five or six things in. Hold them by the top of the hangers so they can't count the hangers. Then you watch out for cameras and things and fill your purse or wear your own clothes on top and go."

"You walk in the dressing room with a bunch of things, you walk out with a bunch of things. Nobody pays attention. You get $75 bathing suits, $200 dresses..."

(Asked if she felt guilty about stealing, she replied, "Sometimes. If I take, like, a $100 dress or something. Nobody misses little things; they don't make any difference. I wouldn't ever feel bad about $10 or $20 worth of something, but sometimes I do feel guilty if it's a lot of money. Sometimes.")

Shoplifters sneak small items into fitting rooms by concealing them in bulky merchandise. Once in private, they transfer the loot to a container. Slothful or busy clerks don't give merchandise an even cursory inspection. They trust thieves to show them what's taken in and out. They don't remove discarded clothing from fitting rooms and leave trash, hangers and discarded clothes tags in fitting rooms, concealing evidence of stolen items.

And if *dishonest* clerks monitor dressing rooms, thieves are assisted in *innumerable* ways. Dishonest clerks even stock dressing rooms with merchandise from all over the store for theft by friends ostensibly trying on clothes. Honest employees or security don't know what went in, so they can't nail thieves when they come out. (See App. 07, pg. 161)

**3. Discards.** Just put on new clothes or shoes and leave the old behind. (Notice what people are wearing; at least the color!) Shoes worn in for this purpose are usually obvious "trash shoes." Some thieves take your clothes into the fitting room, put them on, then put their old clothes on hangers or carefully fold them, then carry them out and put them on your rack as though they were yours. Women engage in a novel variation: Wearing nothing beneath a raincoat, they take clothes into a fitting room, then just get dressed and leave.

> "Lose yourself in the crowd." Most thieves enjoy crowds. Lots of activity allows them to enter, steal, and exit unnoticed. Crowded fields favor predators, but just as the confusion helps a thief conceal theft, it also provides cover for security personnel.

> A 24-year-old "regular customer" was clothes-hunting. He left a bag from another store with the regular clerk who then went about her regular business. If he wanted help, he'd find her like he usually did. That particular day, he settled on three pairs of socks, three pairs of underwear, two pairs of pants, and a shirt. Like always, he stepped into the *unattended* dressing room to try things on.
>
> A second man was also hunting in the area, but not for clothes: handcuffs hidden, he was a hawk in the guise of a dove. When the regular customer reappeared with only one pair of pants in his hands, the second man--waiting just outside the door--stepped immediately into the fitting room. It was empty.
>
> The "regular customer" was a "regular thief," and admitted stealing from this store "once or twice a week." He wore the missing clothes under his own, and in his bag were $127 of clothes he stole from other stores. On a previous visit to this store--he said--he stole the belt he was wearing. He refused to give it back, though, because "nobody caught me stealing it."

**4. Package Switching.** The possibilities are endless. A thief can remove a $10 item from a box and replace it with a $30-item. Most clothes-irons fit in the same sized box. Will the cashier know the difference? If so, the thief will plead ignorant. Few cashiers check boxes that have obviously been opened, or investigate opened or ripped packages.

**5. Snatch and Run.** Also referred to as **"hit and run"** or **"grab and run."** Shoplifters simply take something and run out the door. This can occur so quickly that employees who notice often have no idea what was stolen and can rarely provide a decent description of the runner. Positioned correctly between employees and the door, thieves shield merchandise from view with their bodies, a box or some other "prop." If a door is involved, an accomplice may be there to open it and then innocently--or not-so-innocently--hinder pursuit. (A car may be right outside.)

It's seldom necessary to run, though, and most thieves just walk. Few employees notice, chase thieves, or even call management if they see it happen. In fact, many prefer to believe nothing was stolen and generally ignore it rather than "get involved" or "create a scene." Others simply couldn't care less.

> **4 minutes, $99.00.** Three women select a microwave oven. One carries it while the other two obscure the busy cashier's view as they walk out the main door.
>
> **8 minutes, $90.00.** Two men take a boxed vacuum cleaner to a position near a check-out and "browse." When the cashier is distracted *and* other shoppers are leaving the store, the two men just stroll out, box in plain view.

**6. Legs. (Also called "tight-leg.")** With practice, a small television, VCR, or case of beer can be "got" by stealing with legs. Under skirts or coats, large items are gripped between vice-like thighs. Those who steal this way are invariably professionals, and their gait appears normal to casual observers. (Watch for short steps or a semi-shuffling gait.)

**7. False stomachs.** With a technique "meant" for women, merchandise is stuffed up under a skirt into a strong girdle or home-made "apron." This works best with long, loose-fitting "flowing" skirts, and is a Gypsy specialty. (You *must* look at people when they enter the store or area, and before they enter dressing rooms.)

**8. Multiple Pick-up.** He picks up several items and wanders around. He gives anyone watching a chance to become distracted, and then he steals one item, dumping the rest in a pile. You probably won't know what, *exactly,* is missing, and by the time you sort it out, your eyes have been off the thief too long to make a decent stop.

Often, these thieves steal a bit at a time. They do a lot of touchy-feely, picking things up and setting them down out of place or constantly replenish items in their hands or buggy. It's all part of their deception. If the thief is a "regular customer," he'll probably buy something before he leaves.

**9. Counters and Displays.** Store personnel create *"blind spots"* while stacking boxes, moving merchandise, or arranging displays. A good location for a thief obscures your view of his hands and bag. Some blind spots are obvious and could hide a troupe of thieves, but others are not so obvious. In a narrow aisle, for example, one person just standing there might block the view of three bag-stuffing chums.

> Look down aisles when patrolling a store. Don't focus on the person at the end of the aisle closest to you; let your peripheral vision handle him. Look beyond him to the *next* person on the aisle. What's *that* person doing? What's he holding?
>
> Did the one who saw you first say anything to the other as you approached? Or make a noise or sudden movement? You know...sound the alarm?

**10. Diversions.** Occasionally a "sure thing" roams your aisles. He "looks like a thief," handles high-risk merchandise, and does everything a thief should do. Quite naturally, he gets your undivided attention. Oddly, he leaves without stealing, but you later discover something *was* stolen; just not by *him*. He was a distraction; an illusion of danger to divert personnel--especially security--away from the actual thief. (See "Creeper," pg 61.)

Distractions can be well planned. A man and woman arguing, a child misbehaving or tripping a fire alarm...anything to draw attention away from the *real* action.

It's not necessary to attract the crew of "Unsolved Mysteries" or set fire trucks rolling, although fire is always an excellent diversion. Nothing need distract you for more than a moment or two, and even a simple conversation can often do just that.

If there's some question as to who or where security people might be...create a problem and see who drops in. Distracting is still another area of Gypsy expertise. They have *specialists*. Try to approach "weird" situations from a direction that is not obvious. If possible, swing around the sales floor on the way and have someone check other areas, too.

> Satisfied shoplifters, like satisfied customers, return again and again where employees are cooperative and the price is right. They enjoy stores where employees bury themselves in "things to do," and "don't have time" to even *look* at shoppers. Employees who don't move around are easy for thieves to keep track of.

**11. Portable Walls.** Picture in your mind a man carrying a 2-by-4-foot bulletin board (properly bagged and tagged after having been purchased) under his *left* arm. He walks past a cashier, keeping her to his left. She's unable, of course, to see the boxed VCR on the other side of the larger item. (And wasn't it nice of that lady to hold the door open?)

Thieves use their bodies or those of accomplices to create "walls" (blind spots). At a checkout, a thief will stand with his back to a display, then discreetly reach behind him and load items into his back pockets. (Preventing beats losing, so if it's difficult to monitor a situation, move in and take a close look: "What can I help you find?"

**12. Repacks and Nesting.** OK, maybe the right boots are in the right box, but what's inside the boots? Are both boots the same size? Commonly used for this type stealing are items that no one closely examines. Excellent prospects for repackaging are things like winter coats, 50-pound bags of dog food or quilts packaged in plastic zipper-bags. With a box cutter, thieves slice the bag and insert small items.

At the checkout, they chirp, "Don't forget the dog food." The price tag is conveniently face-up, of course, so the cashier won't need to move the bag and find hidden items. If ice chests or trash cans are sold, cashiers should routinely look inside.

Thieves unfold quilts--ostensibly for examination--and insert smaller items (sheet sets, crystal, anything quiet). Next (maybe then, maybe later), someone buys the stuffed quilt with a rubber check and the quilt is returned for a refund before the check bounces back from the bank. One thief rolled a car stereo into a sleeping bag. Would a cashier unroll it to see if it concealed a two-hundred dollar stereo? She could say, "We've had some of these returned with rips inside, so let's make sure this one's all right."

> Follow me with this: Two hundred bucks in free merchandise (concealed inside a quilt), plus $100 cash for a refund on the quilt. He got $300 in cash and prizes for just one hour's work. Then, of course, a week later his check bounces back from the bank.
>
> And are you the only store in the mall? In the city?
>
> It's bad enough that many stores won't prosecute shoplifters, but some businesses (including some regional and national retail chains) won't even prosecute hot checks!

If a store has sales fliers, thieves put slim items such as hosiery and jewelry in a cart and cover them with a sales paper. To someone just glancing, the cart appears empty except for the papers on the bottom. Luggage, of course, provides the classic example of "nesting:" smaller pieces inside large ones. The possibilities are limitless.

Ten dollars here, ten there...like the congressman said: "A billion here, a billion there, and pretty soon you're talking real money."

**13. Questions.** Some shoplifters request customer service. "Do you have size 10 in the back room?" The "wild-goose chase" is an old, old trick.

And in response to a "customer's" request, would any cashier be so stupid as to take her eyes off an open cash drawer? (Sure they do.) Or turn around long enough for a thief to steal merchandise off a check-out counter? (All day long.) Would she even notice anything missing? (And if she does, will she do anything? *Really*?)

A question commonly heard in many retail stores is, "Do you work here?" Some shoplifters ask this when they find someone suspicious. It can be unsettling, and some plain-clothes security actually answer "*yes*." (Wrong answer, but thanks for playing.)

**14. Sales Receipts.** It's easy to get cash refunds with a receipt because it "proves" the item was purchased. Often, though, the item never left the store. Receipt in hand, a thief strolls in, grabs the item he needs and carries it to customer service. Sometimes he needs to be sneaky, but it can be very easy. Dishonest employees *give* receipts to their friends.

With or without an accomplice, employees withhold receipts from honest customers to use for fraud voids or refunds. "The customer left because he didn't have enough money (or didn't have any more checks, etc.), and we were really busy (or the manager was busy, etc.) so I didn't call you right then."

**15. Children.** Many things--especially candy or toys--are handed to small children to carry out. If stopped, the adult says he didn't notice. To make you think he's honest, he gives the child a chewing out. Also, kids are used to distract employees away from adults.

> A suspicious "customer," about 10 feet away was examining watchbands and asked if I worked for the store. I told him "no" and then asked him if he'd mind helping handicapped-me read some fine print on a watch. (I had an eye infection, you understand, and couldn't see well. Close up, I told him, was bad, but anything more than about 3 feet away was just a blur.)
>
> The nice man obliged, and, convinced I was harmless, this careful thief walked straight back to the watch bands and immediately pocketed one. He was <u>so</u> easy.

**16. Dumpster Diving.** It is sometimes difficult to get receipts without active employee-cooperation. One way is **"dumpster diving."** If a thief is detected in a dumpster or while rooting through trash cans, he says he's looking for empty soda cans. Who cares?

They want merchandise or paper trash from offices, checkouts and customer service. (Often neatly packaged in trash bags.) They want addresses, phone numbers, credit card and social security numbers, and employment information. Kiss your good credit good-bye if a knowledgeable dumpster diver surfaces with your info. He'll buy things and wreak all kinds of havoc. Make it an injury or insurance liability issue to evict them; or call the PD.

Some want store bags to help with stealing or to make it appear credible when returning stolen items for exchange or refund. Some recover damaged merchandise to return for cash and some fetch merchandise put in the dumpster by friends who are dishonest employees.[23]

**17. The Sting.** Now you see it, now you don't. Think of movies in which one briefcase is switched for another. Same thing. Two or more thieves work together and a bag of stolen merchandise is switched with another, seemingly identical, bag. The switch is either a blind drop or hand pass, but it must occur out of the employee's sight. It takes only a second, and can be done in the store, in another store, or in a fitting room or restroom. (Even under the dividers from one stall to another.)

Once the stolen merchandise is safe with an accomplice, the thief might wait for you near totally uninvolved witnesses because he *wants* to be detained and arrested. When his bag is searched, nothing incriminating is found and unless you pull rabbits out of hats, you've got big trouble.

**18. Creepers.** One person seems to enter a store or area, but "duck-walking" or bent low is a second thief who "dips" left or right into nearby displays. This "creeper" pulls a bag from a pocket and begins stuffing. Meanwhile, his partner pretends to examine nearby merchandise, but is a look-out feeding information to the creeper. When the creeper is ready, they exit. Employees satisfied to see just the tops of people over racks and counters never even know the creeper exists. Putting high risk merchandise near doors is just plain dumb. (A variation is a "salt and pepper team." A "suspicious-looking" black stereotype enters and intentionally draws attention while an ignored white does the actual stealing.)

## 6.03 Intimidation

**Illegitimi non carbundum.** (Don't let the bastards grind you down.)

Intimidation is a tool and psychological tactic which is often successful against people who are ill-prepared or inexperienced. It includes shouting, cussing, and threatening body-language. Some victims fear immediate harm. Others just want to avoid "a scene," or repercussions such as a "customer complaint" to the home office. Some victims are afraid of getting mugged some night in the parking lot, and others are embarrassed or humiliated.

Intimidation is used by shoplifters and many others. These include people attempting fraud refunds or exchanges, and writing bad checks ("paper hangers," they're called).

It may begin with "Why are you watching me? or "Do you think I'm stealing?--which are pretty mild--or more aggressively with "Why don't you get the hell out of my face?" One "customer" may say loudly to another, "If that ---- starts watching me I'll slap her face off." Initially, it can be impossible to ascertain if an intimidator is a bully, a person with low self-esteem, someone just having a bad day, or a thief.[24]

If you work in a place, you can look at whatever you want (*except* where a reasonable expectation of privacy exists, such as in fitting room or restroom stalls). Thieves know it's legal for you to watch them, but even if you're 20 or 30-feet away, one occasionally looks over and makes wise-cracks (loudly, so you will hear). If they want to play Tom Sawyer starting mischief, *fine*. I might be their Huckleberry and play: I walk over and with a little edge to my voice politely say, "Pardon me?" Or--depending on how I read the situation--not-so-politely say, "It's a free country. I look at what I want to. *Especially* in here."

If one escalates, I might tell him that I was happy over there, but they wanted my attention, so now I'm over here. "I'm confused. So I won't be walking back and forth all day, I think I'll just stay right here. For right now." Or I might ask a question: "Are you *suggesting* that when you're in this store, other people have to *stand* where *you* want them to?" (Let the words drip sarcasm.)

I might just silently stay with them. (They hate the silent treatment.) Or I might ask a different question, "Are you *suggesting* that when you come in here no one is allowed to *look at you*?" If they don't back off, they'll probably say, "I just don't like you looking at me like you think I'm trying to steal." That's easy: "So you're saying that people in here have to *keep a certain kind of look on their face*?" (Have some fun!)

Grasp this: they have no legal right to tell you not to stand nearby or not to look at them. If they even say it, they are violating *your* rights. Many managers and LP now accept the unacceptable, but whether you do or not is up to you. If you don't want their nonsense, just don't put up with it. Many of them are initially confused if someone explains the house rules, but are actually quite polite once they understand the program.

> Some years ago, American embassies abroad were frequently stormed and ransacked by foreign "students" who made "statements," issued demands, manhandled employees, and burned flags. It was terribly inconvenient for the embassy staff, and not a little humiliating for the nation.
>
> During this period, an official of the Soviet Union was asked why their embassies weren't attacked, too. He laughed and responded, "Because we don't allow it."

Encounters have four areas of information: (1) what you know that the thief doesn't know, (2) what he knows that you don't know, (3) what both of you know, and (4) what neither of you knows. A thief or bully worries when #2 is smaller than he thought. His thinking can be manipulated, and the four areas change size as encounters progress.

*Think.* Know your options and limitations and the outcome you want. Then figure out how the situation must be handled to get it. Then figure out what the first step must be. Shoplifting and disorderly encounters are ninety-nine percent "mind games," i.e., *brain* games. Be afraid or be angry, but *think.*

Even if they're big, bad and experienced, thieves *always* have fears. Use their fear and control your own. When we are afraid or embarrassed, more blood goes to those muscles involved in "fight or flight." More blood to the legs and arms, less blood to the brain; less blood to the brain, less oxygen and less ordered the thoughts. (Remember though, that fear is Nature's wake-up call. If you're not afraid, maybe you should be.)

**Environments of Disorder.** In most cities, fear has resulted in entire city blocks and neighborhoods being surrendered to hoodlums. In those areas, most retail stores are gone and those convenience stores still remaining have barred windows, extensive camera systems, and very high prices, even for a 7-11. They're dangerous places to work or shop and are often hang-outs for prostitutes, street dealers and derelicts.

> **The Wilson and Kelling "Broken Windows Theory" (Paraphrased)**
>
> If a broken window in a building does not get fixed, someone eventually breaks another. More broken windows are followed by graffiti and more severe damage. People hang out with booze and drugs. Pedestrians and motorists are harassed. Over time, the entire block becomes shabby and down-right dangerous.
>
> Few things decay overnight. Whether you're talking streets, stores, or behavior, large, unwieldy problems usually begin as small, manageable ones.

"An environment of disorder--broken windows, graffiti, shoplifting--threatens civility and leads to major outrages like robbery and murder" (*Time*, 11 May 1992).

Is this a philosophical or macro-economic idea with little bearing on a single store? No. Example: If a sex pervert frequents your store and you allow it because of "policy" (or, more likely, because of no policy covering that exact situation), your inaction empowers the man to continue. Over time, more and more customers and employees are affected. It's like spilled water on the floor. Do you just ignore it until it evaporates?

Suppose this pervert asks a female clerk for sex. She complains to you. You don't ban the "customer" from the store, but do politely ask him to quit doing it. He does it again, she complains again, and you ask him harder, but you continue to let him in the store. Finally, he actually touches or grabs her. Your insurance had better be better than your action verbs and impotent reasons for letting him be there, because it could reasonably be argued that you *allowed* her to be sexually assaulted in your work place.

Even in a free and diverse society where everyone must absorb, without significant protest, an occasional minor insult or harassing comment, a line does exist between acceptable and unacceptable. When that line is crossed, it's no longer a little thing.

Insulting, intimidating words and crass behavior are the thin edge of a very large wedge and, if ignored, things *will* degenerate. People will use fitting rooms for restrooms, and use restrooms for things you don't even want to know about. It will be all you can do to keep the store half-straight as every existing problem worsens; and as more and more good customers and employees are run off by the bad ones, even more problems will arise.

"The deviant--criminals who assault, rape, rob, murder and deal drugs--ruin their neighborhoods by making local business, development and economic transformation impossible. Where the deviant rule, conservatives can forget about the magic of enterprise zones and liberals can forget about the promise of new social welfare measures." (John J. DiIulio, Jr.) No matter what the symptoms are, when inventory comes, you'll feel the disease.

## THE SINGLE ISSUE OFFENSE

Our society has few "sacred cows," and very few things are universally condemned. "Cussing around ladies and little kids," though, is still considered a "no-no" by just about everybody. When a problem-person uses the first curse word in a "public place" (inside a store) and it could--even possibly if amplified to the 10th power--be overheard by *any* female, senior citizen, or child, the Single Issue Offense is an option.

*Any* profanity will do. Immediately, say, "Look! In here You can't use filthy language around ladies and little kids." Say it forcefully. Whatever his response, say the same thing again. Use variations, but don't vary much: "There's no excuse for talking filth around (old) ladies and little kids." If uninvolved people hear you, that's fine. Very fine.

If he continues to cuss, he validates your position. If he becomes louder, he's obscene and loud: clearly "disorderly." Hammer away, and let nothing take the focus off obscene language. Debate nothing, acknowledge nothing. This is a *"single issue"* offense.

He'll be like a vampire with a cross in his face. He'll be embarrassed and frustrated at his inability to change the subject or even apologize and go in peace. People will look at the two of you like you're the Keeper of the Faith and he's a foul-mouthed pervert abusing children. Even his friends will distance themselves. He *will* look for a way out.

At the same time that he's trying to figure out how to handle "this cussing thing", he's worried about being there if police arrive. Witnesses will all agree: "He was cussing at some women and kids, and the other guy told him he couldn't do that."

If he stops cussing (which they normally do pretty quick), no matter what he says, stay close to him and keep at it every time he opens his mouth: "You used filthy language around ladies and little kids and we don't tolerate that." If you want him to leave, ignore any apology. Stick with "we don't *tolerate* filthy language around little kids."

If he wanted to steal, he will go somewhere else. If he tries speaking quietly, keep on with the same thing. If he says no one heard him or he didn't cuss at all, ignore what he says and stay with the Single Issue; loudly, if necessary, and until you get what you want.

**Bravery: Who needs it?** I was off-duty one afternoon when a criminally insane prisoner overpowered a courtroom guard, escaped, and was seen crawling under an antebellum house a few blocks away. Although the house was surrounded, *I* was appointed in absentia to crawl in and fetch him. (I was "on call," you see, so it was "my turn.")

On arriving, I quickly sized up the situation and swung into action, pointing out to the captain in charge that I was off-duty, not dressed for the occasion, and wasn't the fool who lost a lunatic in the first place. Also, although I didn't say so, the fact he was cornered bothered me immensely. To *my* way of thinking, situations like that call for cops with nicknames like "Meat," or "Sandman." (I don't even play legal poker machines because my philosophy is to avoid <u>anything</u> with its back to a wall and taking on all comers.)

The captain's wordless response to my whining was to poke a flashlight in my stomach, and a minute later I was squirming through a crawl-space door into a dark, musty maze of under-pilings, support walls, debris and madmen. "Bravery," I assure you, had *nothing* to do with it.

Meanwhile, deep in the maze, our lunatic had entertained himself by gathering a jagged assortment of broken glass and brickbats. With those laid out neat in a row, he was ready for some fool to find him. Technically, though, the fool didn't find him at all: I was crawling along when a voice from the dark said, "Here I am." I shined my light in that direction and, sure enough, there he was, sitting cross-legged, about fifteen feet away. All I could think to say was, "Time to go," and his disappointing reply was, "I don't think so."

OK, I tried to fetch him and failed. Tear gas sprang to mind. We hadn't used the stuff in a year or so, and even the captain would admit we needed practice. The last time we used it was during a shoot-out and hostage situation. Instead of the shooter, a half-dozen cops were gassed, the chief of police nearly shot dead, and the stand-off finally ended when a drunk hostage brained the shooter with a beer bottle. We *definitely* needed practice. So, just back me out the way I came in and...*damn!*

To my horror, I discovered that, as it was, I *couldn't* back out. My sole exit lay through the slasher, so either we *both* left or I'd be tucked in for the night with Hannibal Lecter. And *that* cozy vision crystallized my thinking.

It came to me that he didn't want to be there any more than I did, but here we both were. Why? I knew why *I* was there, but how about him? Why would he run in the first place? To get away. Why would he hide? Fear. *Fear?*

Freud said every man's decisions are based on the deep inner needs of his nature, and if he was right, then I must have plunged the right depth: even Pavlov's dogs couldn't have slobbered their way out as fast as that guy did.

In case you missed my point (an easy turn to pass), it is this: you don't have to *be* brave to *do* "brave things." Cops unbraver than me were surely rare, but I had long before discovered a quirk in reality: When I do whatever it seems ought to be done, things usually work out better and I get hurt less than when I place purely selfish or personal safety considerations above all others. Odd, but whatever I run away from, I often seem to catch.

It may sound simplistic, but ninety percent of the time whatever you worry about just doesn't happen. Who cares why?

## 6.04 Profiles and Red Flags

Can you know a person is going to steal just by looking at him? No. Can you tell a person is going to steal by looking at him and analyzing what you see? Sometimes, yes. Some thieves can be spotted as soon as they walk in the door.

In one case, a **"profile"** entered, walked directly to a display, looked left and right, stuffed an item into his coat, and was arrested. All in less than a minute. He had failed to notice just one more body flowing in a river of moving shoppers.

But why didn't the manager--standing with me--also know? How do cops spot prostitutes? Or one person know "something's going down" before others have even a vague suspicion? "I don't see no Injuns," says Tenderfoot, and the veteran of a thousand encounters responds, "That's when you got to worry, Pilgrim, is when you *don't* see 'em." To recognize shoplifters, you train yourself to relate normally unrelated things.

---

**"How can I tell the signals and the signs?"** -- H.W. Longfellow

One hot, summer afternoon, a man and woman caught my eye as they entered a store. Both were about thirty-five and wore matching jackets. They went directly to the perfume department, declined assistance, and examined boxes and bottles, spraying some and talking quietly. As they continued their harmless play, a pile of boxes collected on the counter between them. As the clerk became occupied elsewhere, I asked another clerk to get the store manager *quickly*.

The two stopped fiddling and stood facing each other, but looked beyond one another, scanning the store. Then they both leaned against the counter and looked left and right. Show-time.

In *seconds*, a dozen boxes of perfume were gone; and seconds after that they were arrested. We learned later that Jack and Cathy were wanted in the Midwest on felony larceny warrants. They were just passing through town.

---

What went wrong? They racked up too many points. Jack's shirttail was out, both were in the shoplifter's age-bracket, and both had sorry haircuts. They studied customers and employees, but declined assistance. Then, on a June afternoon in South Carolina when people in T-shirts and shorts were wilting, these two fools wore jackets. You don't need a NASA technician to spot a flaw in *that* picture.

Different flavors of thieves have certain constants just as all of Mr. Baskin's 31 flavors have certain things in common. Anyone who thinks all ice cream is chocolate-color is an idiot: a particular color is *not* common to all 31. Temperature is. Texture is. If you find a row of refrigerated, steel boxes full of colorful, semi-hard things, an excellent guess is you're in an ice cream shop. Or a morgue. (You won't be right every time.)

Despite limitations, profiles are effective. The DEA, for example, has profiles for "mules" smuggling contraband, and the FBI uses them for terrorists. In retail, there is no definitive shoplifter profile. Many stores have several profiles, depending on what merchandise is being "shopped," so their LP might bust a suburban housewife and a tattooed gangbanger both on the same shift.

Why aren't you terrified to go through an intersection when you've got a green light? Because *as a rule* other people stop for red lights. *Rational* people live by rules, *not* by exceptions. "Gang-bangers" commit burglary and strong-armed robbery in a New York minute and, to most of them, shoplifting comes natural. So *the rule* is that any particular hoodlum in your store might well shoplift. One might *not* shoplift (be an exception), but the safe bet (the rule) is that *he will*. So watch him. If a uniformed cop and priest walk in, it's a safe bet they *won't* shoplift. Exceptions exist, but exceptions do not invalidate rules. Don't bet heavily against the odds *unless* you don't mind losing.

---

One national retail chain's Red Flag short list:
- » People dressed inappropriately for the weather,
- » more interested in watching employees than merchandise,
- » unconcerned with prices,
- » using their own clothes to conceal merchandise they hold,
- » carrying open handbags or shopping bags,
- » setting merchandise down in places other than where it belongs, (particularly if they set it near a door),
- » who have a car waiting for them outside with the motor running,
- » carrying quantities of merchandise into a fitting room.

---

Danger signs ("red flags") are rated like movies. Three stars are a "must see."

\* \* \*

A person who
1. examines merchandise and gives equal attention to employees,
2. watches customers and employees while a friend examines merchandise,
3. stands stationary, facing merchandise and looking left and right.
4. "paces," "kills time," or scans the ceiling (for cameras),
5. says anything to the effect of, "Do you think I'm stealing?"
6. treats merchandise in a manner indicating interest in something other than what's being handled; puts items down when employees come near,
7. takes a "concealable" item to a relatively deserted or inappropriate area,
8. wears "trash" shoes where shoes are on sale (or holds a small, shoeless child where children's socks or shoes are sold),
9. suggests an employee leave the area, or
10. wears a coat in "short-sleeve weather," or raincoat if it only *might* rain,
11. "stacks" or otherwise separates merchandise; or holds or carries a stack,
12. removes a price tag (or--duh!--an EAS or ink tag, or any security device),
13. uses a worn or tattered shopping sack,
14. does a little dance or jig at a display,
15. folds clothes down to a size suitable for quick stuffing, or rolls clothes like a newspaper, or rolls an item (shirt, pants, etc.) around their arm,
16. holds a small item in hand so that it's out of casual view (especially if taking it from the display to *any* location other than a check-out).
17. A *pair* of same-sex teens or young adults. (Not one or three; two.)
18. A person who returns to an item again and again, or shops, leaves, shops, leaves,
19. doesn't seem concerned about prices, or
20. makes a purchase, gets a bag and begins "shopping" anew,
21. stands with his back to a wall (facing customers and employees) and then begins looking down and then up, down and up, or crouches or bends down,
22. is in a high-theft area.

\* \*

A person who
1. holds an apparently empty large purse or back-pack,
2. stands *very* close to a display,
3. head "snaps" to see who's walking nearby,
4. acts drunk or drugged,
5. shops with an open purse or a bag with an "open" top,
6. taps merchandise like a drum stick,
7. takes off his backpack,
8. wears two pairs of pants;
9. after looking at customers and employees, declines assistance,
10. damages packaging to "see" the merchandise,

11. wears sunglasses indoors (excepting elderly shoppers),
12. is positioned so that a view of his hands and bag is very limited,
13. people together who entered separately,
14. holds merchandise up against a bag, purse, or stomach,
15. holds a greatly folded-down bag or sack,
16. holds "keys" at a display case,

\*
A person who  1. wears an ankle-length coat, or
2. takes something out of a bag or purse while in the store,
3. has a bag that obviously has room to conceal much more than is in it,
4. uses words not allowed on television or has such words on his clothes.
5. has a baby-buggy,
6. holds a medium or large bag or sack,
7. takes merchandise out of a box or package, or
8. asks a particularly "stupid" question. (As if to say, "Oh! Hi, there. Please just think of me as just an ordinary honest shopper.")

> **"White Flags:"** Interestingly, these shoplift less than others: [25]
> 1. People wearing prescription eyeglasses.
> 2. Adult women in traditional church or business attire *and* wearing high heels.
> 3. Men and women with traditional-style, professionally-cut and styled hair.
> 4. Very attractive women (Cosmo and McCall types).

## 6.05 Site Hardening

Much can easily be done to make theft difficult, and many measures are cost-free. Store fixtures, displays, and merchandise, for example, can be arranged to help shoplifting or to hinder it. In a typical clothing store or department, hangers on racks are uniform, all facing either left or right. A defensive technique is to "alternate" hangers on the same arm: the first hanger faces left, the second, right, and so on. Then, even with two hands, try to "snatch" three or four off the arm at once.

Employees routinely provide opportunities for thieves by leaving merchandise or stacking boxes "just for a little while" in poorly chosen locations, especially when bringing freight to the sales floor. Shoplifters appreciate these hideaways and "blind spots."

Hard-to-monitor areas should contain bulky or low-theft items. Small, expensive items should be under lock and key or easily and closely monitored. Popular items for shoplifters should be in areas *easily* monitored and employees *required* to watch them. Also, these areas should be obstruction free.

Thieves commonly steal store bags and fill them with stolen merchandise. If you have distinctive store bags, can a dozen (or hundred) be stolen by a quick thief? Do cashiers watch for this? Do they give bags to anyone who asks? (They shouldn't.)

Freight from the stockroom can be taken to the sales floor packaged so thieves can carry it out *in plain view without arousing suspicion*. I once watched forty-eight neckerchiefs (all "gang colors") stroll out because they arrived four dozen per bag in plain, white plastic bags, thank you. Cashiers assumed they were from another store.

If possible, use ink-tags for soft lines, and put tag removers at check-outs. If pried apart by a thief, the tag releases permanent ink. (These can be circumvented, but still deter most thieves.) Security cords (cables)--plastic coated wire--can be run through coats and dresses. Available in 4 to 10-foot lengths, a loop at each end allows the cables to be intertwined or locked together with a tiny padlock.

A good layout enables employees to monitor customers. Can thieves access the stockroom without notice? The office? If an area's sole employee also uses a cash register, can he see his register from anywhere in his area? Walk around and see. While ringing a sale, is he a significant deterrent to thieves on the sales floor? Or to thieves carrying merchandise out a door? Employees *must* see what comes in and goes out of the store. If they don't, you have NO security; you're "wide open." Smaller businesses in particular need a bell or buzzer on the door to announce every entry or exit. Hearing it, an employee *must* move to see what's coming or going. (Have *good* people near the doors.)

For less than $30, a colored light can be mounted high on a pillar--or on the ceiling of a sales floor--that alerts the staff to a problem. A switch somewhere at ground level activates it. Use multiple lights for a large area. This system can increase cooperation by ensuring "confidentiality" to clerks who would otherwise be reluctant to get involved.

Does your LP staff have a cell-phone so they can monitor situations *while* communicating with other employees or police, or do you live in 1930? (Most LP units currently operate with technology that is best described as state-of the-art...for 1980.)

If you have display cases, test the locks and hinges with a knife or screwdriver, then try odd keys on your personal key rings. Can a top or side be lifted with a knife or screwdriver? With sliding glass doors, can some pressure and a tug carry one panel past the lock, or even lift a panel out of the frame? Can a small, hand-held, pump-action suction cup--used by any glass/window-repair company--lift a heavy glass pane smack out of the frame of your best display case *quietly* and in just *5 seconds*? (Borrow one and see!)

Can a whole display case be picked up and carried out? (*It happens every day.*) If thieves can carry it out, then somehow attach it to something that *cannot* be carried out.

Some thieves are unnerved by *any* unexpected action, so look around, see what other stores do, and be creative. Even the old "bellhop" bells, still sold in many hardware stores for under $10, can convey information *and* deter thieves. At checkouts, for example, hit it once for assistance or twice to alert others to a potential problem.

Finally, remember this: display cases, boxes and rooms have *six* sides. Check *all six!* (Think of any enclosed thing as a box.) If an area is sectioned off (even by walls), can items pass through, perhaps at junctures? Or *over* barriers? (Ah, the stories I could tell...) After hours, can thieves bypass alarms by coming through ceilings or *through walls* from stores next door? That can be particularly easy in older "strip" shopping centers.

---

### "A little dab'll do."

While a thief is in the store, he expects everyone to let him behave pretty much as he pleases. He will become *very* confused if--inside--an issue is immediately made of ripping open a package or otherwise damaging an item in such a way it no longer brings full retail; or of using hand lotion or after-shave from a non-"tester" bottle.

Many people who do this sort of thing actually say, "I thought it was OK." Think about it: has *anyone* a right to intentionally devalue others' property? The bottle says 8 ounces, not, "6 to 8 ounces depending on what got consumed in the store."

If it was clearly not a "tester" bottle, I often handle it by saying, "We charge the same for a squirt as we do for a bottle. Will that be cash, check or charge?"

After that, I might let it slide if they humbly apologize. If not, I get not nice and--depending on circumstances--may even arrest them for shoplifting. There's no difference between that and going into a grocery store, pulling one slice of bread out of a loaf, and popping it in your mouth. (Yeah, pal...tell the judge you thought it was OK.)

---

**To secure yourself against defeat lies in your own hands. The good fighters first put themselves beyond the possibility of defeat, and then wait for the opportunity to defeat the enemy. That opportunity is provided by the enemy himself.** -- *Sun Tzu*

# Chapter 7

# The Shoplifting Act

Shoplifting is not always shoplifting. Many people simply forget what's in their hands and walk out of a store. They drive away from a self-serve gas pump and realize an hour later they forgot to pay. Things happen. Don't precipitate a travesty where someone guilty only of a memory lapse finds himself with a criminal record.

Carefully examine the totality of the circumstances to see if a *reasonable doubt* might actually exist. Make a truly conscientious effort to find it. You *must* distinguish bona fide thieves from absent-minded shoppers. It's not just something you're *supposed* to do, it's something you *ought* to do. It's the moral, ethical, and professional thing to do.

## 7.01 Location

Generally speaking, theft occurs when merchandise is intentionally concealed or is removed from the store, unconcealed. Within the confines of the store, theft occurs either **at the display** (where the item was located) or **elsewhere**.

"At the display" can be the exact display *or* the area immediately around it from which there is unobstructed access to the display. "Elsewhere" is a different aisle, around a corner, in a dressing room...anywhere. The location of the theft often determines how and where the shoplifter is approached, and the time available to get help and make the "stop."

Assuming an absence of security cameras (a given), when you actually see merchandise being concealed, it is usually near the original display. A good position for your surveillance provides a clear view of what a suspect removes from a display, of his hands and pockets, and of any tools he uses. These examples occurred at the display:

- 4 minutes, $12.00. A teenage boy enters a store and walks to a hamster cage. After looking around, he takes a hamster and puts it in his pants' pocket. Closing the cage lid with his free hand, he leaves the store.

- 8 minutes, $49.00. Two men enter a shoe store. One browses, facing employees, while the other takes off his own shoes and puts on a pair. He puts his own tattered shoes in a box, puts it on the shelf, and out they stroll.

- 5 minutes, $9.00. Three women stand at a perfume display, all wearing jackets. The one in the middle has jacket sleeves with elastic at the wrists. A perfume bottle is slid up her sleeve and held in place by the elastic.

- 10 minutes, $60.00. Two teenagers stand shoulder-to-shoulder at a display case. The lock is on the front of the case, and employees see only the boys' backs. One produces a ring with dozens of keys. One by one, he tries them in the lock. Eventually, a key actually unlocks the case, items are loaded into pants, and they close the case.

> Shoplifters constantly allege that store employees don't watch them and don't pay attention to things that thieves consider obvious.

**Certainty.** Most shoplifters (and their families) believe that to make and prove a case, you must actually *see* a thief conceal merchandise. This is simply not true. Besides, you can know if merchandise was concealed even if you didn't actually see it go in a bag. For example, if you see an item in a suspect's hand *and* he brings it near his bag or pocket *and* you then see the hands (plural, both hands) are without the item, you can be pretty sure it's been stolen.

But "pretty sure" is never "sure and certain." Anything at all less than "certain" is, by definition, "uncertain." Reality: "99.999 percent certain" equals "uncertain." (You must remember that!)

"Pretty sure" is one thing, being right is another. "Proving it" is something else entirely. "Certainty" and "proving" ordinarily require some degree of investigation. Did he *really* put it in the bag? You must be certain where it is not. Did he discard it while you moved? Be certain of what you see, and just as importantly, know what you don't see.

At accident scenes, traffic cops hear this tired story over and over: "I didn't see anything coming." They patiently explain: "That's the problem: you *didn't see* anything coming. It's your responsibility--before you pull into traffic--to *see nothing coming*. 'Don't see anything' isn't the same as 'see nothing.'"

It's not a play on words, *it's reality*. When "is" is confused with "ought to be," situations go "fubar." (Pronounced *foo-bar*; "fouled up beyond any redemption," or "fouled up beyond all recognition.") You see it go into a pocket (or whatever), or you *must* see there is no other possibility. I did *not* say, "You *don't see* any other possibility." I *said*, "You must *see* there is no other possibility."

**"Eliminate the impossible,"** said Sherlock Holmes, "and whatever remains is the answer." This proven technique is called "investigation by process of elimination."

---

Batteries are high-risk merchandise. I observed a man select a 6-pack of large D-cells from a display and then step back from the counter. In one hand he held a plastic bag (containing a box about the size of a shoe box), and the batteries were in his other hand. His hands went up in front of him, but from my position I couldn't see what he did. He looked left and right, and when the hands came back down, the batteries were gone: "disappearing merchandise." I hadn't lost sight of him for a second.

I didn't see him conceal the batteries, but I was <u>certain</u> he didn't discard them. Following him, I looked for tell-tale bulges, but I saw nothing. I walked up behind him and tried looking in his bag. No luck. I then stopped him and pleasantly asked if he had changed his mind about buying batteries. He smiled and said he might get them later.

Too polite. Pushing it, I asked where he left them so I could put them back where they belonged. He replied, "Back on the counter." A lie. I didn't know where they were, but I was certain where they weren't.

Although I didn't suggest it, he casually opened the bag for inspection. In it was a box, obviously taped shut, but nothing more. Bag and box were both from a shoe store about a minute's walk from where we stood. It wasn't unreasonable that he came from there.

"See?" said Mr. Cool. "I don't steal. If you don't mind, I'm in a hurry."

Once confronted or having already concealed their loot, thieves are invariably in a hurry, so I had no doubt he was anxious to move along whether I minded or not. No bulges in his clothes and the bag was definitely empty except for the box. He hadn't had time to open the sealed box, insert the batteries and close it again. Besides, I would have seen it.

His eyes were darting now, and he appeared *very* uneasy.

Truly, there were only two possibilities: Either Scotty beamed 'em up--and I ruled that out--or somehow this guy had some batteries. I told him I'd like him to come back into the store "and talk about batteries." He stepped back, saying, not unpleasantly, "I need to go." I stepped forward and took him by his free arm (clutching his sleeve, not actually his arm) and said, "I'm sure you do, but I insist." (He then had only limited use of his free arm, and if he dropped the bag in his other hand, it would signal he was about to fight.)

Crumbling, he asked, "Can I just pay for 'em?" Back in the office, I discovered his box was a garden-variety "booster box" with the batteries inside. He claimed the theft was a fraternity initiation, and I claimed I didn't care.

## Theft Away From the Display

Stealing "elsewhere in the store" means anywhere other than at the original display. If a thief carries an item and wanders around, he can "bag" it, "drop" it somewhere for another person to bag, give it to another person, put it somewhere to retrieve later, discard it and steal something else, or discard the item and leave the store.

While walking, he might remove store tags, discard packaging, or time the theft (waiting for just the right minute). He might be strolling around looking for what he feels is a "good place" to bag it, or he might be trying to see if security is on his tail. Whatever he's up to, after a long walk it's sometimes difficult to prove an item's true origin. [26]

He might eventually get together with friends or family as a calculated strategy to involve innocent people and confuse the issue. The others may provide a chorus of righteous indignation if he's approached, and that's assuming they're totally innocent. If they *know* he's stealing and choose to help him, it can be much worse.

A constant refrain from shoplifters is "nobody misses" one dress off a rack of twenty, or any single item from a large display (like packs of batteries). That's true. But you *can* notice an item in a customer's hand. Not only "can notice," but you *must* notice what people hold in their hands.

It's often easy to identify thieves who walk around holding what they plan to steal. You have a chance to see how many items and what they are. You have time to plan and organize. If they have clothes, but you can't tell exactly what, note the colors or count hangers. If they have different types of items, note which are most likely to be stolen.

If a thief carries some jewelry and a dress, she might pay for the dress or just put it down before she leaves, but you can already be pretty sure of what--if anything--she's going to steal. You don't have to stay real close or follow her up and down aisles. She might pick up more things, but you don't need to know exactly what they are. Just wait and see if the jewelry disappears.

> What kind of thief would walk around, attract attention and not mind it, and then purchase the item or just set it down and leave? A professional. A "dry run" measures employee reaction, "smokes out" security people and gets a handle on security in general and see how good it is. First, test action and reaction; *then* set up the kill.

## 7.02 Examples of the Act

A man got out of a taxi, told the driver to wait, and entered a store. He passed three employees (standing just inside the door, talking), walked to the back of the store and picked up a 6- by 33-foot roll of plastic (at $3.99 a yard). Carrying it up-right, he walked back out the front door past the same three employees. (I arrested him outside.)

None of the clerks remembered seeing him *or* the plastic.

You'd think that experienced employees would notice, but think football or basketball. A flagrant foul committed in front of ten million television viewers, may be *noticed* by only a handful. It's the same principle, and employees--like referees--are *paid* to *notice*. What does the NBA do with referees who ignore or don't notice flagrant fouls?

The following examples show the diversity of shoplifting, the use of various tools, and how shoplifters depend on employees.

1. 10 minutes, $112.00. A man and a woman take folded plastic bags from their pockets and, having stacked small appliances in a "blind spot," fill the bags. It takes an entire minute to do the bagging.
2. 3 minutes, $5.00. A woman enters a store, walks directly to a counter, takes an item and strolls through the store. While walking, she casually stuffs the item into the front of her blouse and takes the empty box back to the display.

3. 10 minutes, $10.00. A woman takes three pairs of earrings off a display. While browsing, she takes two pairs off their "cards," puts them in her pocket, and hides the empty cards among some merchandise. She returns to the earring display where she selects several more pairs and some miscellaneous merchandise. Then she dumps everything on a counter and quickly leaves.

> Where's the suspect taking the item? To a register? Is he standing *near* a checkout line or actually *in* the line? Will he stay there or, after a minute or two, just mosey out the door?

4. 5 minutes, $5.00. A boy takes a G.I. Joe figure from the counter, turns to face a wall, and drops it down the waist of his pants. The tight elastic at his ankles keeps the toy from coming out the bottom of the pants.
5. 3 minutes, $14.00. A man enters, goes directly to a counter, takes an item, looks around, and stands with his back to a wall. As he watches customers and employees he stuffs the item into the back of his pants, his shirttail covering the bulge.
6. 8 minutes, $4.00. Only five feet from a cashier, a 10-year-old girl picks up one piece of candy after another and drops them down the front of her blouse. She keeps her back to the cashier and leans against the counter.
7. 10 minutes, $15.00. A woman takes cosmetics from a display and meanders up one aisle and down another. On a deserted aisle, she faces a wall and stuffs the items into the front of her pants.

> Is he messing with his pants (stuffing merchandise in them)? If he has long sleeves, can you see his hands, or are they drawn up into the sleeves clutching merchandise?

8. 5 minutes, $20.00. Two women enter a store and one says, *"I need to look at the lotion."* While she does that, the second woman walks to a cosmetics display, pulls four items from a rack and slips them in her pocket. She then rejoins her unsuspecting friend.
9. 5 minutes, $20.00. Two women look at athletic shorts hanging from a rack. One has a large black purse, the other a large, paper shopping bag. The woman with the purse holds it in front of her, supported by a shoulder strap. With her left hand held below the top of the rack, she pulls shorts from their hangers. Her right hand is in plain view of any observers, moving other clothes.

    Standing close to the rack and never looking down, she stuffs the shorts into her purse. Her right hand was constantly, visibly moving clothes and her eyes were always on the clothes being moved. (They weren't rookies, and her friend escaped.)
10. 4 minutes, $4.00. At a lotion display, a woman selects a box and takes it to another aisle. As she walks, she removes lotion from the box, stuffs it down the front of her pants, then makes a great show of putting the (empty) box back exactly where she found it.

> Should the item in someone's hand be loose, on a card, or in a box? Is it a single piece of a multi-piece pack? If so, where's the rest of it? *WHY* is he holding it at all?

11. 3 minutes, 50¢. A man picks up two candy bars and reaches into his pocket with the same hand. When it emerges a second later, he's holding only one candy bar and a one-dollar bill. He goes to the checkout and purchases just one candy bar.
12. 12 minutes, $3.00. A woman with a baby takes a pacifier from a display and strolls around the store. She strips it from its package, hides that on another counter, and, a moment later, puts the pacifier in the baby's mouth.

13. 15 minutes, $160.00. A woman with a small child gathers two blouses, two pairs of pants, and a dress. Near an exit she drops the clothes on the floor. From nowhere, a man appears with a plastic sack. Crouching, hidden by display racks, he bags while she scans for trouble. Staying low, he leaves with the loot while she remains, browsing away. He was in the store less than a minute.
14. 6 minutes, $21.00. A man chooses a day-planner, checks to assure he's not being watched, then stuffs it down the front of his pants and heads straight for the door.

> Why is a girl with a pair of your earrings in your garden center? Think about it! What 16 year-old girl drives to Sears with this in her mind: "Oh, I think I'll get some earrings and look at chain saws. La-di-da-di-da." *No, no, no, no, no!*

15. 5 minutes, $20.00. Two juveniles are handling earrings. One "watches" for trouble while the other pops earrings in his mouth. In the parking lot, he spits them out.
16. 3 minutes, $475. Two women enter. One grabs five jackets and runs out a door held open by the other. A car is at the curb, motor running and doors open.
17. $5 a minute. At checkouts, candy bars, cigarettes, batteries and other impulse items are on racks in plain view. A teenager backs up to a rack--like a truck to a loading dock--and puts an arm behind his back. Facing cashier and customers, he stuffs cigarettes from racks into his back pockets. By coincidence, two of his chums are in line making nickel-dime purchases, dropping things and creating confusion.
18. 7 minutes, $200. Two men browse in one department while furtively watching a clerk in a different area. She leaves that area, and the two men move in. One pulls a folded plastic bag from his pocket, *and in less than 120 seconds the bag is filled and the men are gone.* The clerk--engaged in customer service and not thirty feet away--never saw the men.

Shoes, vacuum cleaners, toys, microwave ovens, books, live animals...is there anything you assume is safe or sacred? They steal *Bibles*. Any shoplifter "on the job" can easily clear $20 an hour and steal dozens of times without being caught. Then, if caught, he'll probably be released or otherwise dodge a criminal record. *Gee, why do they do it?*

## 7.03 Shoplifting Rituals

Before dogs attack, they normally perform a **"ritual."** (Thank God.) They snarl, hair bristles, fangs flash, muscles tense. All of that demonstrates a situation exists, and whether or not it's convenient for you, personally, doesn't matter in the least.

Shoplifting rituals nearly always include looking to the left and right.

Regardless the number of thieves involved, in nearly every case there *is* rubber-necking. *Or* they may walk a tiny circle; or stand in one spot and turn their body slightly and look, then turn a bit more and look, until they cover every direction.

> "Left and right" means looking in both directions or in all direction(s) from which trouble might come. Generally, a shoplifter faces a wall or display, or has his back to one when stealing. In actual practice, then, he *does* look left and right.[27]

The human eye has a fantastic capacity to notice slight movement against still backgrounds. On the other hand, it's difficult to spot a single individual among a flowing or milling crowd. Thieves are extremely alert when they actually do business, so movement on your part is dangerous and should be carefully timed and executed.

Once he has an item in hand, you might assume he'll immediately conceal it. Your assumption can trigger an adrenaline kick that makes you move, and many a surveillance is "blown" because of that. I once had a sign at my rancho that read: "Please don't spook the horses." In stores, don't spook the thieves.

I arrested a young woman whose "ritual" was typical and transparent. She admitted to shoplifting in the past ("....fifty times. A hundred. I don't know.") and was amused to learn I "picked up on her" as soon as she entered the store. While we talked, she told me she knew (this) store had "security." How? "People talk." Why chance it? "I never come in here, but other places I go have security and they don't do anything. I figured you'd be the same as them."

Mark Twain strikes again: "It's not what you don't know that gets you in trouble, it's what you think you know that just ain't so."

Webster defines ritual as "a set of acts." Shoplifters commonly perform rituals, and that is very important: When stealing, shoplifters commonly perform rituals. Professional shoplifters know that rituals are dangerous, but unavoidable, so they try to keep it subtle.

> **A man on a mission.**
> Rituals may begin at the door--an "Entry Ritual"--where a thief "places" the employees and tries to spot plain-clothes security. Neither of you wants eye contact, but if you let it happen, it probably will. If he has a bag for stealing, he often alters his grip. He's entering "the ring;" his subconscious fidgeting is like a boxer tapping gloves together. But, since most thieves--non-professionals--make the decision to steal *after* they are inside the store, there is no obvious "Entry Ritual."

Rituals vary from thief to thief, but, fortunately, most of them share common elements, common *acts*. To untrained eyes, these acts can seem so insignificant they don't even register with the conscious mind. Without prompting, an employee won't independently recall the act even when questioned only a minute after witnessing it. Viewed in a shoplifting context, the acts help you to identify shoplifters, ascertain what's to be stolen, where, and how.

Some people who plan to steal do the "**Shoplifter Slide**" when they enter a store: a sort of smooth, purposeful walk. When they do it, they cast sneaky glances at everyone in sight. Face set and serious, it's obviously a business call.

Once at a display or particular department, there's no telling how long the selection process might last. Some thieves solicit opinions or information from employees. (Like everyone, thieves want to make a wise selection. The item might be for personal use, but if it's special--perhaps a birthday present--they want to make a good impression.)

Once he decides *what* to steal, the next step is *"taking"* (removing the item from the display). *Then* comes *"stealing"* (concealing or taking it out the door). After taking--but before stealing--the window remains open to abort the theft. While all this is going on, most shoplifters do a *lot* of rubber-necking. Watch for that.

Also, a thief seldom grabs an item to steal while he's on the move, so he probably stops walking at least long enough to select his item. Then, for a few seconds, his attention is divided between the merchandise and watching for trouble. You can sometimes use that time to set up, move, or call for help.

If he intends to conceal then and there, he *will* look around. He knows his window of total innocence slams shut the instant the item's concealed, so his look-around just prior to concealment is sometimes a little more thorough. The faster his head and eyes complete the arc, though, the sooner he can bag the item, so these two acts--1. final security check, and 2. bag the loot--take place one after the other (or simultaneously) in as little time as possible. He's so busy right then that the theft is sometimes incredibly obvious.

In addition to looking around just before concealing an item, shoplifters ordinarily look around while the item is being concealed. And, usually, again just afterwards. Obviously, all these neck exercises *should* draw attention.

While rubber-necking, he gets other ducks in a row. For example: the empty package (if an item was stripped out of one) must be disposed of. He may carefully put it back on a display, toss it, or go to some length to hide it. For these things, too, he might "run up the periscope" to see if anyone's watching. Your job: look for them looking for you.

> Honest shoppers seldom watch employees and survey the surrounding area for signs of a surprise attack. Shoplifters look for trouble nearly always, and may even scan the ceiling for cameras. (Do honest shoppers study ceilings?)

Just before concealing an item, a thief often fiddles with it or with his bag (or whatever is used to conceal the loot). Merchandise is brought near where it will be concealed, or a bag will be pulled out of a pocket and unfolded. At this point, most thieves "telegraph" their next move, so watch carefully to see what follows.

Even the best shoplifters get nervous, and nervous people standing in place often move their feet and fumble things. Watch for people acting like a small kid in bad need of a restroom. He takes a few steps, comes back, pauses, walks and returns. He turns this way and that as though terribly undecided about which way to go. His movements may be jerky. He might look over counters and around corners, for cameras, people approaching, and mirrors. All this activity is a combination of security and bad nerves. He's worried that someone might be watching.

> If you see a theft about to go down, but are in a poor position, can you get some one to move near enough to the suspect to *delay* the theft? He can walk up, fiddle with anything, mentally count to 60 and then nonchalantly walk away. This interference can buy you a minute to get to a better position.
>
> *After* a thief has concealed an item, it can be a good idea to have someone hover nearby until the actual stop. Even if it's obvious to the thief that the person is a store employee, this step assures the thief doesn't discard the item.

## 7.04 Counter-Surveillance (Also, see the Thieves Manual, pg 161.)

While you look for their rituals, they look for yours. They look for "security rituals" such as "walking with a purpose," paying no attention to merchandise, and maneuvering through aisles with no conscious effort. They look for people who look down every aisle they pass and crane their necks left and right; who focus on other people and what they're doing; who peek around walls and counters. They look for people who appear to know employees. And, quite naturally, they look for walkie-talkies and handcuffs. Like you, they look for anything *not* part of normal shopping.

Experienced thieves try to spot sneaky employees by "flushing them out," by forcing or enticing them to move. They walk in one direction then suddenly do a U-turn ("double back"); or just stop and look behind them, maybe pretending to be interested in something they passed. Or they move from one display to another that "makes" them face the opposite direction (so they can see anyone behind them or trying to *stay* behind them). They look for a body that moves when they do: a **"shadow."**

Careful thieves sometimes make "dry runs" before stealing. With fitting rooms, for example, they take merchandise in, leave it and walk out. Then they watch (or a partner watches) for the reaction; to see who, if anyone, was watching or will check things out.

Those are "counter-surveillance" measures. Remember, though, that their counter-surveillance is ordinarily *very* limited. They lack patience and poise. They *scan* an area, but not in detail. If you are face-to-face with someone and talking while *discreetly* looking over their shoulder, a thief will ordinarily assume your primary interest is the person you're talking to, *not* in what's happening behind him. Most professional thieves won't make that assumption, of course, but most shoplifters aren't professional-quality. Blend in and don't show too much of your body (or use a mirror or peephole), and they won't focus on you. Even if they see you, they won't really *see* you.

One thief may bag an item while another "helps look," i.e., looks for trouble. The lookout may be mobile (walk around) or stationary (position himself at some location where he can spot trouble in time to warn his chum). If he sees an employee coming, he can, whistle, speak, drop something, or distract the employee, maybe by asking a question.

If you suspect a "customer" is an accomplice (distraction), say something like, "I'll be right with you, but I've got to help another customer first." Then move *quickly* to the "bagger" to offer "help." Muddle their plan *quickly*. If you see you can't catch the thief, at least prevent the theft. Of course, prevention may be your goal anyway; but if you waste time with the distraction, you cooperate with their plan. You'll lose.

You want to see the bagger's hands before a lookout has a chance to warn him (or very soon thereafter). You can catch baggers in the act if your approach is *quick* and from a good angle. Use the "come-at-them-from-out-of-the-sun" concept: descend rapidly from a direction difficult for thieves to watch.[28] (Sometimes, to fool them you move slowly and play dumb. It depends. There's no sure-fire tactic for every occasion.) At any rate, to get to a thief you may have to brush past an accomplice who may "innocently" try to block your approach. Don't be surprised if he gets irritated. After all, it's his job to prevent your unpleasantness. "It riles them to believe that you perceive the web they weave." (The Moody Blues band, circa 1970.)

> In the action movie "Colors," a veteran cop (Robert Duvall) attempts to counsel a rookie (Sean Penn). Having no success, he tries a story: Two bulls come across a group of cows. "Wow!," says the younger bull, "Let's charge on down there! "
> 
> "No! Wait!," says the older, wiser bull. "I've got a better idea. Let's *walk* down there and get 'em *all*." If you move too quickly, chaos ensues and cases fall apart.

## 7.05 *DEE-fense ! DEE-fense !*

There are three "musts" for an excellent defense:
1. Excellent customer service **must** be embraced as the Number One Priority.
2. Customers **must** be *properly* greeted. (Not only to deter and foil shoplifting, but to *increase sales*. (See Greeting, pg. 83 and Appendix 10, "Put Wind in Your Sales!")
3. Employees **must** deter thieves *and* help honest shoppers. (*Simultaneously*.)

While talking with the owner of an exclusive (read: expensive) ladies' store, she mentioned that from time to time shoplifting was a terrible problem. Questioning her, I discovered her surveillance was pitiful. She was shocked to hear that it doesn't suffice to see only the heads of suspicious shoppers protruding above display racks from across the store. "I can't believe someone would steal if they knew I was watching them." Patiently, I explained to her the difference--to a thief--between being "looked at" and "being watched."
29 (Chapter Notes, pg. 146)

Gene Tunney, the great boxer, once said that in a boxing ring, the greatest bar-room fighter--however "natural" a fighter he is--cannot cope with even a 4th-rate professional boxer. Same with shoplifting. Without training, managers and employees do not cope well with experienced thieves. "There's nothing we can do," becomes a common sentiment.

But that sentiment is not reality. Too often, it's overlooked or not taken seriously that sales floor employees are the first and most important line of defense. With that in mind, one thing that can be done to decrease shoplifting losses *and* increase sales is to turn "routine customer service" into loss preventing, *excellent* customer service.

If there's a shoplifter around, or someone who wants to give cash to you instead of your competition, it's more profitable for the store if things like stocking, signing, and pricing are put off for five minutes...or don't get done. Deterring and preventing *begins* with rank and file employees, and their vigilance and cooperation are *imperative* to shrinkage control, sales, and profit. EVERY employee must become de facto LP. (Or is it felt that customer service is not the Number One priority; or that self-service is OK?)

> A man once told his dentist that he didn't have time to properly floss all his teeth every day. The dentist--probably Charlie Wade of Rock Hill--replied, "That's OK. Just floss the ones you want to keep." If you don't have time to properly greet every customer, that's OK, too.

As often as they can, employees must walk over to see what customers are doing with their hands. Whenever possible, even if working or talking, they should stand facing the customer who seems to pose the greatest potential risk. (Just shift a little this way or that. It's no major inconvenience.)

If a current task won't allow watching curious people, employees <u>must</u> call a manager or security, or find something to do to get near enough to discourage theft. (Straighten a display? Sweep a floor? Chat?) Three or four minutes is usually all it takes.

In 1994, the 1,600-store Dollar General Corporation initiated a program designed to increase interaction with customers. Employees <u>must</u> ask customers they come within ten feet of: "Are you finding what you're looking for?" (D.G. studies show that, as a result, more shoppers ask for assistance which, in turn, generates sales and decreases shrinkage.)

D.G. definitely took a step in the right direction, but thieves easily handle "yes or no" questions. Use "open-ended" questions such as, "What is it you're looking for?" (Incredibly, thieves sometimes tell you what they want to steal.) If a customer is holding a blouse, try, "What else do you need besides the blouse?" <u>That</u> sends a message.

> If you are hit again and again and suspect the same thieves, get a good description of the customers who engage the sales staff at the time(s) of the theft. One of them may be an accomplice. Watch for that person. His arrival may be a "tip off" that your thieves are nearby. If the same employee is hit again and again, take a *real* hard look at *him*.

The success enjoyed by professional shoplifters (*and* those successful in preventing shoplifting) is traced to a single, fundamental concept: Think like your enemy thinks. Ask yourself, "If this guy wants to steal, how can I help him?"

One thing you could do is walk away. If he needs to rip packaging, you could ignore the sound. You want to talk on the phone? *Fine.* Price merchandise? *Please do.* Gab with a friend or another employee? *Go right ahead.* He doesn't care what you do as long as you ignore him. *That* is what he wants. Thieves don't need you, and they want you to feel the same. And if you do *not* cooperate with them? Well, they mostly go somewhere else to play. (Will that bother you?)

When asked what will likely make thieves leave a store *without* stealing, one professional shoplifter said, "That constant 'can I help you' crap. If they won't stay away and leave me the hell alone and let me steal, I'll cop an attitude and leave." His wording reveals a very important point: "If...they won't let me steal." In effect, he says that he can steal only if employees *let* him, i.e., provide the opportunity. If the employee stays with the suspect (or someone quickly arrives who will), then there will be no theft (*or* if covert loss prevention [LP] is called, the thief will almost surely be caught.)

That same professional thief went on to say that most shoplifters belong to loose groups or "**cliques**." (See pg. 112.) They share information about apathetic and dishonest employees, and about security and opportunities in different stores. His group's favorite stores? Those that don't prosecute, those with employees who are "cool" (who help thieves or ignore them), and, of course, stores that give cash refunds without receipts.

## 7.06 Employee Sabotage

The <u>American Heritage Dictionary</u> defines sabotage as the "damaging of property *or procedure...*" Expanding on that, employee sabotage could be defined as: "Any intentional active *or passive* act that harms or obstructs a business and/or its personnel, customers, productivity, policies, procedures, or normal functioning." The key is intent.

Methods used by employee saboteurs can vary day to day as different opportunities arise, but common goals include (1) frustrating and demoralizing other personnel, (2) doing actual damage, and (3) generating unnecessary expense. Their sabotage is misdirected, highly inappropriate, and often criminal, but that doesn't stop thousands of people (perhaps hundreds of thousands) from engaging in it. And sometimes *daily*.

The actual cause may have nothing to do with the company, but vindictive employees "act out" rage, disgruntlement, or frustration in large incidents and various small things done again and again. They seek concrete retribution, and in sabotage, find the perfect weapon: easy, low-risk, and--at times--high-impact. Plus, of course, it's on the clock.

> **A Passing Thought:** Could any bad LP stops *possibly* be the result of a dishonest loss prevention or security officer working a "con" with a friend or business associate?

In war, sabotage results in spectacular happenings that people are sure to notice. In the business world, however, sabotage is insidious and usually calculated to avoid serious inquiry. In virtually every instance, it appears non-criminal: "lost" paperwork, water faucets left running for hours, derailing efforts of others, "not-seeing," work slow-downs, damaged, wasted or trashed merchandise, materials and supplies, <u>and</u> such things as a lack of "suggestive selling," being rude to customers on the phone, and poor customer service.

**Motive Unknown.** Occasionally, we all do a little "goofing off" on the job. For some employees though, doing nothing (especially while encouraging others to do the same) is <u>intended</u> to waste time and money. (Salary costs increase as labor productivity decreases.)

Signs of sabotage are noticed by management, but instead of being recognized for what they actually are, they're dismissed as being "just carelessness" or, perhaps, a training or discipline issue. ("No big deal. We'll cover it in a store meeting.") Or they're misdiagnosed as an accident or coincidence; or perhaps as incidental to something else.

Unlike missing cash, sabotage seldom seems to profit anyone *personally*. Plus, few managers can even *think* in terms of sabotage; it is simply incompatible with their own mental software. *Therefore*...before telling a manager that sabotage exists, ask yourself this question: "What would he think if I told him the Loch Ness Monster was operating in the store?" Clearly, the 'bottom line' is don't even *suggest* it. Instead, focus the manager's attention on something he can get his mind around, like "customers are being ignored."

> Awareness is critical. To help employees develop and increase their level of awareness, *frequently* ask them these five questions:
> - "What (does) did that man have in his hands?"
> - "What merchandise did that woman take out of your area?"
> - "Did that man (already) have a bag when he got here?"
> - "What, exactly, does the person have in the dressing room?"
> - "Don't look! Just tell me if there's anyone in your department right now."
>
> (When an employee has his back to his area of responsibility, I love that last one. Really...how can he *possibly* provide excellent customer service or *possibly* deter theft?)

# Chapter 8

# SURVEILLANCE

If catching (apprehension) won't work, you *must* rely on prevention. (Or just let it slide.) Theoretically, prevention is easy. It's intervention prior to the actual theft. Since few thieves steal if they know they're being watched, it's obvious what needs to be done. Prevention can be *passive* (merely standing nearby) or *active* (*doing* something like asking if you can help).

After three or four minutes of observation, you can usually tell if a suspect *probably* intends to steal or *probably* doesn't. A good educated guess is the initial goal. And that's not the same as an assumption. There's a difference. Like boomerangs, about the time you think you're OK, assumptions come full circle and hit you in the back of the head.

If you start out "to catch him stealing," your mind-set is wrong. Initiating an investigation with a predetermined outcome is foolish (or dishonest), because an investigation is, by definition, an *objective* search for *truth*. Professional private detectives don't like to be asked to "catch my husband (or wife) running around," but will gladly accept a retainer to see *whether or not* a spouse is cheating. What if she's *not*? What if she did, but stopped before the P.I. got involved; how does he "catch her in the act?" Lie?

> Tommy Lee (not necessarily his real name) is a thief, a "usual suspect" for any larceny in his part of town. While I was a rookie, a veteran officer told me how to tell if Tommy Lee was lying: his mouth opens.
>
> Later experience verified that Tommy Lee makes such a habit of lying that he has almost forgotten how to tell the truth. In all fairness to that accomplished liar, however, I grudgingly admit that even the deceitful Tommy Lee does--once in a great while--say something that's not exactly a bald-faced lie. Similarly, however habitual a thief some particular man might be, he *might* not steal this *particular* time.

See this line? _____

Most people see a line, but it's actually *two* lines separated by a small space. If you didn't notice the space it's *not* because you didn't see it. Your eyes saw it and notified your brain, but your brain considered it insignificant and subconsciously "filtered it out." In addition to deleting information, the human brain works to fill gaps and holes with subconsciously manufactured "filler." Instead of what actually exists, it's common for us to "see" what we expect to see, which means we don't always see reality, but rather what we're conditioned (programmed) to see. Or we see what we *want* to see...or what we fear.

This natural utility device keeps life simple and prevents trivia from overwhelming us, but it also creates confusion, perpetuates problems, and turns people into doctors' work.

It is *not* your job to create facts and neither should you blindly cram facts into molds. They fit or they don't, and it's your job to figure which and why. Fortunately, intelligent people can consciously train themselves--or be trained--to collect and analyze information, note and file seemingly insignificant data, *and keep "filler" out of the process.*

> That a person *may* be stealing is a painfully inadequate thought; he either *is* or he *isn't*. LP resolves the issue through surveillance and investigation.

If you can't watch everyone who may need watching, surveillance becomes an exercise in priorities. When that happens, use a 10-point system. Maybe this person's a 5 on the 10-point scale. If an 8 comes along, drop the 5 and go with him. (Clearly, this is not an exact science, so keep in mind that "bird in the hand" thing.)

We all have shortcomings and occasionally become complacent. To compensate for one and to combat the other, I do an exercise--a sort of game--I call "Pick a Number." A couple times a day, I pick a number from 1 to 10, then count customers coming in the store. If the number I picked was five, it doesn't matter if the fifth person through the door is nine or ninety; I tail him.

## 8.01 Technique

You don't want honest, paying shoppers thinking they're being "spied on." That hurts sales, and sales pay salaries. Also, some people take *major* offense. Ordinarily, then, rule those people out ASAP and stay clear of them. (However, I do sometimes watch people whom I *don't* suspect as a way to sharpen my skills, test a "profile" or simply spot check.)

If you want to deter or prevent theft, jump in whenever you like, and the sooner the better. Otherwise, it's assumed you're on the offense and out to catch a thief.

The Three Golden Rules of Surveillance:

1. Don't make eye contact.
2. Don't make eye contact.
3. Don't make eye contact.

*Just (don't) do it.*

Shoplifters are extremely interested in who watches them "shop." They look for "the heat." They look back to see if you look back to see, and eye contact gets their attention. Thieves categorize people who make eye contact as *probably harmless, maybe a problem,* or *a problem ("a danger")*. They do the same thing you do, but in reverse.

"Hookers" (prostitutes) use eye contact to initiate negotiations. Then comes a nod or wink and things develop. For "working girls," drug dealers, and thieves, eye contact equals interest. Make eye contact twice--demonstrate interest twice--and, to a thief, you're a danger. At that point, you should usually go overt and try prevention; or just pack it in altogether unless he does something *extremely* provocative. Even then, be *very* wary. He may be a trickster.

Do not lock eyes. Not only does that blow your cover, but in some circles it signals hostility and aggression.

How to avoid eye contact? Aside from the obvious, concentrate on *hands,* which is the priority anyway. (With eyes, thieves steal only glances.)

If a thief might have noticed you, *don't* react immediately. Act disinterested and play stupid. Keep walking without breaking your pace and *do not rubber-neck*. Quickly--but without setting off a thief's radar--"double back" and discreetly work your way to a good position. Try not to let him see you turn around on him. That's a clear warning. Some thieves will ditch and split if they even *think* they *might* smell what *could* be trouble.

An old ball park adage is, "You can't tell the players without a program." Since you lack a Shoplifter Directory, you may not be aware of all the players. While you concentrate on one, his chum may notice. You're burned. All bets are off. (If anyone might see you turn around on a suspect, make them think you're interested in something else. Anyone--even a total stranger or employee--who sees you "spying" on someone might suffer Big Brother Syndrome and warn a thief he's being watched. It happens.)

Once you have a suspect, *don't become distracted*. Don't take "just a second" to watch something attractive nearby or look around to see what made a loud noise. Imagine a shell game: a pea *might* be placed under one of the shells that, eventually, are scrambled. Your job is to keep the pea in sight and *if* it's put under a shell, to keep *that* shell in focus.

Are you reacting to something that *could* be a distraction for a theft in progress? What all can be seen? What *can't* be seen? Who all is tied up? What's not being covered? Think. *Right now,* is someone covering the safe, jewelry, cash tills, high-risk anything?

> You're "under cover." You want people *not* to notice you. You want to be H.G. Wells' Invisible Man; a vice-president, ready and waiting, but nothing anyone pays attention to.

Long ago, hunters used to blend by creeping along on the blind side of their horses in order to get near unsuspecting deer. *Of course* the deer could see the hunters' legs under his horse, but that didn't matter; deer don't know how many legs a horse is supposed to have or what they're supposed to look like. How can you fool *your* quarry? Can you sit or stand behind a display and see through it or *around* it with a mirror? How can you *blend*?

If you cannot blend with something, then you must find some way to discount your existence. Perhaps you can talk with someone, and watch the thief over your friend's shoulder. Whatever you do, *something* must give the suspect the impression that he does *not* have your attention. (If you wear plain clothes and stand with an employee, thieves associate you with the store. You might be able to finesse your way out of the association, but it's not wise to assume any particular thief is that careless or stupid.)

*Blend.* It's not uncommon for women to shop for men's clothes, but a man checking sizes on women's lingerie doesn't blend in with nearby shoppers. He needs a better "cover." Your activity should appear age and sex appropriate to you personally. Anyone, for example, can appear "innocent" looking at postcards or most sporting goods..

> When "stalking," don't walk at a fast pace if you can avoid it, and don't set a firm, serious look on your face. People (innocently) shopping have "soft" looks. You want that same sort of look on *your* face.
>
> An average person won't normally recall another person's face just a couple of moments after passing. If an average shoplifter pegs you as just another customer, he quickly forgets enough about you.

When you walk, don't rubberneck. If walking side by side with someone else, use each other for cover; watch the side of the aisle you see as you face your friend.

Consider your suspect a bird: hold him too tightly and he suffocates; hold him too loosely and he flies away. Until you pounce, make no sudden movements and no abrupt stops. Don't scare him. The object is to get him safely and quietly into the cage.

Where are you standing? Can you move in reaction to a thief's movement *without* drawing his attention? Go where thieves often stand and look around. Why do they like to be there? What racks or merchandise can be arranged or realigned to put the thief in a less advantageous setting. Moving something just a few inches this way or that might help. Seize every possible edge.

You need to see the suspect and remain unseen by him without appearing to be a Keystone Cop to anyone else in the store.

It's best to "pick up" on thieves without them knowing you exist, and then remain invisible, tailing them while using all available cover. You don't have to hide while you move, just keep something at eye level somewhere between you and your thief's head so if he glances your way, something will break his line of vision. (If you know what they want to steal, get there first and forget the tail.)

**Peripheral vision** is a key to "tailing" a suspect. Keep your focus on your target and let your peripheral vision pick up on closer things.

Stand in one place and practice using peripheral vision. Hold something in front of you about chest-high (like shoppers do), and keep your elbows bent. Hold it about like you would if you were standing there holding and reading a magazine. When you look directly at it, you can see things above it, below it, and off to the sides. That's *peripheral* vision. Keep your nose pointed straight at the item, but *cut your eyes* above it and to the sides and focus on things twenty feet away. Then turn your shoulders and head slowly just to the left or right. To anyone just glancing at you, you should appear to be examining the item or reading the label. (If poorly executed, this can be *extremely* obvious.)

Watch for this tactic from thieves! When looking for security and employees, they often hold the item too high, at odd angles, or with their arms straight out; or sometimes their head is held back instead of keeping their nose pointed down at the item. But whether tailing an individual or watching for a specific act, focus on that and let your peripheral vision keep track of everything else, i.e., all the non-essentials.

**Noise.** Don't make it. Keep loose change out of pockets, keys quiet. Wear quiet shoes. Don't whistle, sing, or smack chewing gum. If you carry merchandise as a "cover," carry *quiet* merchandise; no cellophane, no Tic-Tacs in a plastic box. *Don't* have your beeper start up.

*Practice* sneaking. See how close you can get to people and look in their hands, bags, and pockets. Move away without their knowing you were there. *Practice* being quiet.

**Colors.** The color of clothes is important. Wear quiet colors. The color red registers with the conscious mind while brown may go unseen. White, too, is highly noticeable. Avoid bright colors and bold patterns, and go instead with the darker earth-tones. Be subtle or, if appropriate, appear a little dressed-down.

**Ears.** *Listen*, and you can *hear* packaging being ripped. Amazingly, you hear shoplifters discussing their operation. (I actually heard a pair debate how many of a particular item they needed to steal to fill a buyer's order.)

Being near enough to hear might be near enough for inadvertent contact. If you happen to get *too* close, give a polite "excuse me" and maneuver around or past. *Don't make eye contact.* He *will* look at your eyes, so let him see that you're just browsing, uninterested in his face, and oblivious to whatever he's doing. But see what's in his hands, what's on the floor, and what's amiss within his reach.

Thieves generally give avoidance of eye contact a favorable interpretation *so long as you're not obvious about looking at hands and bags* or unless you "blow it" some other way. (Like if you chat with employees.) Take in the scenery as if you were shopping in a grocery store, as if you couldn't care less who's around. *Don't spook the horses.*

> Carpenters have their favorite hammer; mechanics, their favorite wrench; and shoplifters have a favorite bag or purse used over and over because it works so well. It's just the right size, it "feels" good. Maybe it's "lucky."

Are children separated so they won't see Mom's larceny? (Few people steal if their children in the five-to-ten age bracket will see it.) If a group has your attention, watch for one person to go off alone. That's common with honest shoppers, but a Red Flag with a thief. He might feel uncomfortable stealing around an honest friend. If one separates to steal, he usually acts *quickly*. Whether he steals or not--maybe he just went looking for a restroom--you can rule him out quickly and get back to the group.

Dealing (confronting, watching...) is easier with an individual than with a group or pair. You're at a *severe* disadvantage with a group, and the chance of getting "burned" is great. You can handle only so many things at a time, so go with what appears most promising or most pressing. (A good "cover" in some situations is to take an item to a close-by checkout, have the cashier ring a no-sale, hand you a receipt, and bag your item. This fools *many* thieves.)

If more than one is stealing, try to take them one at a time without the others seeing the arrest. This requires assistance, but it can make individual arrests easier. If you can't get one alone, perhaps one will drift somewhat apart, giving you a bit of a head start--*an edge*. Be alert, *think*, and watch for every advantage and opportunity.

## 8.02 Looking, Watching, and Seeing

A store manager asked a man if he needed help. The man reared up and asked if someone thought he was stealing. When the manager said that he was just trying to be helpful, the man apologized: "I come in here a lot, and nobody ever asked me if I wanted any help before." Had they even *seen* him? Richard Pryor--who once set himself ablaze--said that a nice thing about being on fire is people notice you.

Surveillance is pointless if you don't see what you're watching. Ask employees, "What did that (man) who just walked past have in his hands?" Sadly, they often answer, "What man?" *Rarely* can they say what he held or what he wore. Average store clerks notice individual customers no more than drivers on a road notice individual trees. (Incidentally, professional vision is 20-20. Get new glasses if you need them.)

***Everyone must be noticed.*** You simply cannot have blind employees or invisible customers. In one store, I asked the first 32 shoppers I encountered how long they had been shopping and if any employee had said hello or in any way had asked if they needed help. All but four had had ample time to steal, but only *two* of the thirty-two had had their existence acknowledged *in any way*. What did the employees say? "I have too much to do to get tied up with customers." Interestingly, this company fantasizes that they provide good customer service. That's either self-deception or hallucination, because their *reality* is pure "self-service." With no front line against shoplifters, thieves pour through.

That sad commentary leads into "the greeting." If you can be readily identified as an employee, it's good P.R. to give every customer a hearty greeting. If a suspect has obviously spotted you, this formula deters theft *and* greets the customer:

O.H.O. + (E.C. + G.) = G.C.S. + T.D.

This reads "Obvious Hand Observation plus Eye Contact and Greeting equals Good Customer Service and Theft Deterrence." Notice: hand observation comes *before* eye contact. A shoplifter will always look at your eyes, so he sees your eyes travel from hands and bag up to his face. When he notices your eyes are on his hands and bag, he assumes you may be on to him even though you may not have the slightest suspicion.

That greeting is unusual and makes a thief's radar go berserk. A thief instinctively knows he's in trouble if you see what his hands are doing. You create *serious* questions in his mind and an uneasy feeling in his gut. If he already stole something, it may scare him into "losing" what he concealed. Professional thieves detest odd happenings, and they know there's always a safer time or easier store. (See App. 10, "Put Wind in Your Sales.")

If a suspect puts something down, see what it is. Is it out of place? Is it torn or tampered with? Is he repositioning merchandise on a display? Are price tags on the floor?

> With practice, little tell-tale curiosities rivet your attention. You scratch surfaces and see shoplifters beneath. Chris Hodgdon, a college administrator and longtime friend, said to me, "Your book has totally ruined my shopping. Everywhere I go, I see thieves. It's distracting as hell." He's right: they're everywhere.

*Why* is he standing or crouching *where* and *as* he is? Does his head snap around when someone approaches? How large and full is his bag? Is it nicked, wrinkled, and worn as though used many times? Did he have it in his hands when he came in? Is it sealed at the top? Is it a ridiculous size for the contents? How large is her purse and how full?

Did she already have an umbrella when she walked up to the umbrella display? If you don't know, find out *quickly*. (On rainy days, always watch umbrellas.)

I was in a grocery check-out line. Three cashiers were operating with three or four customers each. Standing there with my groceries, I watched a guy come in, look at cigarette lighters *at a closed checkout*, walk away, return, look all around, and then stuff an entire peg hook of lighters into his pocket. He wasn't 10 feet from a cashier and people in line! In plain view of everyone, he was invisible.

I immediately told the nearest clerk who looked at him and said to me, "That's terrible." I went to a second clerk who called the manager, but by the time he arrived, the thief was long gone. The manager told me the store is swarming with thieves since they eliminated security as a cost-reduction measure. (Whatever *that* means.)

Sometimes "seeing" takes extra effort. If you notice a man with a large bag--the open-at-the-top type--what prevents you from walking up behind him and glancing at what's in it? Or what *isn't* in it?

Ideally, you approach from behind or from an angle allowing you to scan the situation prior to the suspect seeing your eyes or noticing your approach or proximity. Do a casual "walk by;" stroll down the same aisle and discreetly check him out. Did he stop what he was doing or begin doing something else? Did he put something down?

*Practice.* Feign interest in a nearby display; pick something up, walk away with something. If it looks as if you really have his attention, ask him what time he's got; anything charming or disarming to get you where you can see what is in his hand or bag. If you have a watch, ask what time it is, then look at yours and say, "I knew my watch was slow." Appear stupid; thieves *love* that.

Grasp what constitutes "normal" for honest shoppers. Learn how they hold purses and bags, how they examine merchandise, what they do with their eyes, and how they stand. A trick with thief-spotting is to see the abnormal (a thief's action) in a basically normal (honest shopper's) situation. Illusion is a thief's stock and trade and it's your job to see through it. You're a detective...so *detect*.

**Two examples of aggressive "wading in."** I suspected a woman was trying to steal socks. Half the time I couldn't see what she was doing and the other half she was looking around at customers and employees while handling her purse and our socks. I finally couldn't stand it, so I walked directly to her and stood at her side. I looked at the socks on display, then down at her purse, then up into her eyes. Then I said, *"Socks."* Just that one word.

She looked at me like I was acting strangely and said, "What?"

"Socks," I repeated, like it was some new and fascinating thing.

Without another word, she opened her purse and held it open for me to see inside. There were socks, the same as we sold and the same as she'd been handling. But I couldn't see a price tag. I had no precedent, so what to do next? Ask a logical question, of course.

"What are you doing?"

"I'm going to pay for them." *(Now* I've got her!)

"What'd you do with the price tag?" Pure bluff, but harmless, since she admitted the socks hadn't been paid for, but were in her purse. Also, I still couldn't yet prove that they belonged to my store. I felt sure they did, but I like to touch bases. By asking about the price tag, I hoped she'd show it to me.

"I thought if I took the tags off I might get a better price." (This is a true story. Highly unusual, for sure, but less surprising than a royal flush in an honest poker game, and I've seen *that*.)

"Well, you need to tell the manager, and we'll see what he wants to do."

And I knew what *that* would be. She didn't answer the price-tag question, and I didn't want to get hung up on that. Keep the ball bouncing.

She told the manager she stripped the price tag off and kicked it under a counter, then concealed the socks in her purse. She was even kind enough to retrieve the tag. By the time she was done, even a jury of Spruill Avenue whores would have been too embarrassed to find her not guilty.

Another day: I came upon a man (about 40-years-old) standing at a vitamin display. As I walked past, his head jerked in my direction and his right hand shot out of his right pants' pocket. I stepped over to him, grinned, and asked, *"What's going on?"*

"I'm just looking at vitamins."

"Really?"

"I might buy some." No way. A normal shopper would tell me to buzz off. This guy was trying way too hard to be Mr. Friendly.

"What's this all about?" I looked down and, with an exaggerated motion, scratched my own right pants' pocket. (Scratching an itch is perfectly legal in South Carolina, and pure coincidence that my leg happened to itch at that particular moment.) Then I looked him in the eyes and waited.

In response, he reached in *both* his front pockets, pulled a bottle of vitamins out of each, and set them back on the shelf. If I arrested him right then, I felt the municipal judge would convict him. *But,* I was having a good time, he seemed eager to help me build a stronger case, and I wanted more to show that they were ours and not paid for.

"What's up with that?"

"I'm thinking about buying them."

"You got money to pay for 'em?"

"I'd rather not say."

"I'd rather not pull out a badge. You <u>better</u> show me ten bucks."

"I don't have any money."

Good enough for now, so off we marched. Once in the office, I asked his name.

"I'd rather not say."

"What would you say if I told you I was arresting you for shoplifting?"

"I'd say you're being an ass-hole."

A few minutes later he asked for a smoke, and I told him not until he apologized for what he said. (Whatever else it might be, nicotine is powerful motivation.) After the store manager drifted in, my thief admitted to him that he had put our vitamins in his pockets and couldn't pay for them. (That nailed his coffin tightly.) I asked again for his name.

Calmly, he replied, "I am a reincarnation of the noble Saint Bernard." He obviously believed it, and I don't recall which bothered me more: memories of past fights with berserk mental patients, or being called a dirty name by a saint.

In court, Miss Socks pled guilty. The judge then asked if I had anything to say, and I didn't. (What would be the point of saying anything? *She pled guilty.*) She was fined $148.

Charley pled *not* guilty, and my testimony was brief. "(He) came in the store and stuffed bottles of vitamins in his pockets. I arrested him and he had no money."

**Notice!** I did not make an issue of whether or not I saw the vitamins go into his pockets. 1) Don't create issues, and 2) Legally, it didn't matter anyway. I stated the results of my investigation, confirmed to witnesses at the scene by the thief himself.

Charley admitted putting them in his pockets and having no money. (Thank you, Charles.) Then he rambled on and on until a uniformed nurse came forward and spoke to the judge. Found guilty, Charley's fine was waived on condition he return with the nurse to the hospital from which he had wandered and resume his therapy and medications.

## 8.03 Physical Descriptions

Accuracy is *extremely* important. Begin *immediately* to develop skills in observation. How? Look at the next person you pass. A minute later, double back and look again. Did you remember his shirt color? Pants? What was in his hands? Gradually increase the time lapse between first viewing and second.

Don't worry about race and sex; you'll remember. *Try* to note tall, short or medium (or how tall in relation to yourself); age (teens, 20,s, 30's,), hair, hat; fat, thin. *"Try"* to note these things, but *know* the color of the shirt and pants and what was or was not in their hands.

A simple way to remember clothes is "shirt first, pants second." *Always* shirt first, pants second. Fix it in your mind: shirt first, pants second. If he wears a red shirt and blue pants, repeat "red, blue" over and over until you write it down. Two people, one with red shirt and blue pants and the second with blue shirt and white pants: "red, blue; blue, white" over and over in your mind. Keep it simple. (And always carry a pen and notebook.)

If one gets away, query witnesses and write as much detail as soon as you can. Note gold or missing teeth, facial hair, hat (and color), shoes (and color), and memorable jewelry. Finally, don't forget Mat Dillon's favorite question: *"Which way did he go?"*

For a car, get the license plate number, if possible, but surely the color (2-tone?). Two-door or four? Two brake lights or three? Any noticeable, distinguishing marks like a bashed-in door, bumper sticker, or broken tail-light? Write it down ASAP!

With two basic clothing colors plus sex and race you have a chance. If you ask police to find someone and your description is, "He was a white guy," *you* should be punished.

## 8.04 Security Windows

Evidence viewed or obtained illegally is said to be "fruit of the forbidden tree." *It* falls under **"The Exclusionary Rule"** and cannot be used in court. A police rule of thumb is, "If you have a right to be, you have a right to see. If you have a right to see, you have a right to seize." Creativity often provides a right to be where you need to be so that you can (legally) see whatever there is to see.

Security windows are often the most effective item in a security repertoire. For our purposes, a "security window" is any window, hole, or opening that provides for lengthy study of a situation without much chance of the viewer being detected. *They are essential.* Things are seldom ideal, but, ideally, from a window you see not only merchandise, but the thief whether he stands, couches, or sits. Naturally, the better the window is placed, the less of your body will be visible from the target side and the more thieves you'll catch.

With a formal security window--glass and all--you're totally out of sight, but physically removed from the sales floor. The view can be great, but distance creates a problem: if you move from the window, you lose sight of the thief and merchandise. Using a phone or walkie-talkie to direct another employee might avoid problems arising from a lapse in surveillance. (Some companies use mobile booths with mirrors: a Trojan Horse.)

Some windows are "peepholes" cut in counters with a jig saw or razor. *Excellent* peepholes can be created, too, by an imaginative arrangement of merchandise or displays. Whatever the type, peepholes are dirt cheap, easily constructed and remarkably effective.

The following examples are successful peepholes.

1. Small, quarter-sized holes cut in a counter. About three feet above floor level (kneeling-height) or at eye level, allowing you to be on one side of the counter and observe activity on the other side.
2. A 6-foot rotating post card rack. Maintain an empty slot on one side of the rack at eye level and stand on the full side. Look between the card slots. The "window" through the backside of the empty slot seems enormous. The rack is portable and provides "cover." Casual observers think you're just passing time looking at post cards. (Jewelry or necktie racks? Think!)

3. A display of stacked boxes separated at eye level just enough--about an inch--to see between them to the sales floor beyond. Boxes are high enough *so the top of your head can't be seen from the target side of the display.* It's best if the boxes contain items of interest to males or females so to a casual observer--or a thief's chum--an employee standing there can appear *appropriately* interested *for a prolonged period of time.*
4. Freestanding racks. Racks are pulled slightly apart or placed nearly together (about 1- to 3-inches apart is enough, depending on the configuration of the racks) so while you *appear* to be looking at merchandise on the racks, you can observe the sales floor beyond the space. The closer together the racks, the better they hide your presence from anyone on the target side, but the more they restrict your field of vision.

The closer your eye is to the peephole, the greater your field of vision will be. From a hole no larger than a half dollar, you can see thief, bags, merchandise and display, all without a thief knowing you exist. But whether you stand, kneel or stoop, you must appear inconspicuous and innocently occupied; not like Larry or Curly spying on Moe.

The location of the items you're worried about determines where the peephole needs to be. Work the problem backwards from the "point of theft." Go to that item and look around for likely peephole locations. Look near and far, high and low. First, decide where a peephole needs to be, then decide how to make it.

Can merchandise be rearranged, or do you need a hole in a counter or display? Can merchandise more suitable to "peephole construction" be put nearby? Can the problem-display itself be moved to a more easily monitored location? Need a mirror?

Some peepholes are at natural eye-level, others not. Some require a "step" of some sort. As a rule, the lower the peephole, the less apparent it is from the target or "business" side. Camouflage the target side. If a casual observer can easily recognize your side of the hole for what it is, cover it with something when not used.

Check peepholes regularly to make sure they're ready for instant use, and keep the target *area* clear of empty packages or out of place merchandise.

Probably not a Harvard grad, the shoplifter will, nonetheless, have brains enough to look around; to scan. But he does not take time to study his surroundings, so with a little thought on your part, his quick scans won't do him any good. Without time to focus on detail, he's at a major disadvantage. It's a beautiful thing to witness a thief look right at you without seeing you and then craftily stuff merchandise in his pants.

> A thief will casually select merchandise and do prep-work while other people are in the immediate area. Once he thinks he's safe, though, he normally acts *quickly.* If a suspect thinks no one is watching, it's usually clear after just a minute or so whether or not he's a thief. If you've seen no indication in five minutes, he's usually OK.

## *Security windows have a pitfall*:

***First,*** you observe a thief select an item and conceal it. You leave the window (you *move*), and go elsewhere to follow up.

***Second,*** while changing positions you lose visual contact and cannot observe his actions. It's *possible* that during this lapse the thief became fearful he'd been seen by an employee or passing customer. Some noise may have startled him. He may discard the item (or even hide it) among other merchandise.

***Third,*** you stop him and accuse him. He's happy to prove you wrong and, later, you get a certified letter.

A second good-guy should pick up surveillance before the first person breaks visual. (That's *if* you're fortunate enough to have a second good-guy.) He stands near the thief to see that nothing gets discarded. Knowing the thief still has the concealed item, the good guys can confidently get on him. An important aspect of all this is that you must not fly on automatic pilot. If the surveillance is broken, for even a moment, you exit the world of certainty and enter the realm of *uncertainty*: the Land of Lawsuits.

With few exceptions, if there is an interruption in surveillance, it's conceivable that something was switched or was dumped, or you're otherwise being set up for a fall.

But even if the continuity of surveillance was broken, you have several options. You can watch for another item to be concealed, or overtly encourage the thief to leave. You can huff, puff, rattle, and bluff him into a mistake, or diplomatically induce him to produce the merchandise. And your options can change minute by minute.

Obvious things are often overlooked. If a suspect had something in his left hand that disappeared, look at his left pants pocket for a tell-tale sign or bulge. If you're quick, you might see merchandise protruding from the pocket. *Too* simple.

What you *do* depends on the totality of the circumstances and the thief. At the very least, you know he's a thief; remember his face, and you can get him next time. Also, you can sometimes determine an item is still concealed by its physical impression on a bag or pocket, or by it's size. If so, there's no problem; unless, of course, Murphy comes knocking.

**Deep Thoughts.** Ever misplace your keys or a letter? You know, *lose* something, then find it the last place you looked? The reason people always find things the last place they look is because that's when they quit looking. You sometimes see a thief steal, but he sees you coming, pulls the concealed item out of his pocket, drops it, and then tries to leave. You lost the bust, but got your merchandise back, so that's that, right? Wrong.

Drug traffickers give up decoy loads to slide larger loads through the pipe while everyone's looking the other way. Or a yacht full of marijuana is seized, the pot burned, and the boat sold at government auction. The dealers buy it, take it home, and then take it apart to recover a hidden cache of counterfeit money or cocaine worth ten times the pot.

If a drug ring wants to get a particular police officer or agent promoted, what better way to help their man than feed him juicy busts? But that's law enforcement...plots within plots. The point is that when you think risk and loss, think *depth*. Don't *assume* you got all there is, or that they came clean the first time around. Beware of anything obvious or that seems "too easy." And certainly beware of *anything* an enemy gives you.

> The best way to avoid trouble with security, says Alethia, is "get somebody who works there to steal for you. They have more opportunity, and they know how to do it."

## 8.05  Fire Lanes (Kill Zones)

The Smithsonian Institute estimates systematic hunting began about 300,000 years ago. Today, predators of a different sort roam city streets and businesses in much the same fashion that tigers roam jungle paths. Our predators are shoplifters, profit killers. Most shoplifters depend upon store personnel to ignore them or, at worst, *maybe* say something. Few thieves expect anyone to *try* to catch them. Fire lanes--called "kill zones" in the military--are retail tiger pits: primitive, but effective. Without cameras, *they're essential*.

Like your ancestors, you are a hunter. First, find bones; signs like discarded wrappers, price-tags, empty hangers, etc. These provide an idea of *what* is consumed (stolen) and *where* stealing occurs.

In large stores, there may be a number of locations. In a small store, thieves might constantly use one particular aisle. Begin with a known bad place, or make your best guess. Go there. What is it about the place that draws thieves? What direction do they come from? How would they stand when they steal; which direction would they face? How would they exit? Then look around until you see where *you* need to be or where a peephole or mirror needs to be.

Your goal is to create a visual funnel with an observation point at the small end. (Grocery store aisles are *naturals*.) Eliminate things that obstruct your view. Can a display be lowered, moved or realigned? Think observation window, peephole, and mirror. Think hands. (And once a thief is in place, can you get to your "stand" without spooking him?)

By making it difficult to steal at some locations or with obvious (but functionally useless) dummy cameras or mirrors, thieves are encouraged to enter a chosen area (the funnel). Stealing there should seem "safe," so provide that illusion. (And since stealing was happening there anyway, that impression shouldn't be too difficult to make.) The idea is if he chooses to steal, let him do it where *you* can see it happen and make the bust.

Incidentally, this is not "entrapment." You don't bait a field with toys and whistles and tempt honest people to steal. Thieves steal, and this is just one of the better ways to catch them.

---

**Time Bombs** Some shoplifters will purchase what they want to steal *if* employees provide encouragement. This type thief often has a "time bomb:" a limited amount of time to steal before something bad happens. For example: Mom and teenage daughter, Angel, are in the mall when Angel says she wants some $10 lipstick. Mom hands her $11 and says be back in twenty minutes.

Angel has a time bomb with a twenty-minute fuse. If she steals the lipstick *quickly*, she can use the cash for something else later. Mom will never know.

If arrested, Angel will say, "It's a mistake. Why would I steal it when I have the money to buy it?" Then, when Mom arrives, you hear it again: "This must be a mistake. Why would she steal when she has money to buy it?"

---

## 8.06 Mirrors

Cheap, versatile and easy, a small mirror can be more effective than a first-rate security window. If well placed, it provides an excellent field of vision at odd and seemingly impossible angles. It can be hung on a wall, counter, or display, and can be wired or taped in place, freestanding, nailed, or propped on a shelf or desk. Mirrors can be effectively mounted at any height, including on the ceiling, and a mirror on one aisle can provide a view of a different aisle. They allow tactful, lengthy observation (is it reasonable for you to be where you are?) and a good position. (Don't restrict yourself to mirrors; *any* reflective surface can help. Find things to use!)

Size is almost immaterial. Huge mirrors deter and make a statement, but my best *case-producing* mirror was only 3- by 4-inches. Literally wired to a display at (my) eye level, it was in an area unrelated to and physically removed from the area it monitored. Standing at the mirror, *I couldn't be seen from the target area* and I could fiddle with the merchandise around it for five or ten minutes without anyone becoming suspicious.

Because most mirrors are uniquely positioned to view singular locations, the angles involved make them practically useless to thieves.

---

The day this page was originally written, I caught three shoplifters in two separate incidents with the mirror mentioned above. One wore a huge gold ring on every finger, gold chains Mr. T.-style around his neck, and a big gold earring. Six-feet tall and 195-pounds, he was 18 years-old, had several known aliases, a street nom de guerre, and a criminal "rap sheet" longer than a loan-shark's memory. It included *"Lynching."*

(Some people say there's no such thing as a bad boy.)

Experiment: Take hand-mirrors from place to place. Find some likely locations, examine things from different angles, and then hang a few. Honest customers love to check hair and make-up, but thieves hate 'em (and that's reason enough to hang a few).

One professional thief claims to have been at it for years. She says she's never been caught and steals as much as $600 a day. Why has she never been caught? "For one thing, I don't go in places with cameras and lots of mirrors. You can't ever be sure no one's watching. If you don't want to get caught you got to be smart."

But what if she wants merchandise from a place with mirrors? "Pay someone stupid to take a chance." She says many shoplifters ('stupid ones') just don't know any better. What if someone stupid is not available? "Crackheads will do anything for money." What if her crackhead "friend" gets caught? "Too bad. It's not my problem." (Especially when they need a 'fix,' crackheads--crack cocaine addicts--are *extremely* relentless, hyperactive, and driven to gross stupidity. In short, they're freaking *crazy*.)

Because of cameras, mirrors, and plain-clothes security, she shops small and specialty stores and avoids "big stores" like Sears. *However*, she avoids even small stores that have many mirrors: "I get people to steal (there) for me, but I won't do it myself."

> You can't eliminate every spot where shoplifting might occur, but with some work you can eliminate *some* spots and make others *very* inconvenient. One step at a time...

## 8.07 Cameras

If you can afford an electronic surveillance system, multiplex monitors, and humans to handle it and watch countless hours of tapes, CCTV might be a good idea. Even a 30-grand system, though, is only as good as the human working it. Does he know how to pick suspects? Does he mostly use the zoom when sexy women are walking around?

Another problem with sophisticated electronics is that some operators don't develop skills necessary to shake and bake on the floor *in person*. A security room becomes their element, but it's the sales floor where things happen. Also, if electronics (cameras, sensor tags, etc.) were *all that*, it seems companies using them wouldn't be getting sued all the time. (However, even a single hidden video camera hooked into a VCR aimed at one particular location can be *extremely* revealing and effective; and cost less than 500-bucks.)

Anyway, the type camera needed by everyone is for instant photographs. Second best is the 24-shot, 110-type. Shoplifters and disorderlies *abhor* having their picture taken and usually leave soon after a bulb flashes. Descriptions given to police are often inadequate, but pictures are frequently excellent evidence and proof. Plus, they can be copied and distributed, thereby increasing the likelihood and variety of trouble for the suspect.

And speaking of the law, it varies from place to place and from adults to juveniles. Talk to a solicitor and police to learn what you can and cannot do with a camera.

## 8.08 Projections From Observation

At times, sowing a little hate and discontent is unavoidable, *but the goal is control*. While watching someone, you need to figure out how to handle things if he steals. If prevention is the goal, how aggressive must you be? Is he in a "holding pattern," just waiting for an employee (possibly yourself) to be distracted by a telephone call or honest shopper? How long can you "baby-sit"? What can you do if he tries to walk out *now*?

(Speaking of telephone calls, if someone calls the store and asks for "security," or for an officer by name, would you tell them that there is no security in the store? Or that security left and will be back in about an hour? Isn't that a way of telling them that it's a good time to steal? When you disclose where security *is*, you may disclose where it is *not*.)

If a customer wants to talk to security in person, maybe about a lost wallet or keys, could it be a distraction or diversion, or could the "customer" just want to see what your security people look like? Or see what the procedure is or how long it takes to respond? (I handle most such requests by phone or have someone else handle it.)

Watching a suspect is one phase, preventing the theft, actual stealing, leaving the store, and the actual stop are other phases. Know your limitations, then anticipate and be better prepared than the thief for each subsequent act as the drama unfolds. If there's no practical recourse if he steals, then an ounce (or ton) of prevention is definitely the priority.

If he appears likely to run or fight, what can be done *prior* to the stop to lessen the chance? Which aisles will he probably use? *Where* would it be best to make the stop, and *how?* Stay calm and focused, and remember the overview (which includes who or what else might be involved in the current situation) *and* the "four areas of knowledge." (Pg 62.)

You must think ahead and factor input from your eyes *and* ears. If he does this or that, what will you need to do? Then, how might he respond to what *you* did? And how can you handle *that?* Thinking a move or two in advance allows you more control in each new phase. People are people and bring a certain consistency to whatever they do, including shoplifting. *If* you keep your head, you'll find virtually everything they do is predictable.

## 8.09 Second-Hand Information

The unsubstantiated word of a witness is usually worth its weight in gold. (Speak a word, snatch it out of the air, put it on a scale, and see how much it weighs.) When some excited person claims he saw a theft, listen carefully, but *never* allow his sincerity or air of urgency to cloud your judgment. Be Marshal Dillon: "Now, Chester, just calm down and tell me exactly what you saw."

"She stole something and put it in her purse," usually boils down to something like, "I saw her hand come out of the purse and she had this real guilty look on her face," or "She was in your ladies' department and I saw her put a blouse in her shopping bag."

Well, maybe it's hers and she brought it in to compare colors. Maybe a dozen other things, too. Did Chester actually see anything in her hand? Does he know *exactly* what it was? Does he know *for sure* it belonged to the store? Was it already paid for? *How* does he know? After listening to events in chronological order and examining the details, you normally find no concrete evidence of theft.

> Non-professionals, however intelligent and well-intentioned, often leap from A to C. Or, having seen B and C, they *assume* A preceded.

If you think it's nothing--but want to humor Chester--handle it like you think he's *really* on to something. Begin a surveillance. Collect first-hand information, then chart a reasonable, legal course.

(Even if you have witnesses by the yard, it won't help if they're useless in court. One common problem is "amnesia," also called "recent memory deficit." It strikes about the same percentage of witnesses as the Black Plague did European villagers.)

What if you can't independently justify a stop, or the "thief" is walking out the door? What if you *must* act *right now*, and the stop *must* be based on the word of a third party? It happens. So...if you know the witness personally, AND his credibility in this particular type situation has already been established, AND you discount a major lapse in observation, AND you choose to ignore my advice to the contrary, AND a majority of the Supreme Court is in your pocket...hey, go for it.

Anything less than 100 percent reliable is, by definition, unreliable. Before you confront someone, you want more than a third-party advisory. You can use their input to help develop a situation, **but** *never* let your case hinge solely on third-party testimony. If it hurts, you'll get over it.

## 8.10 Know When to Let Go

"Today a peacock, tomorrow a feather duster." Life can be merciless. Many people often forget that the business of business is money: making it is good, losing it is bad. To win in the long run, you sometimes must let a little money (or even a lot) just walk out the door. Regardless how well you've played in the past, one wrong bet can wipe you out, so before you bet the farm make sure *all* the stars are lined up just right.

When four people sit down to play poker, *three* are usually there to gamble and *one* is there to make money. The sales and LP game runs 12 months; then, come inventory, you count chips. Along the way, you want to win what hands you can, including the occasional big one, but you must *avoid* large, singular losses. That means don't get sued.

Some hands you play to the end; others you just fold before a suspect even knows you exist, or you begin to play, but fold before things get serious. As any stop progresses, it becomes apparent (and quickly) if things are going your way or not. There's no strictly defined "right" time to let go, but if a stop is bad you will back off either *before* it's too late *or after*. (High stress comes when you just have to play out a bad hand. It happens.)

Many thieves--most, in fact--get away, and a few get away laughing. You can't see them all, deter 'em all, prevent 'em all, or catch 'em all. Even if you could, you'd never convict 'em all. Such is life.[30] Bide your time, play the good hands, don't push your luck, and learn as you go. (See "*Lesson de Jour*," page 192.)

> Each situation is a single hand where you bet each time a card's dealt. If a poker hand's going nowhere, get out. Not losing is very important. Where's the profit if you win twenty hands and $1,000, but then lose a biggie and *ten* thou?

Somehow, some way, a suspect might discard the item before you reach him. Not only that, it's *possible* he's *innocent*. Your demeanor must reflect these possibilities. If there's *any* degree of uncertainty (or, perhaps more accurately, any degree of less-than-total certainty), your actions and words should reflect your appreciation of the possibility he is *not* a thief. (Or that you won't be able to prove it.)

A stop is a de facto investigation, albeit the end game, and is a means to an end, not the end product. You proceed step by judicious step, *beginning with an approach that allows you a no-lawsuit exit*. As Benjamin Franklin advised: Make haste slowly. Every word and action should be a decided step forward, every reaction another; you accelerate and decelerate as twists and turns appear in the road. Screw up, and you crash and burn.

The writer Annie Dillard tells of a photographer who each year took a stack of pictures to a friend who put the photos into a "good" stack or a "bad" one. Noticing the photographer always brought one particular photo that invariably hit the "bad" stack, he asked why the photo returned every year.

"Because," the photographer said, "I had to climb a mountain to get it."

It doesn't matter how hard you work on a particular case: it's either good and worth pursuing or it's not. Your job is to make the right call.

> Kenny Rogers' hit single The Gambler condenses volumes of relevant philosophy into terse verse: "You've got to know when to hold 'em, know when to fold 'em, know when to walk away, and know when to run."

## 8.11 Uniformed Security vs Plain-clothes

Few stores use uniformed security or uniformed off-duty police officers, so this manual deals almost exclusively with management and plain-clothes LP. These personnel can do *many* things that uniforms generally do poorly or cannot do at all and, perhaps ironically, well-trained employees and LP do as well, and often much better, with generic retail crime.[31]

Who would you expect to make more vice arrests: uniformed cops driving black-and-whites, or cops in T-shirts and jeans driving Nissans? Uniformed officers--like marked squad cars--are easy to spot, and that makes it difficult for them to catch thieves. In larger stores, most shoplifters can work around them. Even the attitude, "presence," mentality and disposition required for successful plain-clothed security differ from those required for most successful police and uniformed security operations

Uniformed security officers and uniformed off-duty police have little (if any) training in customer service, increasing sales, refund fraud, or anything else germane to retail, but they have tremendous value as a "specialty tool," doing extremely well at the small ends of the retail Bell Curve. Their mere presence, for example, can bolster everyone's confidence. And like security lights, they definitely deter crime in their immediate area.

> Unless you truly have the pick of the litter, keep uniforms--and new or inexperienced plain-clothes officers--on a relatively short leash until they demonstrate that "they got it or they don't." It's not unusual for it to take weeks or even months for a good one to get the hang of it and begin producing, but you can usually see in just a week or two if you have one who's wrong for the job.
>
> If a new one flirts with the help, does not report obvious problems, or quickly creates problems or complaints about "arrogance" (from personnel whose opinions you trust and whose performance is good), he's probably wrong for the job.

Uniformed officers too often put a formal, legal slant on routine conversations, even when they only stand and say nothing while others talk. In situations calling for a low-key, no-big-deal approach, uniforms draw attention and make for allegations of embarrassment, detainment, and fear. A manager or store detective can play off a demand as a request, whereas a request by a uniform is routinely interpreted as a legal order. Initially, at least, most situations are best handled by supervisors or plain-clothes personnel.

If a person is disorderly, get a uniform involved. If he won't leave or act civilized, get the police involved. Once police are on the scene, the person either calms or is arrested. If arrested, the officer is the plaintiff (the one who prosecutes), so the case is a police thing, not a store thing. It rarely reaches that point, though, because rowdies usually leave if they think police are en route.

Because in-store disorderly conduct cases are wormy in court, if there was no physical damage or assault worth prosecuting, they are routinely a "let go." It is, however, an excellent pretext to confront an individual when your primary goal is to make him some other store's problem. Other immediate goals for making an issue of disorderly conduct might include banning someone from the store, checking ID, or issuing a criminal trespass notice. (Most problem-people don't return once their faces--and names--are known.)

- **Store employees** are in their element with customer service, watching customers' hands, and noticing what they carry. They alert management to worrisome shoppers and situations. They should be good witnesses and provide a presence, if desired. Their functions are overt.
- **Plain-clothes security (and management personnel)** are in their element monitoring customer service, store standards, and policies. They are trained for security stops, making the determination to arrest, arresting, processing, and prosecuting. They can work overtly or covertly.
- **Uniformed security of any type** watch shoppers and handle disorderly conduct and other odd or criminal situations. They work overtly and back up other store personnel.

### 17 Ways to Maximize the Effectiveness of Plain-Clothes Security:

1. Never forget that the essence of plain-clothes security is the appearance of "doing nothing" and "being nobody." Don't point, wave, or shout.
2. Do not walk up to "undercover" security if it might draw unwanted attention.
3. If LP attention is wanted, be *very* discreet in every way.
4. Stay away from anyone LP may be observing, and stay away from LP.
5. If LP is staring in a particular direction, do not walk through (or stand in) their field of vision.
6. Do not block (the view) of security windows, peep holes, or "fire lanes."
7. If calling LP, do not refer to them as "security," except, possibly, for a real emergency which is clear and present.
8. If LP is engaged in a physical struggle, help or get help quickly. (If you only stand and watch, at least scream or shout loudly for help.)
9. Be a good witness to elements of a crime (activity) that you can see or hear.
10. If LP confronts a suspect, be able to describe that person and his clothes.
11. Do not distract security from a surveillance or a prisoner for even a second.
12. Generally, say nothing to security, especially if any customers are in sight.
13. Do not stand near LP, in front of them, or behind them. (Do not help a thief find them; don't even bring a thief's gaze in LP's direction.)
14. If you speak to LP, don't blow their cover (don't identify them as an employee) to <u>anyone</u> who might hear what you say.
15. If LP carries pagers, use "911" for an emergency. Otherwise, expect them to be a while getting back to you (Five or ten minutes is not unreasonable.)
16. If there is a phone call for LP, take a name and number. Do not interrupt them on the sales floor. (Exceptions: police, loss prevention/security, emergency.)
17. If someone asks, "Is that a security person?" the correct answer is NOT "yes." Ordinarily, pointing out security personnel to anyone is taboo; doing so creates nasty situations. Try, "He has some friends who work here. If you need security, I can call them." Let it go at that. No need to lie.

⇒ It should go without saying that LP work-schedules should never be common knowledge and should never be posted for all to see (unless the purpose is to intentionally deceive someone).

It's by the way, but corrupt police officials and supervisors invent special details for honest officers and assign them to specific areas in order to keep them away from drug sales and known drug areas (KDA's). Officials then point to dropping arrest rates as proof that anti-drug efforts are successful or that the drug problem has decreased in severity. (That makes a mayor look good for November.)

Plots within plots... If a manager or supervisor seems disinterested, resentful, doesn't take appropriate action, or takes inappropriate action if presented with evidence of wrongdoing, maybe he's involved. Or has a "hidden agenda." Or "secret orders" from above.

*Or* maybe he just doesn't grasp the significance of what he sees or hears.

*Or* maybe your presentation is lacking and, if improved, would be more effective.

*Or* maybe he operates with this philosophy: "Big case, big headache. Little case, little headache. No case, no headache." (Typical among bureaucrats.)

The root problem could be one or more of many things, so don't jump to conclusions.

**"Diligence is the mother of good luck."** --B. Franklin

# Chapter 9

# BEYOND PREVENTION

> Most adult thieves, if not prosecuted, will continue stealing; if not from you, then certainly from others. By prosecuting, you *might* end it. At the very least, other thieves might be warned away and other innocent people spared a theft.

In some cases, prevention is moot because the theft is a *fait accomplis*--a done deal. In that case you can try subtly or not so subtly to get the thief to "ditch" the stolen item; or question him or arrest him...lots of things. If a thief thinks you saw him steal, he might be fear-driven (fight or flight), or be more calculating. He can discard the item and walk away, or stand there and see what you do. If you don't seize the initiative *he* will.

Few things in life manufacture more adrenaline than serving police "no-knock" search warrants. Without warning, you explode through a door into a mad scene of screams and motion that a nano-second before had been someone's living room. People wet their pants and jump for weapons; naked bodies snatch clothes and crash through windows. It's so shocking for the home team that even the house Doberman scrambles for a place to hide. I loved it.

Routinely, though, few raids are "no-knock." Police-work is often described as ninety percent boredom, nine percent fun, and one percent sheer terror, and most of the time you just walk up to a door, knock, and the nice folks inside open up. You make a peaceful approach, but always assume trouble is only a heartbeat away.

That principle applies in retail stores, too. Any fraud or shoplifting encounter--like any raid--can unwind. Even if you just want to deter or prevent, if a thief steals anyway (or won't stop trying), you have to confront him. And confrontations are Risky Business.

Ideally, stops are quiet and minimally disruptive of normal business. It may boost employee morale to see a shoplifter trounced, but brawls are detrimental to sales, and sales pay your salary.

## 9.01 Location of the Stop

An officer of a large discount chain told me that their policy is to maintain uninterrupted surveillance of a shoplifter after an item is concealed, then make the stop only *after* the thief *exits* the store. Amused, I asked for reality. What they *really* do is maintain as good a surveillance as possible; then, if they "feel good about it," they stop the thief when he leaves the store. In reality, about 10 percent of stops conform to policy.

"Hell," he continued, "ninety percent of the time, you can't possibly maintain a 100 percent surveillance." Why? "There's the time lapse between when they bag it and the time they reach the door. There's too much time involved. Too many things happen: they turn too many corners; they get up with other people; we get distracted; things come up."

Are mistakes made? Are people stopped outside *without* stolen merchandise? "Oh, yeah," he said. "It gives you a <u>reeeeeeal</u> bad feeling in your stomach." Does it happen even if you maintained what you thought was a 100 percent surveillance while they walked around the store? "Yeah, sometimes. Even then you can't be right all the time."

Do they let people leave unaccosted even when they're fairly certain merchandise was stolen? "Sure. We have to. We let more walk who we saw steal than we stop."

Reality: Once a customer is past the check-out or out the door, there are really only three things to say. 1) "Excuse me. Did you forget to pay for something?" 2) "Excuse me, but I think you forgot to pay for something, and you'll have to come back in the store," or 3) "Excuse me. You're under arrest for shoplifting."

"I think you forgot to pay for something," clearly implies unpurchased merchandise. If he keeps walking and ignores you or says, "I don't think so," what do you do? Little choice, really, but swing into an aggressive mode and quick, or just let it go and return to the store to worry or brood.

If you're mistaken, it's difficult to convince *anyone* the reason for stopping him was anything but suspected theft, and it's virtually impossible to float an apology in what immediately becomes a nasty squall. You're either *real* right or *real* wrong, *too* wrong to harmlessly extricate yourself. With only these options, you let most of them walk.

> Think football: A team loses a big game because of an off-sides call. The next season, the coach tells his defensive line not to react until the ball actually crosses the line of scrimmage. "It's safer," he says. "By doing it this way, misjudging the intent to snap will never cost us another game."
>
> What he says is true, but it's called 'throwing the baby out with the bath water.'
>
> The object is don't let 'em see daylight. *Don't* let a runner find a hole and open field before you react. A shoplifter's hole is the store door. *Don't* let him reach the hole. Once the ball is snapped, church is out.

**"At the Door" and "Outside" Stops.** A bad thing happens when a thief gets near a hole in the wall filled with glass. The Great Out-of-Doors looms larger and larger in front of him. As he nears the door, his adrenaline level rises. His temptation to "fight or flight" increases in direct proportion to the decrease in distance between himself and the Gateway to Freedom, and his temptation achieves critical mass at the door. Location-wise, there or *outside* the door is the farthest extreme possible for a stop; and where things most often degenerate into a foot race, fight, or curse-fest. [33]

Shoplifters *expect* to get to the door or out of the store before anything happens. In that, these tricky parasites with insatiable appetites have been conditioned to expect cooperation. Even though it creates problems, forces mistakes, is frequently impractical, and isn't even required by law, many businesses don't allow employees to react until the thief leaves the store. It's as if "Thou shalt suffer a thief to leave" were carved in stone.

**"Indoor" Stops.** In any situation, you have to analyze what becomes known as things unfold. Plus, you have to factor in all the *unknowns*. Calculations are frequent and tricky, and the more people, the more variables. Inside the store, you at least have more control, fewer unknowns, *and more legal rights*. Even if a thief has friends outside, as long as he's inside he has to worry about who *else* might be outside: is there a cop outside writing a traffic ticket or someone else who will *enjoy* grabbing him? [34]

A thief stopped before he reaches the door is disconcerted by the jolt of unexpected action. He feels very much alone. *You* have the initiative, and he's forced to improvise.

> **The Achilles Heel**
>
> The single most important element in an average shoplifter's demise is purely psychological: he feels it is important to present himself as a bonafide shopper.
>
> While still inside the store, he will go to almost any length, however absurd or self-defeating, to maintain his "customer persona." When his own illusion is turned against him, he has no defense.

## 9.02 THE THIRD OPTION

A thief must do certain specific acts before he can be successfully prosecuted. Store personnel, too, must do certain specific acts before they are guilty of things like false arrest. The **Third Option** solves or obviates problems arising from security stops by providing a worst case scenario of "unfortunate, perhaps, but essentially harmless."

Designed for encounters *inside* the store, a Third Option stop is *ostensibly* a *housekeeping function*. You become a cleaner, watching for misplaced merchandise so you can keep the store tidy. This is a *pretext* for non-libelous encounters. (You'll see the logic shortly.) But before a suspect is approached, follow Sherlock Holmes' example: eliminate the impossible. That sets the stage for the encounter, helps prove "intent," determines the exact location of the stop, and makes the Third Option so *very* effective.

**Eliminate the Impossible.** Ordinarily, each item of merchandise has a single display: shoelaces here, Rapidograph pens there. If a shopper takes shoelaces, wanders around the store, and then returns to the shoelace display and plays with more laces, you can't be sure what happened to the ones he took for a walk. The shoelace display is the *only* place where *irresolvable* confusion may exist if a shopper says, "I put them back."

If he removes them from the display, walks away and never returns to that spot, confusion seldom exists. He, *personally*, could not *possibly* have returned *anything* there. If he later says he put them back, his assertion--obviously--puts a strain on credibility. *Grasp this. It is very important.* [35]

> The primary objective is ordinarily *investigation*; a search for facts and truth which answer the questions, "Was something *really* stolen *and* can I *prove* it?" Secondary objectives include "hardball prevention," recovery of merchandise, or arrest.

If the item is no longer in his hand, and you're certain it's not at the original display, then where is it? Hidden, perhaps? That's getting ahead. *First,* eliminate the possibility that the item--any way at all--was returned to its display. Make that absolutely and utterly impossible. If it's not in its "home," then it is out of place. That makes it unique; a one of a kind item in some unrelated display, and probably easy to spot *quickly*.

"I put it back," is a thief's initial lie (but can also be a poor choice of words by an innocent shopper). When told that his story is impossible, a thief's confidence *visibly* shatters. He has no Plan B. Ideally, the stop is timed so that it was impossible for him to "pass" the item to another person. "Where did you leave it?" is a much better question than "What did the two (or three or five) of you do with it?"

The more people to consider, the more can go wrong. And the more *time* you need. In most situations you have a few seconds--perhaps a minute--for "charm" to carry you. After that, you better know something or get back on the porch.

> **Points to ponder before making contact:**
> First, are you acting to fill some real or imagined "quota?" That is *not* a good idea.
> Second, are you, at the moment, *maybe* a little emotional? (Do you hear yourself saying, "I want to see this guy spit blood.") If so, you may be unconsciously "forcing" a situation, and *that* can lead to beaucoup troubles.
> Third, *could* he have ditched (or passed) the item? Until you recover the merchandise, there's a *doubt*--a possibility, however slim--that this *will not* be a <u>demonstrable</u> case of shoplifting. It is *always* rash to dismiss or brush that possibility aside.

Consider again the four basic areas of knowledge: (1) What he knows that you don't know, (2) What you both know, (3) ) What neither of you know, and (4) What you know that he doesn't know. Let's say you saw a man walk from a display with an item in hand--a wallet--and you're certain it's yours. He meandered down aisles, turned a corner, and reappeared without the wallet. It's gone. The four areas:

### I. What he knows that you don't know:

- The wallet's exact location.
- If he has friends outside.
- If he is armed.
- If he's got a criminal record or is already "wanted."
- If he is a thief.

### II. What you both know:

- He had your wallet.
- He didn't pass it to another person.
- He's in "customer persona"-mode.
- The wallet *wasn't* returned to the original display.
- He *couldn't* have returned the wallet to the original display.

### III. What neither of you know:

- How the other will handle a confrontation.
- Who may happen by, such as family member, policeman, or preacher.

### IV. What he does not know (when you confront him) that you do know:

- That *you know* the wallet is gone.
- If there was a witness.
- If there was a hidden camera.
- That you know it's impossible the wallet was returned to the display.
- Whether or not police have been called.
- Whether or not there's anybody "in the back room" to assist you.
- If you think he's a thief.
- Whether or not you know the wallet's in his pocket.
- That you need his cooperation to arrest him and prove his guilt.
- If you're an off-duty police officer or deputy, or if you can/might/will arrest him.
- If he's already *"surrounded"* or if police are already at the door.

Clearly, much of what he knows (that you don't know) won't help him if he's confronted properly *inside* the store. Also, while you have only a couple of unknowns to worry about, he has *many*. Many unknowns make for much stress. *So* much stress, in fact, that some thieves simply can't handle it. They surrender before even a word is said.

While a thief believes himself undetected by store personnel, the item he concealed is a thrilling, exciting thing. Easy money. Once his plan goes awry, however, the concealed item is like acid eating painfully at its container. Seconds seem like hours. Like a bird circling overhead, he can stay in the air only so long before he *must* come down.

The more he has to struggle to fool others, the more stress he feels. And stress manufactures fear and mistakes.

Once merchandise is concealed, you can approach the thief or position yourself so that he comes to you. Determine which is best for *this* situation. If he thinks you're not interested in him, he won't worry about walking near you. He strolls along ignorantly (arrogantly) thinking, "All I have to do now is walk past Stupid, there..."

Another rule of surveillance holds that if you know where they're going, don't follow them. (Get there first.) But that doesn't necessarily apply if they might ditch merchandise or engage in other serious mischief along the way. At any rate, *you* must appear harmless.

When you get near him, you might see the item in his hand or, for some other reason, might not want to confront him. If so, continue walking. Also, up to the last possible *second,* carry some piece of merchandise to make him think that your interest is in *things,* not people, and least of all in *him.*

He desperately wants to believe that you have no interest in him, and until you convince him otherwise, he'll believe his "customer persona" has fooled you. He believes it because he *wants* to believe it. If he notices that you walking *at* him instead of simply 'in his direction,' he might spook. If he spooks, there's liable to be a stampede.

> Once merchandise disappears, a suspect is usually asked a question that allows for a dishonest response: "Would you mind telling me where you left the (whatever)? I'd like to put it back where it belongs."
>
> His response and demeanor help separate wheat from chaff. Yes, he might lie *because* he's scared, but a lie is a strike against him and might be helpful later.

If you can *quickly* trace his path before the stop, do so. You might find the missing item or evidence such as a discarded wrapper. Your primary focus, however *must* be on the suspect. He may notice you while your attention is divided; or something you're not even aware of might cause him to discard what he stole or otherwise change his plan. It's nice to have a partner.

The Third Option, by definition, is a stop of a *suspicious* person, *not* a guilty one. An *innocent* person's perception of your intent should be that your interest is locating discarded merchandise that *he* removed from its proper display. His perception should be that your goal is "putting things back where they belong."

If he turns out clean, the *worst* ending you want is for him to think (or say or scream) that you are a theft-*implying* pain in the butt who surely deserves the obscene tongue-lashing he's giving you. You can live with that and be good company at dinner. More relevant, you can live with that out of court and without lawyers.

*At worst,* the result of a stop must be "unfortunate, perhaps, but essentially harmless." If the words you spoke are put on paper, or repeated to others and taken literally, they must appear legally harmless. If you are accused of something because of your words, it should be only that you dislike people moving merchandise around and messing up displays; that maybe you're obsessive-compulsive about neat counters.

> Being nice pays surprising dividends. Most situations need only *nice* and a little *insistence.* So begin nice and stay nice until something (like violence) happens that calls for *not*-nice.

If there's *any* doubt whether something was or is still concealed (and that's usually the case), your opening line is *polite.* Even if you're certain he's a thief, you want his help. Opening lines vary and have differing degrees of "push." Ultimately (*always*), your actions depend on the *totality of the circumstances.*

A. "Excuse me. Would you mind telling me where you left that (whatever) so I can get it back where it belongs?"
B. "Excuse me. Would you mind showing me where you left that (whatever) so I can get it back where it belongs?"
C. "Excuse me. Where'd you leave the (whatever)? I want to put it back where it belongs."
D. "Excuse me. If you show me where you left that (whatever), I can put it back for you."

Do not say, "Show me where it *is*." Say, "Where did you *leave* it." All four openers (A-D above) state the item was *"left,"* and they all imply that your interest (your pretext) is *housekeeping*. (At this point, by the way, if a thief is inclined to flee it's usually damn your implications and full speed ahead. Many, though, just give it up. Total surrender.)

> A beautiful misconception among most shoplifters is that if they surrender the stolen merchandise before they leave the store (or before being told that they're under arrest), you must forgive them and cannot prosecute.
>
> Often, if they *think* they're caught, they will just pull concealed items out and give them to you. They arrest themselves.
>
> Take the ones that are in *your* game plan, and don't worry about the others.

If you're not certain exactly what he took, use ambiguous words like "merchandise" or "item." *He* knows what he took, and he assumes that you know too. You may have seen him steal a pen, but maybe that's not everything he has. If you say "merchandise" instead of "pen," he may surprise you and cough up a whole catalog of things. But if you say "sweater" when he actually took "pants," you might confuse him and create a problem. (Rightly, too, if you think about it. He might think you're dishonest and trying to "frame" him for stealing a sweater that he doesn't *even* know anything about.)

His answer to your question "Where is it?" is critical. "I put it back," is practically a confession, but stay cool. Play dumb: "Oh! You mean over there where you got it?" Point to the original display where he picked it up. If he answers "yes" to that, it's all hands on deck, because you *know* for sure and certain that *he didn't*. Still, stay cool.

"I don't mean that one. I mean the one you had when you were standing over there. (Point to the last place where he had the item in view.) How 'bout show me where you left <u>that</u> one." At this point, few thieves can hide their anxiety. Many give it up here.

> If he says he discarded the item, he's verbalizing a legal defense. On-the-scene explanations need to be addressed to protect *you* in case you made a mistake. Also, checking his story might help keep you safe if the situation is a setup. Be very careful!
>
> *Do not* ignore possibilities that weren't covered before the stop. You have a right to conduct a brief investigation, so do it (and use a pretext whenever possible).

If he insists he returned it to the original display, tell him, "That's impossible. Someone's been watching that display and there's no way you left it there. You must have left it somewhere else. You had it over there." Again, point to where he last had it.

If you initially asked him to *tell* where it is, act a bit confused and say, "How 'bout *show* me." Try to sound like the gullible person he wants you to be; the kind who forgives and forgets or can be manipulated. You want him to *think* that if you get the merchandise back, you'll just let him go--or might--so long as he doesn't jerk you around too much.

> In my experience, only one shoplifter figured out that she had arrested herself.
>
> Waiting for police, we sat and chatted--quite pleasantly--when suddenly the *"Ah, ha!"* light flashed in her eyes. Shaking, she blurted, "Oh, my God! You didn't know, did you!?" I just smiled, and a few days later she pled guilty in court.

Remember, *the suspect* doesn't know how much you know (or don't know). If he says, "I'm not sure where I left it," you can say, "I'm sure we'll find it. It's not lost." A thief will assume the worst: "Someone saw me. He wouldn't stop me if he didn't know." Few shoplifters try to bluff beyond this point. They just pull the item out and give up.

In every case, "the totality of the circumstances" and your overall degree of confidence dictate your options and choices. After you approach a thief, he might collect his wits and then act dumb or innocent while trying to figure out what to do. Meanwhile, you might *also* be stalling and trying to figure out what to do. That's OK.

If not yet confident enough to arrest him, you might want him to try to ditch the item. If so, walk with him to "look" for it. Stay very alert, but seem stupid. Give him enough distance so he *thinks* he can pull it out and get rid of it without your noticing. Don't let the "search" drag on more than a minute or two. (Don't give him time to think and plan.) When he pulls the item from wherever he had it, you *must* see it happen. And pounce.

When he pulls it out of a bag or pocket, he demonstrates--proves--that he committed a crime (assuming, of course, it's yours and hasn't been paid for). The law does *not* say you have to actually see him conceal it, only that it must *be* concealed, and not by accident or act of God. Make sure you see it come *out*: that's usually proof enough that he put it *in*.

> November 1st, 1995. In a Harris Teeter grocery, I noticed a man take two packs of Marlboros from the front checkout and walk toward the back of the store. I pointed him out to a nearby clerk and told her she was about to lose some cigarettes. *Maybe* she cared, but rather than call a manager, she just watched the guy walk. I waited, and a minute later he reappeared with no cigarettes, walked past her, and straight out the door.
>
> The cashier explained that even though she saw him walk off with the smokes, she couldn't do anything since she didn't see him hide them. {But she *could*, of course, have asked him where he left them *so she could put them back where they belong*. That would *not* have been libelous, but *probably* would have saved the cigarettes.)

Perhaps he says he set it down. If you saw him stuff a shirt into the crotch of his pants, the odds are very slim that he pulled it out and put it down during a one-second lapse in surveillance. But, since the Prime Directive is "Don't get sued," *check his story.* Follow him like hell wouldn't have it, keep his hands in sight and don't let him have space enough to successfully break for the door.

If he *did* discard merchandise before you stopped him, it will usually be found. Bear in mind, however, that even if you can't find it it's still possible that he didn't steal it. A third party (accomplice, employee, or stranger) might have intervened and the merchandise is just gone. It happens. If, somehow, the shirt is on a counter, smile, tell him *"thank you,"* and immediately take the shirt back to where it belongs. (Then stay far away from him.) Again, it's best to make the stop *immediately* after concealment. Fewer surprises.

If they lead you around, unable to find it, they eventually enter an aisle you know they didn't traverse *or* you finish covering all the territory. Say, "Stop. This has gone far enough." A thief hears that differently from someone who truly forgot where he left something. A thief hears, "Stop. Cooperate now or we put you *under* the jail." For nearly all suspects, this marks the spot where they capitulate and produce the goods. If they *don't*, there's a good chance they're not guilty. *Remember that!*

If he says, "What if I have it? What will happen?" he's afraid. An apt response is, "Please don't jerk me around." A real die-hard may need something like, "Look. You can give it to us now or give it to a uniform." (Then shrug and *wait*. See what he does.)

"If I give it back, can I go?" You do *not* (ordinarily) say you will let them go, but it *could* be a good idea. (View the totality of the circumstances.) A good response is, "I don't have a problem with that, but first you need to apologize to the manager. He needs to see your face and if you come back in here, he'll arrest you for trespass." You're not lying. He *will* go after he apologizes, but it'll be with the police. This tactic gives you a chance to get help, obtain a confession for witnesses, *and* avert violence until police arrive.

Some say, "Do you want to search me?" Don't. Not even a frisk (pat-down). Search comes *after* arrest, *not* before. If you don't have enough of a case to arrest, don't search. Instead, say, "No. There's no point. I just want the merchandise back where it belongs."

The immediate goal is to get evidence. Do that, and the Prime Directive *will* be upheld. Get the evidence first, *then* decide what to do with your thief. [36]

After getting the evidence--and as soon as you arrange a decent witness--ask a quick question: "Why'd you put it in your bag?" *Any* reason uttered is a confession that he intentionally concealed it, i.e., an element of shoplifting. If he confesses his intent to steal (and some do), so much the better. Even if he doesn't answer, the Prime Directive is covered anyway because you recovered unpaid-for, concealed merchandise.

Throughout all this, a thief is not *called* a thief, nor is the word "steal" used. These words can cause trouble, and what's the point?

> One consequence of stopping shoplifters inside the store ASAP is *smaller dollar-value arrests*. A thief is nabbed before his heist is complete; therefore, he has less merchandise than if he had finished and left. Do not allow small dollar totals to dissuade prosecution. If he'll steal an egg, he'll steal a chicken. *Do him.*

Many shoplifters enjoy displaying their cleverness and flaunting authority. You can often use that to your advantage. If one claims innocence because he *only* concealed an item but did not take it out of the store, he's not only wrong, but he's also insinuating false arrest. Do *not* educate the fool. Instead, humor him.

Thieves tell half-truths and whole lies, whatever seems to fly. If you tell him that concealing the item made him guilty whether he left the store or not, he'll begin lying about that, too. Your job is getting confessions for witnesses, police, and court, *not* helping thieves fabricate credible stories. Don't be a chump.

Let him impress others--and the more the better--with his legal savoir-faire. "Oh, that's right! You didn't go outside, did you? Maybe we'll have to reconsider this. For now, though, I need you to come to the office." If possible, record these conversations *without* the subjects being aware of it. Taped confessions are insurance.

Each time he admits to concealing merchandise, he admits to an element of shoplifting. *Encourage him* to repeat his clever defense to police. As soon as they arrive, tell them--very politely--that Mr. Waller put the item in his bag without paying for it, *but* he did *not* take it out of the store. "Isn't that right?" If he agrees, he confessed to police.

Police sometimes cannot ask questions unless they "read 'em their rights" (Miranda warning), but the officer--an excellent witness--will be happy to listen and testify if *you* get the thief to confess. (See "Confessions" and "Confessions Made Easy," pgs. 114-119.)

Remember, if you're not 100% certain of theft, the stop begins as "housekeeping" (and that's usually a good way to begin even if you *are* sure). Since most thieves *assume* that you know what they stole and can already prove it, trust the Third Option technique to net the majority. An occasional sly or really stupid one wiggles off the hook, but *don't press it*. Do not get pulled out of your game plan.

## 9.03 Whoops! (Exiting a bad stop)

I stopped two girls (both about fourteen) and asked them about some cosmetics that had vanished. (I wanted to put the items back where they belonged.) The girls led me to a counter where they had hidden the merchandise among some clothes.

Had they started to steal them and lost their nerve? I don't know, but I told them that they had no right to go in a store, take merchandise from its display, and hide it. "You need to shop somewhere else. Maybe you can come back tomorrow."

In another case, two girls (again, about 14) were unable to find cosmetics where they claimed to have discarded them. Considering their very real tears, near panic, and willingness to be searched, I felt that something screwy had happened. Was I being set up? If so, how and by whom? Were they telling the truth? Whatever happened, it was clearly outside my game plan. That being the case, I wasn't about to search anything, even though they offered to have purses and pockets checked.

I told them I didn't think they had anything, but that they did take something from where it was supposed to be and now it was lost. "If I walked in your house and played with something, and when you asked for it, all I could tell you was, 'I had it and it disappeared.' What would *you* do? I don't know what's going on, but I'd appreciate it if you wouldn't move anything else while you're in the store *unless* you want to buy it."

> **"No sense have they of ills to come, nor cares beyond today." – T. Gray**
>
> A 13-year-old swore he was as pure as the driven snow, did "real good" in school, and tearfully described how an arrest would break his poor, disabled mother's heart. *Real* tears and lots of 'em. Not that I believed a word he said, of course, but I *love* that particular art form and it was a truly inspired performance.
>
> As behooves an appreciative audience, I encouraged him with a nod here and there, and the occasional *"Is-that-so?"* (Since Loss Prevention provides the opportunity for these young actors to perform, I consider myself a sort of Patron of the Arts.)
>
> Looking forward to another ten minutes of theater, which, I figured, was about how long it would take the police to arrive, I casually picked up the phone during one of his more lengthy sobs and dialed the (seven-digit) number for the local police department. Sitting across the desk all teary-eyed and looking at the telephone upside down as I dialed, he suddenly jumped up and shouted, "Hey man! Why you callin' the PO-leese?!"

What if the person discarded the item before you stopped him? What if he's actually *honest*? What if you're wrong? Don't panic. Remember what you initially said: "where you left it so I can put it back where it belongs." If the item is found, pick it up, *be pleasant* and thank the person for saving you the trouble of looking for it. Sound and appear appreciative of the person's help.

Act as though the whole thing is a casual, perfectly innocent, common activity. Then go put it where it belongs. Ideally he sees you do that. (Don't look back.) Then, if something else is handy, put that away, too. (Didn't you already have something in your hands?) After that, stay away from the person and, eventually, do a report.

If you're all smiles and low-key and the encounter is brief, even a bad stop is usually come and gone before a suspect can organize a show for bystanders. If you leave before he unwinds, no one's the wiser a stop ever occurred. Except the suspect, of course, and once you clear the vicinity, his best chance for mischief is gone. (If he becomes loud while you're still there and insists on babbling, invite him to follow you to a nearby place where business is less disturbed; only a few feet away will probably do. Another benefit of walking is it has a way of quieting people. Even then, keep it short.)

A plain-clothes LP officer approached a man after some jewelry seemed to disappear. *"Excuse me,"* he said. "Weren't you carrying some merchandise over there just a minute ago?" The man responded that he didn't know "a damn thing about it," and followed with, "Do you think I stuck it in my pocket? You think I stole something?"

It struck the officer that this man had "Wilson" on the front of his black athletic jacket, whereas the man with jewelry had "Bulls." Both men wore jeans; both were about the same height and age with the same hair color. Close, but it wasn't the right guy. *This* officer, though, knew how to back-pedal.

Hiding immense anxiety, he calmly said, "I don't think a TV would fit in your pocket. Are you the man who wanted help with a television?"

*BAM!* Deep into his opponent's back court, the shot was simply unreturnable. Confused and visibly rattled, the man muttered something that sounded like "no." The officer then said, "Excuse me," and quickly walked away.

Of course, there *was* no man with a TV.

A necklace is jewelry, something from that aisle, merchandise, an item, etc. When that officer approached the suspect, he said "merchandise" in lieu of "jewelry." His choice of words allowed him to peacefully cover an honest mistake *in a non-libelous manner*. Weird things happen, so hedge your bets and never stray from your game plan.

The pretexts for those three "bad stops' were "housekeeping" and customer service. Each stop was taken as far as it could *reasonably* go and then *ended*. No one was accused of stealing (or "having" anything), and it's good they weren't. (Also, depending on the situation, it might help to diplomatically remind the person--while you're disengaging--that no one said he did anything *wrong*; that your interest is simply keeping things where they belong, thank you, and sorry for their inconvenience.)

There is no "One Way," but if things aren't going your way or begin to look too odd, *end it quickly*. Don't be Brer Rabbit with a Tar Baby.

## 9.04 In-Store Codes

A code system is a valuable tool that allows police and others to communicate discretely among themselves. For example: "We have a 10-96," alerts others to the presence of a mental patient who may require special handling or additional back-up. Employees, too, need means to communicate covertly. For example:

"Phone call for Beth." (Trouble at the back door.)
"Phone call for Frank." (Same, but at the front door.)
"Call Mary and remind her to come in." (Call the police and ask them to come.)
"Jane, line one." (Trouble in area #1.)

> After stuffing small appliances into plastic shopping bags, a shoplifter walked toward the rear exit of a store. Over the P.A. came, "Code Blue to the back door." The thief-- just smart enough--turned and raced to the front door. He escaped (but without his loot).
> *"Phone call for Beth"* may not have spooked him. "Code Blue" is a bit much.

Codes can be strung together, but should not be transparent. If a P.A. is used *and your goal is to keep a thief ignorant,* avoid words like "security," "zone," and "code."

Shoplifters listen to P.A. systems, so a thief in cosmetics should not hear the word "cosmetics" in *any* context. Keep a thief unaware he's a target. "We have a spill in 201, please," won't panic a thief. Be creative. Initiate a system that works with your particular lay-out and personalities. But remember: intelligence and common sense levels vary.

Codes also serve a psychological purpose by "scaring" thieves who fear "hidden messages." (You're not paranoid, though, if they're really after you.) To unnerve someone, use a fairly overt message. Otherwise, whatever is said must seem unrelated to the actual problem. Soft, fuzzy words are good, and "please" is a nice touch. "Hard-color" words like red and blue are associated with danger and police. Even by children.

When speaking person-to-person or on a phone, "Please get me some aspirin" can mean "I need some help" or "Call the police." A "bad headache" can mean an urgent need or *immediate* help. Keep codes simple, few in number, and discreetly posted, i.e., *not* where just anyone can read them.

## 9.05 Necessary Roughness

Forget Ghandi. Your store's not India and that gang tearing your display apart sure ain't a political exercise in non-violence. In this business, passive resistance doesn't always cut it. Physical force can be necessary and justifiable whether it's in self-defense or for holding someone until police arrive. Sometimes you *can't* walk away, sometimes you *won't*. Either way, the law permits *reasonable force* to attain legal ends.

Technically, force comes in two flavors: physical and psychological. "Reasonable physical force" is, short of deadly force, that force necessary to defend yourself, effect an arrest, and prevent the escape of an offender.

To thieves, shoplifting is a game--maybe even a job--but fighting is something else. Fighting *takes time* and brings a hotter pursuit by more people. That increases the chance of being caught, and they do *not* want to be charged with or convicted of a violent crime. When things run amuck, they want *fast* distance between themselves and the scene.

Most thieves know that to weasel clear of consequences from a shoplifting arrest all they have to do is convince fools that, yes, it *looks* bad, but, truly, they were just tripped up by circumstances (just a mental lapse; we all have 'em, you know); or maybe you'll believe that they're sad victims of a Big Mistake. *But*, if there's an assault and injury, a manhunt, and he was dragged back in chains...well, explain *that* to the boss.

> In some places, thieves who use physical force during shoplifting are charged with *"Strong-arm Robbery"* rather than *"Shoplifting."* It flies. If your local law enforcement personnel cooperate in doing this, it's an excellent option. Being a new, innovative approach, though, there are still more skeptics than practitioners.

As a rule, you can use more force than the thief uses. If he tries to walk away, ordering him to stop and taking hold of an arm or sleeve is all right. It would *not* be all right, at that point, to hit him on the chin. Taking his arm or sleeve "invades his personal space" and issues a clear warning. (Warning to *you*: It can also precipitate a fight.)

If you have a sound case and he tries to walk away, you might get in front of him and talk *without* making physical contact. If *he* makes contact by pushing you, grab his arm, or snatch him up. If he tries to squirm or wrestle free, pin him. If he tries to hit you, slam him against a wall, drop him to the floor, or jack his arm up behind his back.

Consider this: "I went to talk to him about cussing (or making a mess, or being real loud and disturbing our harmony, or *whatever* legal pretext you have). He pushed me (kicked me, hit me with his foot, etc.). At that point, I told him to wait for the police and he hit me again. I subdued him and held him for the police. Stolen merchandise was found in his pockets."

The following Case of the Slippery Man illustrates (again) how witnesses confuse one thing for another. This can be good, and it can be bad.

Before arriving at the mall, a shoplifter actually *greased* himself in anticipation of trouble. While trying to subdue him I latched on to him twice, but he shed his shirt and the grease allowed him to slip away each time. Foot chases aren't my long suit, and he should have escaped. Looking back at me as he ran, however, he failed to see a stout, brass Chick Filet sign directly in his path.

Witnesses later agreed that the explosion of the thief into the sign within the confines of the mall corridor sounded like a gunshot. And *that* got the attention of a former semi-professional football player. Hearing my screaming and seeing the chase, he joined in. Long before I got there, Lickity-Split tied up with my thief in the parking lot, but--like me--couldn't hold him because of the grease. The thief was slipping away when I arrived on rubber legs.

As I got within reach, the thief swung an elbow at my face. I was able to duck, but because my legs wouldn't do right, I fell towards him and grabbed at his legs to keep from smashing onto the concrete. Then, tangled, everyone went down. Luckily, he landed on the bottom and grease became moot.

Witnesses present exclaimed my "tackle" deserved a spot on Monday Night Football. When I tried telling the truth, they thought I was being modest. Rule: Excited witnesses frequently see what they like and often prefer that you don't rain facts on their parade.

A really gnarled grip on someone's shirt sleeve--instead of holding an arm--deters running and is often the best safeguard against a sudden jerk. It's a low level way of letting them know you mean business. If they resist and the shirt's torn or ruined, well...I've ripped many a thief's shirt--even Tommy and Ralph Lauren--but I never had to reimburse one. If they don't resist, things don't get torn. Besides, they probably stole it anyway.

Pushing or letting a fist fly are offensive moves, i.e., *attacks*. If someone attacks, use whatever force is necessary to make him quit and submit. (And perhaps a bit more since fighting is not an exact science.) If he tries to put a beating on you, stop him cold.

All that aside, the norm is peaceful surrender. Sprains, bruises, a few cuts and stitches aside, in dozens of scuffles and fights with shoplifters, I've neither suffered nor inflicted any serious injury. Use force if necessary, but not "unreasonable" force.

At any rate, when talking fails, you *must* use force or cut bait. There's no doubt that a bit of brute force can be worth a thousand well-chosen words--the thin red line, and so on-- but from cradle to hearse, Isaac Asimov was right: "Violence is the last resort of the incompetent." (Then again, if you're like most people, some days find you a little, oh, *less competent* than usual. On those days, I revert to Captain Thrasher's Throat Snatch Primer and his inspiring words: "Where the head goes, the body follows.")

## 9.06 Offensive Tactics

**The Numbers Racket.** Numbers impress shoplifters and give you a psychological edge. Since it also helps keep thieves peaceful, get help whenever you can. At times, it's best for helper(s) to be visible, but not closer than five or ten feet away. Other situations call for close-in support.

My helpers are normally no help in a brawl and, since I don't want the thief to know that, I stay in front of the suspect with my helper behind him. If the thief tries turning to face my helper, we shift to maintain our relative positions. I bring the suspect's attention immediately back to me with a sharper voice than I was using before he moved: "I'm talking to you. Pay attention to what I'm saying." I may move a bit closer.

If I have stout help, we can wedge a thief in tightly if it appears he might try fight or flight (and, of course, if we're ready to get hurt). I want a for-sure thief to feel that his only reasonable course of action is *what* I say, *how* I say, and *right* away. (If I *don't* want to dance with him, I make certain he has an obvious, open escape route that *will not* require smashing into employees.)

> Thieving Alethia considers it extremely important to know which employees are "*dangerous*" (and must be avoided) and which are "*stupid.*"
>
> "Stupid" employees (to her) aren't *literally* stupid, but their work habits make stealing easy and risk-free. "Stupid" employees ignore thieves whereas "dangerous" employees pay attention to people which makes stealing around them a risky business.
>
> How does she know which is which? "You check it out before you steal. You just watch and see. Then you go in (steal) when the stupid ones are there."

**The size of the dog.** I'm 5'10" (well, maybe 9½) and this morning weighed 150 pounds. Neither big nor bad, I routinely arrest larger men. Annette Allen is intelligent, unusually versatile, has a well-developed eye for thieves, and stands just 5'3" tall. While working for a national retail chain she made quite a few arrests, including an 18-year-old gang-banger standing 6'2". Unquestionably, she was out-gunned *physically* (and no doubt concerned about that), but she plunged madly ahead and sank him with *mental torpedoes*.

Annette and I help illustrate that confrontations, for the most part, are "mind games" with results not necessarily dictated by brawn. As Winthrop University's philosophical Christopher Hodgdon dryly observed, *most shoplifters swim in the shallow end of the gene pool*. Those we oppose are often fast, big, or strong, but, thankfully, *not* very smart. When faced with intelligence, they often react with astonishing stupidity.

Especially if I think a fight that I might lose hangs in the balance, I often give the thief every reason to think I'll let him just walk away after a bit of conversation. This drops his adrenaline level considerably, and if it jumps again, it won't go as high.

Then, while chatting, I ask if he's got ID; then I ask to see it. I read it and then put it in my pocket or pass it to someone else. This has a *tremendous* psychological effect on everyone. Now, even if running might help, he has to mug me (first) to get his ID back. And even then, I still know his name. In short, he's mine now *or* later. His best chance to avoid arrest, of course, was to run like hell in the first place. (He'll brood about that later.)

**Lions, and tigers and bears...oh, my!** Even imaginary numbers can intimidate thieves. More than once--a lot of times, in fact--I've gestured or talked to an empty aisle that was out of a thief's sight, behind him or not accessible to him. ("Hey! I've got him. Wait a minute.") If he turns and looks...well, my guy just moved...so what?

Do they fall for stuff like that? Like in the movies! They're confused. After all, they didn't see *me*. They think, "This guy's not scared. Is it because of that guy he was talking to?" Is the Invisible Man a cop or nightclub bouncer? And *what* is *this* guy?

I've temporarily planted doubt and *fear* in his mind. He can do what the perplexing guy in front of him wants *or* he can take a chance with Door Number Two. It's pure sales: play his emotions, tell him what you want, and ask for the order.

I might tell the Invisible Man to call the police or ask him if that cop is still out front. Sometimes I toss an instruction at him or actually converse: "No. Just stay there a minute. Let me see what he wants to do." The thief assumes the Invisible Man said something, and he's frustrated that he didn't hear it. He knows he's having a bad day, and what *did* I mean by "let me see what he wants to do"? He has no plan, he can't process all the incoming information, and he feels very *not* in control. *I* take control

I may say, "Are you going to give me my watch (or whatever) then get out of here, or what?" Then again, I may tell the Invisible Man to get ready, and tell the thief, "I'm tired of playing around. Face the wall and put your hands behind you. You're under arrest." What I actually *do* depends on the totality of the circumstances.

So much *always* depends on how your opposite number (the thief) is responding. When asked if Lee was responsible for the Confederate loss at Gettysburg, even General Pickett once replied, "I always thought the Yankees had something to do with it." You've got to develop a feel for these things, be a pretty fair actor, and be *real* careful.

**The Sting.** My father was fond of the adage, "Old age and treachery will overcome youth and skill." That's usually true. And what do shoplifting, loss prevention, and advertising all have in common? *Perception is more important than reality*. So *think*.

I followed a 6' 2" thief through a store while trying to figure out what to do. He seemed sure to fight (and probably win) if I stopped him, so I wanted a better plan than just lose my stuff, and get beat up. Eventually, I spotted a totally uninvolved shopper who, by all appearances, could take my thief apart, piece by painful piece. An Arnold Schwarzenegger look-alike: he was huge, dressed in weight lifter's clothes--big leather belt and all--and his cut-off shirt was emblazoned with the name of a popular gym.

"My God," I thought, "Manna from heaven!" He was a perfect 'ringer,' and perfectly positioned between my shoplifter and the door. Time for a slam-dunk, but *first* I needed my shoplifter to glance at my ringer just long enough to be sufficiently impressed.

I stepped close alongside my thief and half-shouted to the weight-lifter, "I wanna do it myself!" This made no sense to either of them, of course, but my thief did look at Arnold and the puzzlement on Arny's face passed easily for a scowl. Gotta move fast...

Jumping directly in my thief's path and right in his face, I said (quietly, so Conan couldn't hear), "My partner and I'd like you to know you're under arrest for shoplifting. Don't <u>even</u> say a word, just turn around and put your hands behind your back. Do it <u>now</u>." As I said *"now,"* I grabbed him, roughly faced him away from the ringer, handcuffed him as fast as my shaking hands could do it, and dragged him in the direction of the office.

Did he resist? *What?!* And tangle with The Terminator? No way. In fact, the word "docile" comes to mind. Did he learn he'd been suckered? Of course not; I want him to fear us. Besides, why add insult to injury? And what'd Arny think of it all? I have *no* idea.

### If you can't dazzle 'em with brilliance, baffle 'em with bull.

Domestic disputes are dangerous *at best*, and my police partner and I once arrived at one where it was immediately apparent that the husband had to go to jail. Unfortunately, he was big, bad, and drunk, and tempers in the house were already hotter than grandma's waffle iron. His antagonism and blunt refusals to cooperate--interspersed, as they were, with unpleasant promises--had us fondling our night-sticks. To take him, we'd probably have to hurt him, and--being true Children of the 60's--we weren't keen on that.

Prior to going medieval, we decided to give Peace a chance.

We agreed with him that she probably did deserve a beating. He, in turn, agreed with us that he couldn't do it proper with cops in the house. We made it clear to him that "our boss said we can't leave without him," that there would be no cops in the house when he got back, *but he had to come with us before he could get back. SO*...the sooner he got in the squad car, the sooner he could beat his wife. With a logical program laid out neat enough for his drunken mind, he walked peaceably to the car. Maybe all he needed was a face-saving way out, I don't know, but he was fine after he sobered up.

The admittedly obscure point to *this* story is that even if you have the *capacity* to "win," violence comes *only* after imagination is squeezed dry. Also, you can't argue with a fool or drunk, but you *can* be agreeable and helpful. Pretexts help gain control. Our *pretext* for taking him *was to help him do what he said he wanted to do*. And it worked. If you think a man will fight if arrested, try "I can't let you go till you apologize to the manager. He's over there." *Imply* no arrest. Get his adrenaline level down, *then* do him.

I often call uniformed security or police without the arrestee knowing it. Since I want order, not chaos, I use finesse. If he goes crazy, I want it to be *after* location and numbers are on my side. (It pays to have an excellent rapport with area law enforcement, security, and all miscellaneous able-bodies.)

### "Whatcha gonna do when they come for you?"

In May of '93 I approached a thief in a crowded store and the instant he thought I was a problem, his right hand went behind his back. He hadn't said a word and there was no indication of a weapon, but I jumped on him anyway, driving him backwards into a counter, and there followed quite a brawl.

Quick calls based on "hunches" or subconscious calculations are risky. Was I too hasty? Was it too great an assumption that he intended me harm? What was in his head and heart? And, oh, what *will* the witnesses say?

While we were fighting, I kept shouting he was under arrest and, fortunately, an off-duty police officer happened to hear me. My thief was soon handcuffed, and in his right, back pocket was a lock-knife, blade out. *But did he actually intend to stab me?*

The local magistrate was unimpressed by William's knife, the fight, the fact he gave police a false name, and his long criminal record. William's bond was low, and a few days later, he carried his 29 year-old, pony-tailed self to another department store.

Again, he put something in his pocket and was approached by a security officer.

Before a word was spoken, William whipped out a knife and stabbed him.

I can't tell you when to jump. I don't even know how *I* know. But I've already got more scars than Henry Taylor's dog, so if I'm worried about someone hurting me, I'd rather get sued for too fast than stabbed for too slow. It's a personal preference.

## 9.07 Stops and Detention

**Helpful Bystanders.** Bystanders sometimes help, but when they're verbal, it seems they sympathize with thieves. If you want a witness or you're unsure if you can physically "handle" a thief without help (as he wonders if he can handle you), you can certainly ask someone to lend a hand. *But*, understand you probably won't get much help, *and* you may be liable for adverse consequences. If you do ask, speak *quietly* (so the thief can't hear) and explain that you don't want anyone hurt, you just want a good witness.

If a bystander is injured after he agrees to help, the medical bill may fall on *your* shoulders. (Can you afford it?) Or he may be some kung-fu hot-shot and create a major legal problem by drop-kicking the thief. Excited people do unpredictable things which can create beaucoup additional problems.

Police are usually the best help of all, and the sooner you call, the sooner they arrive. Therefore, call them ASAP if a showdown appears imminent.

**Consequences of Force.** One common result of physical force is "sudden-onset injury:" trauma. If a thief is injured in even a minor way, his whining--if nothing else--will likely drive you crazy. If *truly* injured, that becomes a greater issue, legally, than his shoplifting. "The system" gets distracted, and it's musical chairs for the medical bills.

Fights are great sport in a ring, but bad business in a store. Customers come to shop in peace, and even loud arguments have negative effects. To avoid fouling my own nest, I've called police, followed a shoplifter and had him arrested blocks away inside a classy Omni Hotel. (What can I say? That's where he happened to be when the troops arrived.) On another occasion, I followed one into a mall restroom and arrested him as he exited a stall, trying to button his pants.

Try to avoid violence. Even under the best circumstances, it's a tool of inescapable or last resort. And once begun, it can escalate beyond anyone's intent or expectation.

**Judge Colt and his Jury of Six.** If you fire a gun at a man 100 yards away, the immediate result of that irreversible action is realized about a half second later. Weighing 105 pounds, Luchenbach II was my partner for three years. In about two seconds, that German shepherd could latch hold of a man, throw him to the ground and splinter his wrist under more than 500 pounds of pressure per square inch. A critical difference between shooting "Luke" at a bad guy or firing off a .357 hollow-point was I could *stop* Luke after I launched him. Usually. [37]

Force. You can use whatever is *necessary*--including deadly--to defend your life or that of another from an (illegal) attack. But don't go crazy. Someone ten feet away with a knife is *not* an immediate threat. Shooting him would put you on shaky legal ground because he can't hurt you (*unless* he tries to throw it).

*However*, if he approaches with a knife and another step or two will bring him close enough to cut you all three ways, it's clearly bedtime for Burney. *Shoot* the son-of-a-bitch! If it takes a combined team of world-class surgeons and Swiss watchmakers to put him back together, you'll be guilty *only* of poor marksmanship. (According to Capt. Jerry Wolfe of the MPD, you can be badly cut three ways: long, deep, and forever.) [38]

It's a rare situation, though, where things take that sort of turn. In over 15 years, I've been stabbed--by shoplifters--only once (that I recall off-hand) and only once did a thief pull a gun. (Oddly, both in 1993.) Philosophies and laws vary from court to court, so check with police and solicitors before you go shooting people. Even obnoxious people.

> **Grasp this:** When a thief pulls a weapon like a knife or gun, your ideal weapons are a good pair of legs and a fast start.

## 9.08 Weapons and Accessories

**Guns** God made men, Sam Colt made 'em equal. I'm not adverse to keeping a gun in the store as long as it is carefully hidden, knowledge of its existence controlled, and anyone who may use it is trained and even-keeled. However, *carrying* a concealed gun has a psychological effect that makes people forget what's really worth killing or dying for; and what's *not*. There's infinite danger here, and carrying a concealed gun probably won't deter anything, anyway. In 16 years, I've never needed one (in a store).

**Nightsticks and blackjacks.** Tools for self defense. Keep one concealed and handy near a door. Remember, though, if you *hold* it there's a possibility someone will take it from you and break *your* head. Even a stick is a weapon, and any weapon is serious business. If you hit at all, don't hit softly (if they're worth hitting, they're worth hitting hard), and never *threaten* to hit anyone. If you're holding it, your threat's implicit.

Note: If you hit someone with a stick or a club, don't aim above the shoulders unless you are truly desperate. The head is a "kill-zone." Besides, a hearty whack to a shin, wrist, or hand--with a follow-up in the mail--usually does the trick. (See Glossary: *"Location"*)

**Chemical Mace.** Great stuff--especially if you give 'em a bath--but along with the miscreant, even employees and loyal customers run out the door. Aim carefully: the first time I ever used mace, I sprayed Keith Wiggins, another officer, by mistake. (We were both rookies.) If you're determined to have a weapon, mace is probably the best choice. Another lesson I learned a couple years after spraying Keith is to *read the label*. Mace does *not* always work. If it ever fails--like mine did--your next meal could be served up--like mine was--in a hospital recovery room after the ether wears off.

**Pen and Pocket Notepad.** They are powerful weapons (and can be literally so). Keep them with you at all times. If it's not on paper, it didn't happen, and even if it did, you'll probably soon forget. Write physical descriptions, license plate numbers, dates, times and incident types. (Some things require additional, formal reports.) It's one thing to go to a manager and say, "Susie is <u>always</u> out of her zone" or "Herman has <u>too many</u> personal visitors;" it's another thing to rattle off dates and times. I keep a 3.5 x 6, 100-page notebook in my pocket and fill one about every three or four weeks. Sample entries:

> 12/16    6:15 Martha (fired for theft in Sept) in store talking to Susie x 10 min.
> 7:35 Herman personal visitor 7:05-7:35. Ignoring customers.
> 8:35 4 leather coats x $175 not locked down. Were locked at 7:15. All are size XL. Emp=Susie. (Ding! Ding!)

Jot down who always seems to ring up the same people (and vice versa), who was there and who wasn't when ten dresses flew out the door; what hint was dropped about this or that and by whom. Sooner or later, little tid-bits can help sort out major problems.

While on the subject of pen and paper, I should mention that written statements are extremely useful. When thefts occur, immediately list everyone who was there, should have been, might have been, or who might otherwise have relevant information. Obtain written statements. In some cases you just interview them and they initial your notes. Then the work begins. (Every statement is a potential future handwriting sample; gather lots.)

Compare known facts to statements and see if statements are mutually supportive (descriptions, times, people involved, etc). It may be necessary to go back and re-interview people, but more on that later. (Also, try to find and study info on "statement analysis.")

**Handcuffs.** A "must-have" item for well-heeled security. Handcuffs are a real boon to your safety and that of the person detained. Whether you cuff hands in front or police-style behind their back, serious resistance and attempts to flee normally abate once the bracelets are on.

But only a moron would use them in every situation. I can't think of *any* reason to handcuff an 8- or 80-year-old, but I usually handcuff anyone over fourteen or so who resists, is verbally abusive, or who eyes the door and appears to make mental calculations involving relative speeds and distances. If I even *think* "foot-foot-save-the-body" is on their minds, handcuffs go on their wrists. I don't like fighting, but I positively *hate* foot chases.

Handcuffs can be applied too tightly or too loosely, and some prisoners intentionally tighten them to lure you within spitting or kicking range or to get silly you to take them off. Get a pair with a "double-lock" (they won't tighten after being put on), then buy as many keys as you need, but **never** use handcuffs without a key.

Check prisoners and key-rings for handcuff keys; they're common. Also, even if he's right in front of you, check cuffs every ten minutes or so. Don't get complacent. If he squirms in the chair, be ready for a trick. (If a prisoner is "double-jointed,", he can slip his hands out easily.) Have him stand up and turn around before you get too close to him. Finally, if you switch handcuffs, put the second pair on *before* the first pair comes off.

**Identification.** Some companies provide their store security with only an identification card. Frankly, this is somewhat under-whelming. A badge (*a police-shaped shield*) in a small black ID wallet with an ID card *does* get attention. In the criminal mind it creates confusion, hesitation, and fear.

Learn regulations concerning a badge *before* you flash it. Likewise, know which words had better not cross your lips. *Serious* laws govern impersonation of police, and the line is mighty thin between acceptable and unacceptable, legal and illegal. Flashing a badge or spouting psychobabble can get you arrested, sued, or both.

Aside from a badge and ID card, all loss prevention managers and LP officers--all professionals of *any* kind--should carry (and distribute) sharp business cards.

**Electric Stun-guns.** These are very popular in some circles, especially Communist mental hospitals and Banana Republics. My personal experience is limited to using them on unruly bulls at my rancho. There, I always had one of two results: the bull started doing right or it was Katie-bar-the-door.

**The Fat Lady.** The old opera reference that "the show ain't over till the fat lady sings" has never been truer--or easier--than today. Every business owner or manager and certainly anyone in loss prevention or law enforcement (just about *everyone*, in fact) should carry a pocket mini (micro) cassette recorder. It's practically essential for political and economic survival in some environments, and it's good insurance in any. Most micro-recorders now measure about 2½ by 5-inches, with no cord or external microphone needed: just drop it in a pants pocket and go. (And *always* keep fresh batteries handy.)

What types of things might you want to record? Conversations with suspects and thieves, with their families, with personal or business adversaries, and with disgruntled employees; investigative interviews or exit interviews. Basically, conversations that might significantly damage or inconvenience you if words are forgotten, twisted, taken out of context, or flatly denied. (And don't forget to record what people say at accident scenes. "Slip-and-fall guys" and others looking to con you out of money often change details in their stories from one telling to the next. The Fat Lady *never* forgets a detail.)

"I *never* said... I don't recall saying...You should have said something at the time..."

We all encounter these things, and the damage ranges from a little inconvenience to thousands of dollars. It's amazing who lies (and about what) for even trivial reasons if they think you have no witness or proof. Well, the Fat Lady--as a witness--is *merciless* with liars and--unless her battery was dead--she never forgets a word.

Recorded conversations are 'trump cards,' played or not depending on short and long term interests. But consider and remember: if it's learned that you covertly record 'private conversations' without the knowledge and approval of those involved, it can (and probably will) put a *serious* strain on more relationships than just the one on tape.

As with other things, before you begin building a tape library, check the civil *and* criminal laws with a state-level solicitor *and* with a *couple* of experienced law enforcement people. (*Security tools*: Also, see Mirrors, pg. 89, Cameras, pg. 90, and Appendix 13.)

### 9.09 Retail Gangs & Cliques: *The wave of the future*

Loosely organized, non-traditional gangs and "cliques" (generally, an opportunistic group of criminal friends and their relatives) pose a truly insidious security threat. While not confined to the retail industry, gangs and cliques are ideally suited to it.

Gang (or clique) members seek employment and go through the hiring and training process with selected businesses (commonly, large retailers). Once "on the inside," the dichotomy is often to be honest to a fault, work hard and earn the respect and trust of management and loss prevention. (Or just steal like hell and quit when they feel heat.)

Their goals--initially--are (1) gather knowledge of policies, procedures, personnel, and security, (2) infiltrate and assume low level supervisory roles and functions, and (3) help more members of their clique gain employment. (God help you if they infiltrate LP.) Once entrenched, the store becomes the gang's de facto bank ("cash cow"). Through it, they:

- launder and process stolen, fraudulent and counterfeit checks, credit, and gift cards,
- obtain credit numbers, info, and actual credit cards from transactions and customer credit applications (used later by gangs in the same store, and other stores and cities),
- obtain cash by laundering stolen or worthless (garage sale) merchandise through fraudulent refunds and exchanges (or just scan loose price tags they keep handy), and
- feed cash into their own credit card accounts (often through false charge-credits).

In addition to banking activities, several gang members employed in a single store can easily arrange massive conventional theft (shoplifting, "sliding," under-rings, etc.).

**Prevention begins with the hiring process.** In addition to the "standard" information on job applications, obtain the following information *before* a new-hire begins work: (1) Complete name and all names (and maiden name) for the past 15 years; (2) *all* home addresses for the past 7 years; (3) jobs and complete job addresses and phone numbers for the past 7 years; (4) any schools (or "other") and complete addresses and phones during the past 7 years; (5) <u>three</u> "emergency" names, addresses and phone numbers; (6) photocopies of DL or state ID and SS card. (Be wary of and verify any ID issued within the past 6 months.) Verify *everything*. If the applicant "can't" produce it, don't hire him.

Next, the "release" on the application: Your goal is the legal authority to check a person out from A to Z by gathering whatever information is reasonable and deemed necessary for purposes of bonding, insurance coverage, liability, hiring, training, staffing, and promoting. If you use a "generic release," have a qualified attorney draw up a new one. The release (which is signed and dated by applicants) will ideally include, all school records, local, county, state, and federal motor vehicle, civil and criminal records; and hospital, clinic, and Workers Compensation records. That about covers it.

**Too much trouble?** One clique in a Florida store made off with $19,000 of merchandise in *14 days*. And they were just high school kids. A clique in a South Carolina store stole over $1,000 in cash and merchandise every day. <u>That</u> is trouble.

**"Well done is better than well said."** -- B. Franklin

## StealMeBlind

# Chapter 10

# REPORTS AND PROCESSING

**Physical Location.** After an arrest, a high priority is getting your thief quickly and safely to a *secure* location for interviews and processing. Some degree of danger--perhaps a lot--still exists.

The prisoner is *your responsibility.* You *don't* want customers or employees gawking like he's Barnam's Bearded Lady. You *don't* want them hearing his sobbing and cussing. You *do* want his undivided attention. Distractions can be very costly during this crucial period, so a remote or isolated location is best.

Wherever you take him, he *sits.* If there's no chair, he sits on the floor. In addition, if he's not wearing handcuffs, you might take a minute to tighten his shoelaces (so shoes can't be kicked off) and then tie his shoes together. (No running allowed.) Keep things safe and tidy till a uniform walks through the door.[39]

Try to avoid a male employee being alone with a female detainee *especially* with a door closed. A reliable female witness should be in attendance of a female thief until police arrive. If you have two thieves, try to keep them separated, particularly if one is an adult and the other a juvenile. (Some states require it.)

During the entire interview process, only one employee converses with a thief. If two good-guys are present, the most skilled talks while the other takes notes. Any question a prisoner asks the note-taker should be referred back to the primary interviewer or just answered, "I don't know." At least one person should be physically located between the thief and the door. Once detained, first things first: are we safe and secure and in control of the evidence? Everything else depends on the totality of the circumstances.

## 10.01 Searches

This activity is a legal mine-field. Opinions vary, but even if an arrestee is OK right now, that doesn't mean he won't suffer a panic attack ten minutes from now. Or maybe the drugs he took a little while ago kick in. Point is, I'd rather have him go crazy *without* a razor. If you arrest someone, a search for weapons *should* be done.

Check with a local city prosecutor to learn how much you can do and what you shouldn't do whether the law allows you to or not. One good rule--if not the law--is that males check males, females check females, and have a witness whenever possible.

> If not "charge-able," they are not "searchable." Keep your hands to yourself. If you haven't arrested them, they are merely *suspects*. Unless you make an arrest, don't search or even "pat down" suspects. Look at anything they show you, but *do not touch*.

<u>Always know where a suspect's hands are and never assume there is no danger.</u> Before searching, *ask* if he has a weapon: *"You have a knife or machine gun, anything like that?"* Most don't, some lie, and some say they have something. If he says a knife's in his pocket, don't be stupid. *You* fish out the knife. Thieves' hands *do not* go into unchecked pockets. If they do, they don't come out. Grab the wrist (or keep the hand in the pocket by jamming his elbow to keep the arm straight). Keep the hand in the pocket until you're convinced it's not fetching a gun or knife. Then it comes out slow and empty.

After a cursory check ("frisk"), if you're *really* in control, you can ask him to empty his pockets on a desk. Be pleasant and insist, but don't "demand:" "Would you mind going ahead and emptying your pockets and pulling 'em inside out?" Say it so they do it, but phrase it so you can later say you merely "asked." Carefully check bags, pockets, etc. *for weapons*. Weapons include razor blades and small plastic box cutters.

A weapons check is a pretext, too, for searching anything (purse, bags, coat, etc.) that you will leave in possession of someone you've arrested if they will not be handcuffed or are cuffed with their hands in front.

Look *closely* at knickknacks on key chains, and beware razors in wallets, socks and shoes. Knives are disguised as fountain pens, and sharp, pointy things are built into belt buckles.

Look for bulges in clothing. Hats and coats come off and trousers are pulled up to see if Mr. Tricky has anything at ankle level. Feel socks and ankles, and inside shoes and boots. Run a thumb along the inside of the waistband and belt. Hats and coat linings get checked, and check heads for sharp combs, razors and needles.

> After arresting a gangbanger for shoplifting, separating him from his playmates, and getting him into the privacy of an office, I had to wrestle with him when he suddenly pulled a .32-caliber revolver from his waistband. Fortunately, I was more experienced at *taking* guns than he was at *pulling* them.

If you reach into a pocket or bag and take nothing out, hold your hand out open and say, "See? Nothing came out." Be careful with cash. Ask how much he has and make a big show of holding it out in front of you while saying, "Now watch closely..." Let *him* keep it after you count it, so neither of you has to worry. (While all this is going on, it's a more relaxed situation for everyone if a thief is handcuffed.)

Before anyone leaves, ask in front of a reliable witness (a police officer is excellent), "Do we have anything that belongs to you?"

You can't check everything. For example, *do not* allow detainees to remove shirt or pants. A coat, yes, but "strip searches" are absolutely forbidden. Another problem area is the crotch of pants. Don't go there. (Don't be afraid to handcuff females, even teenagers. On the side, part-time prostitutes and druggies are often shoplifters who carry razors in their bras and panties.)

## 10.02 Interviews & Interrogations (What The Shadow knows...)

<u>An untrained or less skilled person who is questioning a skilled or experienced individual usually gives away more information than he gets.</u> At least remember that you ask the questions and he either answers questions or just keeps his bad self quiet.

The first exchange often sets the interview's "tone." If you ask for a name and in response you get only a first name, the thief might not be taking you seriously. Get him on track. Try "That's only half a name," or "Any last name in particular or am I supposed to just pick one?" Anything but a right answer here shows the guy wants to be "hard."

Even young criminals, thirteen year-olds, develop a talent for these conversations. They learn what you *don't* know by evaluating the questions that you ask, or guess what you do know--by inference--from what you *don't* ask. They learn things by how your questions are phrased, tid-bits thoughtlessly dropped, how assertive you appear, and by your facial expressions. Many of these clever little urchins are quick studies, indeed.

**Me and Myself makes Two.** A thief wonders if he can beat the rap, but probably doesn't know how strong a case you have (though he *does* know he's guilty as sin). His thinking and decisions will be based at least a *little* on logic, so give him things to ponder.

Remember, unless you tell them, few thieves know exactly how they got caught, how many people were involved, or if there were cameras. You may have acted alone, but you are security and/or "personnel," and these words are interchangeably singular or plural. If A equals B, and B equals C, then A equals C. (Every time.) In that sense, if "I" am "store personnel" and "store personnel" is interchangeably singular or plural, then I can be "we" if I wanna be.

Use the word "we." "We watched you conceal it. You did it right in front of us." If a thief *thinks* more than one person saw him steal or *thinks* he may be a star on America's Funniest Security Videos, he generally doesn't play "I Say, You Say" which, with these people, is *extremely* tedious. Bottom line: "I" is a summer shower; "we" is a thunder storm. [40]

## 10.03 Obtaining Confessions *(Or, "How to get to yes.")*

Because you want the detainee to cooperate, it's *ordinarily* good to establish a rapport. A prisoner wants a phone call, a smoke, or will be curious about what happens next. *Something.* He'll be more compliant to your needs after it's clear *your* business comes first; that if *he* cooperates, you *might*, if he doesn't, you *won't*.

What constitutes cooperation? Recently, I had a thief who was positively *beside* himself with worry over being arrested. Nice guy that I am, I mentioned that since he didn't fight and was being honest I *might* help him with pre-trial intervention to keep his record clean.

A few minutes later, a police officer and manager were there when I put the acknowledgment form in front of him. "This says you stole two hats and you're guilty as sin. Sign it if you want to." All he said was, "Where do I sign?" *That* is cooperation.

If they confess in the store, they rarely recant in court, so when he asks--as he probably will--what you're going to do, tell him you haven't decided, but you're thinking about it. Pre-trial has begun in earnest. It's time for him to experience "a spring of hope and a winter of despair." It's time to unsettle him; not by making him think, but by making him *feel*.

Don't make promises, but mention options: you may or may not prosecute. If you do, you can suggest that police release him on a personal recognizance bond, or ask that this *not* be allowed. In court, you can ask the judge to be lenient. You can cooperate with soft, fuzzy pre-trial programs that keep thieves on the streets (rather than throwing them in jail with all the other innocent folk) or you can agree to other wondrous things designed to help criminals while--presumably--improving society.

On the other hand, you can obstruct nice things and make it the mission of your life to cause as much pain, trouble, and financial loss as your imagination and the law allow. *Many* options exist; some good, some bad, some ugly.

> The more a thief talks, the more complex his story and lies become. It's sometimes good to encourage lie upon lie until it becomes a story so bizarre that even his mother won't believe it. When a thief denies his theft, see how he answers these questions:
>
> 1. Is there any reason someone would say they saw you with the item?
> 2. *Really?*
> 3. Is there any reason someone would say they saw you put an item in your bag?
> 4. *Really?*

Keep in mind that people usually believe what they *want* to believe. If he believes confessing his theft to anyone with ears is **A GOOD IDEA** and might keep him out of jail, well, he has a right to an opinion. Don't compromise your integrity, of course, but it's not your fault he twists every word he hears. (Incidentally, that you'll probably have him packed off to jail is an unpleasant prospect that shouldn't preoccupy his thoughts until it's time to go, so always be careful how you talk about that.)

Paperwork is pre-trial work. Get his attention, then tell him, "It's one thing to steal, get caught, and tell the truth. It's something else to steal, get caught, tell lies and insult people. Two different things and we handle it two different ways."

Whatever his reaction, ignore it. Ask (as though you're simply curious), "Why'd you do this? Why didn't you just buy it?" (*Don't* use the word *"steal"*; it puts them on the defensive.) You want an answer that equates to a confession. "I didn't have enough money," is fine. *Not* fine is "I don't know," which is the first answer you usually get. The juicy stuff might take a little work.

> Sometimes you can get a thief to confess to a third party right on the sales floor. Tell him, "Look. You tell (Mr. Big) the truth about what you did and then we'll see how to handle it." By "how to handle it," *you* think pre-trial programs, low bond, etc. Let the thief assume a confession will set him free.
>
> Get someone who looks important, and have the thief tell him what he did. Once he says he concealed merchandise, he has confessed. If he confesses to more, that's even better. Get 'em confessing and keep 'em confessing.

"I don't know" is a non-answer. It might be fine if I didn't care and he didn't know, but I do and he does, and it's important that he gives a real answer (articulates a motive). Patiently, as though explaining a new or difficult concept to a child (but with dash of sarcasm), point to a door and say, "See the door? It doesn't know 'why' it opens and closes. You know why it doesn't know? Because it doesn't have a brain. You're not a door. You have a brain, so you know why you do things. Please don't insult me and say you don't know. Now, why did you do this? Give me a reason. Any reason."

Be patient. It may take time and prodding, but some reason usually comes. It begins with, *"I don't know."* Those three words are Part A of a reason. Part B is the good part, and what it lacks in originality it'll make up for in sufficiency. Typical is, "I don't know. I guess I just didn't want to spend the money." (Part A followed by Part B.)

> Confession is good for souls and case dispositions. Do what you can to help a poor, misguided wretch find peace of mind.

You can approach from different angles, but until there's free-flow, keep priming his pump: "The best that can happen for you is we just forget the whole thing and let you go. The worst that could happen is you get prosecuted, go to jail, pay a fine, lose your job, and have a criminal record. And there's things in-between the best and the worst. I want to see how you handle things. Why'd you put it in the bag?"

A shoplifter *thinks* before answering *"Why?"* It feels like a trick question (which, of course, it is). You want him to consider the little spiel you gave him about how you handle "different situations" "different ways." Remind him if he seems to forget. (After all, he *does* have a lot on his mind.) He watches enough television to know that every crime has a minimum and maximum punishment, and he does *not* want the shoplifting equivalent of The Chair.[41] Since thieves always *hope* they can walk away free, encourage that delusion to facilitate a confession.

The operative words are *hope* and *feels*. Thieves are usually *feeling-driven*. They even *think* with their feelings. Whatever the question, they look at what *feels* good as being the "best" alternative. Watch body language (yours and his) and consider your volume and tone of voice as you talk. Work on his instinct for self preservation. Make cooperation seem like a nice, selfish thought; a very good thing compared to the alternative.

If he concludes--feels--that giving you a reason for stealing *might* put you in a good mood and that *that* might help him escape *yet again* the painful consequences of his poor decisions, he'll answer your question, confess, hang himself, and thank you.[42]

When Scarecrow finds a brain and verbalizes an incriminating reason for his theft, *thank him* and go on about your work. Treat it like no big deal, but *eventually* jot his reason down--word for word--in your report. He doesn't know you record it, and don't worry him with that; poor devil has problems enough without worrying about yours, too.

If his answer (his partial or entire confession) is well received by you and it seems harmless to him, he'll normally repeat it to others. (You want him to confess to *at least* two people, yourself and one other.) He may squirm if asked again, but if the question is posed so it appears no big deal (or failing that, act as though an answer's mandatory) the same answer he gave the first time will probably tumble out again.

## "Confessions made easy."

Arrested thieves have so much on their minds that it often pays to be gentle. Don't ask harsh questions like, "Why did you steal this?" Work toward multiple 'mini-confessions' to the *individual elements* of a crime. This is called "walking the cat back":

1. **"Why'd you put it in the bag in the first place?"** Let him lie about that. Any reason he gives is a confession to bagging it. Putting it in the bag (pants, etc.) is *one element* of the crime of shoplifting and infers his intent to steal.

2. **"Why didn't you just buy this?"** Sound as though you're genuinely puzzled. (This is best for inexpensive things.) Does he have enough money now to make the purchase? If so, then why not just buy it? If he says he didn't want to spend the money, it's a confession.

3. **"Why'd you do this?"** (Avoid the word "steal.") If he says "I don't know," he's moving in the right direction. Gently push for Part B. The whole confession might be, "(I don't know), I guess I was stupid." (That's almost there. Don't let up.)

4. **"If you had a chance to buy this, how long would it take you to get the money?"** (Or, **"If you could call someone to come and buy this, how long would it take?"**) Sound nice (i.e., stupid, naive, fool...). After he's hooked, follow it up with #6, below.

5. (If the total dollar quantity is too much for him, ask **"Well, how much of it could you buy?"**) Either way, get his answer and build on it. Let him twist your words into the belief he can buy himself off the hook. Pretend that's the program, maybe jot down who he needs to call, a phone number, etc., and gently reel him in. Sound very, *very* nice, like it's a heart to heart talk. Get the full confession.

6. **"Shoplifting could ruin your future. Not everybody's as nice as me. Why'd you do this?"** You can make it easier for him by making it "multiple-choice:" Did someone make him do it, or put him up to it? Was it "his friend's idea?" Was it a prank or some kind of initiation? *Get the "reason" (the confession), then have him repeat it to others.*

And don't worry about Miranda warnings. Police (on-duty or off) must often "read 'em their rights," but store managers and employees *do not*. Again, it's important that a second person sees some concealed merchandise come out of a bag *or* hears the thief's "reason for doing it." (If a thief refuses to verbalize a reason, he probably plans to fight the case legally. Either that, or your presentation isn't effective. He might be confused.)

All this delicate business really consumes only a few minutes and is concluded before distractions--police or family--arrive. When police arrive, pretend--for a moment--that you sympathize with the thief. Tell them (in front of the thief), "He didn't give us any trouble, and he only stole it because he didn't have enough money. If he had the money, he would have paid for it." Then to the thief, "Isn't that right?" If he agrees, it's *another* confession, and this one to the law. Very, very good. Then it's the officer's show, and you just pretty much sit back and pour coffee. (Become good at interviews. Take a Wicklander or Reid course, or at least invest $30-$100 in some of their books and instructional tapes.)

## THE PRISONER'S DILEMMA

By definition--and inclination--thieves victimize others and are *very* selfish. They adopt "Looking Out for Number One" as a religion, and converts become zealots. When a member of this congregation is arrested, he feels a moral responsibility to wiggle himself off the hook as painlessly as possible, and any tactic will do (however back-stabbing or treacherous it may appear if measured by more...conventional standards).

People under arrest (or who might soon be) feel stress, and the better you become at interviewing (interrogating) the more you can use their stress to your advantage. Amateur interviewers often rely on threats, but threatening a thief can nullify his confession and create legal problems later. Also, threats cause some thieves to "clam up." That's bad.

In addition, few thieves confess to a highly critical interrogator, and many won't confess if their accomplice is in the same room. If two are detained, cooperation is easier if they are kept apart in physically removed areas. Then, sometimes you play a "nice guy," sometimes a "hard guy," and sometimes you're back and forth; whatever works.

Confessions can be spontaneous or result from questioning and suggestion. When you hear a confession, don't be obvious, but write it down (unless you're on the ball and have a hidden tape recorder with fresh batteries; even then, write it down later).

Some thieves actually *want* to confess and, beyond that, actually provide useful information or confirm information you already have. They mention novel ideas for thievery, identify other thieves, and brag about past thefts. Some even identify employees who need an adjustment.

If a pair of thieves is separated and neither cooperates, they hope you don't have a solid case. Others--"usual suspects"--are accustomed to being snatched up, questioned, and then released, and may even appear bored by the whole routine. Initially.

Appearances aside, to one degree or another they all *do* fear a good case. They may not fear a longer record and serving jail time, but they at least don't want it; life is more fun "on the outside." They know if they confess, there will surely be punishment, but maybe less severe than if they played "hard." Are they receptive to suggestions? You bet.

In the rigidly prioritized thieves' world, Number One is Number One and Number Two is not only second, but a *distant* second. Inexperienced spectators are often astonished by police setting one criminal against another. In fact, it's often business as usual for cops *and* robbers: "Honor among thieves" is a myth. The casual--if painful--sacrifice of friends, business competitors, personal enemies, and those lower on the food chain is *common*.

Given the right motivation and opportunity, thieves often torpedoes other thieves, *even best friends*. Handcuffs and imminent incarceration are motivation enough for most people, so only opportunity remains...and good form. (The sacrifice of a dear friend, understand, is delicate business.)

A thief knows he's a liar and a thief, and he knows what sort of friends liars and thieves have. Betting your freedom on the loyalty of a chum--the sort of guy who'd just as soon steal from Mom as eat breakfast--is grim business for any and too nerve-racking for most. Therefore, thieves usually trust people with legal authority more than they trust each other because authorities, for the most part, play within legal, ethical lines.

Cooperation with authority--sleeping with the enemy--is not done every day only because it lacks profit. After an arrest, though, cooperation *may* provide substantial benefit. Not only that, and more importantly for many thieves, cooperation *definitely* eliminates the potentially disastrous possibility of being played the sucker by a partner.

Once physically separated, Laurel has no idea what Hardy might say. Nervous and open to suggestion (to deals and bargaining), both thieves are particularly receptive to ideas that appear reasonable, i.e., selfish. To thieves, the right thing to do is what's most attractive *personally*. Like children are drawn to puppies, thieves are drawn to selfish things and then go belly up precisely because it *is* the selfish thing to do.

Whether it's time in jail versus cooperation, or Daily Special versus buffet, many thieves define issues with arithmetic. A South Carolina shoplifter faced the consequences of being caught: $634 cash fine, $149 restitution, and a criminal record. The slower of two thieves, he was caught while his best friend escaped with jewelry. I wanted the loot and the friend. (If you're young and want to be a thief, you better be able to run *fast*.)

*The Dilemma.* If the arrested thief refuses to cooperate, his friend gets away clean, *but* the sure wrath of authority falls on himself. *Or* he can sacrifice Number Two (his best friend) and save Number One (himself).

As he weighed the complex ethics for about ten seconds, his thinking went like this: "OK, if I don't rat-out my cuz, I'll have a criminal record. Also, it'll cost me, um, let's see here...six thirty-four plus one forty-nine? Dang! Eight hundred dollars for that fool?!"

**The Few.** Most thieves who won't answer questions are just stupid or plan to get a lawyer. There are, however, a few who simply *won't* bend over unless you go medieval. Even if talking is in their own best interest, they'd rather do a year standing on their head than give you the satisfaction. If you need a confession from one of these, forget about it.

## 10.04 Special Requests

When a thief asks for something, remember that the reason he was arrested in the first place is because he wants the whole world dancing to his own personal tune. He takes from others without caring that they worked for what they have. He abuses people, swears to naked lies, wreaks havoc with all that's holy, and then fairly *demands* sympathy and cooperation to remedy the problem he creates. This Democrat is *not* your friend.

One simple question handles most requests: "Is there some reason that can't wait until the police get here?"

(If he's in handcuffs because he resisted, don't take them off until police arrive. Thieves often "give up" after a brief fight just to catch their breath and lull you into a false sense of security. They use the time to think, then unleash Plan B and the dogs of war.)

**Telephone Calls.** What's the purpose? To gather reinforcements? Call a lawyer? If an adult needs to check on children or call someone to bring medicine, it's probably reasonable to let him. Otherwise, most calls can wait until police arrive. (Check with local police to make sure you're not legally required to let a thief make a call.)

**Calls of Nature.** "Nature calls" are a common request, but I've never had a thief over twelve who couldn't hold it. Occasionally, one whines and says he's about to soil his pants (or words to that effect). I remind him they're *his* pants so he can foul 'em if he wants; but in a little while he'll be in the back seat of a cop car and the driver might be particular about the upholstery.

> The criminal justice system--as it applies to youthful offenders--is a wonderland full of Mad Hatters. Sadly, you and every other victim are Alice in a bureaucratic asylum designed by social scientists and manipulated by teen-aged hoodlums.

If you let a thief into a restroom, check it for things he could use for mischief: razors, sticks, matches, paper-clips, light bulbs, spray-cans, etc. If he'll be alone--which, *please*, is *not* a good idea--remove the trash can before he goes in. Will he take advantage of privacy to destroy merchandise or price tags? (Or drugs?) If there's a window, someone must accompany him, or a solution found for "window options." (Can he fit through the window or break some glass and use a shard to slice you to ribbons?) Be careful not only in the restroom, but also walking to and from. Don't relax, even when back in the office.

When I was a compassionate, naive, rookie cop, I let a young woman use a bathroom after she was brought to the station for booking. Fifteen years later I *still* remember the look on the captain's face when he came in and asked where his prisoner was. Her offense was drug possession and she *hadn't* been searched. Don't be a sucker.

## 10.05 Juveniles

If a juvenile wants to call a parent, he waits until *you* are ready. You'll do it soon enough, or the police will. I usually make that call personally, but if a kid wants to, *and* he's been confessing, *and* it seems uncommonly important to him, *and* he's been well-behaved, *and* I doubt he'll spout a mouthful of lies, I might let him break the bad news himself. Then I get on the phone and explain the program.

**Calling home.** Be circumspect on a telephone. You can't know who you're talking to, really, or what mood or condition the person on the other end of the line is in. Or what crises he's already had that particular day. You should sound like someone he can deal with personally, so he doesn't show up later with the neighborhood "sidewalk lawyer."

Even when talking to the parent on the telephone, don't say the words "shoplift" or "steal." Tell them who you are and that, "So-and-So has a problem and we need you to come here as soon as you can. He's not injured, but we need you here as soon as possible. How long do you think it will be?" If they ask more pointed questions, cushion it: "Well, he did something he shouldn't have done." If pressed harder, say, "He's not hurt, but he's in a little bit of trouble. Can you tell me about how long will it be till you get here?"

Adults don't need it spelled out. No matter how shocked they sound, many of them have been through it with the kid before. If you know you're going to prosecute, you want police on hand before parents, but you don't want the officer waiting half an hour for Mom to arrive. (With a uniform in the room, parents exercise more self-control and are less likely to beat the kid doofless on the spot.)

Work on your timing. Ask the juvenile where his parents are and how long it will take them to arrive. Allow about 15 minutes for police, then adjust the time up or down as experience dictates. Often, the police dispatcher can give you an "E.T.A." (estimated time of arrival) if you ask. [43]

**Others.** You owe thieves no favors. But, if an arrested juvenile shoplifter has an adult waiting somewhere you should probably make at least a cursory attempt to contact that adult within a reasonable period of time just to let him know what's going on. You're a Good Guy and it's a simple courtesy to the adult.

If one or more kids accompanied a juvenile that you arrested, what do you do with them? Were they involved or rowdy? Will they be a problem if they stay? Can they wait elsewhere in the store or at the door or leave? What would their parents want? Offer them age-appropriate, legal alternatives that fit your program, and don't discuss the case. Just tell them their friend can't come out and play.

When you detain one of a young pair (perhaps 9- to 12-years-old) their parents may have told them to "stay together." The innocent may be more scared than the guilty. After all, the thief may have been through this fifty times. Help kids, but don't be a sucker. Liars, thieves, thugs and hooligans usually have the kinds of friends you'd expect.

**Do Not Call a spade a spade.** Whether it's an adult or a kid, there's little point in calling a thief a thief. It's not appropriate--technically--until *after* a person is convicted in court. Also, you want him to feel "bad," but not angry. Even though he knows he's a thief, he takes personal offense at being called one. Don't stir him up without good reason.

## 10.06 Friends and Family (and other sightseers, visitors, and well-wishers)

You have work to do, so people hanging around are a distraction at best, and generally a liability. No thief needs an "amen corner," so if friends or family ask about a prisoner, tell them there's a problem and the police will arrive any minute. For now, though, they can't see him. (Exceptions are inevitable: If the detainee is a juvenile and a non-parent adult or relative is there, I might let him wait with the juvenile if the adult is well-mannered and respects all rights of the store and employees, and he's squarely "on my side," and it won't interfere with my priorities, and it "feels" good, and the kid is confessing up a storm. Then, maybe.

Even if the thief's friends just sit there and talk, they will probably share information and work against you. You don't want anyone helping your thief concoct a story. Also, friends might help friends fight their way out of trouble. You're the enemy, and if you're dealing with teenagers, you might be considered an enemy that can't be reasoned with.

In some cases, a thief's friends help you. When they come for their friend, ask them who he is; first and last name. If it's different than the name provided by your prisoner, then--obviously--someone's lying. Who? "If you're telling me the truth then the guy in there is telling me lies. If he's telling the truth then you're telling me lies. Are you lying or is he?" Their program goes no further until you're satisfied. Repeat the question if necessary. If they refuse to answer, tell them to leave and call the police if they won't.

If they give you the same name as the thief gave, keep playing. Ask for their friend's phone number or where he works, etc.

If they don't give a name, but say, "It's the guy you just took in there," tell them a lot of people go in there. "If you're looking for someone, tell me who. If you don't know his name, you need to look somewhere else."

Given the chance, detainees and their visitors pass things back and forth. Things like false ID's, stolen merchandise, drugs, and weapons. Don't say that a thief's friend can't have the car keys or whatever; say they just need to wait till the police get there (which--always--is "any minute now"). Don't make it appear that you personally won't give up the keys, but make it a company thing, a legal thing, a "we" thing. And don't debate it.

I arrested an 18-year-old who wanted to give car keys to a friend who demanded them and threatened to sue me if I didn't turn them over. I told him to have his barber call mine. When the police arrived, they recognized my thief as the subject of a "BOLO" (Be on the look-out) in reference to a pawn shop burglary and stolen weapons. Gee, where were the guns?

> Most thieves, regardless of age, are far more experienced than you imagine. If any employees have contact with a detainee or his family, make sure they know not to say anything, *especially* if you, personally, are not there to hear everything that's said.

## 10.07 Acknowledgment and Release

The **Acknowledgment** (Appendix 01) is a confession, and eliminates most risk of false arrest suits. It says, in essence, "I came, I saw, I stole." Anyone not prosecuted should voluntarily sign it. Promises or threats can invalidate a confession even if the person is unquestionably guilty. Be subtle. (Naturally, if a person cannot read English, the value of his signature on an English-language document is highly questionable.)

When dealing with a juvenile and his parent (or legal guardian), it's important that they understand that the form is an *in-house* tool which does *not* go in some official file that ruins the kid's future. This can be a determining factor in their willingness to sign. Of course, some parents don't give a rip what's signed as long as it's quick and without police. That's OK. Let 'em sign.

The **Release** (Appendix 02) further reduces the possibility of a civil suit. Neither the Acknowledgment nor Release is necessary if the case is prosecuted. However, if a thief or his family wants you to consider pre-trial intervention or other relatively painless programs, the acknowledgment should be signed beforehand. (Always get it if you can.)

If you don't want to prosecute a juvenile, tell parents, "We prefer to work with families whenever we can. In this case, our intention--if you agree--is to release him to you instead of filing a police report. How do you feel about it? Would you rather take him and deal with him, or do you prefer the police?" If they want the boy: "Fine. We need to get the store paperwork done and then he's all yours. Please read these over and sign them." (Having forms filled out and waiting keeps the line moving.)

> Sisters, brothers, aunts, uncles, adult friends of the family, cousins, and ministers are *not* qualified to sign a Release. It doesn't matter if they volunteer, they just can't.

If parents question the formalities, give a brief explanation: "Some people think the reason a child's not prosecuted is that he didn't do anything wrong. They don't understand somebody trying to work with a family. This (form) says we're going to let you handle it and you won't sue us if we do."

If parents want a copy, that's reasonable enough. If you don't have a copy machine, tell them they can get a copy after you've had a chance to make one. (I've only had this become an issue once: they went ahead and signed and returned the next day for a copy.)

If they say anything like, "I need to see a lawyer first," that's a sign they could be on the wrong track and need an attitude adjustment. Response: "The purpose of doing it this way is so you don't need a lawyer like you might if we turn your son over to the police and prosecute him." Bottom line: sign the forms now or go to court later. (Exceptions, exceptions: if the parent is too scared to make a decision, patience and extra effort is nice.)

If you choose not to prosecute an adult thief, make short work of procedure. Hand him the forms, explain them if you want to, and tell him to read and sign if he chooses. If you have a strong case against him and he whines and stalls or wants the program changed to suit his preferences, tell him that it's OK not to sign the paperwork. Just prosecute him.

Write a report for any incident that even *might* create trouble downstream, and that covers a lot of territory besides shoplifting and disorderly conduct. (Many things demand attention and are more fun than reports, but don't let paperwork and notes pile up.)

## 10.08 Records and Report Writing

**Stop Log and Incident Report** A Stop Log is an in-house list of incidents (App. 04) used in conjunction with an Incident Report (App. 05). They are *indispensable*. Much hinges on how well these reports are done.

Complete them even if some facts are unknown. If you lack a name, use "unk." If a first name is known, but not the last, use "LNU" (last name unknown). Height, weight, and ages may need to be guessed, but remember that guess-work is just that. Insert "(?)" after a guess or questionable entry.

Don't assume an ID is genuine. (Naturally, ID that's been torn or defaced to obscure even a single letter or numeral is highly suspect.) Carefully study the card and person. The ID could belong to someone else or be false (forged, etc.). Laminated cards can be pulled apart, another picture inserted, and relaminated. Blank ID cards of all types (including, of course, drivers licenses) are routinely stolen from state offices for resale on the Black Market. Criminals and other people in dire need of documentation (but unable to obtain it legally) are happy to pay whatever amount the going rate might be. It's big business.

Professional criminals and con artists use multiple names, and often have supporting ID and documentation for each. Forged social security cards and birth certificates are ridiculously easy for criminals to come by, and the current generation of copiers, scanners, digital cameras, ink-jet printers, and laminating machines do very good work indeed.

While interviewing, interrogating, and processing, don't let a thief read what you write. Get a name (first, middle, and last), street address including zip code, a phone number, date of birth, parent's names, etc., and have him spell it all. Later, ask the same questions again and check these answers against the first, spelling included. If you have two thieves or a thief's friend is waiting outside, keep them apart and ask them both the same questions, then compare answers. Thieves don't need the truth to get into police custody, but, usually, they do need the truth to get out.[44]

**Narrative Reports.** Reports are for your use and use by others; sometimes years after you're gone. Handwriting must be legible, abbreviations consistent, and meanings clear, at least when viewed in context. The following are commonly used and more are in the Glossary (page 179).

| | | | |
|---|---|---|---|
| B...... | black | ccw..... | carrying a concealed weapon |
| W...... | white | S.O..... | Sheriff's Office (department) |
| O....... | other | f/n/u... | first name unknown |
| H....... | Hispanic | l/n/u.... | last name unknown |
| F....... | female | merch.. | merchandise |
| M...... | male | comp... | complainant (often "victim") |
| juv..... | juvenile | DOI.... | date of incident |
| perp.... | perpetrator | Sub..... | subject (a person) |
| dept.... | department | L, R.... | left, right |
| C#...... | case number | o/a...... | "on or about" |
| emp...... | employee | veh...... | vehicle |
| PD...... | police department | w/m.... | white male |
| R/O.... | reporting officer | b/f...... | black female |
| re....... | concerning | wit...... | witness |

Reports can be written in the "first person" ("I was approached by a lunatic") or "third person" ("R/O was approached by a lunatic"). Either way, make it crystal clear who's who and who did what. The narrative is *your* side of the story; the police have theirs, and the thief has his. What you tell police may be recorded, so do be careful what you say. Then check to see if they understood. The following is a sample of a brief report.

"R/O observed a w/m juv enter the store, walk to men's dept, and take a ball-cap off a rack. He looked l. and r., and stuffed the cap into his pants. He was stopped by emp Lois Lane and R/O. He was arrested and taken to the office. Sub had no money."

A manager or supervisor may want to hear (but not necessarily read) about what happened during that little stroll to the office. The oral report might go like this: "I told him he was under arrest and he tried to fight, so I threw him up against a counter and jerked his arm behind him so high that if his shoulder's not dislocated it's not my fault. I handcuffed him and dragged him to the office. You should have heard him scream."

That might sound a little extreme, but people sometimes exaggerate their war stories. Whether the oral account is accurate or not, the written report is short: "He was arrested and taken to the office." If someone wants more detail about any aspect of the case, a supplemental report can be written. (See App. 05, Part 03, Supplemental.)

> Many people file "honest mistake" in alphabetical order between Easter Bunny and Tooth Fairy. Some incidents call for brevity, some for length and detail, but all reports require care in choosing words or phrases. Be truthful, but it's not necessary to record your thoughts or every detail. If you make a bad stop or have a bad feeling about one, it's best to do a carefully worded report, maybe in detail. Think, and C.Y.A.

"It was a dark and stormy night. I was drinking a cup of coffee with too much sugar in a cup I got at the office Christmas party last year. I was near the south entrance to the store when suddenly the door burst open and I saw it was raining cats and dogs outside and this stunning, mini-skirted blonde bombshell with legs up to her armpits exploded into the store. I was wondering why such a beautiful woman would dye her roots black when..." Forget the frill and write this: "I observed a w/f enter the store."

"It rained cats and dogs," is, "It rained." Unless the actual quantity of rain is relevant, it just rained. (Speaking of rain, who cares about "inches?" I want to know how many gallons came down. Same with snow; it's like ice cream and I can picture a gallon.)

Incident reports are not 9th grade History exams where you fill space in May or it's summer school in June. Keep words and sentences short. Write in "story" form, all events from beginning to end, and write or collect all reports and statements as soon after the event as possible, *not* days later. Keep everything simple and objective; just the facts.

---

### A few Who, What, When, Where, How and Why's

- Who are you? Who is the thief? Who were witnesses and police? Who has the evidence? Who was nearby, (why there and what were they doing)?
- What happened? What did you, personally, see? What did witnesses see? What was taken? What did the thief do and say?
- When did it happen? When did you first see the thief? When did you approach him or when did he leave? When were police called? When did they arrive? When is court? When was the incident or suspect first reported to you?
- Where did it happen? Where was the item concealed? Where did you stop him? Where is the evidence, where is court?
- How did the thief act? How do you know the item did not belong to the thief?
- Why did he say he stole it? Why did you let one go but prosecute the other?

---

Have someone check reports for readability, particularly if you're new at it, but consider privacy issues. Consider what you share, and have a *reason* for sharing it.

After things quiet down, related facts may surface, phone calls are made, or something else may happen germane to the case. Record it on a separate sheet of paper and staple it to the original report. Keep all case paperwork together.

If witnesses know nothing, make a note of who knows nothing and have them initial it. (See Appendix 05, Witness Narrative.) I've had witnesses say, "I heard what the customer said, but I didn't hear anything you said." That's fine; have him write that. (If, later, the "customer" says you embarrassed him, you can respond that nothing you said was overheard. Maybe he embarrassed himself by intentionally creating a loud scene. Sometimes, of course, you want the whole world to hear what you say.)

How long was the person detained? A minute? Ten seconds? Get a watch with a second hand, then read the following aloud and see how long it takes: "Excuse me. Would you mind telling me where you left that sweater you were holding? I'd like to get it back where it belongs. Oh, that was my sister, not me. Ah, I see. Thank you very much. Do you want to look in my bag? Oh, no. I just want to get the sweater back to the right counter. Thanks a lot."

10 or 15 seconds. That's how long it lasted and that's what the report reflects.

If it was a bad stop, have a witness (or two or ten) write that the person wasn't touched, searched, verbally lambasted, or unduly delayed. If a customer or his associates were loud, insulting, or cussing, that goes on paper, too. All paperwork is attached to the incident report.

**Assumptions and conclusions.** If you write that Miss Bombshell concealed merchandise under her clothes in a dressing room, how do you know? Is there a peephole? Do you have peepholes in restrooms, too, or only in dressing rooms? How long have you been a voyeur? Have you ever even heard the term "reasonable expectation of privacy?"

She entered with items and exited without items. An immediate search of the fitting room revealed no discarded items. Of course she concealed the items under her clothes; but, unless someone saw her do it, that's a conclusion or an assumption. If you later see her pull the items out of her mini-skirt, that's a fact that supports your conclusion (about what happened in the dressing room).

Avoid assumptions and conclusions, or be careful how they're used. When testifying about concealment in the privacy of a fitting room, it's probably best not make an issue of whether or not you actually saw her conceal clothes: "She took clothes in the fitting room and came out with the clothes concealed. At that point, we stopped her and she pulled the clothes out from under her skirt." Or leave out the fitting room and just say she concealed merchandise and was arrested. Probably, no one will make an issue of it. However you choose to do it, present facts and findings in a simple, non-controversial manner.

## 10.09 Evidence

Evidence for a particular case must be relevant. Shoplifters commonly say they had enough money to buy what you say they stole. They say the fact that they had money is proof--evidence--that they weren't going to steal. However, the simple fact that they had money is not relevant to their defense, because having it is not prima facie evidence of a willingness or intent to spend it. (Most shoplifters could pay, but steal anyway.)

If they did not have enough money to pay for what they concealed, that *is* relevant because it proves the person did not have the ability to pay. That points to an intent to steal. In addition, besides evidence being relevant, there must be enough evidence to prove the case beyond a reasonable doubt.

Evidence is divided into two basic types, each with two categories. One is Physical, which embraces Real evidence (physical objects such as a knife or stolen property) and Circumstantial. (Fingerprints found in a room are circumstantial evidence suggesting that a particular hand--and perhaps, by extension, that entire body--was in the room.) The other basic type of evidence involves People. People-evidence is testimonial (verbal statements about something they know), or direct (eyewitness testimony).

> Evidence proves an allegation, and most lawsuits stem from a lack of sufficient evidence (usually physical evidence). Gather it carefully and preserve it properly. If you screw up badly, you'll learn what Archie Bunker meant when he said, "That's what's wrong with our legal system, ya' need evidence!"

Television and movies often imply that cases built on circumstantial evidence are weak. But if a case goes to trial a year from now, would you rather count on a lone eyewitness to identify the perp in court, or would you rather have his fingerprints all over the crime scene, murder weapon, and getaway car? (All circumstantial evidence.)

Witnesses develop amnesia and selective memory and otherwise blow it in court. They move away and leave no forwarding address, decide they no longer want to be involved, are bribed, intimidated, lie for a variety of reasons, or just die a natural death. Lots of things go wrong with witnesses, but fingerprints don't change. They don't forget, they don't move away, and--while they sometimes mislead--they never lie.

But don't misunderstand me: I like having a good witness. Just don't think that circumstantial-only cases are necessarily bad or automatic losers, or that eyewitness cases are sure winners. Life just ain't that simple.

Stolen merchandise is evidence, as is the packaging that contained it. A knife used to remove price tags is evidence, as is the bag, or whatever was used to conceal the item. (I don't normally keep a purse or backpack as evidence unless it is demonstrably a tool used habitually or primarily for theft.) Evidence goes to court.

---

**Paper Shredders:** Once exotic, crypto security devices, good shredders are now available in the $40-$80 price range and should be used for <u>anything</u> with credit account numbers, social security numbers, addresses, and other personal information. Take no chances.

---

**Evidence Handling.** Most evidence is "bagged and tagged" and, if possible, multiple items from the same incident are kept together in a single bag. (For convenience, see-through bags are best.) Once the bag is sealed, nothing is added or removed without a notation being made on the report explaining when, what, why, etc. If more evidence is (later) discovered for the same case, bag it separately, tag it, and note on the report (and on all bags) that a new bag exists. Keep the case bags together and label them "1 of 1,""1 of 2," "2 of 2," etc.) Check with police about unusual items or perishables.[45]

Some courts allow photographs in lieu of physical evidence. That saves storage, and the item goes back to stock immediately. If you use a picture, give it all respect due the "real thing." It must not be misplaced. (Since it's helpful to be able to identify the thief in court, if you took his picture staple it to the report with the evidence photo.)

A torn shirt or cut hand is evidence of a struggle. If evidence cannot be otherwise maintained, take pictures. If a good-guy is injured, take gruesome pictures immediately.

Photos have a down side: the actual, physical evidence often makes a better impact in court to demonstrate how a package was torn, how much effort was required, etc. Also, a lower court may accept a picture, but a higher (or appeals) court, for some reason, may not. (That would be such an unusual twist, though, that I nearly decided not to mention it.)

If you have a conversation on tape (recorded), make a copy to keep away from the primary file, then transcribe it ASAP. Keep one copy of the transcription with the original tape (under lock and key), and keep the other with the duplicate tape. If you loan a tape or give a tape up for evidence, try to keep the original in your own safe-keeping.

Evidence *must not* be tampered with (altered) from the time of arrest to the time of testimony. This can be important. It's best to keep evidence under lock and key so it won't get lost, sold, or used. File cabinets are good. You can go years without evidence-handling becoming an issue in shoplifting cases, but if something ever does go seriously wrong, your case can be lost.

Proper evidence handling and good court presentations establish professionalism and credibility. A number of well-prosecuted cases behind you gives you a leg up in the future, particularly with those nasty "I say, you say" contests, which are also referred to as "swearing matches;" basically just your word against that of a thief.

---

Private security extends back thousands of years, but became "big business" in the U.S. in the 1880's through the efforts of such legendary men as former Cook County, IL detective Alan Pinkerton whose company--like Brinks (armored cars)--operates to this day.

Private security--which includes store and corporate security--now employs more personnel (over 700,000) than all government law enforcement agencies combined (over 500,000) and represents an annual expenditure of over $20 billion, roughly one percent of the US Gross National Product (GNP).  *(J.H. Christman)*

---

**"Who has deceived thee so oft as thyself?"** -- B. Franklin

**Steal**MeBlind

# Chapter 11

# Prosecutions, Police and Court

A defendant in a Georgia municipal court was complaining about a police officer's lack of politesse during a traffic stop when Judge Phil Spivey cut her short: "Madame, the police <u>are not</u> the Welcome Wagon."

Not the Welcome Wagon, neither are police "Boogie Men" called in to just scare people. That's counter-productive in the long run and besides, police have better things to do. If you think cops just sit around speed traps when not flirting with waitresses, you're *sadly* mistaken. That glazed look in their eyes comes from stress, not donuts.

> Shoplifting is serious, but so, too, are armed robbery, death, and mayhem.
> Twenty minutes before he got to you, an officer may have held a 9 year-old dead in his arms or handled some other gruesome call. If it seems to you that he's not taking your problem as seriously as he should, maybe he's still shifting gears.
> You concentrate on your end.

**Making the call.** If you have someone in custody, police dispatchers ordinarily need to know only the sex and age, i.e., adult or juvenile: "This is the Frame Store at 213 Apple Street. (Say, "two, one, three," *not* "two-thirteen.") My name is Lois Lane, L-A-N-E. We have a male, adult shoplifter in custody and we'd like to prosecute him." (If he's rowdy, say so.) Then answer the questions the dispatcher will ask.

If someone is disorderly--vulgar, threatening, etc.--and you want him gone, call 911 and keep it simple: "This is the Frame Shop at 123 Apple Street. My name is Lois Lane, L-A-N-E. We have a disorderly man in the store who won't leave. He's a white male, red shirt and purple pants. Please send us some help." The type situation determines how much information the dispatcher needs. Police don't like to work blind.

> Understand, clothes might be "purple" or "dark red," but *do not* say a color like "mauve." In the concrete jungle there's plenty of black, white, gray, and red, but there ain't no such color as "mauve." (And only God knows what the fuchsia will bring.)

Police can't make psychic connections, so be patient and provide a clear idea of what's going on. What with emotions high and exciting things happening--strange people under foot and all--it may be difficult to stay lucid, but do your best.

And, before you call, know if you want to prosecute. That's your decision, not the responding officer's, and you should seldom be undecided. Police should not be called--normally--unless you will prosecute. [46] (Also, rather than make an officer wander around trying to find you, try to have someone meet him at the front door and bring him to you.)

**The Stall.** At times, you want to prosecute, but a fight might erupt if you say so. The obvious strategy, then, is be sneaky: call the police, but don't let the thief know you did it. Buy time. One stall is saying that before he can go he needs to personally apologize to the manager; another is to tell him he needs to sign a form saying he won't come back in the store (and then you find out the one you're holding is the last one you have, so someone has to make a copy before you use it...)

**The Big Picture.** Like they say on Dragnet, "There are a million stories in the big city." But they don't tell you that some stories are inter-related because of BBD's: Bigger and Better Deals. As a cop, I traded gram arrests for ounce arrests; misdemeanors for felonies. Once in a while, police can hold a shoplifting charge over the thief's head to elicit cooperation in resolving greater crimes. If your shoplifter helps convict burglars, dropping your charge is *probably* a small price to be pay for the greater good.

One more thing. If you get through a day without being robbed or worse, it's *not* because the gangbangers were intimidated by Thomas or Ginsberg assuming the bench, *nor* is it because some homeboy was dissuaded by an article he read in Law Review. You can debate capital punishment and the joys of rehabilitation until Jimmy Hoffa comes home, but make no mistake: deterrence on the street is a thin, blue line.

If an officer does well, write a note to his chief (and the mayor and newspaper, if half-appropriate). Don't forget to send a copy to the individual officer ("in care of" the department). It's good form, greatly appreciated, and seldom done.

I'm sure that the poet Rudyard Kipling won't mind my taking the following liberty with one of his poems. If you ever feel compelled to become ex officio in charge of criticizing police, think about it:

> "He's piggy this and piggy that, and 'Sue him! He's a brute!'
> but he's 'Savior of the City' when the guns begin to shoot."

## 11.01 When to Prosecute, when not to

Some owners and managers don't prosecute even excellent cases because they feel that "sitting in court is a waste time." But don't they set time aside to go through mail, and read books or magazines? Court is a nice place to sit and read. Do you throw out trash? If it helps, think of thieves as trash and court as a city dump.

Remember this, too: you want thieves to know that you prosecute, and court is a "bully pulpit." In court, in jails, schools, malls, and on the street, word gets around.

Because of age, mental status and other variables, though, some offenders should *not* be prosecuted. Selective prosecution requires judgment calls and even if prosecuted, a case may not get to court. That depends on variables such as age, severity of offense (dollars, damage, and violence), and if the thief is a "first offender" (which is to say he's not been previously caught *and* prosecuted). The entire criminal justice system is highly selective.

A pair of boys (aged 14 and 15, I learned), entered a store and went directly to a clothes rack. It was obvious they wanted to steal trousers, but a clerk offered "customer service" and they left. A half-hour later they tried again, were inconvenienced by another clerk and, again, left. Their *third* attempt was about an hour later and without employees making a nuisance of themselves, it took only a minute to bag some pants.

No spur-of-the-moment temptation, this pair chose a victim and carried out a premeditated crime. They might cry, their mothers might cry, and I might cry too, but just as sure as grits are groceries, thieves like these *must* be prosecuted.

In fact, though, you don't *really* have to arrest *anybody*. Having said that, I usually prosecute the following:

- Adults, *especially* those with no identification.
- Anyone who physically resists or created a "scene."
- Anyone who maintains that the "stop" was illegal or unjust.
- Anyone who refuses to sign the Acknowledgment and Release.
- Anyone who escaped in the past.
- Anyone laughing or treating the experience as a "lark" or treating employees disdainfully or insultingly.
- Anyone using a tool more sophisticated than a bag or pocket.
- Any juvenile whose parent(s) can't or won't come to the store.

- A juvenile whose parents maintain the "stop" was illegal or unjust.
- A juvenile in these categories: hard, violent, experienced, high dollar-value, obscene, threatening, armed, totally don't-care, or with rowdy friends. ("Bad company brings bad luck.")
- Anyone who threatens employees in any way.
- A "regular customer." (Which means he was a regular thief.)
- Anyone who appears to have pre-planned a theft.

In addition, I prosecute shoplifters with friends who even appear to suffer similar inclinations. If they see their pal caught red-handed and released, they have every reason to think they, too, would enjoy an outcome that makes a "game" of theft and a sham of prevention. If you don't prosecute, it's an invitation to steal.

> Little Jimmy and Johnny's mother tells Dad the boys have taken to cussing, and she wants it stopped. "No problem," says Dad. Next morning, little Jimmy sits down at the table, and Mom asks, "What do you want for breakfast?"
> Jimmy says, "I want some damned corn flakes." WHAM! Dad back-hands him and he crashes to the floor. Little Johnny, who witnessed that from the doorway, steps over his brother and sits at the table. When Mom looks at him says, "How about you? What do you want for breakfast?" he looks down at his brother on the floor and thinks about it. Finally, he says, "I sure don't want no damned corn flakes."
> When dealing with thieves and employees, make your lessons crystal clear.

Do I *not* prosecute anyone? Yes: the senile, retarded, and children under twelve.

With juveniles not on the list above, prosecution "depends." I study the case and circumstances, their body language, faces and words. I study their families. And I think real hard and pray. In this unique line of work, one of the greatest sources of personal satisfaction and one of the greatest services we provide to our communities is helping catch that occasional falling angel before his fool butt hits the ground. If a juvenile over twelve demonstrates *sincere* remorse, didn't otherwise "blow it," might actually have "learned his lesson," *and* the dollar-value is small, I'll often just turn him over to Mom.

> A consideration: County sheriffs are elected. They can lose votes if their deputies use handcuffs. By coincidence, deputies are sometimes perceived as, oh, less enthusiastic than city police about prosecuting some "minor offenses" (like shoplifting). [47]

If my standards seem harsh, it's because of grim statistics. To many thieves, a misdemeanor court fine is just a cost of doing business; minor--even negligible--compared to the thousands of dollars between busts. To most juveniles, a bust for shoplifting requires no court, no fine, no time, and no permanent record for even twenty offenses.

Police officers sometimes discourage prosecuting juveniles because it takes much time and paperwork, family court systems are often a shambles, and prosecution might be near-pointless, anyway. In some cities, even violent juvenile cases involving injuries might hit a Black Hole with bizarre dispositions and no reason or notice given to the victims. The upside is you rarely go to court for juveniles. Once the police take them, you're done.

The officer will feel less put-out, though, if you make it clear from the start what you want. If you choose to prosecute (and I usually do) just *insist* and the officer should handle it. If he's frustrated, he'll get over it. Just don't usually expect much to come of it.

The average shoplifter steals for years before he's caught and escapes 49 times for every one time caught. But most are never caught, and of those who are, ninety-eight percent are released without charges. *If* charged, the thief ordinarily enters a pre-trial intervention program that removes the arrest from his record. Consequently, if caught *and* prosecuted *again*--which requires *ungodly* bad luck--it's still just another "first offense."

**Remorse.** As a rule, a thief's show of remorse for stealing is just that: a show. Predictably, they do feel remorse, but only because they were caught. Their remorse is actually self-pity, totally self-centered and divorced from any guilt or shame stemming from being a thief. It's fear (sometimes even shame) associated with the circumstance of arrest that causes the anguish.

With many of them, it's inherently pointless to discuss morals. Don't we *teach* that every person should decide for himself what is right or wrong, moral or immoral? Do *they* have to think it's bad just because *you* think it's bad? Of course not! One of their favorite slogans is, "Who are you to judge other people?"

> "Oh, poor me!" thinks Melissa after being arrested. She actually says, "Don't you feel any remorse locking me up?" Amazing, I thought. I mean, she looked so...lifelike. "Of course," I reply. But I do what I do and sleep the best I can.

Bitter Whine, Vintage '92: "But my daughter will lose the college scholarship she just won! She's learned her lesson." Good. Will she demonstrate her new dedication to honesty by calling the College Entrance Board right now to tell them she suffered a little mental lapse? Or don't we want to be that honest? And maybe the kid she beat out for the scholarship *is* honest and needs the break twice as badly.

Bitter Whine, Vintage '93: "But my son won't be allowed to join the Army. He already has a contract and is supposed to report next week." Yeah, right. Let's put him in position to steal M-16's instead of Bic lighters. That's just what America needs: an army of thieves being all they can be.

Nearly all thieves swear it's their first offense. "But, oh, the trouble this will bring...." That is merely an attempt to manipulate you. It's a con to make you feel guilty. Don't fall for it. Whatever they whine about, it's not your problem. Today they chose to be a criminal. Tomorrow, they'll have the same choice again: don't be a criminal, or *be* a criminal. Whatever trouble an arrest brings, it's just part of the life they choose.

> A woman in handcuffs asked me, "Am I going to be in trouble?"
> "You <u>are</u> in trouble," I said. "You've been arrested for shoplifting."
> "No, I mean am I going to be in <u>trouble</u>? Are you going to call the police?"

If a burglar stole from her house, would she tell police, "Oh, it's OK. Just let him go." If she says, "It's my first theft," follow that one-liner with your own: "What a coincidence! You're the first person I've prosecuted!" Occasionally, they play along: "Why me?" The answer, of course, is, "I don't know. Why'd *you* pick *me*?"

If she maintains that sending her to jail is overreacting, say, "Oh, I see what you mean. Shoplifting is different from real stealing. It's like the difference between unlawful and illegal. Is that what you mean?" If she doesn't know the difference, tell her unlawful is against the law and illegal is a sick bird. (Ill eagle.) Have some fun. There's nothing wrong with taking a little pleasure in your work.

Mean? Nah. Shoplifting is illegal, just like DUI and burglary. *Or didn't they know?* Each encounter is an educational experience. If the lesson is not clear, class time is wasted. Prosecution is not only a clear lesson, it opens the door to unimagined possibilities.

One Henry Trueblood (name changed) was snatched up in a Piggly Wiggly grocery by stocky stockers who saw him steal steaks. The manager called the police, and a few minutes later I arrived to take Henry off the Pig's hands. (Pig's hands?)

En route to the station we talked about life and Karma until out of the blue--and pretty casually, all things considered--he said he was a drug-runner, was tired, wanted out, and would I help? One incredible thing then led to another. It happens.

Sometimes, the more they whine, the more they have to hide. Maybe his face is on a milk carton, or maybe it's a third or tenth offense. Maybe he's on probation. Ever hear of the Patty Hearst kidnapping and the "Symbionese Liberation Army?" That incredibly violent gang ("revolutionaries," they called themselves) evaded massive nationwide, local, state, and federal manhunts *until* two members were caught shoplifting socks. Unless you call the police, you never know what you have. (Of course, calling 911 for shoplifters with machine guns *ought* to be a no-brainer.)

**11.02 Court** During the Civil War battle of Spotsylvania Courthouse, enemy cannons began blasting away in the direction of General John Sedgwick. "They couldn't hit an elephant at this dis--" were his immortal last words. Take nothing for granted. In court, good cases are sometimes lost and poor cases won. In honest courts, preparation is the key; and it begins before a shoplifter is even approached.

**Run-throughs.** Watching Matlock re-runs on TV is no substitute for experience. Before your first big dance, take some free lessons. Attend court a couple of times to get the feel of things. Notice how people stand and dress; how they act and speak. If you want to leave before it's over, leave *between* cases. (Between acts.) Having been to court, you'll at least know your drive-time, where to park, where to sit and what to expect. (Take comfort in the fact--as you'll learn--that most judges expect and forgive minor problems.)

**Dress for Success.** A popular cliché is, "You have only one chance to make a good first impression." A judge or jury may be offended if *they* think you dress like a clown or slob, so avoid flashy clothes, shocking hair styles, and wear nothing dirty or crumpled. Don't let your thief make the better impression. Wear basic blues, browns, grays, and tan (khaki) pants with shoes and socks to match. No blue jeans, shorts, or knee-high pants. There are exceptions, but *the rule* is "conservative."

Men should wear long-sleeved dress shirts (white is always OK) and not-wild ties. Wear a conservative jacket that matches your pants; no purples, oranges, pinks, etc. Women should avoid too much make-up, gaudy and/or too much jewelry, and too-short skirts: calf length is best. Hair colors like purple make the wrong statement.

Sometimes you dress up, sometimes you dress down, but you always dress for the occasion. If you're in loss prevention (LP) or law enforcement (LE) but you don't understand the effect that personal appearance has on others, you're not paying attention. If you want people to perceive you as a professional in your field, at least *appear* professional.

Thieves get amazing makeovers for court. Last seen, they were under-dressed for a Chicago precinct drunk-tank. Now, hair is cut and styled, and they wear nice--if slightly ill-fitting--dress shirts. (After court, of course, it's back to rode hard and put up wet.)

**Before trial.** On court day, arrive early and speak with the "Clerk of Court" to confirm that your case is "on the docket" for that day. You *don't* want to sit for hours waiting on a rescheduled case. Also, try buttering up the Clerk. Or ask if your case can be heard quickly so you can get back to the hospital and your dying mother. Sometimes it works. (It ought to, considering defense attorneys *routinely* go to the front of the line. *Their* time is important, you see.)

Looking good and being early are pointless, though, if you arrive without a case. Check your evidence and reports the day before court (when there's still time to find anything that's misplaced) and *always* contact witnesses to make sure they don't forget the trial. While you're at it, see if they have a transportation or wake-up problem. Witnesses are evidence. Have *all* your evidence in court. [48]

If you oversleep or simply won't be on time, call the courthouse or even the police, but make sure the case won't be dismissed before you arrive. You *must* do that!

**How to Address People in Court.** The judge is "Sir" (or "Ma'am"), "Your Honor," or called by name, as "Judge Bean" (or whoever). The clerk is "sir" or "ma'am." City police are "officer" or addressed by name and rank: Officer Farris, Sgt. Goocher, Captain Josey, Deputy Chief Black, etc. Sheriff's deputies are the same, but substitute "deputy" for "officer." If you don't know an officer's name, refer to him as "the officer."

Do you call everyone "Doctor," or "Captain?" Of course not. Descriptive titles are *earned* by work and submission to certain performance standards. Not every rock is a nugget of gold, and the mere fact of existence does not make *every* woman a lady. By definition, ladies and gentlemen don't shoplift. They hold themselves to a higher standard. Gentlemen might pillage every treasure from an entire culture, but you can count on them at least to leave the knickknacks alone or pay retail.

> In court, never refer to a shoplifter as "gentleman" or "lady."
> **Never, never, NEVER, never,** never, but never.

When you refer to a thief as "gentleman" you imply that he is ordinarily an honorable man of uncommonly high morals and ideals. You imply that--in *your* opinion--the poor fellow merely suffered an unfortunate mental lapse. No! They're thieves, and probably cheap ones. Don't even *imply* there's such a thing as the hooker with a heart of gold.

When you call them "ladies" or "gentlemen," you insult boys, girls, men, and women everywhere who struggle daily to *be* ladies and gentlemen. For thieves, let "Mister" or "Miss" suffice.. Even "this man" or "this woman" is fine, but ***never*** lady or gentleman.

## The Non-Attorney, Non-Jury Trial

The normal, most common setting for shoplifting cases is a non-attorney, non-jury trial. Court is held by a judge or magistrate in the same room with a catalog of other cases. Typically, you see traffic cases, a prostitute or drug possession or two, and some illegal drinking and disorderly conduct. Verdicts in these courts are rarely appealed.

In the courtroom are witnesses, defendants, family, friends, a lawyer or two, a few police, and maybe a howling child. Near front and center is a court clerk, a busy individual handling paperwork for the judge. Getting testy with her is always counter-productive.

At his personal convenience, the judge appears, and probably late. Expect that, and assume it's because the Supreme Court called him for advice. (Cosmic Law: If you are late, that's the one time he *won't* be, and your case will surely be called and dismissed.)

**Show Time.** Loudly, someone orders everyone to their feet, followed by the judge ordering everyone to sit down. This ritual awakens everyone and demonstrates the food chain. Cases and case *types* are called and people for each particular case (or type) go forward. Once properly organized, testimony is heard, evidence presented, and judgment passed. Cases take about 10 minutes each, so you're normally in and out in a couple of hours or less. (Newspapers are noisy and easily spied by court personnel who may become indignant. Take a book or magazine, hold it low, and don't sit *too* near the front.)

When your thief's name is called, you both go forward. Don't miss that.

The judge then asks the defendant for a plea. Before that--as soon as you're in front of the bench--slowly and meticulously take your evidence out of the bag(s) and lay it on the table in plain view for everyone to see. Do it before anyone says anything.

If you brought multiple items, spread them out on the table so each individual item can be seen. This launches a psychological torpedo at the shoplifter that takes only seconds to impact. The bigger your display, the greater the impact. If you have the incident and confession on tape: keep it put away and don't make an issue of it till the thief finishes lying under oath, and get him to repeat his lies several times. (I've never needed my tapes in court for a shoplifting case. Also, I've never had a defense attorney *ask* if I had one. In advance, check the laws and ordinances in your area concerning evidence at bench trials.)

**The Fear Factor.** Stage fright produces physical symptoms such as stammering and hand-wringing; testimony becomes word-salad, and instead of focusing on your words, people wonder why you're nervous. It's OK to be fearful, but not fear-*driven*. Understand that it's only fear, and keep it in the back seat where it won't mess with your steering. Take a deep breath, think happy thoughts, and watch Mary Poppins the night before. [49]

> When the thief's name is bellowed by a bailiff, it shatters the silence between cases and calls him to judgment. The thief feels the chill of Doom's unseen shadow, and he's momentarily confused as to why hearing his own name scared him so badly.
>
> If *you* feel afraid of what people in court may think of you, consider the thief. He's afraid not only of what they think, but he's also scared about what they're going to do after they finish thinking. Money's always short, and some cell-mates are not nice guys.
>
> If he had planned to plead not-guilty, the tidy story he concocted suddenly seems woefully inadequate. He feels unprepared, vulnerable, afraid, and *very* guilty.

**Warrants and Evidence.** A warrant is an affidavit prepared by the Solicitor or police and signed by the complainant (victim) before testimony begins. When your name or the thief's name is called, go forward. Someone (usually the busy Clerk) has the warrant ready. Read the narrative--technical mistakes are not uncommon--and make any minor corrections necessary. For example, it may indicate the person walked out of the store when, in reality, he walked toward the door. If so, draw a line through "out of the store" and insert "toward the door." Sign it when it's right; you'll be swearing to it.

If police took evidence, they (should) return it now. If there's a form for you to sign to acknowledge getting the evidence back, someone will show you where to scribble. They rarely make mistakes handling evidence, but check anyway. Ensure the evidence matches the description on the form and that it's the right evidence for the right case.

**Theatrics.** In centuries past, entertainment in court was provided by a jester who was called "the court fool." He wore mismatched clothes, silly hat, and pointy little shoes with bells on the toes. Plenty of fools will be in court, but *your* title and function is court "plaintiff." Don't forget that.

"Theatrics" include rolling head and eyes in mock astonishment, gasping, shaking your head "no" while listening (to even outrageous lies), stomping feet, or any exaggerated display. Don't dance or turn your face to heaven and, under no circumstance, do you interrupt the judge when he speaks. Showing respect for the judge and the court is a demonstration of respect for law and the System. Showing *disrespect* for the judge is a demonstration of disrespect for the law which equates to a willingness to break the law.

In front of the judge, you stand near or beside the defendant. Don't slouch, and if there's a table in front of you, don't lean on it. Don't glare at the defendant or jab your finger in his direction. Don't talk with your hands, don't put them in your pockets, either. You needn't be poker-faced, but keep it under control.

If you have an itch, ignore it. Don't play with your hair, mustache, or fingernails. Don't be flippant, and make *no* jokes. If someone does make a joke and the judge doesn't laugh, it's not a funny joke. If the judge laughs, you can chuckle, but stop when he does.

When the judge speaks to you or you speak to him, look at him, not the floor or ceiling. If he speaks to the defendant or vice versa, look mostly at the defendant. This makes some defendants feel nervous. If the defendant insults you, look to the judge. It's his job to keep the fight clean, and he deducts points for low blows.

**The Plea.** Defendants must pick one plea and one plea only: **guilty, not guilty, or "no contest."** The last is seldom heard unless a barrister's in the woodpile. "No contest," means in effect, "I'm not saying I did it and I'm not saying I didn't do it. I just don't want to talk about it." Not as pretty as guilty, but if he pleads no contest, you will win unless you get *real* stupid. If the judge then asks for your side of the story, tell the short version covering only the most basic elements of the crime.

If the defendant pleads guilty, the judge may or may not allow him to explain, and he may or may not ask if you have anything to say. He might simply rattle off a sentence (fine or time). If he asks you to testify after a thief pleads guilty, the *only* hope the thief has is your foolish tongue wagging ("bumping your gums"), so keep it *very* short.

If he pleads not-guilty, the judge will ask for your story. You testify first. In this case, you want to present enough evidence (testimony) to convince and convict, but you must say <u>nothing</u> to muddle the primary issue, i.e., he's a thief who stole something. Demonstrate the elements of the crime and provide a minimum of other facts.

Countless books have been written on Caesar's most famous campaign, but he summed it all up in just three words: veni, vidi, vici (I came, I saw, I conquered). Well, maybe six words, but that's what I mean by a short version. "He came in the store, looked all around, concealed our hat in his pants, was confronted, denied it, and was arrested. The hat was recovered."

Then, the clincher. "He said he stole it because he didn't have enough money."

Remember pre-court prep? You want the thief's confession (his reason for "doing it") recorded word for word in your Incident Report (which you have with you in court). If he pleads not guilty, make him eat his reason. <u>Read it</u> aloud from the report. Your witness to that confession nails the coffin by testifying that he, too, heard the (thief) confess.

If he pleads not guilty, he will normally say he didn't steal, or that he didn't *intend* to steal. He might say he never concealed it, or that he was going to pay for it even though he did conceal it and denied having it. He might admit to part of your testimony but deny another part. He might say he stuck the hat under his belt, but it was visible and he was going to pay for it. Or he might say he thought you said cat--not hat--which is why he denied having one. One thing is for certain: if he pleads not guilty, more lies will follow.

**The Defendant's Dilemma.** Fighting and denials at the time of arrest contrast sharply to thieves' behavior in court where nearly always they just plead "guilty." One reason was their hope that *you* could be bluffed or intimidated; but the judge won't be.

The shoplifter must enter a plea before proceedings go into full swing. He knows he's guilty and he knows he'll be under oath. Furthermore, he *expects* to be found guilty and *expects* to be punished *regardless* of his plea or what he says. These realities, combined with fear, present him with a serious dilemma: if he pleads guilty, he screws himself for sure and faces certain punishment. *However*, he wants a ration of mercy from the judge and might not get it if he insults His Honor with lie upon lie. If he pleads not guilty and is found guilty, he'll have told multiple lies under oath. Some judges take offense at that.

Just as the thief (now "defendant") *looks* differently in court, his version of what happened might make people think that you and he are discussing entirely different cases. If he offers any explanation, it's usually rambling and pointless. Also, he may bring his mother or girlfriend. They'll admit they weren't even present at the time of the incident, but still swear that he didn't steal anything; or that American society needs an overhaul.

If the plea was guilty, the judge will order the choir silent and might ask if you have anything to say. As long as the thief didn't stray too awfully far afield, simply say, "No, Your Honor." Leave it at that. You won. Don't blow it.

**Questioning and Cross Examination.** In most cases, you won't ask a defendant questions. That chore is assumed by His Honor. But different judges have different styles: some progress methodically and probe with seemingly insignificant questions, then mold the mass into form; others employ a "slash and burn" approach.

If a thief pleads not-guilty, whatever he says will probably be too much for his own good, *and* he will lie. (Listen carefully and you'll find the answer to a lie is often in the lie, itself.) That, or his testimony will be inherently pointless. I heard somewhere of a man on trial for murder, and the prosecution produced four witnesses who testified they saw him stab the victim. Undaunted, the defendant produced eight witnesses (none of whom had been at the scene, however) who testified truthfully that on the day in question they did *not* see him stab anybody.

I rarely feel obliged to cross-examine, elaborate on testimony or refute lies, but when I do, my approach is to jab, then punch. For example, if the shoplifter says he didn't conceal a hat at all, but just had it in his hand: I jab: "We sell hats to hundreds of people." Then I punch: "If we arrested people for just holding a hat, we'd fill the courtroom. It was stuffed in the crotch of his pants."

If you have no witness and he attempts a blanket denial, it's "I Say, You Say." In that case, you might want him to come up with a credible reason for being singled out of thousands of people. Why him? If you arrested him to provide "numbers," why just one? Why none last week? Why aren't the courtroom benches sagging under hundreds of alleged hat-thieves? (No matter what he says, don't you have a witness to a confession?)

Finally, if he admits he concealed the hat and *also* admits he lied about it while he was in the store, then no matter what else he says, his chance of acquittal (winning) is roughly the same as a cellophane dog chasing an asbestos cat through hell.

## Tips for Testimony

1. Think before you speak.
2. Take your time in answering if you need to organize your thoughts.
3. If asked a "trick question" (a 'yes or no answer' is inadequate for your purposes), look at the judge and ask, "May I answer the question in my own words?"
4. Speak loudly enough for the judge and jury to hear you. Don't make anyone repeatedly ask that you speak up.
5. If unsure or if you don't know, say so. Evading comes across as dishonest.
6. Whenever you ask the judge if it's all right for you to do something and he says "yes," always say: "Thank you, your Honor." (If he says no, say it anyway.)
7. Regardless the outcome (but especially when the judge rules in your favor) before you leave say, "Thank you, your Honor."
8. Avoid "street talk" words like bust, hanging out, chill, etc.
9. A common mistake is talking too much. K.I.S.S. (Keep it simple, stupid.) The more you say, the more someone can "hoist you with your own poniard." (Stick you with your own knife.)
10. Wear a heavily starched, long-sleeved shirt. Crisp, sharp edges help keep you alert.
11. NEVER make a disparaging comment about race, intelligence, origin, or sex.
12. NEVER tell a judge you won't do what he orders.
13. NEVER allow your personal feelings or opinions to become an issue.
14. NEVER tell the judge what he can or can't do.
15. Perjury is a serious offense.
16. Don't create issues.
17. Don't create issues.
18. **DON'T CREATE ISSUES.** *

---

\*  If your hat was in his bag, that is the issue. You want *him* to explain how *that* happened. The issue is not whether or not you saw him put it there. Remember: how you say something can be more important than what you say, and what you don't say can be more important than what you do say. Choose...your...words...carefully.

**The Defense Attorney.** Since virtually all shoplifters know they're guilty, they stoically accept their fate in court and the case is heard by a judge without a jury. There is rarely a defense attorney, a fact which simplifies Due Process immensely. (By coincidence, there's usually little profit for an attorney representing a shoplifter.)

Some thieves do try to contact an attorney and some even have an initial consultation. Most attorneys they consult, however, are anything but shoplifting specialists, and thieves find that calls to F. Lee Bailey or Johnnie Cochran go unreturned. In the end, most shoplifters are asked--in essence--if they really want legal fees added to a fine.

A handful of thieves, however, actually do hire an attorney.

Once retained, the concern most dear to that gentleman's heart (next to a respectable fee, of course) is winning. If, to win, he must make Mother Theresa appear a lying, filthy, fraud...it's OK; even if he knows it's not true. And whether the lawyer is ultimately successful or not, the lady with the blindfold and scales usually takes a hit.

Which reminds me: regardless his obvious good taste in tailors and verbal concern for your welfare, the defense attorney is not a trusted ally. When he says, "I'd REALLY appreciate it if 'we' can give this guy a break...." What he MEANS is, "Since I'm taking the guy's money, I want your help." So what is his appreciation good for? Ab-so-loot-lee nuthin'. For fun, though, do a little ethics and sincerity check.

The suit said he'd "appreciate it," so what did he mean? Ask him how, exactly, he might demonstrate his appreciation. Will he talk to your landlord and get a broken pipe fixed? A quid pro quo? He asked you to perform a service for him, so will he pay you? At least tip? If he offers a free legal service, is that kind of like free money? Don't touch it. Like I said, just for fun.

Before court, a thief's attorney might tell you that it's his client's "first offense." Be skeptical. If you check, you might learn he's on 10 years probation. When you ask Clinton, Esq. about that, he'll say what he meant was "first offense for this particular statute, this particular year in this particular area." (Plus, of course, the fifty times he got away.)

If the shoplifter has an attorney and your case appears decent, the attorney will probably reschedule the case at least once; probably at the last-minute. You'll probably learn about the postponement after you get to court expecting a trial. In fact, that may happen several times. If you once over-sleep or confuse dates, the judge--even knowing you were stood up before--will probably dismiss the case "for lack of prosecution." [50]

> General Motors made six billion dollars in 1995, and Ford made four. Some lawyers, too, make money like the big boys. Those of the assembly line persuasion care about one low budget case as much as Detroit cares about one bottom-of-the-line car sale. Generic shoplifting cases are low budget, so if an attorney takes one on, he probably just wants a quick win, a couple hundred bucks, and outta here.

When dealing with lawyers, remember that most of them belong to a club that's *far* tighter than the Fraternal Order of Police. For all you know, the defense attorney and solicitor are in-laws, former partners, or--God help you--have a shared, bigger fish to fry. If the latter, they may link cooperation now with a future, mutual back-scratch. (You'll never know.) But then again, they may be honest and straight-up.

Regardless of all that, if a defense attorney approaches you before the case is called, he's fishing for information or he wants to play "Let's Make a Deal." Be careful. It's usually best not to discuss the case at all. Say "nice to meet you" and quickly get away. If he presses you, politely tell him you'll think about it, and then quickly get away.

**Court Psychology.** In Pontius Pilate's court, the smart money was not on Jesus Christ. Even today, some judges and magistrates run court as crooked as a first grade lunch line, and not half as amusing.

Where justice *is* served, a courtroom might still invoke thoughts of Alice's Wonderland where stern figures glare and barristers argue From Here to Absurdity: "Ladies and gentlemen, the State alleges that my client bit off the ear of this police officer. However, sympathy for the officer cannot blind us to the fact that no evidence was presented to prove that my client bit the ear or that the unfortunate injury was intentional. The officer himself admitted that he didn't see my client's mouth on his ear and my client testified that he is certain that he didn't intentionally bite anyone's ear that night. You must not allow an unfortunate accident to be compounded by an emotional rush to judgment."

Pure fabrication? No, no, no. A Georgia attorney actually argued that her client bit an ear off a fully uniformed police officer <u>by accident</u>. Hence, "The One-Ear Rule." (Pg. 189)

Thieves act, but defense attorneys are *trained* to act. Some even attend acting *classes*. And a manual written for defense attorneys advises them to use fear as a tool, and to use the principles of show business in court. Sometimes, that manual says, you just have to "deal with (a problem) up-front." When taken in context, that appears to mean, "if you've tried everything else, but your case appears lost, consider telling the truth."

Oliver Wendell Holmes: "Lawyers spend a great deal of their time shoveling smoke."
A timeless proverb: "A poor man between two lawyers is like a fish between two cats."

While there's no question that certain aspects of the legal profession and criminal justice system deserve great respect and admiration, "the system" certainly does seem to have misplaced a fundamental principle (or two). Maybe it just needs a little fine tuning.

Once attorneys assume their courtroom persona, they take a Semi-mental Journey. They become actors, and actors are big into showmanship. If their script calls for the appearance of anger or exasperation (to make a point or to intimidate someone), they'll not think twice about acting half-crazy. And they expect you to get over it just as you get over a good scare at the movies. (In court, cops are the only people who don't normally act. They're usually pretty stoic: just do their business, take it all in, and file it away.)

So...don't worry about how attorneys act. Even if one is genuinely angry, it probably has nothing to do with you or the case, but rather has something to do with his wife or girlfriend; something like that. Like I said, don't worry about it. (But don't laugh at 'em, either. That's bad manners and just not smart.)

Back to you: beyond seeming credible, it's important to seem likable. Smile politely and nod to the nice people. You are the Good Guy. If a gate is between the gallery and the judge's bench and you get there first, hold it open for the bad guy. If he gets there first and doesn't hold it open, time your approach so he appears inconsiderate; make a little show of letting it hit you; just enough to show he's inconsiderate. (Did I say lawyers are actors?)

Once in front of the bench, nod politely to the thief, and then say a nice "Good morning" to the busy clerk. (Judges usually like their clerks.) After that, you make no further eye contact with the thief at all. Unless--and this is <u>un</u>usual--he's asking you a question after he's got permission from the judge to do so, or after you have permission from the judge to ask questions of the thief. Questions and answers thrown back and forth between defendant and plaintiff often just muddy the water, so avoid that if you can.

If the thief pleads not guilty, then (ideally), you briefly tell what happened, the thief tells transparent lies, and the judge rules in your favor. And it's usually that simple.

Never seem arrogant. (That is death.) Demonstrate that you're not some corporate hit-man down to notch your pistol, but a stalwart victim seeking justice, may it please His Honor to dispense it. (Most judges like humble pie.)

Project "nothing personal," but carry that too far you'll seem too impersonal; like you're some kind of android. You want people to think you're a warm person; one who wouldn't dream of shafting some poor soul caught up in a Big Mistake.

If a thief hit you and a fight ensued, a defense attorney might try to demonstrate his poor Mr. Ghandi dealt with an easily provoked bully. Don't over-react. Keep cool. If the thief was stopped inside the store, the attorney might try to show that if your jump-the-gun self had only waited, his client would have paid for the item he stuffed into the crotch of his pants. (He put it there--we'll be told--so it wouldn't get lost while he was walking around.) Don't show impatience and don't interrupt.

If he pleads not guilty, he wants to convince the court that (1) It was your fault that there's a Big Mistake, (2) The facts have been misinterpreted and that's why there's a Big Mistake, or (3) You're a bad person and so the facts are bad and that's why there's a Big Mistake. His key, always, is Big Mistake.

A defense attorney (or thief) usually takes either a **denial** or **destruction** approach. If "denial," he denies some single, specific, (but important) point, usually "intent". He sometimes denies and argues multiple points. This is the "shotgun approach" (also called the "spaghetti on the wall approach"): try lots of things and maybe one will hit and stick. With "destruction," he goes after you personally. It's "consider the source": if he makes you appear an untrustworthy person, your testimony will seem untrustworthy, too.

Whatever his approach, your job is to behave in such a way that everyone present perceives you as being credible: that at least you know <u>who</u> you are, <u>where</u> you are, <u>why</u> you're there, and that you know <u>when</u> you are. Psychiatrists call that being "oriented times four" ("O x 4"). Mess that up, and all I can say is try to act civilized until it's over.

## 11.03 Jury Trials

Matlock's jury trials on television resemble garden-variety non-jury trials about as much as an expensive restaurant with a maitre d' ("major-domo") resembles McDonald's. They're both eateries, but jury trials have more players, formalities, and atmosphere. Courts and restaurants, both, keep their doors open with O.P.M., Other People's Money.

With jury trials, judges do much less questioning and infinitely more refereeing. For the lawyers, winning the case--their immediate goal--often takes precedence over abstract concepts like truth and justice. And the jurors and their verdict? They're like boxing match score-keepers, tallying points in ways discernible only to themselves and managing at times to slip even those bonds imposed by such trivial things as evidence and law. [51]

Judges and lawyers might stick pretty close to "legal points" (especially when there's witnesses), but juries decide the outcome and juries consider "people points" and common sense. (And one thing common sense dictates is you don't anger unpredictable committees engrossed in the business of deciding your fate.)

Jury trials have more "time-outs" than non-jury trials. The referee (judge) and team captains (counselors) confer to settle weighty constitutional issues and confirm the next day's tee time. Another thing differentiating jury from non-jury contests is in jury trials, lawyers...pardon me...*counselors* do most of the talking. In either type trial, you (the plaintiff) ordinarily testify, but testifying is optional for the thief. (It's usually up to his lawyer and depends, also, on whether or not a "deal" was made before court.)

> **Reality:** In a criminal case, the prosecutor (solicitor) is probably on your side, and the defense attorney is certainly not. In a civil case, the attorney for the other guy is definitely not on your side, but your own attorney is on your side. (Usually.)

If you declined to play "Let's Make a Deal," you'll be among the first to be called as a witness. You'll be questioned first by the prosecutor and then by the defense. When a prosecutor asks questions, it's called "direct questioning." After you say what he wants to hear, he turns you over to the defense for "cross-examination."

On cross, the defense attorney wants to make you and your case look weak or bad. He'll change topics, then quickly change again. He'll ask the same things different ways. If he uses rapid-fire, complex or compound questions, or wants a single response to multiple or interwoven questions, act puzzled and say, "I'm sorry. Could you repeat the question, please?" Ask this a few times and you'll be surprised how often he forgot what he actually asked. His next question will be simpler. (If it's amusing, don't smile.)

Defense attorneys slip trash into questions, so pay close attention to every word. If you testified that his client (the thief) put an item in a pocket, he may ask: "What did you do after Mr. Waller bagged the (item)? Did you approach him right then or did you call the police and approach him later?"

If you skip the first question (containing the word "bag") and, instead, answer the second or third question, you will eat your non-answer later. It might come back like this: "Mr. Smith, in your earlier testimony, you stated that Mr. Waller put the (item) in his pocket, but you also testified just a moment ago--under oath--that he put it in a bag. Mr. Smythe (intentionally mispronouncing your name to distract you), if you _really_ saw him conceal something, you wouldn't be so confused, would you?"

If the attorney changes details, times, description of merchandise or the description or identity of the shoplifter, correct it immediately. Remember, defense attorneys want you to lose. For that reason, they serve up questions with more curves than a bowl of spaghetti.

When the defense attorney is finished, the prosecuting attorney may want to clarify a point or two. If he asks questions a second time (following the defense), it's "redirect," and that may be followed with "recross" by the defense. And, yes, there may be "re-redirect" and "re-recross." Always, though, someone will eventually say, "You're excused," and then you're free to find a restroom. Before you leave the witness stand, though, look at the judge and say, "Thank you, your Honor." Never mind what for.

More witnesses may follow and the same "Direct/Cross," "re-direct/re-cross could accompany every one. Sooner or later, though, the evidence is all presented, or a couple of jurors nod off, or the judge becomes noticeably irritated. When any of these signs appear-- and you can count on this--the proceeding _will_ be wrapped up PDQ.

At that point, everyone takes a break. The jury retires to the "jury room" where, isolated from the emotion-charged atmosphere outside their door, they discuss society, shifty eyes, current events, the case at hand, and last night's ball game. It may take hours, but our sturdy peers eventually tie it all together. Usually.

Eventually, the principal parties all return to the courtroom, joined a bit later by the jury. The judge asks if they reached a verdict, and if they did, someone announces it: guilty or not guilty. The judge then briefly addresses the assemblage, brings in the dog, puts out the cat, and it's over.

No matter how it turns out, a courthouse usually looks best in a rearview mirror.

> *"It ain't whatcha say,*
> *it's the way howcha' say it."*
>
> -- Louis Armstrong "Whatcha Say," 1945

> 12/27/92
>
> Dear Mr. Helena,
>
> I am thirteen years of age, and I am guilty, as you presumed, of shoplifting in your store.
>
> I am extremely ashamed of myself and <u>never</u> intend on stealing again. I am in deep regret of this, for I have lost the trust of those close to me. I am so terribly sorry and hope that you will come to accept my sincerest apology.
>
> I have realized that if one must do something wrong to obtain a thing, then it was not meant to be theirs in the first place. Again, I am so terribly sorry. You can bet on my life that this will <u>never</u> happen again.
>
> Sincerely,
> Chrissy

**(Time will tell.)**

# *Chapter Notes*

## Chapter 1

**1.** The average family of four pays about $300 per year for shoplifting and related expenses; but that doesn't cover the losses. In addition to stolen merchandise, stores suffer time lost to court, increased training and insurance costs, legal fees, damaged merchandise, medical bills, and damaged fixtures and displays. Security is an add-on: a single store might have $30,000 in electronics, an employee monitoring screens and other security personnel on the sales floor. Some stores have security tags on merchandise, removers at check-outs and sensors at doors.

**2.** Millions of people expect rewards for good decisions while fiercely resisting negative consequences for bad decisions. For example: people who make themselves unemployable with foolish choices feel they have a "right" to the same health care as wage earners who *work* for it.

As it is, if anyone commits a big enough crime, or multiple small crimes, their health and dental care is provided in prison free of charge by a presumably grateful society while millions of honest workers cannot afford identical medical treatment for themselves and their families.

Plus, we give millions in "disability" dollars to drug addicts with no requirement to stop buying and using illegal drugs. Disability officials may disagree, but they know as well as anyone that their only *real* requirement is that addicts must *not* get their lives straight. If they do, they are *definitely* punished: the free money stops.

We even pay citizens to become obese. Yes, you can eat your way into a lifetime of monthly "disability" checks and Moon Pies. The requirement? Get very heavy and don't lose weight.

"Something for nothing" is more than tolerated: it is institutionalized. Non-performance in American schools is rewarded with automatic promotions which allow a million functionally illiterate young people to graduate each year. Over time, tens of millions have come to believe that being forced to live with painful consequences is not only cruel, but damned unusual.

**3.** *Having*, though, is fun. Society teaches that everyone has the right to have anything they want. And if you have a right to have it (so the thinking goes) you must also have a right to take it. (Otherwise, you might not get what you have a right to have.) Hence, a right to take whatever you have a right to have; a right to not to have to be without--a handy de facto right by virtue of the double-negative.

With their "Right to Have" and "Right to Take" established, it conveniently follows (to a thief's way of thinking) that store employees are "in the wrong" if they interfere; that employees victimize shoplifters, not the other way around, and that employees are honest-to-God fortunate if merely humiliated for interfering. In practice, many a retail clerk is thumped for the breach.

Whether it's a gold necklace or pound of shrimp, millions of people just steal it if they want it. They don't have an ingrained ethic that "having" is a product of "earning" or "working." (Of course, some thieves point out that stealing *is* work, and dangerous at that. But that sentiment demonstrates the importance of semantics more than anything else.) For many people, "earning" is an alien concept involving responsibility, self-discipline, and other uncomfortable things.

## Chapter 2

**4.** One loss prevention firm in Orlando, Florida, reports that older citizens are being caught far more frequently. Another Florida source, a pre-trial intervention program, advises that of 600 cases handled annually, 60-70 percent of their shoplifters were older than 60 years of age.

**5.** "Class" involves *much* more than personal finances. In fact, money--or lack of it--has little to do with class: if you give a poor scumbag a million dollars, what have you really done other than create a *rich* scumbag?

**6.** At the police academy, we were taught how to use handcuffs; how to have the suspect stand, how we stand, etc. After the first training period, the cadets returned to a classroom where we were shown a film videotaped by a prison staff.

Fascinated and not a little shocked, we watched convicts in the prison yard teaching other convicts how to <u>avoid</u> being handcuffed.

7.  I was flabbergasted the first time I saw a teenager steal an item and just throw it in a trash can outside the store. Once they start, kids can quickly escalate out of control. I've watched shocked parents struggle with the reality of Sweet-never-been-in-trouble-and-makes-straight-A's being arrested for a stealing frenzy from *numerous* stores.

Juveniles lack emotional maturity, but have unprecedented, unsupervised access to stores. I've even heard a group call themselves "Theft R Us Kids."

8.  That leaves 80 percent of employees. (Some say it's 25-50-25.) They steal, or don't, from one month to the next. Many are situationally tempted depending on whether they feel "taking" is justified: "I worked two hours last week and didn't get paid for it. They owe me ten bucks, and this pen (or whatever) is only five bucks. It'll make us even and, what the hell,...they're getting the best of the deal." And so it goes.

Another common rationale used by dishonest employees is a unilateral decision to get a raise. If they feel they "should" get $7 an hour, but make only $6, they steal what they feel is enough "to make things right." Two reasons most expressed are (1) children's needs, and (2) lack of appreciation of work by management. Good employee relations and a watchful eye keep the usually honest 80 percent a usually honest 80 percent.

## Chapter 3

9.  While researching, I called a police duty officer in Detroit. She said shoplifting wasn't shoplifting (there) until a thief left the store. I explained SC law, and she put me on hold to "check with someone else." A moment later, she said she'd been mistaken; in Michigan it is *not* necessary for a thief to leave; arrests are legal inside the store. A duty officer with another major police department in a different state told me that a credit thief cannot make use of an account number and other information unless he actually has physical possession of the credit card itself. Of course, this is patently untrue. Over the years, how many victims have they misled?

Do not--*do not*--speak with only one officer. If you have a question, *ask* an officer, but double-check with a captain, deputy chief or chief; *and* a judge or solicitor. Take notes, and obtain copies of applicable laws and ordinances. Resolve inconsistencies between sources.

**Seminars:** About 90% of counterfeit money in the US is imported from other countries. We all know the Secret Service handles that, but did you know they also handle many types of credit fraud? I learned that and much more during a highly informative loss prevention seminar in Charleston (SC) where Special Agent Joe Ravenell was guest speaker.

Another LP seminar that I attended featured veteran agent Joe Livingston of the SC Law Enforcement Division. A nationally recognized expert on transient criminal groups and non-traditional organized crime, he provided information about a criminal technique that enabled me to identify a potentially disastrous--and previously overlooked--hole in a store's diamond and gold security. The "window" for theft existed only to those who knew exactly what they were looking for, but it was *soooooo* simple. But in three years of looking right at it, I hadn't seen it.

Seminars "sharpen your saw" and provide quantum leaps in knowledge. They also provide opportunities to network with specialists...*and to ask questions.* Many areas have local loss prevention associations, merchant associations, and law enforcement programs that provide excellent seminars free of charge. (A good starting point in locating such groups are local police "crime prevention officers.")

I suggest attending every germane seminar that time and finances allow. For advice on starting an LP association, write Noah J.R. Moore, Director of Security, Citadel Mall, 2070 Sam Rittenberg Blvd. #200, Charleston, SC 29407.

10. In SC, "Code 16-13-140, Delay to investigate ownership of merchandise," would be referred to as "The Merchant's Privilege." Quoted here is 1996 criminal law: "In any action brought by reason of having been delayed by a merchant or merchant's employee or agent on or near the premises of a mercantile establishment for the purpose of investigation concerning the ownership of any merchandise, it shall be a defense to such action if: (1) The person was delayed in a reasonable manner and for a reasonable time to permit such investigation, and (2) reasonable cause existed to believe that the person delayed had committed the crime of shoplifting." (continued next page)

(continued from pg 142)

If jerks feel they have a right to act suspiciously without question, what other "rights" do they fancy they have? The answer is "quite a few." How you handle it depends on how severe the tirade becomes. They probably expect you to "retreat." If you do, you accept and reward their crude behavior *and* you give them the opportunity to steal.

Many people see nothing wrong with ripping packages open. In fact, they consider it a "right" (presumably incorporated somewhere under "Pursuit of Happiness.") The appropriation of others' property, to them, is a demonstration of individual freedom (not entirely unlike the freedom we all have to vote for whichever political candidate promises us the most from other peoples' paychecks).

**11.** Even a parrot can say, "If it feels good, do it." Nevertheless, most people who mouth "slogans" think ("believe," actually) that their slogans constitute intelligent conversation.

But are slogans even true? Example: "People have a right to say anything." Really? Is slander a "right?" How about shouting "Fire!" in a theater?" Of course not. We all know that *no one* can legally say anything he feels like saying, wherever he happens to be. But slogans feel so good to people who use them that truth and common sense take a back seat.

America's favorite slogan might be, "Everyone should be treated the same." But is it even *possible* to treat everyone the same unless everyone *is* the same? Same skills, same age, same religion, and same natural abilities? Emotionally, physically, and intellectually the same? Don't different people *need* different kinds and degrees of attention, treatment and motivation?

Would you treat your worst employee the same as your top producer? A lazy rookie the same as Michael Jordan? Do you want crackheads doing brain surgery because they're "just as good" as doctors? Get a grip!

"Just because you think it's wrong doesn't make it wrong. Who are you to judge?" Do people using that slogan believe we should legalize rape, sex with children and cannibalism? If not...well, who are they to judge?

"Oh, but that's different." No, it's not different; just the other side of the same coin.

Most slogans are idiotic and virtually all are only half-true (which is "the Devil's favorite kind of lie"). Demagogues such as Hitler *love* slogans; "Say a lie loud enough and long enough, and people will believe it." After hearing any particular slogan enough times, people stop examining or thinking about it. Then they subconsciously accept it and unconsciously react to it.

To see how people use slogans and react to them, watch any TV talk show. Herds...I mean crowds...adore slogans. They cheer and applaud as though someone actually said something. Or they nod solemnly as though the slogan is some sacred Ultimate Truth.

In reality, slogans are simple tools, often used to justify, promote or attack. They allow us to avoid having to consider uncomfortable, opposing, or new ideas, to dodge personal responsibility, to trample rights of others, and to end honest dialogue by replacing logic with feel-good rhetoric.

Unfortunately, slogans are here to stay and will continue to create no end of trouble. When you hear a slogan, just realize what's happening and react intelligently. (Shoot the speaker.)

## Chapter 4

**12.** Corporate executives who comfortably refer to shoplifters and other types of thieves as "customers" must feel that shoplifting is essentially harmless; a pedestrian form of "income redistribution."

After a dozen employees and an FBI stakeout team witness a man smash a display case, snatch twenty gold watches, shatter a glass door and shoot a clerk on the way out, some executives will say "...and the customer then exited the store." People like that are too insulated.

**13.** The young lady in question, so her manager said, allowed two cheeky thieves to stuff "many" earrings into a shopping bag and leave. "Policy's policy," thought the naive clerk. What do shoplifters think about this place? Melanie says, "We go there every time we're in the mall. It's so easy!" (Fortunately for the store, Melanie & Company have no idea that the store's policy prohibits stops and arrests. She thinks her success there is a result of her crafty self outwitting stupid employees.)

## Chapter 5

**14.** A jury is composed of adults, supposedly more or less average. Consider for a moment how situationally-dumb an "average person" can be. Then consider that half the population is--by definition--even dumber than that. Does it surprise you that most cases scheduled for a jury are settled before court, even if it means hammering out a compromise in a courthouse bathroom?

**15.** If police arrive before she leaves, they may ID her, check for warrants, or issue a Criminal Trespass warning. If things go exceedingly well, they might even arrest her for disorderly conduct.

**16.** One result of this change in American attitudes has been a change in our working definition of "victim." It's now, "One deserving of reward or preferential treatment by virtue of actual, implied, alleged, reported, perceived, imagined, widely believed or verbalized offense, trauma, delusion, hallucination, affront or slight, such cause not needing to be experienced, witnessed, understood, or articulated by plaintiff or others, and which cause falls within an appropriate statute of limitations, being currently retroactive to the Dawn of Time." (Author)

**17.** One day, Geraldo may host "Children of Survivors of Retail Security Stops." America is dying for new and innovative victims, and TV talk shows advertise for them with 800-numbers. Unless the national trend is reversed, victims may eventually be classified like food groups. Class 10 victims, for example, might be gulag survivors; Class 1 victims, those surviving a burger where a cook forgot to hold the mustard. (An allergic reaction to the mustard would move him up, you know, to maybe a Class 5.)

Each offense will have a designated fine, and we'll print manuals with offenses and punishments so everyone can know exactly how offensive he can afford to be.

Speaking of Geraldo, his show on October 21, 1993, featured "Female Shoplifters Who've Come Clean." One "guest" admitted to shoplifting over $81,000 in merchandise, and Geraldo announced retail losses to shoplifters during Christmas would exceed $7 billion, with shoppers paying markups of up to 20 percent to cover it. About a month later, Riki Lake, too, featured shoplifting "guests." Riki and a psychologist present on the show agreed that shoplifters "need help," but didn't mention that shop owners need help, too. (Yeah, probably just an oversight.)

**18.** Don't be "wishy-washy" in the presence of the family unless it serves a purpose. In some cases, you may *want* someone to "talk you out of prosecuting." Maybe your case isn't as strong as you like, or maybe you want to "appear" happy to prosecute, but you'd really rather just be done with it. Sometimes a little wavering back and forth keeps the line moving.

**19.** Contemporary society is witnessing a polarization process with accompanying ill will, mistrust, and violence. Abortion-issue "tribes," sex tribes and a hundred other tribes all have very intense feelings. Our own divisiveness is depressing and frustrating, but look around: millions of Irish hate the English, the Killing Fields of Cambodia are legendary, and mountains of murdered children in Africa continue to grow. As bad as we seem to have it, where would you rather be?

**20.** Karl Sigmund & Martin Nowak of the Univ. of Vienna developed a mathematical theory concerning personality types. One type, the "Tit-for-Tats," mirror others' actions toward themselves. They repay kindness with kindness, but when hurt by others (even unintentionally), tit-for-tat became an eye-for-an-eye. Another personality type, "Relentless Defectors," are often disguised as "nice people," but in truth *feed* on nice people, the unwary and the inexperienced. Relentless Defectors ruthlessly seize any benefit by any means and leave trails of victims and destruction in their wake. And the most effective (profitable) strategy? "Two-Tits-for-a-Tat." When one assumes that an initial hit is accidental and responds cordially, accidents seldom escalate and everyone usually gets along very well. It provides maximum success in the long run.

**21.** As we sat in front of his mother, both of us bloody with shirts torn apart, one thief told Mom that he "didn't fight nobody." On another occasion, my eyeglasses were broken, my face bruised from multiple hits, and the hole where the thief stabbed me poured blood and required stitches. I eventually got him handcuffed with the help of *three* others. Later, he denied fighting "with anybody" and said he had no idea why anyone would even say he fought. (Interestingly, he was one who fought and lost, then faked resignation and waited for another--better--opportunity to escape. Then he unwound like a tornado. Never believe they give up just because they give in.)

22. You become their mother's voice: "Put things back where they belong." You're their 1st grade school teacher or their grandfather. It's "right" to put things back where they belong and it's "bad" if you don't. Seize the moral (and psychological) high-ground.

Before you go seizing anything, though, remember that until you find concealed merchandise your case is not a sure thing. Worse, it may be a major faux pas on your part. If you play the lion, someone may shoot you for sport; play the lamb, someone might decide it's chops for dinner. Ordinarily, the greatest degree of safety lies between the extremes.

## Chapter 6

23. In March of 1995, I did a little dumpster diving and drove away with office supplies (new rolls of calculator tape, boxes of staples, etc.), store fixtures (peg hooks, shelf fences, scan hooks, etc.), dozens of new store bags, *new* merchandise thrown out with trash, and--of course-- damaged merchandise as well. It was a surprisingly clean job since considerate employees had the nasty trash all neatly bagged. (To discourage thieves in the past, I've marked damaged items with spray paint and even poured paint all over trash in a dumpster. Let 'em go through *that*.)

The next day I took some of the damaged merchandise to other stores of the same chain and found everyone cooperative. In exchange for some of the damaged dumpster merchandise, I was given a new coffee machine, new Igloo ice chest, and a smaller cooler. These, along with the undamaged dumpster merchandise, were returned to sister stores for *cash*. Considering time in the dumpster, organizing loot, and driving store to store, I cleared $15 *an hour* in cash and prizes. No one knew my face, of course, and I dealt with different stores *and* different shifts.

I could even justify all this as *honest* activity. What's the difference, one might ask, between pulling it from a dumpster now or from a landfill later? And, hey...no one asked me if I bought it, they just asked if I had a receipt.

24. When intimidators (bullies) feel uncomfortable, they blame others. It's a personality trait. They respond with aggression to even perceived slights. If you so much as look at them, they believe they've been wronged.

I asked one young man if he just stole from stores, or also from individuals, from strangers. Would he steal a purse from a woman shopping with her children? "Yeah, probably so," he replied. "If she did something wrong. You know, like if she looked at me cross or something." Note his use of the word "wrong" and the enormity of the woman's offense. ("Looked at him cross.") <u>That</u>, he feels, is justification to victimize women and children.

25. Throughout this book I present what *is*. Other people's experience may differ radically from my own, and that's OK. In Britain, for example, Scottish dwarfs might account for all theft, and maybe that's why Hadrian & Company collected rocks. But even if that were true, Scottish dwarfs wouldn't make *my* list because *I* haven't found them any trouble at all. The Romans had their barbarians; we have ours.

Since my listings reflect experience, my future lists might change. Meanwhile, though, the moving hand writs what *was*, and never mind should-have-beens.

## Chapter 7

26. Those who intend to steal by just walking out with an item in their hand don't *normally* dally on location unless it's necessary. They might, for example, need to wait for store personnel to become distracted.

27. In kindergarten we were taught to look left and right before crossing streets. Apparently, looking left and right is taught in Shoplifting 101. As though programmed, almost all shoplifters perform this ritual. One young man I watched looked to his left fourteen (14!) times before bagging an item. "Rubber-necking" is a flashing neon sign.

28. I've been able to get to a bagger and arrest him before two lookouts *and* two distractions realized what was happening. (One of the lookouts in that case was a man in a wheel-chair.) The looks on their faces were a painful combination of frustration and disbelief, like first-and-goal, offensive linemen after their quarterback is blind-sided and fumbles, and an opposing player snatches the ball to run ninety yards for a touchdown.

"Surprise" is taught in military colleges world-wide as a **"Principle of War."** "Moss Mouse," the nine Principle of war are **M**aneuver, **O**bjective, **S**implicity, **S**urprise, **M**ass,

Organization, Unity of Command, Surveillance, and Economy of Force. The five thieves mentioned above had numbers [Mass] on their side, but I had all the rest.

If you see a look-out, find a bagger; see a ritual, see a thief. Stay undetected or play dumb while thieves are setting up, and capitalize on their belief that they are much more clever than the next guy. But you have to watch, be patient, and *be* "vewy, vewy, quiet."

**29.** A pity--and something of a mystery--is that shoplifting and security lectures aren't required for business majors in college. M.A. after B.A. enters retail familiar with "offshore banks," but totally ignorant about in-store pranks. They know less about a $50-billion gorilla of a retail problem than they know about King Kong's girlfriend.

Most retail management and corporate personnel lack significant training. It often consists of a 20-minute videotape or thin brochure. A manager for a national chain summed up his security training in eight words: "You just kind of learn as you go." Most small business owners also fly-by-the-seat-of-their-pants.

## Chapter 8

**30.** If an item disappears, I usually ask where it was left so I can put it back where it belongs if he changed his mind about buying it. If he says he left it at the original display--and I'm certain that's not true--I think about it. Perhaps he meant he left it at "a" display. Or maybe he gave it to his wife to put back. If there's a possibility that what he says might somehow be true enough to pass muster in a courtroom, I'll probably say something disarming and just walk away. It all depends on the totality of the circumstances.

Maybe I can check his story, maybe not; but I won't arrest if there's doubt, nor will I push a situation that's clearly not going my way. In poker terms: don't bet heavily on filling an inside straight. It's a suckers bet.

If I can't make a decent case, I sometimes lounge by the front door where the thief can see me. He might think I'm waiting for him to leave to arrest him, and that might rattle him enough to make him ditch any concealed merchandise *before* he tries to leave. Whether I see it or not, the merchandise is saved. Also, I might smile and wave when he exits and give him a hearty "Catch you later". Honest shoppers don't read anything into that particular good-bye, but I love the look on a thief's face when he hears it.

**31.** The distinction between "deter" and "prevent" is important. Locked doors deter burglary, but do not prevent it. The presence of a uniformed officer deters a person from screaming at a cashier; but does not prevent it from happening.

Interestingly, life-sized, full-color cutouts of uniformed police officers at doors, sometimes with a sign announcing shoplifters are prosecuted, have been tested and proven in some cases to significantly decrease the incidence of shoplifting.

**32.** I was more proactive than the average police officer, and I worked off-duty in retail stores. In uniform, I caught no shoplifters. Also, I've supervised dozens of veteran officers--good cops--doing uniformed retail security. How does it work out? Few shoplifting arrests, but uniforms did consistently well running weirdoes out, deterring armed robbery, quieting drunk cowboys and providing back-up for store management and plain-clothes people.

## Chapter 9

**33.** If a stop takes place at or near the door, people outside might see and respond if they see a friend in trouble. Therefore, any stop at the door or outdoors is loaded with potential problems and unknown quantities. Outside the door is no-man's land.

**34.** In-store stops decrease the incidence of a thief resisting, and cut down on interference by others. People generally exercise more self-restraint inside a store than on a street or in the common of a mall. This applies to suspects as well as bystanders.

**35.** Would an honest shopper lie about where he left an item? Not usually, but a thief almost always does. He *has* to. And when he lies, it's usually the same tired lie that worked in the past: "I put it back." Your certainty the item was not returned to the display is crucial. As Ben Franklin noted, "Vice knows she's ugly, so puts on her mask." The thief strives to maintain his "customer persona;" but unknown to him, the item he took in hand is "unique."

**36.** Situations vary. After you recover stolen merchandise, you usually take the thief somewhere for processing. (Usually. If you fought and ended up sitting on his back, then letting him get up might let him start fighting again; or if taking him elsewhere might draw unwanted attention, it might be best to stay put.) As soon as possible, check for weapons (razors, box cutters, any pointed objects like pens or pencils, etc.) and look for additional stolen items from your own and other stores. I often find more than I originally thought they stole.

**37.** Alpha dogs (natural leaders by instinct) tend to exhibit an independent flair, and it's remarkable what a superbly trained and effective $8,000 Alpha K-9 can get away with. Luke, for example, knew full well that he was supposed to bite arms only, and during Sunday afternoon demonstrations for a delighted citizenry he was all Marquis de Queensberry. However, he instinctively knew the difference between parades and street-fights, where his preferred "targets of choice" seemed to be front and back about half way down. (Incidentally, if you think a man will flail and scream if his penis gets detained by a police canine, you're mistaken. In reality, most men can be relied upon to stand very still, speak quietly, and be very, very cooperative.)

Rommel (a white Alpha German Shepherd) and Deputy Sheriff Jerry Whidby were a veteran K-9 team, highly skilled and remarkably efficient. One broiling Georgia summer day, a fugitive was cornered in the crawl space under a house and Jerry sent Rommel to fetch him. There followed blood-curdling snarls and screams until, abruptly, all became silent. Jerry crawled in to investigate and found the fugitive and Rommel just staring at each other about 5 feet apart. Both were obviously exhausted and gasping for air. "What the hell's going on?" demanded Jerry, and in response, the fugitive panted, "We're takin' a break."

While commanding the total respect of even the most dangerous and hardened adults, Luke tolerated rooms full of ear and tail-pulling 1st graders. He delighted kids and adults in schools, churches, and on the streets, and wherever he went (well, almost wherever) he made new friends for the police department. Luke and Rommel were wondrous assets, and every community--regardless of size--would do well to find and maintain K-9s like them. They are priceless.

**38.** The five different types of death are **natural, suicidal, homicidal, justifiable,** and **accidental**. (Personally, I would add **"commendable."**)

I've heard many an otherwise compassionate cop say, "I'd rather be tried by twelve than carried by six." Certainly, a jury box beats a pine box. On the other hand, I've yet to see a piece of merchandise in a retail store worth killing or dying for. Unless you really know what you're doing, when weapons come out, it's time to go. Let the police handle it.

## Chapter 10

**39.** The place you store thieves requires attention. Can they easily escape? Are there weapons: scissors, box cutters or sharp pencils? Is the view minimized so they have no idea who (else) may be around? Look the place over and think. You want these people off their feet and far enough from you to allow reaction time if they get froggy.

**40.** Remember that it's fine to fool bad guys, but don't "imply" camera, etc. when talking to good guys or in court.

**41.** Impress him as someone who doesn't hold stealing against him personally. Sound sympathetic. Make him think, "Gee, maybe this can turn out OK." Encouraged, he flips through his mental files to M, for "Manipulate," and turns to the section entitled "How to..." He then tries to demonstrate that he's really a nice person. (Incidentally, that's the reason he quit calling you all those names.)

**42.** Many shoplifters long ago concluded the question is merely rhetorical and honestly find it difficult to answer. Thieves think of themselves as takers, not stealers, and seldom think beyond that point. To them, "I hit the clerk" is a mechanical process like, "I put it in the bag." (He wouldn't hit her--he says--if she didn't get in the way; so it's *her* fault she was hit.) If pushed to consider issues in depth, they sometimes come up with reasons for victimizing others that surprise even themselves.

**43.** Special laws apply to juveniles, but a "reasonable" amount of time to collect evidence, facts, etc. before calling a parent is allowed. Have police define "reasonable time," and get a handle on any odd laws concerning juveniles that might apply to what you do. Even though juveniles have more rights than adults, they are often treated as though they have fewer. That can cause trouble.

**44.** If police are involved, a copy of their report is available (usually free) after a few days. Attach it to your own report. <u>Officers make mistakes, so check for errors</u>. When police ask for your telephone number and address, use your business info, *not* your home. If more then one officer arrives, a "primary officer" will handle the nuts and bolts. He gives you their case number, and court date, and he answers any questions you might have. He may not be the highest ranking officer present, but he's your contact person until the case is resolved.

**45.** Nothing elaborate; just large enough for the shoplifter's name, police case number, your log number and a date. A standard 3 by 5 index card will do. The top of the bag is folded; the card, folded over the plastic, is stapled to it.

## Chapter 11

**46.** If you're a novice, talk to police before you have a problem. Ask about evidence and court. Work at it and you'll earn their respect and support.

**47.** An odd political twist, even by American standards, was cocaine-smoking Mayor Barry of Washington, DC enlisting thousands of city prisoners and their families to help re-elect him. According to national media, he actually promised them he would go <u>softer</u> on crime.

**48.** If you have a witness, get organized before court. Go through events each from your own point of view. If questions or confusion arise, talk it through till your stories are consistent. Don't coach each other, but watch out for contradictory testimony. Far better to remember over coffee where you were when the butler done it than trying to remember that detail under the impatient eyes of an entire courtroom.

**49.** Most fear boils down to questions of rejection or failure, and in truth, according to Dale Carnegie, 90 percent of what we worry about never happens. (Helena's Corollary: "Most bad things that happen to people are covered with their own fingerprints.") The cooperation that we receive from most shoplifters is positively astounding and it's amazing how smoothly things usually go. If you can demonstrate the elements of the crime, there's little left to go wrong.

**50.** I've gone to city court as many as four times for one case because a lawyer was judge-shopping and stalling. In the end, his strategy of letter-generating rescheduling proved no more useful than no strategy at all. It did, however, provide visible justification for a hefty legal fee, so his client (the thief) felt that he got more for his money than just sympathy.

**51.** On the other hand, an impaneled collection of village idiots might somehow do a *superb* job of separating fact from fiction. Some juries soar far above individual capacities, others plunge record depths. Then, too, sometimes, you get what you pay for.

"Oh, the difference between nearly right and exactly right."
-- H.J. Brown, Jr.

---

### 🔒 Security 101: Dumpster divers must earn their pay.

Have enough paper-shredders to handle all of your offices and work-stations. Good shredders are available in the $40-$60 range. As you feed papers into the shredder, be certain the shred-strips will be perpendicular to lines of information. (Or look into "cross-shredders.")

Shred *anything* with bank or credit numbers, social security numbers, drivers license numbers, codes, etc. If information is particularly sensitive, dump the shredded strips into a plastic bag and dump water, other liquids, or any nasty substance into the bag. Then seal it and shake well.

# APPENDICES

1. Acknowledgment — 150
2. Civil Release — 151
3. Criminal Trespass — 152
4. Stop Log — 153
5. Incident Report — 155
   Supplemental — 158
   Witness Narrative — 159
6. Loss Prevention Checks — 160
7. Professional Thieves' Manual — 161
8. Shopper's Report — 165
9. Refund Report — 166
10. Put Wind in Your Sales! — 167
11. Credit Card Fraud — 170
12. Floor-Walking — 172
13. Covert Tape-Recording — 173
14. In-House LP Newsletters — 174
15. Internet Sources — 176
16. Employee and New-Hire Training — 179

Appendix 01

# ACKNOWLEDGMENT

I, _____, residing at

_____ in the City of _____

and State of _____, do voluntarily and without threats, force,

fear or promises admit and declare that on the _____ day of _____, 199___, I took

from the Company _____,

located at _____, an
item or items of merchandise without making payment for the item (s) and with the intent
to have it for my own use. I know or had cause to know that it was the property and/or
merchandise of the above Company and can be described as follows:

_____

_____

_____

_____

The value of the item (s) is _____

Signature: _____ Date _____

Signature of Parent or Guardian, if juvenile: _____

Date _____

Witness : _____

Appendix 02

# GENERAL RELEASE AND INDEMNIFICATION AGREEMENT

I, _____,

residing at_____

in the city of _____, State of _____

do voluntarily and without threats, force or coercion do release the Company of

_____

located at_____

and its heirs, employees, owners, and assigns, from any and all claims, demands or other causes of action, civil or other, I have or may have against them.

In consideration for the release of any claims I may have against them, the Company likewise declines action for the cause of these events.

This release may not be changed orally. I have read the foregoing release and fully understand it.

Signed: _____  Date: _____

Signature of Parent or Guardian, if juvenile: _____

Date: _____

Witness: _____

Appendix 03

The Criminal Trespass Notice allows for the arrest of anyone who enters the business after signing it. It is not necessary for them to do anything after they enter. If their feet are on the floor, that in itself is reason for arrest and prosecution. Anyone caught shoplifting should sign the form. Anyone convicted in court should be required to sign in the judge's presence the moment a 'guilty' verdict is passed. Write the judge's name on the form.

# CRIMINAL TRESPASS NOTICE

I, _____, residing at

_____, do hereby

acknowledge the demand, agreeing to same, that in the future as of this date I will refrain

from entering the business of _____

located in the City of _____. Further, I acknowledge the demand, agreeing to same, to refrain from personal contact with employees of said business and to refrain from entering onto any property of said business.

I understand that if I violate this agreement I will be in violation of Criminal Trespass law and will be arrested and prosecuted to the fullest extent of the law.

I further understand that this agreement may not be changed orally. I have read the foregoing and fully understand it.

Signed: _____ Date: _____

Signed, Parent or Guardian, if Juvenile: _____

Date: _____

Witness: _____

Appendix 04

# STOP LOG

Month/year _____

| C-Number | Date | Name | Sec Emp | Age | Sex | Race | $ | Rel | Pros | Disp | Internal | External |
|---|---|---|---|---|---|---|---|---|---|---|---|---|
| ___ | ___ | ___ | ___ | ___ | ___ | ___ | ___ | ___ | ___ | ___ | ___ | ___ |
| ___ | ___ | ___ | ___ | ___ | ___ | ___ | ___ | ___ | ___ | ___ | ___ | ___ |
| ___ | ___ | ___ | ___ | ___ | ___ | ___ | ___ | ___ | ___ | ___ | ___ | ___ |
| ___ | ___ | ___ | ___ | ___ | ___ | ___ | ___ | ___ | ___ | ___ | ___ | ___ |
| ___ | ___ | ___ | ___ | ___ | ___ | ___ | ___ | ___ | ___ | ___ | ___ | ___ |
| ___ | ___ | ___ | ___ | ___ | ___ | ___ | ___ | ___ | ___ | ___ | ___ | ___ |
| ___ | ___ | ___ | ___ | ___ | ___ | ___ | ___ | ___ | ___ | ___ | ___ | ___ |
| ___ | ___ | ___ | ___ | ___ | ___ | ___ | ___ | ___ | ___ | ___ | ___ | ___ |
| ___ | ___ | ___ | ___ | ___ | ___ | ___ | ___ | ___ | ___ | ___ | ___ | ___ |
| ___ | ___ | ___ | ___ | ___ | ___ | ___ | ___ | ___ | ___ | ___ | ___ | ___ |
| ___ | ___ | ___ | ___ | ___ | ___ | ___ | ___ | ___ | ___ | ___ | ___ | ___ |
| ___ | ___ | ___ | ___ | ___ | ___ | ___ | ___ | ___ | ___ | ___ | ___ | ___ |

Total month stopped ____ Prosecuted ____ Convicted ____
Total month white ____ black ____ Hispanic ____ Oriental ____ Other ____
Total month male ____ female ____ Total month Adults ____ Juveniles ____
Year to date: white ____ black ____ Hispanic ____ Oriental ____ Other ____
Year to date: male ____ female ____ Year to date: Adult ____ Juvenile ____
Year to date: stopped ____ prosecuted ____ convicted ____

| Total Month Internals ____ Externals ____ |
| Year to date Internals ____ Externals ____ |

**Note!!** The nice thing about detailed stats is you can show them to people. The bad thing is that people can look at them. (Think about it.)

Appendix 04, pg. 2

## Stop Log, pg. 2

| | |
|---|---|
| Number: | Chronological (01 through) for current month. |
| Date: | Current (ex., 05/19/89). |
| Sec Emp: | Initials of employee handling stop. |
| Name: | Per ID, if ID is presumed correct. |
| Sex: | M or F. |
| Race: | White--w    B--black    H--Hispanic |
| | A--Asian    N--NativeAmer.    O--other |
| $: | Dollar-value of stolen merchandise. |
| Rel: | Check if released or escaped. |
| Pro: | Check if actually prosecuted via legal system. |
| Disp*: | Guilty--G    Not guilty--NG    Pre-trial Intervention--PTI |
| | Dismissed--D    Escaped--E    Criminal Trespass Notice--CT |
| | Disorderly, arrested--DisA    Disorderly, exited store--DisX |
| Disposition (Employees) | Written Reprimand in file--W    Terminated--T    Quit--Q |
| Type: | Internal -- Employee    External -- non-employee |

\* Some thieves prefer their record clear of crimes implying "character flaws." If permitted, they might plead guilty to Disorderly Conduct and go happily on their way. Later, they can tell others that the affair was merely a loud argument or some other thing that won't keep them from being hired as cashiers or security officers in department stores.

Appendix 05

Part 1

## Report of Incident or Detention

Name _____ Date _____
     Last            First         M.

Address _____  _____  _____
     Street                              City        Zip

Social Security Number _____ ___ _____  Age _____ Date of Birth _____

Drivers License State _____ Number _____

Other ID Type _____ Number _____

Height ____ Weight ____ Color Eyes _____ Color Hair _____ Race ____ Sex ____

---

Time Record

    Time first observed _____ by whom _____

    Time confronted _____ by whom _____

    Time police notified _____ by whom _____

    Time parents notified _____ by who _____

    Time police arrived _____ Name of officer _____

    Time parents arrived _____

    Time subject released/exited with parent/police _____

Stop Log number _____ Police Case Number _____

Police Officer _____

Criminal Trespass Notice given by _____

    Notice witnessed by _____

    Notice form completed : yes ____ no ____

Appendix 05

Part 2

---
## Incident Report
---

1. Location of merchandise recovered  (Circle applicable):

   Hand     bag     purse     pants     pocket     coat     shirt

   Other (specify/explain)_____

2. Total value of merchandise lost _____   Recovered _____   Damaged _____

3. Total number of persons in group _____      Total number arrested _____

4. Did subject admit concealing merchandise?   yes   no

   4a. To whom _____

5. Did subject admit stealing merchandise?   yes   no

   5a. To whom _____

6. Has sub been in store before this day?   yes   no   unk

7. Has sub been involved in incident before this day?   yes   no   unsure   unknown

   7a. If yes, type incident _____

8. Was sub (already) on criminal trespass notice?   yes   no

9. First reason sub gives for theft _____

10. Second reason given for theft _____

11. Court Date _____   Day _____   Time _____

12. Witness needed? yes   no     12a. Notified? yes   no     12b. By whom? _____

13. Evidence needed: _____   13a. Where stored: _____

14. Officer taking evidence _____   14a. Date returned _____

Appendix 05

Part 03

## Narrative

Case Name: Last    First    M.I.                Case Date _____

(If necessary, use and attach Supplemental Report.)

_____
_____
_____
_____
_____
_____
_____
_____
_____
_____
_____
_____
_____
_____
_____
_____
_____
_____
_____
_____
_____
_____
_____

Witness: _____    Telephone: _____
Witness: _____    Telephone: _____
Witness: _____    Telephone: _____

Narrative of _____           Date _____

Appendix 05, Part 04

## Supplemental Report

Case Name _____
         Last                          First              M.I.

Incident Date _____

Stop Log Number _____  Police Case Number _____  Page ____ of ____

_____
_____
_____
_____
_____
_____
_____
_____
_____
_____
_____
_____
_____
_____
_____
_____
_____
_____
_____
_____

Signature _____   Date _____

Appendix 05, Part 05

## Witness Narrative

Subject: _____

Please include who, what, how, about when, and where. Describe in story form, from start to finish, what was seen, said and/or heard.

_____
_____
_____
_____
_____
_____
_____
_____
_____
_____
_____
_____
_____
_____
_____
_____
_____
_____
_____
_____

Name _____

Signature _____

Date _____

Stop Log number _____ Name _____

Incident Date _____

Appendix 06

# LOSS PREVENTION CHECKLIST
### ( X = Not OK )

**Sales Floor:**

___ 1. Fitting rooms and rest rooms monitored and/or locked at all times.
___ 2. Fitting rooms checked before and after customer usage, and regularly spot-checked.
___ 3. Low-visibility areas closely and regularly monitored.
___ 4. Judicious display of "high-theft potential" merchandise.
___ 5. Observation areas and security windows maintained, clear of obstruction and debris.
___ 6. Boxes, cartons, and bags of merchandise judiciously located.
___ 7. Security and display cases locked.
___ 8. Location of keys and condition of locked cases spot-checked (hinges, etc.).
___ 9. Restrooms regularly spot-checked. (Stalls, **ceiling tiles**, trash cans.)
___ 10. Employees in assigned zones and "spread out."
___ 11. If suspicious persons or activity in area, management or LP notified.
___ 12. Shoppers approached/greeted quickly upon arrival in area.
___ Other _____

**Cash Register Area:**

___ 1. Store bags/boxes not easily accessible to thieves.
___ 2. Pricing guns, security ("paid") stickers and other tools not accessible to thieves.
___ 3. Telephone situated so cashier faces customers to answer.
___ 4. Register placed so customer can easily read sale total.
___ 5. Area orderly: no discarded receipts; trash receipts shredded.
___ 6. Sufficient area to process/bag purchases without mixing with other items.
___ 7. Cash drawer maintained to prevent easy bill-snatching of 20's, 50's and 100's.
___ 8. No merchandise littering area (items for store use, discards etc.).
___ 9. No non-employees "hanging out," bagging merchandise, etc.
___ 10. No merchandise (from any store) in store bags being "held" or "watched" for customers.
___ Other _____

**Stock Room:**

___ 1. High-theft merchandise, particularly if small, sent immediately to displays or placed under lock and key.
___ 2. Trash-holding area, trash cans and empty boxes spot-checked.
___ 3. Back door kept closed, locked, and never unattended if not closed and locked.
___ 4. Delivery drivers, merchandise reps, etc., never left alone in storage areas.
___ 5. Supervisor or security present when trash removed.
___ 6. Access to entire stockroom/office area on a "need to be" basis only.
___ 7. No merchandise "laying around" (loose, out of place, etc.).
___ 8. Outdoor area around trash cans and dumpsters spot checked.
___ 9. Outside trash containers spot-checked (around, under, atop, and inside).
___ 10. Orderly storage of boxes/merchandise.
___ 11. No merchandise "held" or hidden contrary to policy.
___ 12. No clearance, mark-down merchandise; no merchandise stored in store-(logo) bags.
___ Other _____

Appendix 07

# A Thieves' World Best Seller

The following "manual" was given to the author at a seminar. It is printed in its entirety with no changes made <u>except</u> that bold print is added for emphasis, and notes in parenthesis are added for explanation. When received, the manual was prefaced as follows: "This 'manual' was reportedly recovered from an organized shoplifting-gang member arrested in Southern California. It is believed to have originated in Texas, and has since made its way to other states. It is reprinted exactly as found." (Typos and other errors were not corrected.)

# A Shoplifters Manual

### *Dressing Room*

This method should not be used unless you can't "do it off the floor," or the opportunity is obvious. Of course, **many stores have dressing room counters and this prevents their use. The most important thing to remember in working the dressing room is to make sure no one can tell how many and what specific pieces you have taken in;** needless to say, if you are planning to take 4 or 5 pieces, it is necessary to take into the dressing room at least twice that many. Of those that you take in, it is essential that the pieces be similar; this is because if a salesperson or security sees you, they see a certain print or style go into the dressing room and if it is not there when you are finished, it will tip them off. So **whatever pieces you decide to take, make sure you have at least one other of that print. A good way of disguising how many pieces there are, is to hang the piece you want to take on the one you're not going to take.**

Never wander around with any of the pieces you are planning to take because not only will the **salespeople want to help you or hold them for you or put them in a dressing room for you, all of which defeat your purpose,** but it gives security a chance to count how many you have.

Figure out which pieces you want to take and either swing them around to one rack or **when the salespeople are not paying attention to you, quickly gather them up and go into the room.** Try not to look too obvious about this because you never know if security is watching. Once in the dressing room, separate out which pieces you want to take and try to hide them by putting them on a chair, covered by your jacket. Often saleswomen will come in and check on you and when this happens, your pieces are protected. Most dressing room doors have slits in them which face in your direction; these allow people on the outside do see in. These were designed specifically for this purpose because before security can make a bust, they have to be absolutely sure that you have taken something and the best way to do this is to observe you.

One way to guard against this is to hang some clothes on the door itself so they cannot see it. You can see if someone is observing you by bending down low and looking up through the slits or open the door and see if someone is out there. **Once you have taken your pieces, leave the remaining ones in the dressing room.** *(Author's note: Naive employees usually believe that if someone left things in the fitting room, it means they didn't steal anything.)*

**This gives you more time to leave the store undetected because of the time someone goes back there to see what's left, you will be on your way out.**

If you feel uneasy about something and you want to test if security is suspicious, take the remaining pieces out and see if they are paying attention or acting funny. One thing to your advantage is that **when a salesperson is suspicious, they will almost always show it by acting rude or looking you up and down, etc.** *(Author's note: See the Greeting Formula, pg. 83.)*

## *Off The Floor*

This seems a lot more nerve-wracking than in the dressing room because you are practically doing it in front of people around you. The best ones are those that block you from view of any and all people around you; the best ones are those that shield you from both sides. Of course, **you can't have anyone close by, but as long as no one can see you,** *(Author's note: As long as no one can see your hands, bag, purse and see you stuffing them...)* **don't be stopped by other people in the department.** The only thing you have to worry about is observation windows and 3-sided mirrors. Also, many stores have disc shaped mirrors in the corner which reflect down; however, these are not too dangerous unless you are standing close by them, besides which somebody has to be looking close and you should notice if they are. The last thing you must be concerned with is a 2-way mirror observation windows, these are usually **small dark little holes located towards the top of the wall. Most of the time there is never anyone in there, but if they can be avoided, do so. If not, you can usually tell if someone is behind them by standing directly under them.**

One nice thing about working off the floor is that **if someone has seen you, they will let you know because they get crazy.** If it is a customer, they will usually look twice to make sure they saw what they thought they saw, and then run and find a salesperson to tell. If a **salesperson sees you, they will have a suspicious expression on their face and either go tell someone, or pick up the phone to call security.** *(Author's note: Security must be called quickly, not after they steal.)* Security can be contacted by three methods: phone the security office and tell them where the suspected thief is; or they have walkie-talkies; or a system of dings will go off in the store to notify them. I'm sure you've heard them and in a large department store, they are going off constantly. Unfortunately, no one has the code to be able to figure out which department is calling them and most of the time you should ignore the bells; however, if you think a salesperson is suspicious and you see them pick up the phone or push something and you hear the bells go off, then be aware because they could be for you.

If you have gotten your pieces all right and there are no detachers, you can get ready to leave the store. Check in a mirror to see if you look all right and there are no belts or tags hanging out. Remember, because you know those pieces are there, you can see them but nobody else can. **As you're getting ready and getting closer to the door to leave, be double-checking for security because they will not grab you until you are out that door.** How to spot security will be described later, but be suspicious of anyone who is around you a lot or following you; if they were around when you took the pieces and they are around when you're leaving, watch them. **Security almost always gives themselves away be using their walkie-talkie which will be in their purse or some shopping bag.** They will stare at you from behind racks, they will keep looking at you, follow you, etc. Never, ever leave the store without checking for them no matter how cool you thought you were. **If for some reason you think someone is onto you, don't panic because they can't do anything unless you leave the store.** *(Author's note: This is a <u>major</u> misconception in SC, GA, and other concealment states!)*

**Keep walking around from department to department just casually shopping and if they're still around, give them back their merchandise. Quickly go behind a rack and dump it or go into a dressing room and leave it. At that point, security knows what you're doing and you know who they are, but you haven't broken the law. They might even say something to you but just act like you don't know what they are talking about and leave. Do not go directly to your car** because they know you are a pro and that you probably have other pieces in your car, so if they can get your plates, they will call the police and get you searched. Just **walk around and see if someone is following you and if no one is, then go to your car.** If someone is, call "J.S." and arrangements can be made. Your car is very important, it can keep you from getting busted. Always park it as close to the store entrances as possible, the further away it is, the further you may have to run. Leave the door unlocked so you can jump in as fast as possible and as soon as you get in, close and lock the door. Make this a reflex action because **once you are in that car, you are almost home free.**

**After you leave, put the pieces in the trunk and take you** *(sic)* **trunk key off the ring and put it somewhere else. This way if you do get pulled over and they want to search your trunk, tell them you don't have the key.** The police can then either take you and the car in and get a warrant and search your car and you're sunk; or, they will probably bust open the trunk and this is an illegal search and seizure and though you might go to jail, the case will not hold up in court. Always check for people tailing you.
Sometimes, they will let you leave the store but a plainclothes will follow you from store to store, waiting for you to finish so they can bust you and get more charges against you.

**If you are being tailed, get out of the city and if they try to pull you over, ignore them; you could always claim you didn't believe they were police. If you have pieces in the car, rip off the price tags, and throw them out because without these, they have no proof.**

### *Detachers*

These are a royal pain in the ass. They are designed to sound an alarm as you leave the store. As I'm sure you have seen, they are white plastic and must be taken off with the proper tool. At one time, only about 50% of the stores had them, but now all of them do so they must be dealt with. When working off the floor, **take your pieces as usual and then go into the dressing room, but make sure you take some clothes in with you. This is necessary when you take the detachers off-- or you will have no place to put them. Put them on the clothes you have taken in, they clip on. Put them in the seams because that is where the stores place them. Don't put more than one on if there already is one there; if for some reason you don't have enough clothes to put them on, put them in your pocket and then put them in pockets of clothing out on the floor.**

Quite often, you can sort through the pieces and find some that are undetached but always feel the pieces because you may not be able to see them. This brings up another point, there are other forms of this; little pieces of cardboard; however, these can be ripped off. These usually say inventory control on them but sometimes stores, especially smaller ones, try to disguise them by putting them in plastic and putting the store name on them. Because they are small, they are tricky to find, so make sure you check the garment inside and out. **Be extra sure and if you're not, go into the dressing room and double check.**

Finally, some stores have really slick methods; always **check the door to see if they have alarms,** they will take different forms: white or wood pillars, overhanging ones, or things that sort of resemble gates--**if you see any of these, be clued that there is something on the clothes. If you can't find anything on them, hang out by the cash register and see what they do to the clothes when something is bought. If the beeper does go off, you have to make a decision whether to run for it or give back the pieces. In a department store, if you can walk back into the store and drop off the pieces without too much attention, go ahead; if your car is real close, run; but that is a decision you have to make.**

### *Security*

As I mentioned earlier, **security almost always give themselves away,** but nevertheless, there are some that are as slick as you are. The one thing most of them have in common is their mentality. I mean it takes a certain type of person to have a job where you suspect everyone and send people to jail. This mentality expresses itself--most security look like real "pricks"; they get off on the power they think they have. When they're working, **they will be sneaking looks at people, looking over racks, or hiding behind things, trying to spy on whoever. Most often security works in couples** because they can see more that way and more importantly, a man has the strength to grab you and keep you.

**They almost always carry a walkie-talkie,** so if you see a woman sort of talking into her purse, be careful. **The men carry theirs inside their jacket or a bag,** like they bought something. **They also try to dress down and usually wear blue jeans because they are trying to look like your average shopper. If you see a supposed customer talk to a salesperson like they know them, be suspicious; or if you see two customers who aren't together, stop and briefly talk to each other, that is another good sign.** When they are suspicious, they will keep looking because they have to make sure that you have taken something. Sometimes they will even bump into you to see if they can feel something on you. **If you act cool, however, there is no reason for them to be suspicious of you, unless of course, they see you doing something. Security looks for people who look nervous, minorities. They are always suspicious of blacks, chicanos, etc. sometimes this works against you because if there are some around you in a**
store, you can be pretty sure security is around; however, most of the time security will be so worried about them, they won't be paying any attention to you.

One should be more careful when working the dressing room because security is real aware of this method. **When you do into a dressing room, stop and check real fast and see if anyone is watching you go in. If you see someone and then they come into the dressing room, beware; and if they leave when you do, the odds are real high that is who they are.**

I try and make it a practice **never to leave through the men's department. This is because if you are being followed by a man, he will be much more obvious if you're in the women's department than in a man's.** The reason this is important is as I mentioned earlier, he can grab you. **If a woman tries to bust you by herself, you will probably be so scared that you will have the strength to get away and if that involves kicking her or hitting her, do so** because you really don't want to go to jail. Some stores also have security who wear red jackets and although they are obvious, they should be paid attention to. Also, some of the smaller stores have armed guards, and if you can avoid dealing with these, it would probably be better.

### *Where to Go*

You should have a list of stores; when you are first starting out, go to the smaller stores until you build up your confidence for the bigger stores. Remember, you have to keep going back into these bigger stores every couple of weeks so the less attention you draw to yourself, the better. The bigger stores have different departments which helps because you can go in one department one week and a separate department the next.

Mostly, you have to use common sense and act cool and you shouldn't really have any trouble. **If you are careful and alert, you should never get caught. Remember too that it is better to come home with no pieces than to get arrested, don't force it. If, God forbid, you do get caught, don't panic. You will be out in several hours**. Do not tell security or the police anything about your name. They will try to get you to confess, or tell them who you work for, etc. They will also ask you who the pieces are for. Tell them they are for yourself.

Stealmeblind

Appendix 08

# SHOPPER'S REPORT

The Shopper's Report is a test. The person who is "shopping" the store must be reliable and somewhat familiar with proper (and improper) procedures for your business. Results are recorded ASAP, and the names of employees involved are ascertained *if* that can be accomplished discretely. (If not, an accurate physical description is recorded.) Recorded, also, is the exact time of day. (Keep your cash register date and "clock" accurate.)

## I. DRESSING ROOM

Take four items (at least one being "bulky"; like a sweater or coat) to the dressing room.

A. Was the door locked?
B. Was an employee present, and was the checked room *before* you entered?
C. Did an employee physically handle the merchandise, count the items, and check for concealed merchandise?
D. Were discarded garments, price tags, hangers, or empty packages found in the dressing room? If so, describe fully.
E. Was an employee present when you exited?
F. Did an employee physically handle what came out, comparing it to what went in?
G. Did an employee check the room after you exited?

## II. CHECKOUT AREA

A. <u>Single-item purchase.</u> (Also call Exact-change purchase)
   Give employee exact change, and do *not* wait for a receipt. Walk away quickly. Was the sale rung on the register?

B. <u>Booster Box.</u>
   Take a boxed item to the register in which another, smaller item could be secreted. The box must not be sealed with tape, staples, etc. If it was, the seal must be obviously broken. Were the contents checked?

C. <u>Concealed merchandise.</u>
   Take a bulky item (jacket, quilt, etc.) to the register. Was it physically checked in at least a cursory manner to see if it contained other merchandise?

D. <u>Unmarked merchandise.</u>
   Remove the price tag from an obscure item and take it to the register. With conviction, say to the employee, "I'm sure the price is (x)-dollars." Pick a price that's close, but slightly *higher* than the actual price, and make the false price consistent with the store's pricing policy. (Some stores' prices often end with .99, others with .95. Get it right.) Does the cashier accept your price?

E. <u>Add-on.</u>
   Make a purchase and pay, but before the cashier gives change, add a small, insignificant item to the purchase and pay for this item with exact change by laying the change on the counter. See if the cashier rings the added item, puts the money straight in the register, or puts it on or near (but not in) the register.

F. <u>Differential.</u>
   Complete a purchase and receive change and receipt, then change your mind. Tell the cashier you want a slightly more expensive item and hand her the difference in price in exact change. (Don't just happen to have the difference ready to deliver; take a couple of seconds to come up with it.) Is the original purchase voided and re-rung? Is the difference rung? Is *anything* rung?

Appendix 09

# Refund and Exchange

(Print) _____  Date _____
      Name   Last,          First,         M.

_____  Day _____
Address

_____  Time _____
City                State        Zip

_____     _____    _____
Phone           Driver's License / ID Number    State

Receipt: yes _____ no _____

_____  _____
Item                                      Price

_____
Reason for return

_____  _____  _____  _____
Date of purchase  Employee making original sale  Register #  Amount sale/refund

Cash given to: (Signature) _____

Issued by: _____

Verified by: _____

Previous refund: yes _____ no _____

Apology: yes ___ no ___ Employee _____ Date _____

Comments _____
_____
_____

Note: Did a "real customer" exist? Who verified a human was even present, or that merchandise was, in fact, returned? Never ignore the possibility that a sales slip was withheld from a customer by a dishonest employee to use later to fabricate a refund; or was rung up and later voided; or the "customer" is the cashier's cousin or sister and just brought the merchandise to the counter. And who's the expert that determined that the returned item is actually the one purchased rather than a substituted item? Refund fraud can go undetected forever if you focus only on no-receipt refunds.

Appendix 10

## PUT WIND IN YOUR SALES!

- Most shoplifters are between the ages of 16 and 35 and the higher range (30-35) is dominated by women. Ages 16-35 represents, nationally, billions of dollars in sales.
- Many thieves spend money rather than steal if there appears no easy alternative.
- A few thieves won't steal at all if they think employees like them.
- Most thieves are in a hurry, even if they do not appear to be.
- Many thieves will not steal if they know an employee saw the item in their hands.
- If you engage a thief in conversation, many won't steal and *assume* you are suspicious.
- If you engage an honest customer in conversation, most assume you are being friendly.

The shrinkage percentage in any store can be reduced three different ways. First, increase dollar sales and simultaneously keep dollar losses the same as they were the previous year. Second, maintain dollar sales and decrease shrinkage dollars. The third way makes you a hero: increase dollar sales and simultaneously decrease the actual shrinkage dollars.

Every dollar in sales ultimately pulls the shrinkage percent down, so LP personnel must do what they can to increase sales. Since "eye appeal is buy appeal," they can size merchandise on racks for a minute or two or pick up a little litter while they pretend to shop. It's fine to appear to be obsessive-compulsive shoppers. (But LP should definitely not do things like run errands for employees, tote boxes, or other things that mark them as employees.)

There may not be enough staff to greet and service every customer, perhaps not even those who ask for help. Short-handed or not, however, management and employees must engage the 15-to-35's. Since thieves want you to think they're customers or not be noticed at all, individual attention makes them feel exposed.(If employees are "people persons," this isn't difficult. If they are not "people persons," why on earth are they working in retail?)

Cheap flattery is transparent, but there is something about every customer that you can sincerely comment on or compliment. *Find* that something. Doing so carries you beyond the routine can-I-help-you and gives you a chance to gather information and do suggestive selling..

Look at hands, bags, purse, shoes, jewelry, hair, and children. If you can't imagine what to say, try one of the following suggestions. Some will work if you're being covert and want to get in close for a good look. Others are used only if you're already pegged as an employee of the store or wish to be known as one. It just takes a minute, then smile and move on.

**Nine o'clock sharp, you're unlocking a door and in comes the first customer of the day. Obviously, they know you're an employee:**

"Hey! Didn't you forget something?"
"What?"
"It's customary, you know, for the first customer of the day to bring donuts."

**A customer has a small baby:**

"Say, how old is your friend there? Kids' fingers are so neat when they're that little."

**A customer has jewelry that kind of jumps out:**

"Hey. How 'bout sell that necklace and buy me a new car?"
(Of course it's just gold-plate, but so what?)

**Approach a customer on the sales floor:**

"Finding what you're looking for?"
"Yes, I found it."
"That's amazing. Most people go their whole lives without ever finding what they're looking for. You must be living right."

"As long as we're both here, you couldn't loan me a thousand dollars could you?"
"What? I need you to loan me a thousand."
"No, no, no. You can't walk around with a $100 hair style and at the same time say you don't have money. Come on, just a thousand."

**A child wandering around by himself does *not* make a mess:**
Go to the parent and ask, "Is that your son over there?" The parent assumes there's a problem, gets worried, and expects trouble.
"Yes he is. Why?"
"All day long, children his age tear the place apart. I want you to know that he has been the perfect kid. If he picked something up, he put it right back when he finished. Better than a lot of adults. Kinda restores your faith in humanity. Anyway, that's so unusual I really wanted to say something."

**A customer says, *"How are you?"*:**
"I'm all right, but I'd be doing a lot better if you'd brought some tacos and iced tea."
"I haven't eaten yet myself."
"What's that got to do with bringing us lunch? I don't see the connection."

**A child is polite, maybe saying *"Excuse me,"* or *"Thank you"*:**
Same as the non-mess child above, but stress the manners. "Somebody did a good job with that kid..."

**A customer is dressed nicely:**
"A long as you're here, how 'bout loan me a thousand dollars?"
"What? If I had a thousand dollars I wouldn't be here."
"Oh, come on. Look at you in your Saks 5th Avenue blouse and matching pants. If you just went a week without buying clothes, you could loan me a thousand and never miss it." (Sure the clothes are steep discount, but never mind that.)

**A customer who usually shops with children is shopping without them:**
"Hey, aren't you missing somebody?"
"Yeah, they're at their grandmother's house."
"Should you be here? I didn't think you were allowed to shop without child-supervision."

**You see a customer you don't recall seeing in a few weeks:**
"Hey, there. Haven't seen you in a while. You all right?"
"I've been here. You were busy working."
"Well, holler at me next time. You don't get credit for coming in if I don't see you."

Or maybe you think this works better: "Huh? Sure I work here. How nice of you to ask. If you see anything you want, I'll ring it up if you can find me. If you have a question, I'll be around somewhere. Or somebody will. If I'm on the phone or talking, don't be afraid to interrupt if you have to. Just look for me. If I can't help you, I can tell you what you have to do or where you have to go if you have to buy something."

In stores with traditional 'good customer service,' customers are frequently seen wandering around like lost souls in search of God. Their 'good customer service' usually equates to self-service. When customers ask where an item is, they're told where it should be. Or where it might be. Or where they can walk to try to find someone who might know where it should be. Shopping in these stores is time consuming and perhaps even difficult and confusing. To increase sales and decrease shrinkage, that sort of thing must not be tolerated.

The key word with excellent customer service is "easy." Asking questions is easy because customers don't have to find employees. Employees find customers; and quickly. It's simple:

Customer has money. We need money. Go to customer and get money. Every customer must be treated as though the store's very existence depends on his purchase. And it does.

We have screwed up if a shopper has to look around or ask for help, and if they have to ask, "do you work here?"...well, you're in the wrong line of business is all I can say. Excellent customer service is a process, not a thing. I begins with help being readily identifiable (wearing a name badge or other identifier), being readily available, and appearing receptive and cheerful,

Smile at the nice people! Go beyond what thieves want and customers expect. You don't have all day to stand and chat, but neither do thieves, and honest customers are ready, they're ready now. Think. If it takes too long to get through your check-out, shoppers go elsewhere when they're in a hurry. If it takes too long to steal, many thieves go elsewhere. (One by one, one way and another, your thieves will get into the habit of stealing elsewhere.)

This leads into the "24-a-Day Program" for managers and key personnel. 24-a-Day increases sales while decreasing shoplifting and related problems. Every business day, give twenty-four shoppers the impression that the store management personally appreciates their patronage; personally appreciates the fact they came to the store. This appreciation of the shopper's personal value is demonstrated by taking just a moment to chat. 24-a-Day is a win-win program.

I once read that children usually decide where families eat out, so as a retail manager I often supplied a cookie and napkin to kids. I also personally made sure they were treated as valued customers, not non-people. And little humans are always "ma'am", "sir", "ladies" or "gentlemen." They like that. Bag their personal items separately from the parent's items, and hand kids' bags directly to them with an enthusiastic, slightly over-done "thank you very much for shopping here." Kids love it, parents love it, and today's cookie eater is tomorrow's employed consumer.

Talk to shoppers, particularly the 15-35's. Give honest customers a chance to tell you what they need or want; to share opinions. They think, "Gee! People here really like me," (and, buddy, there ain't nuthin' wrong with *that*). Finally, remember that the "24-a-Day" program always concludes with the same words: "It was a pleasure doing business with you," which, also, happens to be what I tell the police when they leave with a shoplifter.

Note: It may not be apparent, but some honest employees are intimidated by loss prevention and management. Some have deeply-rooted parental issues, others simply have "problems with authority." A few just don't like anyone who might rock their boat.

However...some of the employees who seem to "have an attitude" simply have no clue as to how to properly interact with certain other types of people. Little conversation pieces like some of those above can break the ice and bring a smile (of relief) from those folks. It's a start, and many employees happily cooperate with LP programs and pass along fantastic tips if there's an open line of communication. Be sure to go *at least* half-way in making employees feel at ease.

## Spread the word...

A great way to pass along LP-related information, contests, and policies is a large, well-placed, Loss Prevention-dedicated bulletin board in an employee lounge or near a time clock.

Simply increasing employee awareness can go a long way toward increasing compliance and voluntary--even enthusiastic--cooperation. And beyond warm and fuzzy, those maddening instances of "intentional ignorance" radically decrease after employees are convinced that everyone is personally responsible for reading the board postings.

Another excellent motivational and informational tool is an "LP Newsletter." Nothing elaborate is necessary, and an effective way to distribute them is to staple one on every paycheck that goes out. Give new-hires past copies, have the current issue posted on the bulletin board, and remember: the more employees you name and the more entertaining the content, the more they will be read. (See Appendix 13: *Newsletters*, pgs 174-175.)

Appendix 11

# CREDIT CARD FRAUD

**(I am grateful to the US Secret Service for providing this information.)**

How much is involved with the major credit card business? 1.9 TRILLION dollars, and one-*thousand* transactions by VISA and MASTERCARD processed per *second*, every day. And consider this: $2,709 is charged to the average counterfeit credit card, whereas the average bank robbery nets only $800.

## Types of credit card fraud and how to recognize them

**1. Card Theft**   Legitimate cards are stolen and used as is to purchase goods and services, or sold to organized crime rings to purchase goods easily convertible to cash. Cards are stolen from legitimate cardholders in a variety of ways; by pickpockets, from homes, from cars, or by store clerks who, after processing valid transactions, "forget" to return the card.

Signs to look for: Multiple driver's licenses or other items of personal identification, multiple credit cards under one or multiple names, and a person whose physical characteristics do not match the identification being presented, i.e., age, gender, race.

**2. Card Re-embossing**   Crooks alter the embossed information (account number, name and expiration date) on legitimate cards which have been stolen. These alterations enable the crooks to elude merchants' fraud detection mechanisms, such as hot card lists.

This is done a number of ways. Typical alterations are made either by flattening or shaving the original embossing, then re-embossing new information.

Re-embossed cards often bear detectable defects, including: evidence of physical alteration, such as ghost images around the embossed numbers and letters and/or poor spacing and alignment of embossed characters; digits pre-printed above the embossed account number on the card front do not match the embossed numbers, first four numbers; erasures, paint or other signs of alteration appear on the signature panel; the numbers printed on the signature panel do not match the embossed numbers on the front of the card; the unique embossed character (the flying V for VISA cards, or MC for MASTERCARD cards) are missing or altered.

**3. Re-encoded magnetic stripe**   Sometimes, the embossing on a legitimate card is left intact and only the information stored in the magnetic stripe on the back of the card (account number, name and expiration date) is re-encoded. Re-encoding the magnet stripe allows the card to pass fraud detection vehicles such as electronic authorization systems.

Crooks obtain encoding equipment to change the data in the magnetic stripe.

Alterations to the magnetic stripe can be detected by comparing the card's embossed data to the encoded information in the stripe: review the information shown on a point of sale readout/printout, which displays the data in the magnetic stripe, then compare with the embossing on the card; or use a magnetic stripe reader to compare the magnetic stripe date to the card embossing.

**4. Counterfeiting**   Counterfeit cards are actually fake cards manufactured by individual professional criminals and by criminals in organized crime rings. They obtain the equipment needed to emboss, encode and print information onto blank plastic cards.

The earmarks of counterfeit cards are similar to those of re-embossed cards. Defects are often visible to the naked eye: "Valid from (or) to" date might be missing, the hologram (a dove for VISA and two globes for MASTERCARD) does not have a three dimensional appearance that seems to move when viewed from different angles; or hologram appears pasted on. **When in doubt, check signatures!**

## 5. Other types of Card Fraud, Fraud Applications and "Account Takeover"

Things to check:
- VISA begins with 4 and contains 13 or 16 digits. (The first four digits are bank ID numbers.
- MASTERCHARGE begins with 5 and contains 16 digits.
- American Express begins with 37 and contains 15 digits.
- Discover begins with 6011 and has 16 digits.

> **"From a law enforcement perspective, highly paid sales clerks are our first line of defense."** -- US Secret Service

---

**Author's Notes:** Some states issue basic identification cards, and it's fair to say that many official state ID cards are easy to obtain under assumed names (i.e., false names). Some are issued upon application (no waiting period) with only a single piece of documentation necessary. Here's a nasty thought: The "documentation" used might be a police report saying the victim had his wallet stolen. In such cases, police officers, just doing their thing, often write whatever the "victim" *says* is his name, address, SS number, etc. A con man who gets such a report can use that as a basis for obtaining many types of "real" ID. After all, "the police say that's the correct information."

At any rate, even a birth certificate will usually suffice, and counterfeit birth certificates are cheap and easy on the street and can be scanner-created on almost any personal computer.

Personal and business checking accounts can be opened "on the spot" in most banks across the nation with little as $25 necessary to open the account. Official bank "counter checks" for immediate are issued on the spot. In addition, anyone with a computer, printer and scanner can generate bogus business or personal checks, business cards, a business license, and damned near anything else. These criminals--con men--often play on greed, ignorance, and inattention.

Consider the credit card and ID information above. If your store requires no ID or single ID only in order to use a credit card, cash a payroll check, or accept a personal check, then you are a prime, easy target for professional thieves with hot checks and stolen or counterfeit credit cards. You are cooperating with thieves, and they will come to you for precisely that reason.

Some of these thieves travel town to town, working each a few days before moving on. They stay in motels and travel with their computers. Some traveling criminals enlist local addicts and prostitutes, among others, to make purchases and cash checks. (Local criminals use the same people for the same types of things; in addition to paying them to shoplift and get refunds.)

Your defense? Do not accept credit cards (or any type business or personal checks) from anyone presenting a state ID card that was issued the same day or only a few days before. If you accept the card (or check), you may learn afterwards that their "residence" is an empty house and telephones are pay phones or pagers. (To provide an illusion of credibility, they may con or hire a professional answering service into providing a contract phone number and operator.)

If you suspect a driver's license is phony or if a transaction "feels bad," one option is excuse yourself, go to a phone, and call the local police duty officer. Tell him who you are and where you work, and then plead well. Give him the "customer's" name, DOB (if you have it) and ID or DL number. Tell him it's big dollars, the guy's weird, you're worried, and would he at least tell you if the ID is valid. If he'll do that much, he'll probably check a few things more while he's at it. If police help you this way, you must understand that they're doing you a favor. Remember that fact. Police want to help and try to help, but if for some reason they can't, don't hold it against them.

Remember that a check is merely a promise; an agreement. It is *not* money. If it doesn't look good, sound good, *and* feel good psychically, dig quickly. You've got to spoil their play or nail them at the time of the fraud. Nearly always, "afterwards" is too late to react. In only a day or two, these people can make $20,000 in cash and prizes. And then...POOF! Like that, they're gone.

Know your money. (Compliments of US Treasury Department)

# Raised Notes:

Genuine currency is sometimes altered in an attempt to increase its face value. One common method is to glue numerals from higher denomination notes to the corners of lower denominations. These bills are counterfeit by law, and those who produce them are subject to the same criminal penalties as other counterfeiters. If you suspect you are in possession of a raised note, compare the denomination numerals on each corner with the denomination written out at the bottom of the note (front and back). Or compare the portrait to another bill of the same denomination. Raised notes are pretty obvious IF you look. Below is a sample of a $1-bill "raised" to a ten-spot. Obviously, it might work well if a cashier was rushed, the lights low, or the cashier just counted ends of bills.

**-- Where there's something of value, a thief will appear. --**

It's not just 'conventional' retail stores that take hits from theft and fraud. Not just Convenience and Department stores, Grocery and Drug, Clothing, Electronics, and Shoes. These four examples are from Bob Spiel's fascinating *Art Intelligence Newsletter*.

British Gardner Loots 11 Libraries: An English landscaper with a rare book hobby was sentenced for stealing an estimated $300,000-worth of rare illustrations from libraries in Great Britain. He used a knife disguised as a writing pen to cut prints from rare library books.

Professor Suspect in Archive Thefts: An Arkansas professor was arrested in a Texas public library after cramming prints and papers into a notebook. He is under investigation for archive thefts in both states.

Rare Copper Coin Recovered for Museum: A coin expert recognized one of North America's rarest copper coins, known as the 1737 Higley, far from its home vault in the Museum of Connecticut History. It appears the coin was switched with a fake duplicate in 1994 by a thief specializing in Colonial coins who visited the museum.

Rare Stamp Thief Nets One Million Dollars: In the field of stamp collecting...numerous boxes filled with stolen stamps were recovered from home of a thief who had been 'working' Southern California stamp and coin exhibits for two years.

**STEALMEBLIND**

Appendix 12

# Floor-Walking

Watch for signs (clues) of external *and* internal theft including these 31 things. If possible, approach registers unseen by both the cashier and the customer(s). Anything and everything that even appears as though it might be odd should be examined. Address any violations ASAP.

1. Are items being bagged before being rung?
2. Is anything really rung, or does the cashier ring "no sale" or void it all out?
3. Are all items rung? (Or only one of every three or four, or just the inexpensive things?)
4. Does the clerk verbalize the price of each item as it is being rung?
5. Does the cashier verbalize the total *and* the amount tendered?
6. Does the clerk verbalize a price, but ring only a fraction of it (pennies on the dollar)?
7. Does the dollar total seem appropriate for the size and number of bags or quantity of items?
8. Does the type merchandise being purchased seem appropriate to that particular customer?
9. Does the quantity and dollar value of merchandise seem appropriate to that particular customer? (A teenager was purchasing a pile of merchandise by personal check. She already had large bags from Belks and Sears: a shopping frenzy, and the check number was 106. I called the bank first thing Monday morning, and sure enough...a "paper-hanger.")
10. Is change verbally counted back to the customer? (Coin by coin, bill by bill; *very* important.)
11. Is the cash drawer closed immediately after each sale?
12. Is money laying around outside a closed register?
13. Do tidbits such as paper clips and rubber bands collect in the cash drawer? (Some thieves use small things--even loose change--to track how much money they've arranged to steal. A penny or paper clip might represent a dollar, or five, etc.)
14. Is the cashier being distracted by customers' activity, companions or conversation?
15. Do employees chat, joke, or talk on the phone while counting or ringing merchandise?
16. Does someone quickly exit the register area as you approach?
17. Are large purchases in progress spot checked?
18. Are register journal tapes checked for "no-sale" entries, and reasons verified?
19. Are voids verified, authorized and handled per policy? Is approval just "automatic?"
20. Is the customer a personal friend or relative of the cashier? Do you know this by faces, or can you tell by the conversation, etc., that it is not-exactly-business?
21. Is a cashier working on a void, exchange, refund or no sale with no customer in sight?
22. Is a cashier ringing a customer or is she actually ringing something for herself?
23. If the cashier is filling out a charge application or processing a check, is there a customer present? Was there? Does it match the register tape? (Could it be fraud?)
24. When you approach, does a cashier suddenly conceal or trash something? Change a price?
25. When you approach, does a customer suddenly 'discover' she doesn't have enough money?
26. If you suddenly approach a transaction in progress, does the customer suddenly decide she doesn't want everything she has at the counter?
27. Are bags of merchandise "held" at checkouts for absent "customers"?
28. Do the contents of bags being 'held' at checkouts match the receipts on the bags?
29. Are register areas littered with merchandise, loose price tags or discarded receipts?
30. Is someone ringing a register who should not be? Is the cashier logged on to *that* register?
31. Is someone, especially a non-employee, "propped up" and comfortable on the counter?

If there is suspicion of theft or fraud, or <u>even an irregularity</u>, a note or report should be made and included in appropriate files. 'Sensitive' LP-related reports, notes, interviews, and records are best kept under lock and key, and LP files kept separate from 'personnel files.'

Appendix 13

## Covert Tape-Recording

Legally speaking, people don't talk. Rather, they engage in 'verbal audio communication, and there are *many* laws and unresolved legal and social issues pertaining to the 'capturing' of such communication. Laws vary widely from state to state, but one 'captured communication' principle seems carved in stone everywhere: 'Thou shalt not record any conversation thou art not party to.'

That's the National Rule of Thumb. You may not 'tap' phones, 'bug' rooms, or otherwise 'capture communication' *any*where if you're not a party to the conversation. There are exceptions. One, for example, is that (recorded) telephone announcement warning us that our conversation 'might be monitored for quality control purposes.' (Sure, call it that. Why not?)

Basically, there are two types of states: Two-Party and One-Party. Two-Party states require that both parties (persons) in a conversation must be aware that a tape recorder (or whatever) is in use. Otherwise, recording the conversation is illegal, and penalties can be severe. (If multiple people are involved in the conversation, 'two party' usually means 'every party.')

In One-Party states it matters not the number of people involved, whether the conversation is taking place in person or on the phone, business or personal, consented to by both parties or not, admitted to by anyone, denied by anyone or not...in One-Party states, only one of the parties (individuals) involved needs to know the conversation is being captured. (And that one party is usually the one with a hidden microphone. See page 111, *The Fat Lady*.)

You should assume *nothing* about laws that deal with this subject. Check your state laws and with the state attorney general's office and with state and local-level law enforcement. You do not want to make a mistake with this. (Sample question: I can legally record phone calls in my own state, but what about long-distance to an ex-wife in Florida or a nasty bill collector in Maryland?)

The following list, quite possibly outdated as quickly as it was compiled, lists every state and notes whether it is Two-Party or One-Party:

| State | Party | State | Party | State | Party |
|---|---|---|---|---|---|
| Alabama | One | Louisiana | One | Ohio | One |
| Alaska | One | Maine | One | Oklahoma | One |
| Arizona | One | Mass. | One | Oregon | One |
| Arkansas | One | Maryland | Two | Pennsylvania | Two |
| California | Two | Michigan | One | Rhode Island | One |
| Colorado | One | Minnesota | One | South Carolina | One |
| Connecticut | Two | Mississippi | One | South Dakota | One |
| Delaware | Two | Missouri | One | Tennessee | One |
| Florida | Two | Montana | Two | Texas | One |
| Georgia | One | Nebraska | One | Utah | One |
| Hawaii | One | Nevada | One | Vermont | One |
| Idaho | One | New Hamp. | Two | Virginia | One |
| Illinois | One | New Jersey | One | West Virginia | One |
| Indiana | One | New Mexico | One | Washington | Two |
| Iowa | One | New York | One | Wisconsin | One |
| Kansas | One | North Carolina | One | Wyoming | One |
| Kentucky | One | North Dakota | One | | |

> "I had," said he, "come to an entirely erroneous conclusion which shows, my dear Watson, how dangerous it always is to reason from insufficient data."
> *Sherlock Holmes (Arthur Conan Doyle)*

Appendix 14

# In-House Loss Prevention Newsletters
## - - *The* way to spread the word. - -

Newsletters are the cheapest and arguably most effective way to distribute ideas and information within a store or company. (Distribution is assured when they are stapled to pay-checks.) To help assure that newsletters are actually read by employees, post a note on the time-clock and attach another to pay-envelopes stating that newsletters are "required reading."

In the newsletters, include <u>many</u> employee names; mention their hobbies, births, promotions, accomplishments, their husbands and children, graduations, pets, etc....interesting tid-bits.

Newsletters are an excellent--*superb*--vehicle for "stroking" good employees, and for informing everyone of upcoming events, new procedures, new employees, changes in areas of responsibility, new product lines, sales floor problems...the list is limited only by your imagination.

Is special training needed to create a newsletter? Is special equipment needed? Does it take a lot of time? The answer to all those questions is "no!" The example below uses a very simple format that can get you started <u>today</u> on a newsletter that can be distributed next payday...

---

Retail Paradise, Store 119

## **LOSS PREVENTION NEWSLETTER**

September 2000　　　　Pleasant Valley Mall, #1 Happy Street, USA　　　　Vol. 1, No. 1

---

This newsletter contains Company and store policy...
information you *need* to know.
*Please take a few minutes to read through it.*

We all look forward to pay-day, and this particular pay-day is educational. After reading this newsletter, you will be a wiser and more knowledgeable person. Here we go...

**Did you know** that watching TV for an hour burns about 60 calories, so watching TV is a sort of exercise? Want to lose a few pounds? Just standing around doing nothing burns very few calories, <u>but</u> if you straighten displays or vacuum, you burn about 200 calories an hour. Good exercise! (200 an hour a couple times a day, 4 days a week, and in 50 weeks you burn <u>80,000 calories!!</u>)

**Did you know** that our new stereo salesman, Joe Walsh, plays guitar in a local band and aspires to be in the Rock & Roll Hall of Fame?

**Did you know** that give-away and promotional items like Michael Jordan basketballs are considered "merchandise" and cannot be sold, taken, or given to anyone except as stipulated in official guidelines or with a manager's authorization?

**Did you know** that after a Georgia police officer broke up with his K-9 partner, the police dog had to be hospitalized and treated for depression (and then escaped from the canine mental ward)?

- - - - - - - - - - - - - - - - - - - - - - - - - - - -

**Dress for Success!**
Do you know the store Dress Code inside-out and top to bottom?
If you read the instructions attached to your pay envelope, you <u>will</u>.
Looking professional is one part of being professional.

- - - - - - - - - - - - - - - - - - - - - - - - - - - -

**Did you know** that what lies behind you and what lies in front of you
are tiny things compared to what lies within you?

Page 2

> **And did you know** that Mr. & Mrs. Paul McCartney (that's Linda in our Jewelry Department!) are the proud parents of Drayton Wade McCartney, a new baby boy?

**Did you know** that young Billy Gates is not only our top electronics sales person, but also designs computer software "on the side" and says that some day he'll be the richest man in the world!?!?

**And did you know** that the average office chair on rollers rolls 8 miles a year? This means that our office personnel--Rhonda and Maggie--roll their office chairs an average of 20 inches every hour that they're on the clock. Go, girls!

**By coincidence,** 8 miles is also what Lillie Smith, Carolyn Jones, and Diane Sawyer in our hair styling salon walked in the March of Dimes Walk-a-Thon! And while they walked 8 miles in 3 hours, Rhonda and Maggie rolled office chairs exactly 5 feet. What do we learn from this? ...That when we all work together we can really *Walk 'n Roll*. (Sorry...) **Anyway, did you know** that the shoe on your right foot will wear out faster than the one on your left?

> ### THE BEST LITTLE STOCKROOM IN RETAIL PARADISE
> Congratulations to everyone in the Womens' Departments for the best-kept departmental stockroom! Only LP knew there was a secret contest and that stockrooms were being judged. The pizza party for the Womens' employees is a "THANK YOU!" for the extra effort. (Plus a $25 cash prize for Sherry, the department supervisor who dogged them every day)
> How did they do it? "It's not particularly difficult to keep it right," said Sherry, "but it requires constant checking, and immediately dealing with anything odd or out of place." (Now you know.)

**Did you know** that "short-change artists" always begin with a simple request to alter the "amount due" OR by fumbling money OR by walking away while the cashier still owes them money?

**And did you know** that quiet Julie J. in our Customer Service Department is also an Emergency Medical Technician, has delivered three babies in ambulances, and has a pet boa constrictor?

**And do you know** how to tell if two people in a restaurant are in love? Brad--age 8--says: "Lovers will just stare at each other and their food gets cold. Everybody else cares more about the food."

> It took courage, brains and heart to clean and organize the main stockroom. (Just ask Toto.)
> A **HUGE** Tip of the Hat to Barbara Walters for clicking her ruby slippers and bringing mountains of disorganized stuff back home from Oz!

**FREE MONEY...FREE PRIZES...**

$ $ $ $ **Did you know** that since the last LP Newsletter three more of our employees picked up extra cash and floor-prizes for calling LP about suspicious--unusual, abnormal, alarming, strange--activity on the sales floor <u>before</u> a manager or supervisor noticed and notified LP? (The dollar amounts varied from $10 to $50 depending on what it was and how things went.)

$ $ $ $ **Did you know** that LP officers sometimes do spot checks besides their normal poking around? Well, they do! You normally can't tell when they're poking from when they're spot-checking, but when they do a spot check the results get recorded and you win a floor prize or cash <u>if</u>...you are <u>where</u> you're supposed to be, <u>wearing</u> your name badge, <u>doing</u> something constructive, <u>and have no cash wrap violations.</u>

> <u>If you know something everybody ought to know, but might not know...LET US KNOW!</u>
> S. Holmes, Manager -- Alan Pinkerton, LP Manager -- Norman Bates & Hannibal Lecter, LPO's

Appendix 15

# Internet Sources

The resources below are in some way related to Loss Prevention. Many provide "links" to other sites (and those to still more). With some locations a benefit is immediately apparent; in others you may need to dig. The list is not comprehensive, as the number of locations having some relevance to loss prevention is in the thousands, and you are your own judge of relevance, usefulness, and quality. (Addresses checked 03/2000.)

**Internet 101: Search Engines**

There are millions of Internet sites, and no single "search engine" searches the entire Internet. Each has its own "search engine database called an Index, and some of them specialize in subject matter. Your computer may "default" to a single service, but you can "bookmark" others.

For an exhaustive (or even "good") search, you must use several search services (or engines). Common are AltaVisa, WebCrawler, Excite, HotBot, InfoSeek, Lycos, Magellan, and Yahoo!. The following are nine that you may have overlooked. (Always read search instructions!)

    www.internetoracle.com    www.momma.com
    www.dogpile.com    www.savvysearch.com
    www.invisibleweb.com    wwwintellifact.com
    www.accufind.com    http://websearch.miningco.com
    www.infind.com

**Legend:**
- .com — Business, commercial.
- .edu — Educational, often a degree-granting college or university.
- .gov — Usually a government agency or branch of an agency.
- .mil — Military.
- .net — Various types of organizations within the WWW/ Internet.
- .org — Often a non-profit organization.

1. www.fraud.org (National Fraud Information Center) Excellent info.
2. www.rlpx.com (Retail Loss Prevention Exchange; LP specialty site.)
3. www.freeyellow.com/members/jsmis (PI/consultant quite knowledgeable about EAS.)
4. www.acsp.uic.edu (Univ.of Illinois at Chicago; CJS throughout the world.)
5. www.apbnews.com/cjsystem (Much info and links.)
6. www.apbnews.com/resourcecenter (Lots; also produces "crime maps" for zip codes.)
7. www.beaucoup.com (A million links)
8. www.crimeandclues.com (Crime & Clues) Interesting articles and links.
9. www.fbi.gov (FBI) (Ex: Gangs, << www.fbi.gov/archives/congress/gang/gang.htm>>)
10. www.facstaff.bucknell.edu/rbeard/diction.html ("Specialized Dictionaries," such as Internet, Military, Law, Collecting, and Psychology.)
11. www.foia.ucia.gov (Central Intelligence Agency; FOI & declassified docs)
12. www.fraud-watch.com (Fraud Watch) False on-the-job accidents and detection.
13. www.globalcomputing.com/states.html (Path to finding web sites for each state.)
14. www.iapsc.org (Int'l Assoc.of Professional Security Consultants) Enter the library!
15. www.intelbrief.com (Interesting and informative.)
16. www.isoc.org/zakon/Internet/History (Mechanics of the Internet.)
17. www.law.cornell.edu (Cornell University; many law links.)
18. www.nacic.gov (Nat'l Counter-Intelligence Center; interesting reading.)

> **LossPrevention@onelist.com**
> Highly informative on-line discussion group created by Randy Hawk of Las Vegas, Nevada. Questions answered and information/opinions sought; posts by loss prevention personnel at all levels and by professionals in related fields. (Subject to the occasional colorful exchange.)

19. www.ncjrs.org   (Juvenile Justice.)
20. www.parascope.com/articles/0397/kubark06.htm (Declassified interrogation manual.)
21. www.rand.org/areas/CRIM.Toc.html   (Rand Corporation research & analysis.)
22. www.soconline.org/STATS/index.html   (Stats on college and university crime.)
23. www.stopspam.org/general/mlm_rs_pyr.html (IdentifyE-mail and mail order scams.)
24. www.albany.edu/sourcebook (Lots, and lots and lots of crim. justice info and stats)
25. **www.larcenyandfraud.com**
26. www.tollfree.att.net  (Toll-free numbers; spotty results)
27. www.usatracer.com   (Background check specialists)
28. www.usdoj.gov (Dept of Justice; various subs and links)

> **www.homestead.com/lp2000 & www.homestead.com/LPCentral**
> (Loss Prevention OP Center being constructed by Michael Easter.)
> Centralized info and links repository for the LP industry on the Internet. Articles and info on all aspects of LP. Informational resource for the LP Industry and for students of Criminal Justice.

29. www.proskiptracer.com  (Info re *Pursuit*, the professional skiptracer publication)
30. www.lossprevention.org  (Numerous interesting links)
31. www.stopspam.org/email/headers/headers.html   (Deciphering e-mail headers.)
32. www.frc.org  (Family Research Council) Includes crime, drug, and family issues.
33. www.gangsorus.com  (Gangs Or Us)  Info on tattoos, clothes, graffiti and more.
34. www.iir.com/nygc  (National Youth Gang Center)  Gang-related data and analysis.
35. www.kruglaw.com  (Attorney Kim Kuglick) Over 800 links to crim law and related sites.
36. www.nlectc.org  (Justice Technology Info. Network, NLECTC) Crim Justice products & info.
37. www.elsop.com/wrc/complain.htm (Elec.Software Pub.Corp.)  Spam, scams, and fraud.
38. ww.fbi.gov (FBI)  Misc FBI info. One example: fbi.gov/ucr=Uniform Crime Reports (UCR)
39. www.w3.org/Security  (WWW Security FAQ)  Technical security info.
40. www.losscon.com  (Loss Control Corporation) Commercial LP site with links & e-magazine.

> **James Samuel Mintz Investigative Services**
> *Specializing in*
> Criminal, Retail, and Child Custody Investigations
> *Also:*
> Theft & Risk Assessment and Consulting
> Physical Security:  CCTV, Alarm Systems, Electronic Article Surveillance (EAS)
>
> JSMIS@aol.com                                      www.freeyellow.com/members/jsmis
> - - CA PI 19541 -                                       *"Fully Y2K Compliant"* -

Note: While Mintz's box (above) might appear to be blatant advertising, *it is not*. Even though he didn't know me personally and knew nothing of this book, he once volunteered and went far out of his way to help me resolve a major EAS headache...and he did that exceptionally well. In turn, I surprised him with this. If I never have another EAS problem, I'll eventually go back to him with something else; maybe a tricky CCTV question. :)

41. www.ustreas.gov/fincen (FinCEN) Money laundering.
42. www.maineantiquedigest.com/articles/artintel.htm
43. www.uncjin.org (United Nations Crim Justice) Reports, links.
44. www.firearmsID.com Forensic and other info on firearms and ballistics.
45. www.uncjin.org (United Nations) UN surveys of crime, trends, and CJ systems.
46. www.ncpc.org (National Crime Prevention Council) Crime prev. info; McGruff Crime Dog
47. www.tncrimlaw.com/forensic (Tennessee Crim Law Def. Resources) Forensic and other links.
48. www.copmall.com Police products, services, publications; more.
49. www.cjconsultant.com/aboutme.htm (Dr.'s Pelz and Pelz) Gang info and articles, esp TX.
50. www.fire-investigators (International Association of Arson Investigators)

> **Toll-free references...**
> 800-876-7060 National Fraud Information Center
> 800-525-7641 American Express travelers' check fraud hotline
> 888-213-0007 BlueLight Publishing, publishers of *Steal Me Blind!*
> 800-257-5540 EAS (Checkpoint), 101 Wolf Drive, Thorofare, NJ 08086
> 800-221-4424 Nationall White Collar Crime Center, Richmond, VA
> 800-551-9130 RGIS (Inventory service)
> 800-394-4006 US Treasury Dept

51. www.terrorism.net ("The Counter-Terrorism Page.) Articles, including Intel and CIA.
52. www.homeoffice.gov.uk/rds/index.htm (Great Britain) Crime, police, prisoons, stats, reports.
53. www.oecd.org/dist (Science, Technology & Industry.)
54. www.secprodonline.com (Security Products Mag.) Monthly magazine free for the asking.
55. www.treas.gov/usss (US Secret Service) Much information re counterfeit, fraud-credit.
56. www.moneyfactory.com (US Engraving and Printing) Good info re new currency.
57. www.usdoj.gov/criminal (US Dept of Justice) Much info re gov efforts, mandates.

(Non-"www" addresses)

58. http://nsi.org (Nat'l Security Institute) Info on computer and internet security.
59. http://police.sas.ab.ca ("Cop Net") Police resources.
60. http://htcia.org (High Technology Crime Investigation Assoc.)
    Association of security investigators, consultants, and others)
61. http://web.soc.ufl.edu/srp.htm (Publishers of the annual *Nat'l Retail Security Survey*)
62. http://cjwww.csustan.edu/cj/links.html
63. http://csrc.nist.gov/welcome.html (NIST) Computer tech topics; includes info on viruses.

### People, Business, Number & Address Finders

64. www.phonenumbers.net
65. www.populus.net
66. www.teldir.com
67. www.inil.com
68. www.whowhere.lycos.com
69. www.anywho.com (Reverse directories)
70. www.infospace.com
71. www.infousa.com (Reverse directories)
72. www.peoplesearch.net (Reverse directories)

Appendix 16

# Employee & New Hire Training

**"Chieftains must teach their Huns well that which is expected of them. Otherwise, Huns will probably do something not expected of them."**
--Leadership Secrets of Attila the Hun

Every hour you invest in training an honest employee saves ten hours every month in execution, problems and aggravation. Also, many frustrating, unpleasant encounters will never occur...because the situations that breed them never arise. Plus, of course, the positive effects of good LP orientation on sales, shrinkage, profit, efficiency, effectiveness, and interpersonal relations are simply incalculable.

Even in organizations with LP staffs, new-hire and other employee LP-orientation is usually too brief (at least two hours is needed) and rather than convey principles and values, training ordinarily focuses solely on mechanics of individual functions. That is a costly mistake.

Training classes also provide an excellent opportunity to identify thieves and slothful employees. Those individuals often display a marked disinterest in "teamwork," company profit, etc., and an important task during training is to probe for these individuals. Watch to see who sleeps or appears bored, especially those who perk up when security is discussed or display an above-average interest in, and ask questions about, the number of LP officers, "camera situation," etc.

Questionnaires completed by trainees in orientation provide "feedback" for later analysis. In addition, they provide personal information about trainees, and signature and handwriting samples for future reference. Questionnaires are best completed before LP training/orientation begins.

Always use notes in training and organize them so that you can check each point off your list as it is covered. When the points are all checked and questions all addressed, you're finished. Always provide the class with informational handouts. (They have no chance of recalling all that you will tell them without handouts; recent LP newsletters are often good additions to the handouts.)

A simple training outline used in conjunction with some or all of the suggestions below covers most of the LP issues that employees need to know. (Added to that, of course, are any specialty items for your particular operation that need to be covered.) A class size of from one to eight trainees works well, and interaction with the trainer should be strongly encouraged. (When working on your outline it will help to re-read pages 20-22 in Chapter Two.)

In the outline below, 1 and 2 in "Briefly tell 'em what..." might be LP and Teamwork. In the "Tell 'em" section, you would cover not only the topic, but any details or philosophy you want the class to know. The numbers after the letters in the outline above represent "details."

Basic outline:  
    A. Introduction. (plus handouts, paper and pen, joke, etc.)  
    B. Briefly, tell 'em what it is that you're going to tell 'em. (1,2,3,4,5,6...)  
    C. Tell 'em. (1.a,b,c,d, 2.a,b,c, 3.a,b,c,d, 4.a,b, 5.a,b,c,d, 6.a,b, 7.a,b,c,...)  
    D. *--Break for about 15 minutes or break for lunch, whichever is appropriate--*  
    E. Tell 'em some more. (8.a,b,c,d,9.a,b,c, 10a,b,c, 11a,b,c,d...)  
    F. Conclusion.

## A. INTRODUCTION

In this phase, I make sure everyone has handouts, something to write with, and that they all sign an attendance roster. I ask which departments they'll work in, what their position will be, and if they have any previous retail experience.

Get information while it's easy. Do not trust the personnel office to get it right, but do count on a thief or liar to forget some of the lies he told in the past. Before I even *begin* to get them thinking they're in the clutches of Loss Prevention, I have trainees fill out brief questionnaire which I later compare to their information already on file. This little info-exercise is unexpected by trainees, and it's not uncommon to see one or another become noticeably nervous, suffer a memory loss, or even become aggitated. Remember who that was.

- Three (3) different local emergency names (& relationship), addresses, and telephones,
- High School graduated from, city, state and year,
- Current address & dates there, last address & dates there,
- Name of lease-holder/owner of current address,
- Telephone number & who phone is registered to,

I also want a photocopy of their DL (or other ID) and a photocopy of their Social Security card, but that should already have been done by Personnel, so I get it later. <u>After</u> collecting these forms and sign-in sheet, I'm ready to begin. I them who I am, my position in the company, a bit of my history. Then I tell a joke to clear the air..

## B. BRIEFLY TELL 'EM WHAT YOU'RE GOING TO TELL 'EM.

Many new-hires have never heard of "loss prevention," so I tell them we're going to talk about that, what it is, what it does and why we have it. More than anything, though, I want them to leave with an understanding of some essential ideas and attitudes. Among those are concepts of profit and teamwork, minimum responsibilities concerning theft, the integrity of     LP operations, and a few things about getting along with LP personnel.

## C. TELL 'EM.

**1.** I begin with this: **"Loss prevention is like security.** What is one of your personal loss prevention programs?" Whether I get an answer from the first person or not, I pause for only a second, then quickly move on, asking that same question of each person in turn.

I then ask each person one or two of the following questions if they weren't already mentioned by the trainees. The fewer in the group, the more questions I ask of each, but I ask many questions and have trainees verbalize answers:

<u>Accidents:</u>
*Should* you try to paint your fingernails while you drive?
Should you put a baby in a car seat?
Do you stop at red lights?
<u>Theft:</u>
Do you have a lock on your doors at home?
Do you lock the door when you leave home?
When there's a stranger in your house, do you want him to be alone?
Do you sometimes lock your car door? Do you need a key to start your car?
<u>Mistakes that lose and waste money:</u>
When you buy something at a store, do you count your change?
In the grocery, do you check the dates on milk cartons?
Do you close the windows at home when you run the air conditioner?
Do you ever change the oil in your car?
When you get a paycheck, do you check to see if you got paid for all your hours?

Penalties and fines:
Do you keep up with how much money is in your checking account?
Do you pay your tax bills to get a sticker on your car tag?
Do you pay bills on time so you don't have to pay a late charge?

Then, the explanation:

"We don't call those things 'loss prevention programs,' but that's exactly what they are. They are personal LP programs, and I'm sure you can think of many more.

Loss prevention programs prevent theft and they prevent mistakes and waste. They protect lives and prevent accidents and injury. They save time and provide consistency which keeps people from getting irritated, frustrated, and stressed out. They help us live our lives without bad things happening.

Company LP programs make good things happen. What good things? Well...if we don't lose too much or waste too much or make too many mistakes...and we don't have too much *stolen*...one good thing we do is *stay in business*. Another good thing is give people *raises*."

## 2. TEAMWORK.

It took about a hundred years to build the French cathedral in Paris called Notre Dame. It is a truly massive work of art. There's nothing like it. One man in particular who worked there while it was under construction had the job of picking up trash. Day after day, year after year, he picked up trash. That was his job. One day, someone asked him what he did for a living. Without hesitating, he said, "I'm part of a team that's building the greatest cathedral this world has ever seen." Whatever your job is here, you are part of a team.

In the store, we operate with a 'Zone Defense' Everyone has a specific area to cover; a specific job to do. Think baseball; the guy on 1st base can't just stroll over to 2nd base whenever he feels like it; the L & R-fielders need to be spread out; the catcher can't just stroll off the field anytime he wants a drink or a hot dog...No team can win like that. Will a coach get upset if he looks at the field and players aren't where they're supposed to be? You bet. If your job is covering 1st base, when anyone looks that way, you should be there.

With management, supervisors & LP...do what's requested when it's requested. You will never "get in trouble" for doing what LP and managers ask you to do. An explanation of "why" at the time of the request is often an inappropriate expectation. Whatever it is, remember: you get money for it.

## 3. PROFIT

Why are you here right now? The goodness of your heart? Truthfully, why are you here? Don't have anything else to do? You a millionaire working for fun? I think you're here for the same reason we're all here. I think you're here because you want to make money.

**(Hold up a piece of merchandise for all to see. Ideal price is 10, 25 or 100 dollars.)**
When we sell something like a shirt, how much profit do we make?
**(Solicit answers; typical is 50%.)**
We'll come back to this in a minute. Right now, pretend it's your first payday and you think you get $100. You open your check, but it's not a check. Instead, it's a bill that says you owe us $20. You worked a week, but you got a bill instead of a check. Naturally, you ask a supervisor. She says, "Well we take out $40 for parking in the parking lot, $40 for using the break room, $40 for letting you work. It's all right there on your pay stub. You owe us $20.

How would you feel? **(Get an answer from one or two people in training.)** All that time and trouble, but you're worse off than when you started? Now...if you lose money every time you work here, how many weeks will you come here?
**(Get an answer from everyone.)**

Me, too. We need to make a profit, and if we don't, we'll find someplace else to go. And it's not just you and me. The store needs a profit, too. No profit, no you and me. No profit, no store. Very, very important to remember that.

If your paycheck, your take-home pay after taxes is $100, how much of that is yours?

**(Get answers.)**

The money that belongs to you is your profit. But with your paycheck--your income--you have bills and expenses. Food and rent. Transportation and telephone. Clothes and make-up. Profit is what's left over after all your bills are paid. For some people, that's not very much.

**(Hold the sale item up again.)**

Reality: After we pay all our bills, out of every dollar we make, we only have about 4 cents left. For every dollar we make, we have 4 cents profit. That means for every one-hundred dollars, we get to keep about 4. That's pretty normal for a retail store.

But how can that be? Well, look at yourself. After you pay all your bills, how much do *you* have left? Have you ever looked at a paycheck and said, "Man, *PLEASE!*"

So then, if we make $4 from $100 in sales, if we have $4 stolen, we have to have an extra $100 of sales to make up for that loss. $2 stolen, $50 extra in sales. $1 stolen, $25 extra in sales. For every one thing stolen or lost, we have to sell 25 more like it, just to stay even. So...if this (shirt, bracelet...whatever your sample item is) is stolen, how many more to we have to sell just to break even? Yes...25. Just to break even. So if someone steals 10 pairs of blue jeans and a manager seems really upset, it's because to just break even, we have to sell 25 pairs for every one pair that was stolen; 10 pairs stolen is all the profit from 250 pairs that we sell.

### 4. COMMON MYTHS AND FANTASIES: PEOPLE WHO EVEN THINK THESE THINGS ARE LIKE CHILDREN.

#### a. "All loss prevention does is try to catch employees stealing."

More often than catching employees doing things wrong, we catch them doing things right. When the store manager comes to LP and says he needs to promote someone and asks who we recommend, we have to come up with some names. That happens a lot. The only way we can recommend you is if we have checked on you to see how you do things.

To conform with federal, state, and local laws and regulations, we have to check, test, and spot check hundreds of things that range from the shoes you wear to fire alarms for the deaf; from having rubber gloves for emergencies to having certain types of locks on different doors, to checking the amount of time employees work.

And does it surprise you that some people steal? Does it surprise you that some people get jobs in stores just so they can steal? Does it surprise you that thieves try to blame their stealing on honest employees? If there's a thief here, we want them arrested, gone and prosecuted with a criminal record for the rest of their lives. But to say "that's all we do" is just childish, ignorant, or just trying to make trouble.

#### b. "What I do is none of their business."

Really? You're not the Lone Ranger. You're on a team, remember? We depend on you to do your part. In baseball, would you say it's not the 1st baseman's business what the 2nd baseman does? It's not the coach's business to know what the players are doing? Is that what you think? Get real.

#### c. "Loss prevention has no right to ask me questions."

Please! If something happened or you even THINK that something MIGHT have happened in your house while the baby sitter was there, or you're just CURIOUS about something, do you really think you don't have a right to ask about it? If you see your plumber--who you are paying by the hour--do something that you don't understand, do you REALLY think you have no right to ask him about it?

**d. "LP checking what I do is treating me like a thief."**

(See "dead guy" pg 21.) If you buy groceries and check to see if you were charged the right amount for a particular item, are you treating the cashier like a thief? Not hardly.

**e. "LP asking me questions is like calling me a thief."**

If you ask the cashier how much she charged for a particular item, is that the same as calling her a thief? If it seemed to you that the cashier at the grocery store gave you the wrong change or rang a wrong price, if you ask her about it or check it yourself, do you *really* think that's the same thing as her a thief? Get real.

**f. "Checking my bags is treating me like a thief."**

Anybody play poker? In most card games one person shuffles, another person "cuts the cards." That is *not* calling the dealer a thief.

When checking bags, the most common problem we find is people are *missing* something that they paid for. The cashier forgot to put it in the bag. Another common problem we find is that bags get switched at the pick-up desk. People get the wrong bag. That *really* irritates the employee whose bag comes up missing. So, we check bags.

**g. "Watching customers is treating them like thieves."**

(See the third "Explain..." on pg 21.) When an employee in the jewelry department looks at jewelry or hair styling looks at a customers head, they look for things that I can't even imagine. That's because they are specially trained in an area. I'm not silly enough to pretend that I know as much about jewelry as a jewelry specialist or about hair as a hair stylist. The question is, are *you* that silly? When I look at any human in the store, I look at things will never cross your mind.

In a way, we're like plumbers doing a job in your house. What can a plumber do in your house that's none of your business? When you hire a plumber and you're paying him by the hour, you want your business to have his UNDIVIDED attention. If you walk in the kitchen and your plumber--who you are paying by the hour--is on the phone, is it your business? Is it your business who he's talking to when he's taking your money? You bet it is!

The fact is that anything going on when he's taking your money is your business. Think. If you hire a baby-sitter, is it your business what she does? What would you think of her if she told you that what she does while she's baby-sitting for you was none of your business? Would you find a new baby-sitter?

And what is the #1 Reason shoplifters leave? According to at least one professional thief, "All that 'Can I help you' stuff. If they won't just leave me alone and let me steal, I'll cop an attitude and leave."

### 5. PERSONAL VISITORS.

If you're paying a plumber to work in your house, do you want his friends and family keeping him company? Of course not. If you were a carpenter working on a job would your friends and family just drop by and climb up a ladder to talk with you? What would the foreman say?

But everyone has a visitor from time to time. Somebody dropping off car keys, arranging lunch...whatever. We just ask that you hold it down to 2 or 3 minutes. After that, it's your job to, excuse yourself. If they won't leave you alone, call LP or a supervisor. After 2 or 3 minutes, it is no longer OK, and if you did not call LP or a supervisor, that means you con't care.

We have shoplifters, bad check writers, con men, credit card thieves, whackos, computer thieves, drunks, short-change artists, counterfeiters, people using stolen checks and credit cards, people stealing customers bags...you name it. They all come in here and create some kind of problem. And there's a thousand different ways they to do it.

Some thieves hang out at cash registers waiting for the drawer to open so they can snatch money and run. When 2 or 3 or 4 shoplifters come in to steal, one of them often stands around and talks to distract the employee away from thieves who actually do the stealing.

When we watch you talk to a friend (and since you didn't call LP or a supervisor, that means the talking is OK with you personally), when we watch that for 10 or 20 minutes...with cameras, security windows, in person, or a combination of things...if you think you are just chatting with a friend, you are very wrong. You are not just chatting with a friend.

What you are doing is wasting your time, ignoring your job, wasting company time, wasting our time, and our drawing attention away from thieves and other things. You are helping thieves. Remember that: Personal visitors and phone calls hurt us and help thieves. You're taking the money, but you're not doing your job.

### 6. "CONSISTENCY."

Customers must be handled the same way by everyone. EX: A customer makes a purchase downstairs and you do not ask for ID like you are supposed to do. Why? Maybe you think you're doing the customer a favor by saving her a little time. Next, the customer goes upstairs, makes a purchase, and the employee *does* ask for ID like she's supposed to do. What happens then? The customer gets irritated and chews out the employee who did the right thing. Customers really don't care how we do most things, but they do want us to be consistent.

### 7. MISTAKES.

One of the biggest things that loses time, money, merchandise and loses customers is mistakes. Mistakes--errors--are murder. If you got hired, it's because somebody has confidence that you can do your job. But nobody expects you to be perfect. We expect mistakes.

Just because you are doing something wrong does not mean you are making a mistake. How can that be? Ex: We find you doing something that seems wrong. Then we walk around to see how other people are doing the same thing and find other people doing it the same way. Obviously, the problem has nothing to do with you. The real problem is that people are getting trained wrong with that particular thing.

We expect mistakes, and we expect different people make different kinds of mistakes. Don't worry about it. What we need you to do, what we expect you to do, is get better as you go. You're a part of a team and each member needs to do his part correctly, whatever that part may be.

If you do something incorrectly, we lose time, money or merchandise, or it creates a problem later, maybe for a customer.

Usually--not always, but *usually*--problems and errors (mistakes) are easier to cure than to endure. And they're easier to prevent than to cure. That's why we have Loss Prevention programs.

The key word is "prevention." If we just look at things after it's obvious we lost something, that's like just putting oil in your car after the engine is damaged. The key is prevention. We check the oil from time to time whether the red light is on or not. Our goal is prevent problems from happening so we don't have a mess later.

Do you always know the trouble your **mistakes** cause? Of course not. Just because you don't see the work it took for someone to fix it does not mean "Oh, it was nothing." They don't want their time wasted, so they probably will want you to quit making that same mistake. It might look to you like it's "no big deal," but most of the time you have no way of knowing how a little thing ties into something much, much larger.

If you do something incorrectly, it does not mean "you're a bad person." The more we do things wrong--or "less than right"--the more opportunity thieves have to steal, the more problems we create for smooth customer relations and sales, and the more time we have to spend correcting problems.

## D. BREAK

If this is about half-time, it would be a good idea to allow people to stretch legs, hit the restroom, smoke 'em if they got 'em, or just everyone go eat and return later. Another alternative at this point is to take a short recess followed by a video on loss prevention, shoplifting, fraud, or anything germane.

## E. TELL 'EM SOME MORE...

### 8. WORKING WITH LOSS PREVENTION

First, and most important, do not take anything personally. It is unreasonable to expect LP or anyone else to speak and act 130 different, specific ways for 130 different people and 130 different personalities. That's impossible. LP and managers conduct themselves in such a way that a *normal* person can *normally* interact. *Do not take anything personally.*

Decide in advance not to take offense. If someone pushes you aside and rushes past you through a door, you can take offense if you want to. Or not. If someone in a car cuts you off in traffic, you can take offense if you want to. Or not. Maybe they're rude. But maybe they just found out their child or mother was in a bad accident and they're just focused on that. If so, they mean nothing personal by it, so why take it personally? Do not play tit for tat. That is always a losing game. Let it go.

If LP takes an interest in something that you are involved with, don't worry about it: Don't even ask exactly what it is they're working on. It may be nothing, really, just a spot check. Whatever it is, there's a very good chance that it has nothing to do with you personally.

It may involve someone else. It may be just to see who all might be involved or who is not involved. It might concern something that happened hours ago, or days ago, or weeks ago, and checking that particular thing is just touching a base. It might concern a customer or another employee or a customer who was helped by some other employee.

There might be a police, mall, or company "BOLO". That means "be on the lookout" for something. It might concern a check, a checking account, or a credit card. If there's a BOLO out for a white male in a red shirt passing bad checks, if that's all the description we have, we're going to check out any purchase made by any white male wearing a red shirt. If it happens to be your brother, so be it.

But, if you ask why LP is checking the register tape and we tell you why, then you might go to your brother and say something stupid like, "Security says you're bouncing bad checks." Sorry, but we're been through that, and now the rule is just don't ask. If you and Susie are both working a register and you ask what we're doing and we say, "Oh, just checking this sale that Susie did a little while ago," the next thing you know, it's all over the store that Susie is a thief. No. We don't want to go through that, so just don't ask. We don't want to start rumors and if we're doing an investigation, you are asking too much for us to tell you about it.

And don't be paranoid. If you are, it's your responsibility to control it. Whatever LP is doing, it probably has nothing to do with you personally and will probably turn out to be nothing anyway. So...don't ask, don't take it personally, don't take offense.

Written statements. We have to check into many things involving many people. Having people just write a statement about something can be a real time saver for everyone. Often we know that you don't know anything about it, but we need that on paper to show that we checked it out. If I write it myself, my note might not agree with your memory days, weeks, or months later. If you write it, your own note will jog your memory.

Sometimes we just ask, sometimes we need a statement. It depends on the situation, the number of people involved, etc. If we ask for one, please do it ASAP. Not tomorrow, not next week.

### 9. HELPING THIEVES & IRRITATING CUSTOMERS.

Shouting at LP, calling to them, identifying them to customers, attracting attention to them...please...just don't do it. Use a pager to call whenever you can. The essence of plain-clothed LP is the appearance of "doing nothing." They don't fool you into thinking they're customers, but we want casual customers and casual observers to not pay them any attention.

You don't know what they were doing 10 or 20 minutes ago and with whom, and believe me, if some customers or thieves think they're being "spied on"--especially when they're not, but circumstances might make it appear that way--we can have a major problem on our hands.

Taking care of your area and the merchandise is almost Biblical. Consider it like this: you're paid to be a shepherd, and the merchandise and customers are sheep. It's your job to watch them, guard them, care for them, watch for bad wolves coming around, and calling for help if a wolf does come. We don't expect you to fight the wolf. We don't want you to. But if a wolf comes around the sheep, the shepherd needs to see it and call for help. Do that.

Oh, but there are so many customers and there is so much to do. That's true, but consider school. A teacher cannot ignore all the kids just because one is acting up or needs special attention. You cannot ignore 20 because you're tied up with one.

## 10. ATTITUDE

Emotional Baggage. Last boss was unfair? Forget it and move on. It's a whole new job. Here, LP investigates many things, some quite serious, some not so serious. You may be directly involved or indirectly involved. We may need to find out who was or was not involved.

If you are being asked questions about business, remember that it is not your register, it is the company's register. It's not your refund slip, it is the company's refund slip. Whatever it is, we may look at it and ask questions. Or not. Again, don't take it personally.

If you pay $10 for 10 gallons of gas, is 9 gallons 'close enough?' We need things right; not close. Say you pay a baby sitter to watch your child. You drop in and find her outside talking to some friends. You walk inside and find your baby crawling around the house alone. You go back to the sitter and she says, "Your kid is fine. I watch him most of the time. Quit hassling me." How many times will it happen before it bothers you? How many times before you fire the baby sitter?

If you do your job like the company wants it done, is there anything wrong with you getting upset if your money's not there? (No. You work, they pay. That *is* the deal.) It's very simple. The store and you are now team-mates: you with your part of the job, other people with theirs. You trade a certain amount of time and work for a certain amount of money and benefits. You need to trust other people to come up with the money and benefits without you having to make a big deal out of it, and they need to trust you to come up with the time and the work without making them make a big deal out of it.

## 11. POLICIES & PROCEDURES

1. Personal shopping, on and off the clock.
2. Procedures for lost children.
3. Procedures for emergency evacuation.
4. LP Cash-Wrap & Customer checks (Registers, tapes, media, stickers, guns, merchandise, BOLO's, credit checks, personal checks, refunds, efficiency, skills, procedures, policies, consistency...
5. Cash, Purses & Pagers on the sales floor.
6. Alterations Room: Tag filled out correctly, receipt with alteration charge. Everything in the alterations room should have a completed tag or a note attached from a manager.
7. Suitcases, purses, & backpacks must be opened and insides checked at POS.
8. Checks/Credit cards: must match ID & signatures must match.
9. Hand-entered credit card numbers must have ID (SCDL has nine [9] numbers).
10. YOU hold the ID, YOU look at the ID, YOU copy the number.
11. Refunds: Always with no-rec't, get the name and DL number.
12. Approval first, give cash later. No approval, no cash.
13. Credit card purchases get charge-credits, NOT cash refunds.

14. Working off the clock. Here's a law and policy that is carved in stone: You do not work off the clock. Don't carry boxes, don't ring cash registers, don't go in stock rooms, and don't price merchandise. If anyone tells you to work off the clock, tell them you need to punch in first. (You are always free to respond to an emergency or a clear and present danger.)
15. Cash on sales floor, near registers, any changing hands, etc. No personal money on salesfloor.
16. Purse, beeper, and cell phone: Leave them in your locker, in your car...not on the salesfloor.
17. Checks and cards, signature must match. If not, require ID.
18. Fitting Rooms. Logs, falsifying, plastic #'s; physical check of items, both enter and exit.
19. Know what is in area and what they entered carrying. Proper greeting. HANDS!
20. Proper customer greeting (Pg.83)
21. Do not ring family. "Appearances." If commission, another can ring (your) number.
22. Personal shopping: None on the clock.
23. Returning to sales floor after close. Notify mgmnt or LP. No coats, bags or purses.
24. Personal bags out: spot checked or routinely checked at any time. Any bag leaving the store.
25. Items "held:" Nothing should be held at registers, and all holds should be tagged, dated, and have the customers name and phone number and the employee's name.
26. Store bags. Not free for the asking. But, elderly customers...there are exceptions.
27. Parking: in employee area. Rides not parked in front of store doors; no loud music. After close, friends and family wait outdoors.
28. Employee number should be written on exchanges, voids, no-sales, refunds, etc.
29. How to page for help for emergencies; how to call police, fire, EMS, mall security.
30. Location of first aid material, rubber gloves and goggles.
31. How to respond to armed or violent robbery attempt.
32. How to respond if (they) see shoplifting or other theft.
33. Essentials of a "physical description." (shirt color, pants color, age, race, sex, hair & color)
34. Immediate action to being hurt on the job.
35. Location of fire extinguishers, fire alarms (in their particular areas and common areas).
36. Promo items ("free with purchase," etc.) Given away only per policy or with mgmn't OK.
37. Thieves: Stealing is neither tolerated nor forgiven. Arrest and prosecute any type thief; shoplifter or associate, whether cash, services, merchandise, or any type fraud. 5-month case.
38. Theft = criminal record; crime of moral turpitude: bonds, nurse, military, teaching, etc., etc.
39. Employee discounts. Giving or getting unauthorized discount may result in termination and prosecution.
40. Harassment by customers or associates; drunk or obscene customers, harassing phone calls. None at all. Report to LP at once, every time.
41. LP Newsletter
42. Incentive programs, contests, etc.
43. Cash for tips about unusual, suspicious, abnormal, odd, frightening and intimidating things, and for ideas on better ways to do things.

## F. CONCLUSION

Have the trainees sign an attendance roster. It's best for that to be on the same form as the information covered in training. In case they later say "Nobody told me." But! Remember that no one can retain all they hear in training. Give them handouts to read later and have a system in place for follow-up checks and training (mini refresher-classes). Once all that's complete, give them a cheery thank you and good bye.

# GLOSSARY
## A GUIDE TO WORDS, TERMS & USAGE

The following words and definitions are not necessarily legal terminology. The intent is to familiarize readers with principles of loss prevention and some germane legal and pseudo-legal terms, professional terms, "copspeak," and "street talk" (even if somewhat crude) that apply to larceny or the LP field in general. Some may be misleading when applied to other things and certain other situations. You won't use them all--or even hear them all--but it's nice to know what things mean if they do come up at the dinner table. Where it's important that a definition be strictly correct, consult a dictionary or some other technical source. (*Black's* is good for legal terms.)

**AKA** 'Also known as...'
**Accelerant** Substance (often gasoline) used by arsonists to cause a fire to enlarge or to spread more quickly.
**Access Control Device** A key, card, code, account (or PIN) number, or other item that can be used alone or in combination with something else to obtain money, items, services, or anything of value.
**Accomplice** One who intentionally aids a thief in a *significant* manner. He bears equal responsibility under the legal theory, 'The hand of one is the hand of all.'
**Achilles Heel** A significant weakness--generally hidden or overlooked--in an otherwise strong position.
**Acknowledgment** Essentially, a written confession.
**Acquit** (Verb) To acquit is to find not guilty. To set free. ('Acquittal' is the finding of not guilty.)
**Adult** Varies state to state. In SC and GA, 17-years and older. (Check with police.)
**Advise** To notify, tell or say something 'I advised him to stop' In written reports (and even when talking), law enforcement personnel seldom "tell" or "say" anything...they advise.
**Affidavit** Written statement sworn to be true.
**Alias** Name used to deceive; different than a person's sole legal name.
**Ambulance Fraud** Dishonest ambulance company employees submitting fraudulent bills by claiming a round-trip with a patient where, in fact, it was one way; or claiming to have performed a service that was not done, or by 'padding' mileage; they can also receive 'kickbacks' from hospitals or clinics. (Note: There also exist clinic fraud, hospital fraud, pharmacy fraud, lab fraud, physician fraud, medical equipment fraud, and home-health fraud. Even if the initial accident is legit, any of these frauds might result in bills to your place of business by a health-care provider or by your own injured employee.)
**Analysis** The process of taking any type of information and turning it into useful intelligence or 'knowledge.'
**Appeal** Request that a higher court reverse the decision of a lower court.
**Arrest** Legal seizure of a person. (Not necessarily with the use of force.)
**Assault** Threatened or attempted physical attack. (Depending on the State, it may or may not involve contact.)
**Associate** Retail new-speak for 'employee.' Also, people who do business together.
**Assume the Position** (Dated) An order for a suspect to put both hands against a surface and spread his legs prior to being frisked or handcuffed. (Note: For two reasons, plate glass doors and window are a bad surface to use. One: glass breaks; Two: the person you're searching can watch you in the reflection.
**Assumptive Question** Used to minimize denial. Rather than ask, 'Did you break that?' (which often prompts a strong denial), an assumptive question is used, 'How did you break that?' Phrasing the question that way often eliminates the need to 'prove' the suspect broke it. By answering the 'how,' he is confessing to having done the breaking without having to muster much honesty; he can even call it an accident rather than an intentional act. (See Rationalizations.)
**Attain Room Temperature** Die. ('He attained room temperature' is to say he's dead.)
**Attitude Adjustment** An action that alters someone's point of view. A beating, for example.

**B.B.D.** Bigger and better deal.
**B & E** Breaking and entering. Illegal entrance.
**B.O.L.O.** Literally, 'Be on lookout for.' An advisory to watch for specific people, things, or activity.
**Badge player** A con man who impersonates a law enforcement officer.
**Bagger** One who 'bags' merchandise (puts it in a container) for stealing.
**Bag Man** The thief who carries the bag of (stolen) merchandise. Not necessarily the 'bagger.'

**Bail** Money posted to insure he appears in court if released from custody prior to the date he is to appear. An arrested individual raising the necessary bail is said to 'make bail' or 'make bond.' Those who subsequently fail to appear in court are said to 'skip,' or to 'jump bail.' (see bond, bush bond, bush pass, rabbit.)

**Bait and Switch** A method used in swindles, cons, and sales. The con artist uses some type of bait (a promise or prospect of cash or sex are common) to get the initial cooperation of the intended victim. The bait often appeals to a person's greed, lust or natural inclination to obtain a 'good deal.' After the victim is ensnared, and a 'switch' takes place in which the initial bait is replaced with something of far less value (or no value at all). The con artist often escapes with the bait and the victim's cash or other valuables.

**Belly Up** To give up; to submit. ('He first tried to bluff, but later went belly up.')

**Bedtime for Burney** Time to relieve an individual of the exertion of conscious function.

**Bench Trial** A trial where a judge--rather than jury--hears evidence and delivers a verdict.

**Bench Warrant** A court order authorizing police to locate, arrest, and deliver a person to court.

**Billy Club** Night stick; baton.

**Bind Over** The action of one court moving a case to another court. (Often to a higher or lower level.)

**Bitter Whine** A thief's sob story. (Your call: Be sympathetic or ask if he'd like some cheese with his whine.)

**Black and white** Marked police car (even blue ones). Commonly called 'a cruiser' by LE personnel.

**Black Bag Job** 'Secret' work, such as installing hidden cameras and other devices or, perhaps, the opposite. The Watergate burglary that proved so inconvenient to the Nixon Administration is one of history's most famous bungled black bag jobs.

**Blackjack** Leather weapon, 6 to 8-inches in length. Half is held in hand while the other half--filled with lead or steel--is used for behavior modification.

**Black Market** That part of the underground economy dealing in fraud, illegal, or stolen goods or services.

**Blowback** Term for when your own 'disinformation' (or propaganda) comes back to haunt you; or is in some way used against you.

**Blunt** Marijuana; often refers to m. packed into a hollowed-out cigar. (Commonly 'Phillie Blunts').

**BOHICA** Literally, 'Bend over. Here it comes again.'

**Bond** Promissory contract in lieu of cash to attain a subject's release from jail prior to a court appearance.

**Book** To process a prisoner (fingerprint, photograph, etc.) and do paperwork at a police station.

**(The) Bookkeeper who never takes a vacation** A person responsible for recording financial transactions and seems to never want time off from the job. This is indicative of someone 'juggling books or making fraudulent entries and who is fearful that the fraud may be discovered by anyone 'filling in.'

**Boost** (Verb) To steal.

**Booster** (Noun) A thief.

**Booster Box** A specially constructed and disguised box used to conceal stolen items. Often appears sealed.

**Bracelets** Handcuffs.

**Breach of Trust** Legal term for theft by an employee.

**Bunco** Term used to include flimflam, confidence schemes, gypsy crime, other crimes, and non-traditional, transient criminal groups. (From the Spanish *banco*, meaning bank.)

**Burned** Detected. A thief is burned if seen stealing. Surveillance is burned if the suspect notices.

**Bush Bond (Also, Bush Pass)** A thief or prisoner may choose to flee--to seek a bush bond--rather than be arrested. (From past usage when outlaws fled into the wilds; 'into the bush.')

**Bust** (Verb) Arrest. To bust is to arrest. (Noun: An arrest.) Also, 'caught in the act,' discovered, or to reveal.

---

### Interview & Interrogation Tip,
*Compliments of* Randy Hawk, LossPrevention@onelist.com

Be prepared and know the subject; know the crime(s) inside and out, and pick specific details from the case as your "ace in the hole." When "fishing" for the unknown, intermix the known within your questioning. First ask about something that you already know the answer to and see if you receive a truthful response. If so, fish for the unknown with a follow-up question.

Example: "To determine your cooperation, I would like you to tell me how many times this week you passed CD's to your friends? If the subject provides an honest answer, ask a follow-up question that will provide information that is unknown to you. "Now, what do you think the total dollar value was?"

**C.C.T.V.** See Closed circuit television.

**C.C.W.** Carrying a concealed weapon.

**Capper** Con-artist who arranges staged auto accidents. He may hire 'victims,' arrange insurance coverage and false identification and cover stories in advance, and provide the automobiles and witnesses.

**Card** Part of the packaging of a piece of merchandise, such as the card that earrings are attached to.

**Case** (Noun) any type of incident. Verb: to look around.

**Case Number** The number assigned an incident by a police agency.

**Cash Wrap** A counter or booth with a cash register.

**Charge credit** A 'credit' made to a refunder's charge (card) account in lieu of giving cash. (If the refunder has no original sales receipt, there exists a high potential for fraud by refunders and cashiers.)

**Check Kiting** A con man opens a checking account at one bank, then uses a check issued on that account to open an account at a second bank. He then uses a check from the second account to make a "deposit" into the first account. He writes worthless checks back and forth between banks (sometimes several banks) for a few days, then suddenly withdraws as much as he can and disappears, OR he writes rubber checks in stores for expensive items (and then disappears).

**Chill** (Verb) Get control of emotions. Relax. (Also, to 'hang out.')

**Choice Question** Like an Assumptive Question, a CQ helps eliminate denial and bring a faster confession. Example: Rather than ask, 'Did you push your brother down the steps?' one could say, "Did you push your brother on purpose, or was it an accident?'

**Circumstantial Evidence** Evidence implied from things known. Your fingerprints on a wall in a house is strong circumstantial evidence that your fingers, at least, were in the house. Your fingerprints on a jar of peanut butter in a house is circumstantial evidence that you were there, but might mean only that you and the occupants all shop at the same supermarket. CE is stronger that eyewitness testimony in that CE never changes its mind, forgets, or dies. Unfortunately, CE--like a witness--can sometimes disappear.

**Clear a Case** To dispose of a case. (Can refer to any type outcome, including dropping charges.)

**Clica** A gang.

**Clique** A small gang. An opportunistic, usually loosely organized, group of criminal friends and their relatives.

**Closed Circuit Television (CCTV)** Refers to surveillance systems usually composed of 3 elements: camera(s), TV-type monitor(s), and VCR(s). Systems have many 'add-ons' such as split-screens, audio capability, the ability to instantly print still-shots from the video tapes, etc., with most 'high-end' systems having color rather than (only) a B/W picture and recording. Prices begin at about five-hundred dollars, and skyrocket.

**Collar** (Noun) An arrest. If an officer arrested two people, he 'made two collars.' Can also be used as a verb.

**Come Clean** (Dated) Cooperate by providing truthful information; also, 'roll over."

**Community Oriented Policing** Having police in the neighborhoods; 'team policing:' assign a set of police to a particular area and leave them there to learn the people, businesses, local 'ways,' etc. A double-edged sword in that the more police and locals interact, the more the locals report crime. That leads to increased crime stats (and arrests) leading to raised eyebrows at the perceived "increase in crime."

**Competitive Intelligence** Gathering, organizing and analyzing information to develop intelligence concerning (other companies), then distributing the intelligence (or making it available) to those in need.

**Complaint** Allegation of wrong-doing; that an offense was committed.

**Complainant** The party making a complaint against another.

**Con** Noun or verb: Fraud; cheating and deception; a scam. (Also, can mean 'ex-convict.')

**Con Artist (Con man)** One who engages in con games; in fraud and scams.

**Confidential Informant (CI)** Someone who provides information on the condition he remains anonymous.

**Con Game** 'Confidence game.' A fraud or scam. Common scams are short-change artists, diamond switching Three Card Monte, 'slip and fall guys', 'Pigeon Drops,' driveway or home repair scams, fortune telling, 'Bank Examiner' fraud, and--a Gypsy favorite--curse removal (saving people from evil curses).

**Conceal** To hide merchandise on a person or among belongings.

**Connected** Tied in to someone or something more important or more powerful.

**Corroborating Evidence** Evidence supplementing or of a different kind which strengthens evidence already offered or on hand.

**Count** A single criminal charge; a cause of action. Two charges would be 'two counts.'

**Counterfeit Checks**  Usually 'home-made' (on a personal computer with a scanner and ink jet printer).
**Counterfeit Credit Card**  A 'new' credit card, professionally manufactured by criminals.
**Counterfeit ID**  False identification documents often produced by PC, scanner, and ink jet printer. False ID can be a 'true ID' which has been altered or an official ID illegally produced & purchased on the black market
**Counterfeit Sales Receipt**  Usually made by PC with a scanner and inkjet printer, or by photocopy machine, or by artfully cutting and taping two or more store receipts together to alter the method of payment or reason for the transaction (exchange, etc.), or by stealing (or buying stolen) rolls of store cash register tape (then cutting the ends with the teeth of an aluminum foil or plastic-wrap box from under the kitchen sink). These receipts are then used in stores in frauds to obtain cash, credits to charge cards, and merchandise.
**Cover**  See Pretext.
**Covert**  'Undercover;' low-profile and/or not apparent to a casual observer. In the extreme, 'deep undercover,' i.e., hidden and invisible to a casual observer and, ideally, invisible to *any* person without a 'need to know' of the covert personnel or operation. (Some deep undercover operatives, 'moles,' remain so for years, even decades.)
**Crackhead**  Person addicted to crack-cocaine.
**Cramming**  Fraud. Third party provider manipulates victim's primary telephone service provider to bill the victim for communication services (Internet, pager, etc.) that are not authorized by the customer (victim). Fraud charges are 'crammed' among legitimate charges on the victim's bill, often going unnoticed...
**Credit Number Theft**  Often practiced by dishonest cashiers; names, credit card numbers and expiration dates are copied and given or sold to dishonest cashiers at other stores who then hand-enter the information into their own registers to make illicit purchases. The (honest) card holder will not normally learn of the theft until their statement arrives, and the dishonest cashiers who made 'purchases' will naturally say that they don't recall the transaction. (This is only one of many, many ways stolen numbers are used.)
**Creeper**  Thief who moves around while crouched or on hands and knees; possibly enters the store that way.
**Crime of Commission**  Crime which requires *an act* (such as shoplifting or switching prices on merchandise).
**Crime of Omission**  Crime resulting from *not* doing something (that the law requires must be done).
**Critical Mass**  In a store, a situation where active employee-thieves and those not reporting theft equal the number of employees *actively* fighting and reporting theft. (Only fast, radical, effective action can save the store.)
**Cross Examination**  Defense questioning a prosecution witness, or prosecution questioning a defense witness.
**Cuffs**  (Noun) Handcuffs. Verb: to *cuff* someone is to handcuff them.
**Custody**  To have control or personal responsibility of a person or thing.
**Customer**  An honest shopper who spends money. Often confused with potential customers and thieves.
**Cybercrime**  Generally, any fraud or other crime committed through 'electric commerce' or via the Internet.
**Cyberstalking**  Generally, the use of the Internet, email, or other electronic communications devices to stalk another person. Usually involves repeated harassing or threatening behavior.

**D/B/A**  Literally, 'doing business as.' Usually a person's name followed by their business name: 'Mr. Samuel Colt, D/B/A Colt Firearms Company.' The term 'D/B/A' has legal implications.
**Dead Presidents**  Cash money.
**Deep Pockets**  Specially attached, often extra-large pockets used for theft. (Can also mean 'lots of money.')

---

### Interview & Interrogation Tip
*Compliments of Peter Harridge, UK*

Generally, people who provide further information after arrest or disciplinary action usually have a hidden agenda. Some resent that they were the "only one caught," and so supply information concerning their ex-colleagues-in-crime out of pure vindictiveness rather than any change of morals.

In the event that one of a group is caught, the remainder often distance themselves from them, anxious not to prompt any of the guilt "rubbing off." In some cases, the rest of the group (of thieves) express shock and disdain for the one caught, so as to display what they believe is an acceptable reaction.

Naturally, this creates a feeling of being "cast out" for the one caught, and it soon becomes evident to him that the common bond between himself and the group has been broken. A feeling of resentment can then begin to surface, accompanied by a need to neutralize the guilt and shame which often accompanies the "label" of "thief." Often, this neutralization is achieved by transferring the blame to ex-colleagues.

**Default Judgment**  Court decision made against a party who failed to attend court.
**Defendant**  Court terminology for someone who is charged with wrong-doing.
**Defensive Wound**  Usually on hands or arms as a result of a victim attempting to shield himself. (See *Location*.)
**Defer Prosecution**  Put case 'on hold' for a period of time. In theory, if the defendant commits a crime during that period, both cases are tried; if not, the case is dismissed.
**Deprive**  Beyond the common definition, it means to make unauthorized use of, or unauthorized copy of, records, data, information, text, music, trade secrets, computer related materials, etc.
**Desire**  One of the three elements necessary for crime to occur. (Also, means and opportunity.)
**Detain**  To stop; possibly to arrest; to hold for investigation or some other authority.
**Detainee**  Person who is held for a short period of time, usually near where he was accosted.
**Deposition**  Formal, recorded pre-trial questioning of a witness to ascertain facts.
**Direct Examination**  The initial questioning of a witness by the prosecution.
**Disguising the Source**  Maintaining the confidentiality of a source, often by somehow altering or 'doctoring' information, changing the date it was provided, deleting some specific part, or even by adding to it.
**Disinformation**  Inaccurate or bogus information intentionally provided by someone to mislead someone else.
**Disorderlies**  Noun: People engaging in disorderly conduct; incidents involving disorderly conduct.
**Disorderly Conduct**  Broad range of offenses including creating a disturbance, preventing others from going about their legal business, being drunk in public; generally, being disharmonious. ('Disturbing the peace.') In most towns and cities, D.Conduct arrests include some degree of P.O.P. (See P.O.P. below.)
**Disposition**  Case 'disposition' is the status of the case: active, cleared by arrest, etc.
**Distraction**  Person or activity drawing unwanted attention away from another person or activity. It may require only a few seconds.
**Diversion**  Prolonged distraction; lasting from only a moment or two to, perhaps, a quarter-hour or more.
**Ditch**  Discard. To ditch an item is to discard it.
**Ditch and Split**  Discard and leave. To abort a theft; ditch the merchandise and just walk out, taking nothing.
**Do Time**  Serve a sentence. To be incarcerated; 'serve time' in prison or jail.
**Docket**  List of cases to be tried in court.
**Document**  (Noun) Usually anything with a message (handwritten, printed, etc.) or information; includes checks, currency, wills, contracts, money orders, letters, warranties...anything. Also, verb: To record or demonstrate.
**Drama**  A disturbance. (There was a fight.=There was a little drama.)
**Drop a Dime**  Inform on someone by making a phone call. (Originated, obviously, when pay phones took a dime.)
**Dumpster Diving**  Searching trash dumpsters for merchandise, sales receipts, credit information, or other material. Sometimes called 'trash trawling' and (even) waste archeology.

**E**ar hustling  Eavesdropping on a conversation.
**E.A.S.**  Electronic Article Surveillance system with tags on merchandise and sensor units at the doors.
**E.T.A.**  Literally, 'estimated time of arrival.'
**Elements of a Crime**  Individual acts or processes which, together, constitute the legal definition of a crime.
**Eliciting Information**  Obtaining information. Covertly: subtle; obtain info without revealing the intent to obtain or revealing any exceptional interest in the specific information sought.
**Emboss**  Used in a plastic (credit) card context: to melt. Numbers are embossed on cards; melted into the card.
**Embossing Machine**  Commercially available machines (similar to lamination types) used to emboss plastic cards.
**Employee Sabotage**  Deliberate action or inaction, the intent of which is to harm a company or its personnel.
**Encryption**  Methods to distort--and thereby render senseless--messages (such as account numbers) sent on paper or on the Internet from one computer to another. ('Old' encryption methods were often codes or ciphers.)
**Ese**  Slang for 'guy' or 'man.' ('Hey, ese, can you spare a cigarette?')
**Etoh**  Literally, 'alcohol.' Abbreviated term routinely used in medical reports today.
**Event**  An identifiable, significant and lasting (although not necessarily permanent) source of influence upon a person, organization, or operation, regardless of whether the influence is good or bad. An event need not actually occur to create an impact: it may be that even the recognition of a possibility that a particular event *may* occur could have far-reaching effects. (Examples of events: Rumors, anticipated changes in law or policy, changes in leadership or organizational structure, the possibility of an earthquake or riot, or a fight or injury.) For your purposes, an event is something that effects *your* person, people, or operation.

**Evidence**  Relevant testimony, documents, and objects used in the prosecution and defense of a case to prove or resolve matters or questions of fact.
**Exact-change purchase**  Method of identifying a dishonest cashier. (See page 16 of text.)
**Exception Reports**  Fact sheets of information and statistics (usually concerning refunds, voids, discounts, sales, purchases, and credit activity) which highlight abnormal (above average/below average) quantities or use.
**Exchange Fraud**  Any number of criminal schemes designed to victimize stores through the exchange of items for (other) items. (Ex: A thief buys pants from a nice store. Then he buys or steals a pair of the same brand at a steep discount from a thrift store, flea market or garage sale. He removes the tags from the nice-store pants and returns the worn pair (along with the tags from the first pair) to the nice-store for an exchange or full-price refund. (This is one method. Naturally, thieves expand this principle into a lucrative practice.)
**Exclusionary Rule**  The legal principle prohibiting unlawfully obtained evidence from being presented in court.
**Eye Contact**  The premier method of alerting a thief to the fact he has been noticed. (Also, see 'lock eyes.')
**Eyewitness**  One who can testify to what happened because he was there when it happened and saw it.

**F/ I/U**  Financial Intelligence Unit. May be governmental or private industry; analytical, investigative, or both.
**F/K/A**  'Formally known as.'
**Failure to Appear**  Term meaning a defendant did not show up for court as directed; 'skipped.'
**Fair**  Whatever is in my personal best interest; 'unfair,' whatever is not. When employed in a context involving 'just,' 'ethical,' or similar sentiments, the intent is usually to deceive or manipulate.
**Fall**  To be arrested is to 'take a fall.'
**Fall-Guy**  (Dated) Someone who takes (or is awarded) blame. One who is 'framed' or 'set up.'
**False Arrest**  Arrest or take into custody without legal justification. The illegal seizure of a person.
**False Imprisonment**  Illegal (without legal justification) seizure and/or confinement of a person.
**False Pretense**  Trickery.
**Family Court**  The court for juveniles arrested for shoplifting or other offenses.
**Fat Lady**  Hidden tape recorder or recording device. ('The show ain't over till the fat lady sings.')
**Felon**  One who commits a felony.
**Felony**  Shoplifting (stealing) more than a certain dollar-value (varying from state to state). More serious than a misdemeanor, it often results in a fine over $1,000 and/or more than a year in jail.
**Felony Stop**  An approach where it is presumed that the suspect to be detained is armed and dangerous.
**Fence**  Person who knowingly buys stolen goods, generally for resale.
**Filters**  Conscious and unconscious 'maps' in human brains that influence our interpretation of facts and events, resulting in different individuals reaching different conclusions from identical data.
**FinCEN**  Financial Crimes Enforcement Network. Federal agency EST 1990 to support and strengthen inter-agency, national, and international efforts to prevent and detect money laundering.
**Finding**  (Noun) The results of deliberation.
**Fine**  Dollar amount one must pay if convicted of an offense.
**Finger**  (Verb) To identify a person or thing; as, 'A witness fingered the thief.' (Noun) A computer program that identifies the name associated with an email address.
**Finger Glue**  Super Glue, etc., smeared on fingertips to prevent latent fingerprints from being 'lifted' by police.
**Fire Lane**  An area specially prepared to facilitate detection, prevention or apprehension of shoplifters.
**Firewall**  Protective layer in computer software; security measure guarding against malicious acts or accidents.

---

### Interview & Interrogation Tip
*Compliments of* Randy Hawk, LossPrevention@onelist.com

I really mean it when I basically tell thieves during the interview that if they cooperate and tell me what I am looking for, the road will be easier for them. They will probably still face prosecution, but being the "victim," I usually have a lot of leeway with the District Attorney on sentencing.

After I conclude an interview with an associate who I feel has not told me everything, I usually give them my business card and tell them that if they decide later that they want to tell me something more to give me a call. I tell them that a decision on how we proceed against them will be made within a week. It is amazing how many calls I get from the associates saying that they "just remembered something else."

**First Rule of Pigs**  'Never try to teach a pig to sing. It can't be done and just annoys the pig.'
**Five-O**  (Dated) Police.
**Float Time**  The time between writing (issuing) a check and the time it arrives (is presented) to a bank for payment, at which time, if it is a hot check, that fact will become known. This 'float time' used to be days or weeks, but computers have reduced it to days or even hours. (Learn from the bank the day your checks actually 'clear.')
**Floor Walker**  Store employee who 'walks the sales floor.' Part supervisor, part 'loss prevention,' part customer relations, and--as normally practiced--almost entirely ineffective against thieves.
**Flow**  Money.
**Forger**  One who alters, duplicates, or creates documents for fraudulent purposes.
**For no reason whatsoever**  ALWAYS the reason criminals are questioned, stopped or arrested.
**Four Piece (4-piece)**  Slang for complete set of restraints (hands, legs, waist, head cover).
**Fourth Amendment**  (U.S. Constitution) Protects citizens from unreasonable search and seizure.
**Frame**  (Verb) To falsely put blame on an (innocent) individual. To make one a 'fall-guy.'
**Fraud Refund**  Refund supposedly for purchased merchandise, but in reality for merchandise that was stolen.
**Fraud Account**  Checking account opened for the sole purpose of passing bad checks.
**Frisk**  A 'pat down' search; not thorough in scope. Usually for weapons.
**Fruit of the Forbidden Tree**  Unlawfully obtained evidence.  For example: If you find a stolen item concealed in a woman's purse and it is later ruled that you had no legal right to search the purse, then the evidence (the stolen item) cannot be used in court. Legally, it may as well not exist.  It is 'fruit of the forbidden tree.' (Also referred to as Fruit of the Poisonous tree.
**FUBAR**  (Noun, pronounced foo´-bar) 'Fouled up beyond all recognition.' Also, 'Fouled up beyond all repair.'
**Full Retail Value**  The normal or advertised sale price of merchandise. The price in effect at time of an incident.

**Gangbangers**  Members of (street) gangs; also, street thugs, hooligans or delinquents. Usually have self-destructive mentalities; most are Democrats. ('Chronic losers,' per columnist Sydney Harris. Most actual street-gang members range in age from 8 to 22, per Irving Spergel et al, 1993)
**General Sessions**  The court to which felons (shoplifters of over a certain amount of merchandise) are bound over. Also, depending on the State or County, the court that tries multiple-offense shoplifters.
**Get**  Steal, jack, hook-up, snatch, lift..
**Get-go (Git-go)**  The beginning. 'From the get-go' means from the beginning.
**Global Electronic Marketplace**  Anywhere there is a computer tying into the Internet.
**Going Down**  'Happening.'  A theft going down now means a theft in progress now. If 'going down tomorrow,' it will happen tomorrow.
**Good Faith**  Honest belief or honest intent.
**Grab and Run**  See Hit and Run
**Grand Jury**  Group of up to 24 persons impaneled to question witnesses, investigate an alleged crime, recommend action, and/or indict the accused if it finds sufficient cause. Normally composed of 'regular' people (non-legal professionals) who meet in settings that range from formal to remarkably relaxed and informal.
**Grand Larceny**  Theft of merchandise or an item valued at over a certain dollar amount.
**Grey Bar Hotel**  Prison.
**Gypsy (ies)**  Usually refers to the ethnic group, but can mean any who 'live on the road;' mobile. See Travelers.

**H.I.D.T.A.**  Literally: high intensity drug trafficking area. ('Where the drugs are!')
**Hx**  Abbreviation for 'history.' ('Hx etoh' means 'a history of alcohol.')
**Hands**  The Number One shoplifting tool and the tool most ignored. Also a thief's Number One weapon.
**Hearsay**  Second-hand information. ('John said that Jane said that...') Often weak or inadmissible in court.
**Heat**  (Dated) Law enforcement or *serious* loss prevention. ('Time to go. The heat's here.')
**Help Look**  To 'help look' is often to 'help find what to steal' or 'help watch out for security and employees.'
**Heywho**  Term used for any member of the criminal element and those living on the margins of society. (The origins of many terms are lost in time. 'Heywho' originated in the 1980's during a chance street encounter involving confused, drunk prostitutes and an enthusiastic, rookie GA police officer, Jose Diaz).
**High**  On drugs; an 'altered mental state.'
**Hit and Run**  Method of stealing where a thief picks up merchandise and runs out the door.

**Home Page**  The first page of any Web site.
**Hook Up**  To give, or to get. To 'hook me up' is to give (it) to me, or get it for me.
**Hootchy Mama**  A female, flashy, tattooed, dishonest and/or gang-related, dressed to strongly suggest sex.
**Hung Jury**  A jury which is unable to reach a verdict.

**Identity Theft**  Fraudulent use by one person of another person's personal identification, information, financial data, etc., with the intent to commit fraud. Usually includes use of the victim's social security and birth info, and may include counterfeit certificates, identification, etc. (including pictures). In some cases, the social security and DOB of a deceased individual is used.
**Important Matters**  Things that must be done to prevent loss and maximize resources and opportunity for long-term benefit. Things that, if not done, will cause you to lose. (See Pressing Things.)
**Impostor Burglar**  Burglar (con artist, thief, etc.) who gains entrance to a victim's home or business by impersonating someone who may reasonably need entrance (such as a water department employee, person suffering a medical emergency, etc.). Once inside, they commit the crime of burglary (robbery, etc.). (A 'home invasion,' on the other hand, usually includes implied violence or threats of violence--if not actual violence--and makes no pretense of legitimacy.)
**Incident**  A happening, an occurrence, an individual case. May or may not be an 'event;' see above. Typically, a term referring to a single instance of note such as a theft, an assault, an alarm, etc.
**In for a penny, in for a pound.**  'Degree' of involvement is moot: one is either 'entirely in' or 'entirely out.' In England (where a penny is a penny and a pound is a couple of dollars) this means that if you're into something only a little, the consequence of the outcome is the same for you as for 'major players;'
**Information System**  Set of elements forming (or regarded as forming) useful or potentially useful facts or other material obtained through an organized collection process (an information gathering system).
**Injunction**  Court order preventing someone from doing something. For example: a thief is convicted and the judge then issues *an injunction* barring the thief from re-entering the store where he was arrested.
**Ink**  Slang for tattoo.
**Ink tag**  Plastic device filled with ink and attached to merchandise to discourage theft and fraud. If the tag is improperly removed, ink explodes and ruins (or at least marks) the merchandise.
**Intelligence Analyst**  One whose primary function is the evaluation of information. He may also be involved in planning and determining the direction of collection efforts, and may verify information; also, may store and safeguard information and distribute (disseminate) the intelligence 'product.'
**Intelligence System**  A <u>process</u> which takes collected information (the 'product' of an information system or search) for 'weeding,' evaluation and analysis. The Intelligence System processes information into knowledge, and knowledge is then provided to tactical and/or strategic levels of an organization.
**Intent**  A person's true purpose in performing an act. (Acts may be conscious or subconscious-driven.)
**Intentional Ignorance**  A calculated tactic to insure that inconvenient facts are not brought to one's attention or, better yet, do not surface at all. (Ex: A manager doesn't want to know if employee purchases are being made at unauthorized discounts. By assigning an incompetent or naive person to monitor those purchases, he can be confident that violations will not be discovered and reported. If the manager's boss ever stumbles onto the problem, the manager pleads ignorance, says he was told nothing about it, and points a finger.)

---

### – Case Closed –
*Compliments of William R. Thrasher, Rome, GA*

An international airport hotel asked us to help identify a baffling loss in a bar with a customer count of about 600/night and average ticket of 11-dollars. Problem: the average ticket had dropped in half while the customer count remained the same. Examination of cash, credit charges, and liquor inventory produced nothing to explain the sales loss. Thousands of dollars in business had simply disappeared.

Posing as a customer, I noticed that about half the drink orders were filled from bottles from the top shelf, and about half from somewhere under the bar. It was devilishly simple: The employees were bringing their own liquor bottles to the bar, and when a customer ordered drinks, one got poured from the bar stock and the next from the employees' bottles. "The degree of cooperation among the employees was phenomenal and it turned out that everyone on the shift was in on it."

**Interrogation** Generally, an interview with someone who is suspected of having committed a crime and who is expected to withhold information. The object of an interrogation is information, admission and confession.
**Interview** Generally, a controlled information-gathering conversation (which may later result in interrogation[s]).
**Investigation** An organized, methodical search for facts and information; a quest for truth.
**"I say, You say"** One person's word against another person's word. (A 'swearing contest.')
**"It's mind over matter."** An illogical or pointless administrative or official action that has a negative effect on someone. (From 'They don't mind and you don't matter.')

**J**udge-Shopping A fairly common practice in which an attorney or other interested party manipulates court dates and locations in order to arrange for a different or particular judge to preside (or not preside) over a particular case. (Often, the shopper seeks a judge who holds, or happens not to hold, some particular philosophy of interest to the shopper.)
**Judgment** A court's decision.
**Just Drove Up** Newly arrived. Person new to a scene, organization, or operation or with very limited experience.
**Juvenile** Varies state to state. In SC and GA, under 17 years of age. (Check with police.)

**K/D/A** Known drug area. An area known by law enforcement to support drug houses and street dealers.
**Keeping Sheep by Moonlight** Incarcerated over-night. (Olde English term supplied by Prof. Chas. Martin)
**Knowingly and Willingly** Legal term meaning consciously and intentionally.

**L.W.O.P.** (Pronounced 'el-wop') Life without possibility of parole.
**La Cosa Nostra (LCN)** Traditional American Mafia of Italian/Sicilian origin; members sometimes referred to as 'wiseguys.'
**Larceny** Illegal taking of property with intent to deprive the owner of its value.
**Latent Fingerprint** Generally, a print that is not clearly visible; which requires 'dusting.'
**Laugh Now, Cry Later** Gang motto: Accompanying tattoo of two theater faces, one laughing, one crying.
**Legend** A false history presented on an employment application or personal resume. May be based on fact and contain much truth, but conceals or deletes significant data; may be entirely false as in cases of 'identity theft.'
**Lie** The noise heard when a thief opens his mouth. A statement made with the intent to deceive.
**Lift** Steal.
**Limbo** A time of waiting or uncertainty. Slang for time in jail before trial.
**Link Analysis** A visual method of plotting relationships (associations) via charts. 'Pieces' of information (people, places, things, events) are charted, and as relationships become known, individual pieces are 'linked' with lines. (Example: A—B—C demonstrates a direct 'link' [relationship of some sort] between A and B, and a direct relationship between B and C, but that example does NOT demonstrate a direct link [relationship] between A and C. The lack of a link [line] between A and C could indicate many different things: B, perhaps, might be a 'go between' or 'buffer' between A and C; or perhaps A and C [if people] are unaware even that each other exist. If a direct relationship between A and C is discovered, a line will be added to the chart that directly connects A with C. In that case, the shape of the diagram could be changed from linear to triangular, with A, B and C each at a corner.)
**Location** The three most important features of real estate property are 'location, location, location.' These are also the three most important features of peepholes and wounds. (Ex: In '93, I was stabbed in the in the palm of my left hand which is a 'good' location. My face--the intended target--is a 'bad' location.)
**Lock Eyes** To make and hold eye contact. (Some types of people consider this to be a hostile act.)

**M.O.** Modus Operandi. (See below.)
**Mace** Disabling chemical spray used to attack eyes, nose and mouth. Pepper spray (OC) is similar.
**Made** 'We've been made' is to say, 'We've been discovered.'
**Made Man** Someone who has proven himself capable or trustworthy. Often with extreme violence.
**(The) Magic Words** 'You're under arrest.' A mood-altering phrase often precipitating bizarre reactions.
**Magistrate** A type judge or justice who performs low-level court-type functions and tries misdemeanor cases.
**Magnetic Ink** The type used on checks and documents for scanning purposes.
**Make** (Verb) To 'make' someone is to identify him, to realize his true identity or activity.

**Malice**  Conscious, willful misbehavior with the intent to do harm
**Mea Culpa**  (Latin) I am at fault. (My fault; 'My bad.')
**Means**  One of three elements necessary for crime to occur. (Also, desire and opportunity.)
**Merchandise**  Items or goods for sale or display in a retail establishment, regardless of value.
**Merchant**  Owner or operator of any type of retail establishment.
**MICR**  Magnetic Ink Character Recognition. Type ink/cartridge necessary for quality counterfeiting.
**Minor**  Juvenile.
**Miranda Warning**  Stemming from the 1966 Miranda vs Arizona court case; allows a suspect the right to remain silent, the right to be informed that anything he says can be used against him in court, that he has a right to an attorney, that if he cannot afford one, one will be appointed for him, and that he has a right to an attorney present during any questioning. (Verb: to Mirandize.)
**Misdemeanor**  'Minor offense.' Stealing a shirt as opposed to a car. Dollar value of a misdemeanor varies, but at some point, a misdemeanor becomes a felony.
**Mi Vida Loca**  Gang motto: My crazy life.
**Moissanite**  Thermally conductive, synthetic diamond selling for 5-10% of genuine diamond prices. Most low-to-medium-end diamond 'probes' (testers) fail to differentiate between Moissanite and diamond.
**Modus Operandi**  Literally, method or style of operation; 'standard operating procedure.' (Also, see 'Signature.')
**Money Laundering**  Multi-step process which changes cash derived from illegal operations into legal cash, goods, and services. The objective of laundering is to conceal a crime, the origin of cash, avoid paying taxes, avoid detection and arrest by law enforcement agencies, and avoid the loss of illegally obtained income and assets.
**Mule**  Person who transports hidden goods or contraband. (Usually refers to a drug carrier. In that world, a mule is very, very low on the food chain. Some drug organizations make a good profit even if they 'lose' 19 mules out of every 20 they send.) Also, low-level criminals who are paid to return merchandise to stores for refunds, to cash counterfeit checks, etc. In every type criminal activity, mules are expendable.

**N**ail  (Verb) To arrest or otherwise inconvenience someone.
**Naked**  Being or operating alone without any assistance.
**Negligence**  Acting without reasonable caution; carelessness. Putting another at risk. Not doing what one is obliged to do.
**Nesting**  Method of theft where smaller items (those to be stolen) are concealed inside larger items.
**Nightstick**  Billy club. A persuasive argument.
**No Contest**  See Nolo contendere.
**Nolle Prosequi**  A disposition where the prosecutor declares the case will not be prosecuted.
**Nolo Contendere**  'No contest.' A plea by a defendant with the same implications (and, ordinarily same ramifications) as a guilty plea.
**No-Receipt Cash Refunds**  Cash given for merchandise with no requirement of proof of purchase. To routinely give cash refunds without receipts is to invite thieves to come and steal. (It's their ideal situation.)
**No-Sale Ring**  Hitting the no-sale key to open the cash register without a sale. (All no-sales should be explained.)
**No-Sale Ring following a Void Sale**  See Void Sale preceding a No-Sale.
**Not Guilty**  Courtish term for acquitted. The defendant is un-convicted, but not necessarily innocent.

**O**.B.E.  Literally, 'overtaken by events.'
**OC**  Term for 'mace' and 'pepper spray.' (OC are the active ingredients.)

---

### Interview & Interrogation Tip
*Compliments of Dennis Flynn, Loss Prevention Manager*

This has worked well with violent or loud shoplifters: I have an empty CCTV dome in the corner of the ceiling in my interview office. When a shoplifter is causing trouble, I point to the dome and say, "See that? Everybody is going to know exactly how you behaved. Now go ahead and say anything you want."

I'm careful to never say there is a camera in the dome or say that the interview is being recorded, which it isn't. I let their imagination do that for them. This has calmed all of them but one, and he started cursing at the dome instead of me, so at least it got him off my back for a while!

**O.C.** Organized crime.
**O.M.G.** (Outlaw Motorcycle Gang) In recent years, reportedly interacting with La Cosa Nostra (the 'Mafia') and with the Mexican Mafia. OMG's have long been involved in interstate drug trafficking.
**Observe** Law enforcement/loss prevention officers don't 'see' anything at all. They 'observe.' ('I observed the man enter the store.')
**Ockham's Razor** Term named after the 14th Century philosopher which says that 'a problem should be stated in its basic and simplest terms. In science, according to Ockham's Razor, the theory that fits the facts of a problem with the fewest number of assumptions is the one that should be selected. This is the great-grandfather of the K.I.S.S. (Keep It Simple, Stupid) theory...' (From the superb article *Bad Science* by D.H.Garrison, Jr., Forensic Services Unit, Grand Rapids Police Dept., Grand Rapids, Michigan.)
**Offender** The perpetrator; one who commits a crime.
**(The) One Ear Rule** 'Sometimes it just be's that way.' (An observation made in an emergency room by an ancient, nameless gentleman while scrutinizing a bloody, battered police officer who was shy one ear.)
**On the One** Honest. (From G.Washington--who never told a lie--being on the one dollar bill.)
**Open Source Information** 'Information that is publicly available.' This includes newspapers and most public records, in addition to the fabulous wealth of information online.
**Opportunity** One of three necessary elements for any crime to occur or for crime to even exist. (Also, *desire* and *means*.)
**Organized Crime** 'Any enterprise or group of persons engaged in a continuing illegal activity which has as its primary purpose the generation of profits.' (Interpol, 1988.)

**P.**C. See Probable Cause.
**P.O.P.** Literally, Pissing-off-the-Police; bad manners. (Frequently a prime element of 'Disorderly Conduct')
**P.T.I.** See Pre-Trial Intervention.
**Palm** (Verb) To hold or cup an item in hand in such a way that it cannot be seen.
**Paper Hanger** Person passing bad, stolen, or counterfeit checks. (Also, 'check kiter.')
**Pat-Down** See **Frisk**.
**Perpetrator** One who commits a criminal act. Also called 'perp.'
**Perjury** An intentional lie under oath. A typical shoplifter's testimony.
**Petit Larceny** (Also, petty larceny, shoplifting, theft by taking, and concealment.) A minor theft, relatively speaking, compared to Grand Larceny. Normally a misdemeanor, but if repeated, might be a felony.
**Photo Line-up** Rather than a line of actual people, a number of photographs are presented to a viewer.
**Pigeon** A victim or intended victim of a scam or con.
**Plaintiff** Merchant or his rep in a shoplifting case. One who initiates a civil or criminal action against another.
**Play Now, Pay Later** See Laugh Now, Cry Later
**Plea** Defendant's formal answer to a formal charge: guilty, not guilty, or no contest.
**Plea Bargain** An attempt to get a lesser charge (with less severe punishment) substituted for a current charge in exchange for some degree or type of cooperation.
**Pocket Trash** Whatever people have on their person, such as matches, slips of paper with phone numbers, etc. 'Pocket trash' can provide invaluable information for intelligence and case purposes.
**Point of Purchase** Also, **Point of Sale (POS)**. Where an actual sale is done. Normally, a cash register.
**Ponzi Scheme** A con, illegal in most states (and many countries) involving a 'pyramid' sales structure where only those persons originating the scheme (or enlist very early) have any significant possibility of actually making a profit; all others will certainly lose their investment.
**Pop** (Verb) To arrest.
**Pop a Cap** (Verb) To fire a gun. Also, 'squirt metal.'
**Portability and Value Rule** Using the PVR, apply security first to the most valuable and portable objects, and apply for more funds to secure the others in commercially descending order. The most serious threats are dealt with first. (Security consultant Bob Spiel)
**Posse** Group of friends or associates; a gang, often ethnic such as a Jamaican posse.
**Post and Coast** Get just enough information about a problem or activity to make a brief report, then simply file it ('post') and walk away without taking any significant action ('coast').

**P.R. Bond** Personal recognizance; a method of releasing a prisoner from custody without requiring payment of cash or signing a property bond.
**Preliminary Hearing** Pre-trial proceeding where the basic assertions of each party are examined by a judge. Actual guilt or innocence is not an issue.
**Pressing Things** 'Fires.' Activity that distracts from Important Things getting done. (See Important Things.)
**Pretext** An alternate 'cover' or excuse to perform an act which serves to conceal or protect the actual reason..
**Pre-Trial Hearing** Informal; held at a courthouse attended by prosecuting and defending attorneys to "get a feel" for the issues, evidence, and personalities. Seldom is the perpetrator present.
**Pre-Trial Intervention** Used in some jurisdictions in lieu of prosecution of young or first-offenders. An alternate means of rehab. The arrest will not appear on a criminal records check.
**Prima Facie** Accepted on the surface as fact and requiring near-irrefutable rebuttal to prove it untrue.
**Priors** Prior arrests or convictions.
**"Problem with your back door."** Refers to employees, venders and jobbers stealing.
**Profile** 'General description' of physical and behavioral characteristics.
**Profit** The name of the game! (It is *not* evil, nor is it some guy with a bad haircut shouting on a street corner.)
**Probable Cause** Information or facts generating a reasonable belief that a crime was or is being committed.
**Prosecutor** The person responsible for prosecuting a case in court; the defense attorney's opposite number. Depending on the situation, the prosecutor may be called a solicitor, District Attorney, etc. In a trial without attorneys, the complainant or police are usually referred to as 'the prosecutor.'
**Public Records** Usually court, property, and many tax records. Increasingly available online.
**Put on the Street** (Verb) To make public.
**Put Your Pen to the Wind** Start writing; go ahead and write.

**Qualified Answer** A response which addresses or focuses upon a specific detail of the question. Ex: 'Did you steal $100 from the office?' 'I never stole any money from the office.' That answer indicates he may have stolen something from a location other than the office or stole something from the office other than money. Other qualified answers include phrases such as, 'As I recall...,' 'At this point in time....' etc.
**Questioned Document** Any kind of document (see 'Document') that is being examined for authenticity, origin, or significance.
**Quid Pro Quo** To exchange one thing for another; often a service. (I scratch your back, you scratch mine.)

**R/O** (See Reporting Officer)
**ROC** (See Russian Organized Crime)
**Rabbit** (Verb) To run, as, 'He's going to rabbit.' Used also as a descriptive noun: 'He's got rabbit in him.'
**Raised Note** Counterfeit technique involving cutting an end-portion or the corners off a larger bill----a $20-bill, for example--and attaching the cut corners or portion to a one-dollar bill, then passing-off the one as $20.
**Rationalization** 'A good reason for doing a bad thing.' Thieves confess more readily when able to justify their theft with a rationalization that makes their crime appear 'understandable under the circumstances.' Stealing money to buy crack cocaine is NOT a good reason, whereas if the thief admits to stealing money to buy clothes for children he might expect sympathy and understanding from authorities, and--at the same time--makes him seem like someone sacrificing for his children; a 'victim of circumstances' rather then just another thief.

---

### -- The Lesson de Jour --

To some extent, evaluation (debriefing) should follow every incident & event. The purpose is to discover what the incident or event actually *means*. Probe for all possible answers to these questions:

1. What did this tell us about our defenses, equipment, & organization?
2. What did this tell us about our management and other personnel?
3. What did this tell us about our LP department, our training, and our procedures?
4. What lessons--right or wrong, intentional or not--might *everyone* have left the table with?
5. What did this tell us about our enemies?
6. What did this tell our enemies about us? (What lessons did *they* learn?)
7. How might our enemies adapt and respond in the future in reaction to what they learned?

**Reasonable**  Whatever an average, prudent person may think or do when possessing the same facts and faced with a similar situation.

**Reasonable Doubt**  THE standard used to determine guilt or innocence. The judge or jury must find that evidence proves guilt beyond a "reasonable" doubt; beyond the point an average, prudent person would *reasonably* doubt the person's guilt. *Not* beyond an 'imaginable' doubt, a 'fanciful' doubt, or beyond 'a shadow' of a doubt.

**Reasonable Suspicion**  The standard or level of 'evidence', irregularity, or abnormal behavior necessary to initiate an investigation. Actual proof of a criminal act or clear proof of a policy violation is normally not necessary.

**Red Flag**  Indication of danger or imminent trouble.

**Reporting Officer**  When writing reports, particularly narrative reports, police officers or store security personnel usually use 'R/O' in place of 'I' or 'me.' (Ex: 'While on routine patrol, R/O observed...')

**Requirement**  A thing that must be done; negative consequences are suffered for noncompliance.

**Restitution**  Payment for damages.

**Ride**  (Noun) Car.

**Robbery**  Seizure of another person's property by violence or intimidation (or threat of force).

**Roll Over**  (Verb) To give up information.

**Roper**  See 'Steerer.'

**Rubberneck**  Head movements (often, frequently repeated) to the left and right. 'Looking around.'

**Run**  (Verb) Do a computer check. (Run a tag, a name, etc.) Slang, to find information about a person.

**Runner**  Person fleeing authority or arrest; attempting a bush-bond. Also, a 'rabbit.'

**Russian Organized Crime**  Organized criminal groups originating in the former Soviet Union (F/S/U) and exploding onto the world stage during the 1980's and 90's. Specialties include murder for hire, prostitution through extortion, drug trafficking, fraud (including credit) and money laundering. Members travel 'legally' (on legally issued visas) and/or with stolen and forged papers and are active in the US. Has worked in conjunction with the American Mafia, Chinese Triads, the Yakuza, and Columbian drug cartels.

**Salami Theft**  Stealing, 'slicing off,' a bit of a thing from time to time rather than the whole thing at once.

**Salt and Pepper Team**  A couple or group of people consisting of both black and white players.

**Sap**  (Dated) A weapon like a black-jack. Also, anyone who believes a thief who says it's his first time stealing.

**SARS**  Suspicious activity reporting system. Can be used in any organization, but often refers to the reports to the government from US financial institutions of suspected criminal activity.

**Saturday Night Special**  Cheap pistol; one that might easily jam, misfire or be very inaccurate.

**Scam**  (Noun) A fraud, con, or flimflam.

**Scenario Planning**  Brainstorming different possible events and the various ways each might play out. Then, planning precautionary and preventive measures for each, and planning how each might be addressed.

**Scratch**  Money.

**Selective Memory**  Choosing to remember nice details while choosing to forget bad or inconvenient ones.

**Selective Prosecution**  Not all detained shoplifters are referred for prosecution. (For example, if all shoplifters are prosecuted except the severely mentally retarded, it is selective prosecution.)

**Self-Perpetuating Information**  Information, perhaps initiating from a single source, that is reported multiple times by various other sources leading to the erroneous conclusion that it is verified by multiple first-hand sources. 'The more it is repeated, the more it is believed; the more it is believed, the more it is repeated.'

**Self-Revealing Fraud**  One that comes to light naturally, as when a credit card statement is read by the owner and he discovers fraudulent charges.

**Shadow**  Noun: A 'tail;' one engaged in covert surveillance who moves in reaction to another person's movement. (Verb: To follow covertly.)

**Sherlock**  Slang for plain-clothes store security. (Sometimes 'Sherlock Holmes')

**Shooter**  One who shoots someone; who shoots a gun.

**Shoplifter Slide**  Style of walk noticeable by a set, business-type look on a walker's face, eyes searching for employees and potential problems; a slightly hurried gait, and (perhaps) fidgeting with belongings.

**Shop Theft**  Otherworld term for 'shoplifting.'

**Shoulder Surfer**  Thief or con man who loiters near bank autoteller machines and steals access numbers by peeking over the shoulders of (honest) customers. 'Surfers' can lurk at a distance using binoculars, telescopes, or camcorders and other cameras with a zoom lens.

**Shrink** Shrinkage.
**Shrinkage** Dollar amount or merchandise lost to theft; the difference (dollar or property) between a physical inventory and property on record. Total shrinkage includes paperwork errors.
**Sidewalk Lawyer** Derogatory term for someone who thinks they know 'the law,' and commonly heard telling police officers what they 'can' or 'cannot,' and 'must' or 'must not' do. SL's often cause harm.
**Sit On** Conduct a surveillance or to guard. To 'sit on' a place (or person or thing) is to monitor it very carefully and, in some case, to protect it.
**Skim** Remove profits from a business covertly and not declare them for required tax or other purposes.
**Slamming** Fraud. Changing a victim's telephone service to another company without the consent or knowledge of the owner (victim).
**Slide** Steal: A cashier 'slides' merchandise into a friend's bag without ringing the merchandise on the register.
**Slip and Fall Guy** Con-artist whose specialty is 'staged accidents;' falling in stores to collect insurance money.
**Snatch and Run** (Also Grab and Run.) See Hit and Run.
**Snitch** (Verb) To inform, to 'stool' or 'rat.' Noun: an informer, a 'rat.' (These are ordinarily derogatory terms.)
**Soft Information** Rumor, opinion, 'general knowledge;' some projections, assessments; not 'hard verified facts.'
**Solicitor** Generally an attorney charged with prosecuting a case in court.
**Some-Dude Defense** A third party (unknown to a suspect, personally) is said by the suspect to be the perpetrator of the crime. (Ex: A suspect is stopped and searched. In his pocket is a stolen pistol and a bag of cocaine. To invoke the SDD, he claims he was walking along and minding his own business when 'some dude' ran past and threw the items at his feet. Being a good citizen, he recovered them to give to the police and was on his way to do that very thing when officers happened to find him.)
**Source Assessment Sheet** A record that tracks the accuracy of information or quality of service provided by each information or service provider (whether human, animal, or thing).
**Source Tagging** Tiny sensor tags (Electro-magnetic, Acousto-magnetic, RF) are attached to items prior to the items arriving at the store for retail sale. (These can be more difficult for thieves to detect and remove.)
**Split Screen** Single monitor for surveillance cameras displaying pictures simultaneously from multiple cameras.
**Staged Accidents** 'Slip and falls' in businesses and automobile accidents are common frauds perpetrated by con-artists who sometimes pay 'witnesses' to lie about what supposedly happened. Their usual goal is a cash settlement. In a worst case, willing participants include a doctor, lawyer, and medical providers. Staged accidents (and altercations) are also commonly used as diversions and distractions.
**Standard** An thing of known origin or authenticity that can be used by an examiner for comparison to establish the origin or authenticity of a similar thing. (Ex: comparing suspect bills to known 'good' ones.)
**Statement Analysis** Examination of verbal and written statements. (Ex: Abrupt changes of verb tense or pronoun usage or time and space 'balance,' or deleted information could be an indication of attempted deception.)
**Statute of limitations** Time limit for prosecuting a case. (There is no time limit for the crime of murder.)
**Steerer** Someone who 'steers' an innocent party into a con or flimflam; directs buyers to sellers. A 'roper.'
**Stitched Up** (Noun) A problem that has been taken care of. (Verb: Stitch up=to fix.)
**Stoney's Law** 'Anyone dumb enough to have to work for a living must be punished.' (My neighbor and sometime philosopher, Stoney, submitted his Law in response to my complaint of a run of bad luck. It explains a *lot*.)
**Stop** (Noun) An arrest, detention, or confrontation. (Verb) To arrest, detain, or confront.
**Store** Any retail establishment where merchandise is held, displayed, or sold.
**Street Name** Slim, Sandman, Chicken Bone, One-Ear: Name used in lieu of legal name or formal alias.
**Stupid** One who doesn't care, or is naive or habitually blind to what goes on; does not deserve respect. Someone who is chronically inept or otherwise does not have to be seriously reckoned with.
**Subject** 'Sub.' A person.
**Summons** Formal notice to appear in court.

## Lies, Damned Lies, and Statistics...

Curtailing the authority of employees to arrest shoplifters decreases data suggesting that shoplifting is a problem. If a store (or company) implements stringent guidelines resulting in radically fewer arrests (or otherwise impedes such arrests), is it possible that someone--for some reason--wants to demonstrate *something*, and to do that requires new, improved shoplifting stats?

**Suspended Case Analysis** ('Let's see where we are now, and take a look at where we're going.') A study of all information on hand and at the 'direction' of a complex investigation. Conducted during an intentional pause ('time out') in case development. Example used at a seminar: A doctor tells you that prior to surgery or a treatment that could harm you--or doing something very expensive--he'd like to just stop and spend some time reflecting on the reports and progress to date. (So...would you consider that a problem?)

**Suspicious** Any pair of teenage girls looking at cosmetics or jewelry, or a pair of teenage boys at ball-caps or earrings. Also: abnormal, unlikely, curious, odd, or unusual, *especially* when compared to 'normal honest.'

**Suspicious Activity Report (SAR)** Verbal or written account of an unusual ('suspicious') happening.

**S.W.A.T. Principle of shoplifting** Steal What's Available Today.

**S.W.A.T. Principle of Retail** Sell What's Available Today.

**Sweethearting** See Sliding.

**S.W.O.T.** Literally, 'Strengths, weaknesses, opportunities & threats.' Considerations for assessment purposes.

**T.B.T.** Theft by Taking (used in some states in lieu of the term 'shoplifting.')

**Tail** Verb: to follow. Noun: a person who is following; usually covertly. (See Shadow)

**Talking in a cornfield** Talking where you will probably be overheard by others. (Many ears in a cornfield.)

**Talking Trash** Cursing, threatening; verbal intimidation.

**Tape** (Verb) To record, by audio, video or both. (Also used as a noun.)

**Technical Operations Unit** A specialized unit within an organization or individual(s) responsible for such activities as covert audio or video surveillance. (Sometimes called 'spooks' or 'black bag boys.')

**Ten-Codes** Police radio codes. (Ex: 10-10, a fight; 10-4, OK...) Vary from area to area.

**Terry vs Ohio** Supreme Court case affirming the police right-to-frisk suspects for weapons.

**The Magic Words** 'You're under arrest.' Those are powerful words with unpredictable consequences.

**Theft by Taking** Above, T.B.T.

**Thief Takers** In centuries past, Thief Takers were private citizens paid by the government for capturing thieves. The practice encouraged '**thief makers**,' unscrupulous people tricking or encouraging others to steal so they could then capture them and turn them over to authorities for reward.

**Thirteen and a half** Slang for taking a chance with a trial: A jury (12), a judge (1), and half a chance.

**Threat Assessment** The study of a threat (any individual, group, or thing) to determine its current or future potential for doing damage, what, exactly, it could do, and the results of those possibilities.

**Tight Leg** Method of theft where merchandise is held between a person's thighs. Very effective if wearing a long coat, dress or skirt.

**Till Tapper** One whose criminal specialty is stealing money from cash registers, tills, and cashiers.

**Time-Bomb Theft** A theft with a deadline for completion; that must take place within a given period of time.

**Time Served** A possible 'sentence' declared by a judge in court following a verdict of guilty. Many defendants spent hours or days in jail awaiting trial. If they are found guilty, that time can be considered their punishment in lieu of a cash fine or additional time in jail after court.

**Time to Go** Means: 'bad things might be about to happen.' (Can also mean 'no point in staying.')

**Totality of the Circumstances** Everything that could reasonably be germane to a situation.

**Traditional Investigative Techniques** Year 2000: Generally, anything *not* involving a computer.

**Transcriber** Basically, a cassette tape player with a foot control pedal, earphones and extra controls. Used to aid in typing of taped conversations (either normal cassette or micro). Cost is about $200.

**Travelers** Groups of thieves of Gypsy, Irish, Scottish, or English origin; highly skilled 'transient criminals' traveling city to city, state to state, and operating in teams of two to a dozen or more individuals.

**Trend** A long-term, possibly permanent, change in an environment. Not a short-term 'fad.' (Ex: in the retail industry, there is a trend toward increasing dependence on computer-generated exception reports to identify problems with refunds, discounts, etc.).

**Trickster** Thief or accomplice whose job involves tricking, fraud, distracting, and providing diversions.

**Trojan Horse** Computer security: T.H. is an 'attachment' to an e-mail message that contains a computer virus. Once the attachment is opened, the virus goes to work in your computer. It obtains your pass codes, PIN's, and even credit information, then sends it by e-mail back to the originator of the Trojan Horse.

**Turn over** Change mental position. A thief who initially refuses to cooperate with investigators, *turns over* if he begins cooperating. (Also, 'roll over.')

**Twenty-four, Seven, and Three-sixty five** (24-7-365.) All day, every day.

**Under-ring**  Method of stealing where a cashier rings only a fraction of an item's true price, or rings only some of the merchandise that is taken to the register. (Ringing only some of the items is usually called "sliding.")
**Uniform**  A uniformed police officer.
**Usual Suspect(s)**  Someone who typically or habitually engages in criminal activity and who, if a crime is committed in or near his postal zip code, is routinely questioned about it by the usual police.

**Vehicle Ram Theft**  Roll the dice. Finesse-free larceny by driving a vehicle thru the doors of a store (usually after hours), ignoring any alarms, loading up merchandise, then speeding away. (It happens.)
**Verdict**  Judge or jury's finding of fact (guilty or not).
**Verified Information**  Ordinarily, the best (most reliable) kind of information (or 'fact'). It usually has been confirmed by multiple, independent sources which helps eliminate possible contamination by exaggeration, self-perpetuating information, errors, and disinformation.
**Vicarious Liability**  Legal doctrine which imposes liability on employers for actions of their employees.
**Void Sale**  A cashier rings the merchandise, subtotals, collects the money and gives change. After the customer leaves, he hits the void key. The money is pocketed and the register will *not* show a cash shortage.
**Void Sale preceding a No-Sale**  A strong indicator of theft by a cashier. (First, the dishonest cashier rings a customers sale and puts the money in the register. Second, after the customer leaves and when there is no witness, the cashier voids the sale. Third, the cashier takes the money out of the register. Note: the void ring negates the sale which--if the cashier does not steal the money--should make the register come out with too much money at the end of the day.
**Voir Dire Examination**  Jury selection process during which potential jurors are questioned by the prosecution and defense to see if they are 'suitable' to serve.

**Waive**  To willingly and knowingly forego a legal right. **(Waiver)** A signed document foregoing certain right(s).
**Wanna-be**  Not the real or best thing, but acts like it. A pretender; usually held in disdain. Often a reference to a juvenile (by age or mentality) who tries to act or be 'bad,' tough, etc.
**Warrant**  Legal document to arrest a person or conduct a search (and seizure). An order to do something.
**Washing Checks**  Checks are stolen from residential and business mailboxes, then washed (dipped) in a solvent which removes the handwritten ink but NOT the printed information. The signature (photocopied earlier) is traced back onto the check which is made payable to the thief or accomplice.
**Web Spoofing**  A false copy of a reputable web site is created that forwards information (such as passwords, credit card and PIN numbers and personal info) to the thief's computer.
**Well-heeled**  Appearing to have plenty of financial resources. (Also may mean 'well dressed.')
**Wire**  A recording device, usually audio.
**Wired**: Equipped with a recording device. (This term most often references a covert, 'hidden' device.)
**Wit(s)**  Witness(es)

---

### ~ ~ Tips on Grocery Theft ~ ~
*Compliments of Jim C., Quincy, Massachusetts*

- Meats have traditionally been a top theft item in the Grocery business. Add to that, fresh and frozen seafood products such as lobster and shrimp.
- Where large and expanded Health & Beauty Care (formerly HBA) sections exist, they compete with high risk food products because non-perishable items do not have to be "fenced" as quickly.
- From an internal theft standpoint, "sweethearting" is a major problem. With large numbers of items moving rapidly across the belt, it isn't too difficult to slide some items right past.
- In Service Departments such as Deli, Seafood, and Meat, under-pricing or mislabeling product can be very costly.
- And watch those meat cutters who are buying big packages of inexpensive meat that appear from the back chest. Is the ground beef covering some nice Rib Eye's?

**Witness**  Person who might testify in court or deposition while under oath; one who has relevant knowledge.

**Word Count Analysis**  Used to determine the importance or significance of a word, term, or idea. (Example #1: If a teenage boy speaks 100 words in each of 10 conversations and uses the word 'Susie' 20 times in each of those 10 conversations, one can reasonably infer that he thinks 'Susie' is important. Example #2: If a store manager holds 10 weekly employee meetings, but fails to make frequent use of words like 'shrinkage,' one can reasonably infer that he thinks 'shrinkage' is of little importance.)

**World's Fair**  Street term for the welfare system. Alludes to unlimited opportunities for fraud and Easy Money.

**Writ**  Court order demanding that something must (or must not) be done.

**Write Up**  (Noun) Disciplinary report; a report of policy or procedure violation.

**Wrong**  (Noun) Legally, an unreasonable, unlawful or otherwise contraindicated act. (Verb) 'He wronged a man.')

**X**  'Times,' 'for,' or 'since.' Times indicates a total quantity. Ex: 'shirts x 4, hat x 1' (four shirts, one hat). 'Unemployed x 4 yrs' is 'unemployed for 4 years.' Also, 'x 6/15/98,' means 'since June 15th, 1998'). Most common usage is 'by,' as in 3x5 index card.

**Yakuza**  Japanese organized crime group active in the U.S. Reportedly working with Colombian drug cartels in distribution of cocaine to the U.S., Japan, and Europe. Extremely not-nice people.

**Young-blood**  A fairly respectful term meaning 'young man' sometimes used by adults and older teens when greeting or addressing street-wise kids, mostly in the 7-12 age range.

**Zombie**  (Dated) A person who is 'spaced out;' probably very high on drugs, 'strung out,' or organically brain damaged (diminished intellect) due to drug or alcohol abuse. Also, a person who works midnight shifts or habitually 'hangs out' late at night, often until four or five in the morning. ('Creature of the night.')

**"I wish he would explain his explanations."**  -- Lord Byron

**STEALMEBLIND**

# Index

**A**bbreviations 123; also, see Glossary
Access control device 189
Accomplice 13,16, 46, 49, 50, 58-61, 76, 77, 189
Acknowledgment 42, 43, 115, 121, 122, 128, 150
Adult children 4
Allen, Annette iii, 106
Alpha Academy of Dog Training iii
Ambulance fraud 189
Appendix 149
Argument of the Beard 3
Armstrong, Louis 139
Art Intelligence Newsletter 172
Asimov, Isaac 106
Assumptive question 189
Attila the Hun 180

**B**aby buggies 55
Background checks 21, 197
Badge/identification 111
Badge player 189
Bait and Switch 190
Bells (on entrances) 68
Bennett, Wm. 47
Birmingham, "Nita" iii
Black market 9, 190
Blind drop 61
Blind spots 59
Blockbuster Video 30
Blunt (*Phillies*) 190
Boggs, Wade 2
Booster box 12, 54, 70, 165, 190
Booster pants 55
Broken Window Theory 62
Brown, H.J. 112
Bulletin boards 169
Bunco 190
Bunker, Archie 125
Byron, Lord 205
Bystanders 48, 103, 109, 146

**C**ameras 10, 13, 18, 66, 69, 75, 88-90, 98
Capper 191
Carnegie, Dale 147
Cash register (area check) 160,165, 172
Cash shorts & Tracking 11, 15-18, 60, 68, 80, 160,166
CCTV (see Closed circuit television)
Charge credit 21, 191
Check kiting 191
Checkpoint (EAS) 179

Chemical Mace 110
Choice question 191
Citadel, Military College of S.C. iv
Clavell, James 5
CLEO (background check) 21
Clerk of Court 131
Clique 112, 191
Closed circuit television 191
Clothes, court 131
Clothes, LP 82, 163, 164
Codes 18, 104
Cohen, Albert 3
Community Oriented Policing 191
Competitive Intelligence 191
Con, Con man 3 9, 47, 191
Concealment law 23-26
Confess, Confessions 43, 100-102, 114-119, 121,134, 135, 147 (#40,41), 164
Confusion 56
Corbin, Lowell iii, 18
Cornell University 177
Corroborating evidence 191
Counterfeit credit card 170, 171, 192
Counterfeit sales receipt 192
Counter-surveillance 75, 76, 161-164
Court fool 133
Court, prep 131-132 (also, see confessions as preparation.)
Court, theatrics 133
Covert 192
Crackhead 90, 192
Cramming 192
Credit card fraud 170, 171
Credit number theft 192
Creepers 61, 192
Crime (required elements) 53
Crime, two basic categories 20
Crime, three basic types 20
Criminal records/checks 20, 21
Criminal Trespass notice 152
Customer persona 55
Customer service, excellent 7, 57, 76-78
Cybercrime 192
Cyberstalking 192

**D**aise, Isaiah iii
Dean, Ken iii
Death, types & causes 147
Deep pockets 54, 192
Defendant's Dilemma 134
Defer Prosecution 193
Deprive 193
Descriptions 18, 54, 85, 86, 90, 110
Diaz, Jose iii, 195
Dillard, Annie 92
Dilulio, J.J. Jr. 63
Disinformation 193
Disorderly Conduct 20, 27, 28, 63, 90, 93,127, 143, 193

Distractions (diversions) 8,59,76,80,19
Diversion 59, 90, 193
Ditch and Split 193
Document 193
Dressing rooms (fitting rooms) 19, 57, 61, 66, 78, 125, 160-165
Drugs (testing) 20, 21
Dumpster-diving 61, 145 (#23), 193

**E**AS (See Electronic Article Surveilla
Easter, Michael 178
Electronic Article Surveillance 179, 193
Emboss 193
Employee sabotage 78
Employees, screening/training 15-22, 38, 76-78, 85, 86, 112
Encryption 193
English Travelers (See Travelers)
Event 193
Evidence 23, 25, 50, 56, 90, 99,102, 113, 118, 124-126, 132, 133, 193
Evidence handling 125,126, 133, 147, 148
Evidence, types 125
Exact-Change Purchase 16, 194
Exception reports 194
Exchange (merchandise/fraud) 13-16, 46,61,145 (#23), 166, 194
Exclusionary rule ("Fruit of the Forbidden Tree") 86, 194
Extortion 49

**F**ailure to appear 194
Fair, David iii
False pretense 194
False stomach 54, 58
Family Research Council 178
Fat Lady (The), 111
FBI 178
Felony stop 194
Fence 9, 194
Filters 43, 194
FinCEN 179, 194
Finger 194
Finger glue 194
Fire (diversion) 59
Fire lanes (Kill zones) 88, 89, 194
Firewall 194
Fitting rooms (see dressing rooms)
Float Time 195
Flynn, Dennis 198
Force and deadly f. 46, 50, 93, 104-111, 146 (#33,34), 164
Forensic Science Center 179
Fourth Amendment 195
Fraud refunds 13-19, 145 (#23), 195
Fraud Watch 177
Fruit of the Forbidden Tree 195

**G**ames thieves play  45-52, 161-164
Garrison, D.H.  199
Georgia law  23-28
Geraldo  144 (#16)
Global Electronic Marketplace  195
Glossary  189-205
Grab and Run  58  (Also, "Snatch and Run")
Greeting (proper)  83, 167-169
Gypsies  8, 54-55, 58-59, 195

**H**ammarskjold, Dag  22
Handcuffs  39,111,114,141 (#6)
Hand pass  61
Harassment (sexual)  51-52
Hardie, Dorothy  iii
Harridge, Peter  192
Harris, Sydney  195
Hawk, Randy  190, 194
Helena, R.W., Jr . iii
Hearst, Patty  131
H.I.D.T.A.  195
Hit and Run (Grab and run)  58, 195
Hodgdon, Christopher  iii, 83, 106
Hoffa, Jimmy  128
Holmes, Sherlock  70, 97, 174
Honest mistake  123
Honey trap  51-52
Hootchy-Mama  195
Hux, Kevin  iii

**I**BM  30
ID, req for checks and credit purchase  171
ID (LP card, badge)  111
Identity theft  196
Illusion  16, 56
Impostor burglary  196
Incident Report  113-117, 121-126, 134, 147 (#44), 155-159
Information system  196
Ink Tags  196
Insurance  49
Intelligence analyst  196
Intelligence system  196
Intentional ignorance  169, 196
Internet  38, 177-179
Interview/Interrogation  113-122, 197
Intimidation  10, 27, 28, 61-64, 93, 145 (#24)

**J**osey, Capt. James  iii
Jobbers  18
Johnson, Jimmy  5, 6, 8
Judgment  197
Judge shopping  25, 136, 148, 197

**K**ill Zone  see "Fire Lanes"
Kipling, R.  128
Kleptomania  12

**L**ake, Riki  144 (#16)
Law, SC "Merchant's Privilege"  142 (#10)
Law, shoplifting, GA  23-28
Law, shoplifting, SC  23-28
Law, refund  25
Legend  197
Liability  39-52
Library theft  172
Link analysis  197
Lists (in order of appearance):
   Gen. shoplifter characteristics,  8
   Tips from a professional,  13
   Common methods register theft,  16
   Parallels: thieves and guerrillas,  31
   "S" Factors,  35
   Liability issues,  50-51
   Shoplifting tools,  53-55
   Shoplifting tactics,  56-61
   Red flags, short list,  66
   Red flags,  66-67
   White flags,  67
   Examples of shoplifting,  69, 71-73
   Questions for employees,  78
   Golden rules of surveillance,  80
   Successful peepholes,  86,87
   Ways to max. sec. effectiveness,  94
   Categories to prosecute,  128,129
   Tips for testimony,  135
   Methods of credit card fraud,  170-171
   Floor walking issues,  172
   States (recording conversations)  174
   Internet/Web sites,  177-179
   Lesson de jour,  200
Livingston, Joe (SLED)  142 (#9)
Losses (to shoplifting)  1, 2, 144
Loss prevention checklist  160, 172
Loss prevention spot-checks  21,22, 172
Luchenbach II (Luke)  109, 147 (#37)

**M**ace (chemical)  110, 197
Magnetic ink  197
Management's Dilemma  19
Martin, Col. Charles "Fat Jack"  iii, 186
Mea Culpa  198
Merchants' Privilege  27, 142
Michigan  23
Mintz Investigative Services  178
Miranda  102, 117, 198
Mirrors  76, 87, 89, 90, 91, 162
Moissanite (synthetic diamond)  198
Money Laundering  178, 198
Moody Blues  76
Moore, Noah J.R.  iii, 142 (#9)
Moorefield, Bob  iii, iv
Mule  198
Museum theft  172

**N**arrative (report)  123-125, 134, 155-59
Nat'l Crime Prevention Council  179
Nat'l Fraud Information Center  177, 179
Nat'l White Collar Crime Cntr  179
Negligence  198
Nesting  59, 60, 198
Nevada  23
Newsletters  169, 175-176
Nightsticks  110
No-contest (plea)  133, 134, 198
No-sale  16, 17, 198
Notepads  110

**O**.C.  198
O.M.G.  199
Oakham's Razor  199
Obsessive-Compulsive Disorder  12
O'Conner, Sinead  26
Open source information  199
Orientation, new-hire  180
   ...Attitude  187
   ...General  20-22, 180
   ...Mistakes  185
   ...Myths  183
   ...Personal Visitors  184
   ...Policies & Procedures  187
   ...Profit  182
   ...Teamwork  182
   ...Working w/ LP  186

**P**ackage switching  58
Paper Hanger  199
Peepholes, see security windows.
Petit Larceny  199
Photo line up  199
"Pick a number"  80
Pickett, Gen.  107
Pigeon  199
Point of Purchase  23, 40, 199
Point of Purchase Advertising Institute  30
Police (See uniformed security and police)
Police, cooperation  127-128
Policy, shoplifting, effects of no policy  30
Policy, shoplifting  29-34
Policy A, (normal standard)  31,32
Policy B, ("high gross" standard)  33
Ponzi Scheme  199
Portable walls  59
Pretext  25, 28, 49, 50, 97, 100, 104, 114, 200
Pretrial  200
Price guns  57, 160
Price switching  24,57
Prime Directive  28, 48, 50, 101, 102
Principles of War  145, 146 (#28)
Prisoner's Dilemma  118, 119
Profile, shoplifters  8, 65-67
Purse, trash  53

**Q**ualified answer  200
Questioned document  200
Quid pro quo  200

**R**aised Note  172, 200
Rand, Ayn  4
Rationalization  200
Ravenell, Joe (Special Agent)  142 (#9)
Reasonable (defined)  39, 201
Reasonable doubt  69, 201
Reasonable force  104-109
Reasonable suspicion  201
Recording, Devices & Law  111, 174
Red Flags  65, 66, 67, 82, 201
Re-embossed credit cards  170
Refunds (see Fraud refunds)
Release  20, 42-43, 112, 121-122, 128, 151
Relentless defectors  144 (#20)
Reports, writing  122-126
Restitution  49, 201
Rituals  73-75
Rogers, Kenney  92
Roper (see Steerer)
Russian Organized Crime (ROC)  201

**S**ales floor (area check)  160, 165, 172
Salt and pepper team  61, 201
SARS  201
Scenario planning  201
Schwarzenegger, Arnold  107
Scottish Travelers  (See Travelers)
Scott, Alfonso  iii
Searches  50, 88, 97, 101-103, 113, 114, 120
Second-hand information  91
Secret Service  142 (#9), 170, 171, 179
Security (see Uniform Security/Police)
Security bells  67, 68
Security cables  67, 68
Security lights  67, 68
Security windows (peepholes)  86-89
Security windows, pitfalls  87-88
Selective prosecution  44-45, 201
Self-perpetuating information  201
Self-revealing fraud  201
Shadow  75, 201
Shoplifter (The word "shoplifter" is found throughout this manual.)
...Amateur  11, 12
...Categories  8-12
...Mentally Disturbed  11, 12
...Professional  8-16
...Profiles  8, 65-67
...Recreational/Social  11
...Situational  12
...Statistics  1, 7, 8, 141 (#4)
...Tactics  56-61, 161-164
...Tools  53-56

Shoppers Report  165
Shop theft  201
Short-change  11, 13, 17, 18
Shoulder surfer  201
Shrinkage box  44
Sidewalk lawyer  120, 202
Sigmund, Karl  144 (#20)
Single Issue Offense  63, 64
Site-hardening  67, 68
Skimming  16, 202
Slamming  202
Sliding  15, 16
Slip and Fall  202
Slogans  130, 143 (#11)
Smith, Steve  iii
Snatch and run (see grab and run)
Soft information  202
Some-Dude defense,  202
Source Assessment sheet  202
Source Tagging  202
South Carolina law  23-28
Spiel, Bob  172
Spivey, Phil  127
Staged Accidents  202
Standard  202
Statement Analysis  202
Statute of Limitations  202
Steerer  202
Stockroom  19, 160
Stokes, Carl  2
Stop Log  122, 123, 153, 154, 158, 159
Store buggies  55
Strong-arm robbery  105
Stun guns  111
Sun Tzu  5, 8, 68
Supplemental report  123, 158, 159
Surveillance  31, 32, 37, 69, 70, 73-91, 94-101, 145 (# 27, #28)
Suspended Case Analysis  203
Suspicious activity report  203
S.W.A.T. Principle  3, 203
Sweethearting  See Sliding

**T**ape recorders  111, 174
Technical Operations Unit  203
Testimony  125, 132-135, 137-139, 148 (#48)
Texas  23
Texas Southern University  45
Thief makers/takers  203
Thieves' Manual  161-164
Third Option  97-104, 146 (#30)
Thrasher, Wm  iii, vii, 30, 53, 106, 196
Threat assessment  203
Tight-leg theft  58, 203
Till tapper  16-18, 203
Time-bomb theft  89, 203
Time served  203
Tit for Tat  44, 144 (#20)
Totality of Circumstances  203

Training, security  20-22, 146 (#29) 179-187
  Employee Orientation  179-187
Transcriber  203
Trash shoes  57
Trash, store  19 (Also see Dumpsters, D.Diving)
Travelers (Also see Gypsies)  203
Trend  191
Trespass (notice)  152
Trojan Horse  203
Tunney, Gene  76
Twain, Mark  74
Twenty-four a Day (customer service/deter)  170

**U**nder-rings  15-16, 204
Uniformed security/police  92-94, 98, 1 104, 108, 111, 114, 117-125, 127, 1 132, 146 (#32), 163-164
University of Florida  178
USATRACER (background checks)  2
Usual suspects  204

**V**ehicle Ram Theft  204
Vendors (also, 'jobbers')  18
Verified information  204
Victimhood  4, 39, 42, 44-47, 144 (#16, Void Sale  204
Voir Dire  204

**W**ade, Dr. Charles  77
Washing checks  204
Washington (state)  23
Weapons  109, 110
Web sites, various  38, 176-178
Web spoofing  204
West, Mae  11
Whidby, Jerry  iii, v, 147
White Flags  67
Who Screws Who?  45, 46
Wiggins, Keith  iii, 110
Wilson and Kelling  62
Wilson and Hernstein Study  1
Wind in your sales  168-170
Witnesses  9, 18, 39, 41-43, 45-48, 51, 6 63, 74, 85, 86, 91, 93, 94, 101, 102, 10 108, 109, 112-114, 124, 125, 131-139 148 (#48), 159, 162
Wolfe, Capt. Jerry  iii, 109
Word count analysis  205
World's Fair  205
Wright, Pete  iii
Wronged  39-52, 205

**Y**akuza  205

**Z**one, Zone defense  19, 181

# Steal Me Blind

# *CLEO* from USATRACER

The far-reaching USATRACER system offers on-line, real-time identification and tracking data based on a name or Social Security number. With an average return time of only twenty seconds, the *CLEO*-USATRACER report is possibly the single most powerful weapon available to those with a "need to know."

CLEO was originally designed to assist law enforcement agencies in tracking fugitives. It immediately proved to have unparalleled applications in the private sector as well.

## *What does CLEO provide?*

- Year and State of issue of the input Social Security Number (SSN)
- The reported owner of the SSN you input, and an address history
- Any other reported users of that SSN and their address histories
- Automatic scan of the Social Security Administration Master Death Index file
- Fraud Detect: An automatic scan of our Fraud Alert database, alerting you to possible "red flags" and deception
- SSN locator: when you absolutely, positively have to have someone's SSN
- Subject verification with closest neighbors: Locates your target at a given address and also tells you who all their neighbors are as well as their addresses, length of time in neighborhood, and phone numbers
- Change of address: Search of countless databases to find a subject's most recent and/or new address
- Address Verification: Same as above, but concentrates on confirming a valid address as opposed to an empty lot; also shows as many as five neighbors
- Telephone number ownership: Learn who a phone number is actually owned by, plus their address and other information about the owner

- One-time software license fee that entitles the client to all future program upgrades

Businesses, corporate & industrial entities are welcome to apply.
All clients must have a current business license.

For a free analysis of your status regarding secure connection to the CLEO network, please contact us toll-free at 1-877-295-5777.

## World wide, visit our web site at
## www.usatracer.com

*THE RETAIL THEFT BEST SELLER!*

# STEAL ME BLIND!

The Complete Guide to
Shoplifting & Retail Theft
...and how to stop it
*without getting sued*

For retail owners, managers & loss prevention professionals coast to coast

**How to end thieves, cut shrinkage, and increase profit!**

---

Return this form (or a copy) to:

## BlueLight Publishing

Box 39205
Northbridge Station
Charleston, SC 29407

Please rush me the title above. Enclosed is my check or money order for $34.95,

*Save 20%--order two for just $56.00!*

**Price includes postage and handling!**

Allow two weeks for delivery. **(Most orders shipped within 48 hours!)**

NAME _____

ADDRESS _____

CITY _____ STATE _____ ZIP _____

-  -  -  -  -  -  -  -  -  -  -  - To order with **Novus - Discover** -  -  -  -  -  -  -  -  -  -  -  -
*simply complete this form!*

Account number _____  Expiration date __ __
                                                       Mo. Yr.

Authorized Signature _____  Date _____

(Print) Authorized User _____  Telephone (___)- ___-_____